Seabiscuit

Charles Howard, Red Pollard, and Tom Smith
(KEENELAND-COOK)

Seabiscuit

The True Story of Three
Men and A Racehorse

LAURA HILLENBRAND

FOURTH ESTATE • *London* and *New York*

This film tie-in edition first published in 2003
First published in Great Britain in 2001 by
Fourth Estate
A Division of HarperCollins*Publishers*
77-85 Fulham Palace Road,
London w6 8jb
www.4thestate.com

1 3 5 7 9 10 8 6 4 2

A catalogue record for this book is available from
the British Library

ISBN 0-00-716704-0

Typeset by Rowland Phototypesetting Ltd, Bury St Edmunds, Suffolk
Printed in Great Britain by Clays Ltd, St Ives plc

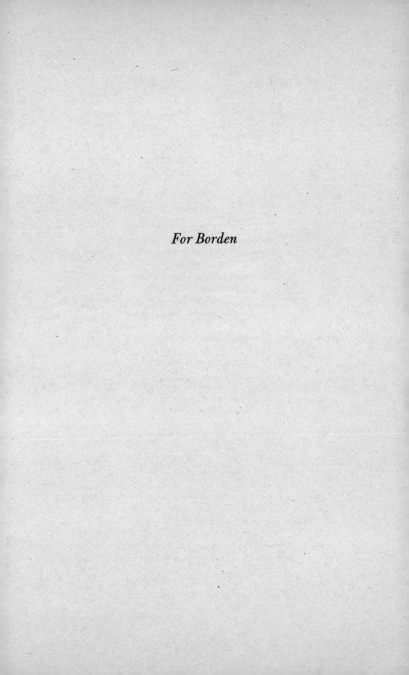

For Borden

"Nobody ever lives their life all the way up except bullfighters."
—Ernest Hemingway, *The Sun Also Rises*

Contents

CONTENTS

Preface

In 1938, near the end of a decade of monumental turmoil, the year's number-one newsmaker was not Franklin Delano Roosevelt, Hitler, or Mussolini. It wasn't Pope Pius XI, nor was it Lou Gehrig, Howard Hughes, or Clark Gable. The subject of the most newspaper column inches in 1938 wasn't even a person. It was an undersized, crooked-legged racehorse named Seabiscuit.

In the latter half of the Depression, Seabiscuit was nothing short of a cultural icon in America, enjoying adulation so intense and broad-based that it transcended sport. When he raced, his fans choked local roads, poured out of special cross-country "Seabiscuit Limited" trains, packed the hotels, and cleaned out the restaurants. They tucked their Roosevelt dollars into Seabiscuit wallets, bought Seabiscuit hats on Fifth Avenue, played at least nine parlor games bearing his image. Tuning in to radio broadcasts of his races was a weekend ritual across the country, drawing as many as forty million listeners. His appearances smashed attendance records at nearly every major track and drew two of the three largest throngs ever to see a horse race in the United States. In an era when the United States' population was less than half its current size, seventy-eight thousand people witnessed his last race, a crowd comparable to those at today's Super Bowls. As many as forty thousand fans mobbed tracks just to watch his workouts, while thousands of others braved ice storms and murderous heat to catch a glimpse of his private eighty-foot Pullman railcar. He galloped over Manhattan on massive billboards and was featured week after week, year after year, in *Time*, *Life*, *Newsweek*, *Look*, *Pic*, and *The New Yorker*. His trainer, jockey, and owner became heroes in their own right. Their every move was painted by the glare of the flashbulb.

They had come from nowhere. The horse, a smallish, mud-colored animal with forelegs that didn't straighten all the way, spent nearly two seasons floundering in the lowest ranks of racing, misunderstood and mishandled. His jockey, Red Pollard, was a tragic-faced young man who had been abandoned as a boy at a makeshift racetrack cut through a Montana hay field. He came to his partnership with Seabiscuit after years as a part-time prizefighter and failing jockey, lugging his saddle through myriad places, getting punched bloody in cow-town boxing rings, sleeping on stall floors. Seabiscuit's trainer, a mysterious, virtually mute mustang breaker named Tom Smith, was a refugee from the vanishing frontier, bearing with him generations of lost wisdom about the secrets of horses. Seabiscuit's owner, a broad, beaming former cavalryman named Charles Howard, had begun his career as a bicycle mechanic before parlaying 21 cents into an automotive empire.

In 1936, on a sultry August Sunday in Detroit, Pollard, Smith, and Howard formed an unlikely alliance. Recognizing the talent dormant in the horse and in one another, they began a rehabilitation of Seabiscuit that would lift him, and them, from obscurity.

For the Seabiscuit crew and for America, it was the beginning of five uproarious years of anguish and exultation. From 1936 to 1940, Seabiscuit endured a remarkable run of bad fortune, conspiracy, and injury to establish himself as one of history's most extraordinary athletes. Graced with blistering speed, tactical versatility, and indomitable will, he shipped more than fifty thousand exhausting railroad miles, carried staggering weight to victory against the best horses in the country, and shattered more than a dozen track records. His controversial rivalry with Triple Crown winner War Admiral culminated in a spectacular match race that is still widely regarded as the greatest horse race ever run. His epic, trouble-plagued four-year quest to conquer the world's richest race became one of the most celebrated and widely followed struggles in sports. And in 1940 after suffering severe injuries that were thought to have ended their careers, the aging horse and his jockey returned to the track together in an attempt to claim the one prize that had escaped them.

Along the way, the little horse and the men who rehabilitated him captured the American imagination. It wasn't just greatness that drew the people to them. It was their story.

It began with a young man on a train, pushing west.

PART I

Howard at the wheel of his Buick race car, San Francisco, 1906
(LT. COL. MICHAEL C. HOWARD)

CHAPTER 1

The Day of the Horse Is Past

Charles Howard had the feel of a gigantic onrushing machine: You had to either climb on or leap out of the way. He would sweep into a room, working a cigarette in his fingers, and people would trail him like pilot fish. They couldn't help themselves. Fifty-eight years old in 1935, Howard was a tall, glowing man in a big suit and a very big Buick. But it wasn't his physical bearing that did it. He lived on a California ranch so huge that a man could take a wrong turn on it and be lost forever, but it wasn't his circumstances either. Nor was it that he spoke loud or long; the surprise of the man was his understatement, the quiet and kindly intimacy of his acquaintance. What drew people to him was something intangible, an air about him. There was a certain inevitability to Charles Howard, an urgency radiating from him that made people believe that the world was always going to bend to his wishes.

On an afternoon in 1903, long before the big cars and the ranch and all the money, Howard began his adulthood with only that air of destiny and 21 cents in his pocket. He sat in the swaying belly of a transcontinental train, snaking west from New York. He was twenty-six, handsome, gentlemanly, with a bounding imagination. Back then he had a lot more hair than anyone who knew him later would have guessed. Years in the saddles of military-school horses had taught him to carry his six-foot-one-inch frame straight up.

He was eastern born and bred, but he had a westerner's restlessness. He had tried to satisfy it by enlisting in the cavalry for the

Spanish-American War, and though he became a skilled horseman, thanks to bad timing and dysentery he never got out of Camp Wheeler in Alabama. After his discharge, he got a job in New York as a bicycle mechanic, took up competitive bicycle racing, got married, and had two sons. It seems to have been a good life, but the East stifled Howard. His mind never seemed to settle down. His ambitions had fixed upon the vast new America on the other side of the Rockies. That day in 1903 he couldn't resist the impulse anymore. He left everything he'd ever known behind, promised his wife Fannie May he'd send for her soon, and got on the train.

He got off in San Francisco. His two dimes and a penny couldn't carry him far, but somehow he begged and borrowed enough money to open a little bicycle-repair shop on Van Ness Avenue downtown. He tinkered with the bikes and waited for something interesting to come his way.

It came in the form of a string of distressed-looking men who began appearing at his door. Eccentric souls with too much money in their pockets and far too much time on their hands, they had blown thick wads of cash on preposterous machines called automobiles. Some of them were feeling terribly sorry about it.

The horseless carriage was just arriving in San Francisco, and its debut was turning into one of those colorfully unmitigated disasters that bring misery to everyone but historians. Consumers were staying away from the "devilish contraptions" in droves. The men who had invested in them were the subjects of cautionary tales, derision, and a fair measure of public loathing. In San Francisco in 1903, the horse and buggy was not going the way of the horse and buggy.

For good reason. The automobile, so sleekly efficient on paper, was in practice a civic menace, belching out exhaust, kicking up storms of dust, becoming hopelessly mired in the most innocuous-looking puddles, tying up horse traffic, and raising an earsplitting cacophony that sent buggy horses fleeing. Incensed local lawmakers responded with monuments to legislative creativity. The laws of at least one town required automobile drivers to stop, get out, and fire off Roman candles every time horse-drawn vehicles came into view.

Massachusetts tried and, fortunately, failed to mandate that cars be equipped with bells that would ring with each revolution of the wheels. In some towns police were authorized to disable passing cars with ropes, chains, wires, and even bullets, so long as they took reasonable care to avoid gunning down the drivers. San Francisco didn't escape the legislative wave. Bitter local officials pushed through an ordinance banning automobiles from the Stanford campus and all tourist areas, effectively exiling them from the city.

Nor were these the only obstacles. The asking price for the cheapest automobile amounted to twice the $500 annual salary of the average citizen—some cost three times that much—and all that bought you was four wheels, a body, and an engine. "Accessories" like bumpers, carburetors, and headlights had to be purchased separately. Just starting the thing, through hand cranking, could land a man in traction. With no gas stations, owners had to lug five-gallon fuel cans to local drugstores, filling them for 60 cents a gallon and hoping the pharmacist wouldn't substitute benzene for gasoline. Doctors warned women away from automobiles, fearing slow suffocation in noxious fumes. A few adventurous members of the gentler sex took to wearing ridiculous "windshield hats," watermelon-sized fabric balloons, equipped with little glass windows, that fit over the entire head, leaving ample room for corpulent Victorian coiffures. Navigation was another nightmare. The first of San Francisco's road signs were only just being erected, hammered up by an enterprising insurance underwriter who hoped to win clients by posting directions into the countryside, where drivers retreated for automobile "picnic parties" held out of the view of angry townsfolk.

Finally, driving itself was something of a touch-and-go pursuit. The first automobiles imported to San Francisco had so little power that they rarely made it up the hills. The grade of Nineteenth Avenue was so daunting for the engines of the day that watching automobiles straining for the top became a local pastime. The automobiles' delicate constitutions and general faintheartedness soon became a source of scorn. One cartoon from the era depicted a wealthy couple standing on a roadside next to its dearly departed vehicle. The caption read, "The Idle Rich."

Where San Franciscans saw an urban nuisance, Charles Howard saw opportunity. Automobile-repair shops hadn't been created yet —and would have made little sense anyway as few were fool enough to buy a car. Owners had no place to go when their cars expired. A bicycle repairman was the closest thing to an auto mechanic available, and Howard's shop was conveniently close to the neighborhoods of wealthy car owners. Howard hadn't been in town long before the owners began showing up on his doorstep.

Howard had a weakness for lost causes. He accepted the challenge, poked around in the cars, and figured out how to fix them. Soon he was showing up at the primitive automobile races held around the city. Before long, he was driving in them. The first American race, run around Evanston, Illinois, had been held only eight years before, with the winning car ripping along at the dizzying average speed of seven and a half miles per hour. But by 1903, automotive horsepower had greatly improved—one car averaged 65.3 mph in a cross-European race that season—making the races a good spectacle. It also made for astronomical casualty rates. The European race, for one, turned into such a godawful bloodletting that it was ultimately halted due to "too many fatalities."

Howard was beginning to see these contraptions as the instrument of his ambition. Taking an audacious step, he booked a train east, got off in Detroit, and somehow talked his way into a meeting with Will Durant, chief of Buick Automobiles and future founder of General Motors. Howard told Durant that he wanted to be a part of the industry, troubled though it was. Durant liked what he saw and hired him to set up dealerships and recruit dealers. Howard returned to San Francisco, opened the Pioneer Motor Company on Buick's behalf, and hired a local man to manage it. But on a checkup visit, he was dismayed to find that the manager was focusing his sales effort not on Buicks but on ponderous Thomas Flyers. Howard went back to Detroit and told Durant that he could do better. Durant was sold. Howard walked away with the Buick franchise for all of San Francisco. It was 1905, and he was just twenty-eight years old.

Howard returned to San Francisco by train with three Buicks in tow. By some accounts, he first housed his automobiles in the parlor of his old bicycle-repair shop on Van Ness Avenue before moving to a modest building on Golden Gate Avenue, half a block from Van Ness. He brought Fannie May out to join him. With two young boys to feed, and two more soon to follow, Fannie May must have been alarmed by her husband's career choice. Two years had done little to pacify the San Franciscan hostility for the automobile. Howard failed to sell a single car.

At 5:12 A.M. on April 18, 1906, the earth beneath San Francisco heaved inward upon itself in a titanic, magnitude 7.8 convulsion. In sixty seconds the city shuddered down. Fires sprang up amid the ruined buildings, converged, and raced toward Howard's dealership, consuming four city blocks per hour. With the water lines ruptured and the sewers bled dry, there was nothing to check its course. Wagon horses ran in a panic through the streets, snapped their legs in the rubble, and collapsed from exhaustion. The horse-drawn city was in desperate need of vehicles to carry firemen and bear the injured, 3,000 dead, and 225,000 homeless out of the fire's path. Fleeing citizens offered thousands for horses, but there were none to be had. People were fashioning makeshift gurneys from baby carriages and trunks nailed to roller skates, pulling them themselves. There was only one transportation option left. "We suddenly appreciated that San Francisco was truly a city of magnificent distances," wrote one witness. "The autos alone remained to conquer space."

Charles Howard, owner of three erstwhile unsaleable automobiles, was suddenly the richest man in town. He saved his cars from the flames and transformed them into ambulances. By one account, Howard himself served as a driver, speeding into the ruins to gather the stranded and rush them down to rescue ships on the bay. His cars were probably also employed to bear massive stacks of army explosives, which were used to create firebreaks.

On April 19 the fire drove the soldiers and firemen west into Howard's neighborhood. Van Ness Avenue, half a block from

Howard's dealership, was the broadest street in the city. The fire-fighters chose it as the site of their last stand. As the fire bore down on them, they unloaded dynamite from the automobiles, packed it into Howard's dealership and the surrounding buildings, and blew it all sky-high to widen the firebreak. That evening the fire roared over the rubble of Howard's dealership and reached Van Ness. The exhausted firefighters refused to give. Though it burned for two more days, the fire did not jump the road.

Howard lost everything but his cars, but he had been insured. The reimbursement check that arrived at his door offered him a painless way out of his automobile venture. But Howard was certain that he could coax his new city into the automotive age. The earthquake had already done half the work for him, proving the automobile's superiority to the horse in utility. Two weeks after the quake, a day's rental of a horse and buggy cost $5; a two-seated runabout cost $100 a day. All Howard needed to do was prove his automobiles' durability. He put up one of the first temporary buildings in the quake's aftermath, moved the cars in, and set out to craft a new image for Buick.

Few men have demonstrated a better understanding of the importance of image than Howard. He could probably thank his father, Robert Stewart, for that. While accumulating a vast fortune in his native Canada, Stewart had become the focal point of a business scandal. Though his role in it remains unclear, his subsequent behavior suggests a spectacular fall from grace: He left the country, changed his last name to Howard, and spent the rest of his life in exclusive hotels and clubs all over the eastern United States. Listing his occupation as "traveler," he never again owned a permanent home or stayed in one place for long. He married and divorced repeatedly, gaining notoriety among gossip columnists for slugging one of his wives and engaging in public shouting matches with the others.

Charles Howard was never close to his father. Growing up in a Victorian upper-class America in which reputation was social currency, he must have felt the sting of the family's ignominy. He made himself into his father's antithesis. Whereas Robert Stewart Howard was wealthy, his son evidently refused to base his life on its advantages, embarking on his westward journey with virtually no money to his name. Whereas his father lacked the interest or discipline to save his reputation and that of his family, Charles measured himself by his image in the minds of others. It was a preoccupation, verging on obsession, that would inform his decisions, and guide his energies. By instinct or by study, he had an exceptionally firm grasp of the human imagination and how to appeal to it. Habitually putting himself in other people's shoes, he was in his private life charming and engaging, generous and genuinely empathetic. In his public life, he demonstrated a prodigious talent for promotion and manipulation.

Howard knew that to get his automobiles into the public eye, he had to get his name into the press. He also knew that car salesmen didn't interest journalists. Race-car daredevils did. Donning a gridiron helmet, a white scarf and goggles, Howard slipped behind the wheel and put on a holy show. He drove his Buicks in breakneck speed races at Tanforan and hare-brained hill climbs up the harrowing grades of Diablo Hill and Grizzly Peak. He ground through twenty-four-hour endurance tests and "stamina runs," in which contestants looped up and down local roads until their beleaguered automobiles exploded or shed their wheels—the last one rolling was the winner. He was reportedly the first man to send a car down into Death Valley and the first to push over the snowbanks of the Sierra Nevada, performing the feat on an annual basis. The ventures were not without risk. Drivers were killed all the time. The cars also came to sad ends; the joyous celebration after the first Skaggs Springs economy run came to a tearful halt when the winning car spontaneously burst into flames and burned to the ground. Howard was utterly fearless and wildly successful, especially with his sturdy new Buick White Streaks. When he wasn't winning other people's races, he was organizing his own and pressing other Buick agents to join him.

The reporters ate from his hand. Here was the dream subject: daring, dashing, photogenic, articulate, a man who was always doing something stunning and always saying something quotable afterward. Out of the rubble of San Francisco, a perfect marriage arose. Howard gave the press a banner headline; the press gave him the public. He and his Buicks became local legends.

Where the press fell short, Howard and the Buick management filled in by papering the city with full-page ads and brochures trumpeting every win. Critical to the publicity's success was Howard's shrewdest decision. He recognized that the common practice of competing with specially outfitted racing cars muted the promotional effects of victories, given that the consumer knew he was not buying the race car. So Howard opted to race unmodified stock models, exactly the same cars customers could buy off the dealer floor. He also made the transition from horseman to auto driver as easy as possible for prospective buyers. Because virtually none of his customers had owned a car before, he gave free driving lessons. Most important, he began accepting horses as trade-ins. The experience he gained in judging horses would be invaluable to him later, though he would have scoffed at the idea at the time. "The day of the horse is past, and the people in San Francisco want automobiles," he wrote in 1908. "I wouldn't give five dollars for the best horse in this country."

The promotion worked. In 1908 Howard sold eighty-five White Streaks for $1,000 each.

In 1909 he paid a visit to Durant. The new GM chief was grateful; Howard had virtually created what would be one of the industry's leading markets. With a handshake, Durant gave Howard sole distributorship of Buick as well as GM's new acquisitions, National and Oldsmobile, for all of the western United States. Howard began ordering multiple trainloads of cars, some three hundred at a time, and printing his orders and the company shipping confirmations in full-page ads. He was soon the world's largest distributor in the fastest-growing industry in history. Throughout the West, frontier regions that had long revolved around the horse were now dotted with sleek, modern Howard dealerships.

He wasn't done yet. Durant, for the umpteenth time, took a huge financial leap before looking, and emerged bankrupt. Howard bailed him out with a reported $190,000 personal loan. Durant repaid him with GM stock and a generous percentage of gross sales, guaranteed for life. A poor bicycle repairman just a few years before, Howard soon had hundreds of thousands of dollars for every penny he had brought to California.

In the mid-1920s, Howard began to live like the magnate he had become. In 1924 he funneled $150,000 into the establishment of the Charles S. Howard Foundation and built a home for children suffering from tuberculosis and rheumatic fever. It was the first of a lengthy list of philanthropic projects he spearheaded. He also began to live a little. Finding his elder sons, Lin and Charles junior, attempting to play polo with rake handles and a cork ball, he divested Long Island of its best polo ponies and gave them to his boys, who became internationally famous players. A few years later he outfitted a gigantic yacht, the *Aras*, rounded up a crew of scientists, and sailed them all down to the Galápagos for a research expedition. He returned with a rare blue-footed booby and a collection of other animals, which he donated to a zoo.

He also lived out a fantasy that he had probably cultivated since childhood. He stumbled upon a magnificent ranch sprawling over seventeen thousand acres of California's remote redwood country, 150 miles north of San Francisco, near a tiny lumber village called Willits. The ranch had stood uninhabited since the family living there had perished in a diphtheria epidemic. Fulfilling a long-held desire to be a rancher, Howard bought it. Though he stayed in a mansion in the San Francisco suburb of Burlingame whenever he was on business, Howard thought of the ranch as his true home. For all his love of the automobile, Howard was still attracted to the romance of frontier simplicity. He strove to make the ranch, called Ridgewood, a model of rustic self-sufficiency, complete with massive herds of cattle and sheep, several hundred horses, a dairy, a slaughterhouse, and fruit orchards. Dressed in embroidered western shirts, Howard surveyed his ranch from a stock saddle on a cow pony. But he couldn't resist a little modernity here and there; he sped around his lake in gleaming speedboats. On the hills of Ridgewood, removed from his business, "Poppie" Howard watched his sons grow.

On the weekend of May 8 and 9, 1926, Charles Howard took Fannie May to Del Monte, California, to attend the opening of a new hotel. They left their fifteen-year-old son, Frankie, behind at Ridgewood. Early that Sunday morning, Frankie borrowed one of his father's old trucks and set out for a morning of trout fishing with two friends. At about 9:00 A.M., they gathered up a big catch and headed back toward the main house. Driving along a canyon road about two miles from the house, Frankie saw a large rock in his path and swerved to avoid it. A front wheel dipped over the side of the canyon and Frankie lost control. The truck flipped headlong into the canyon. No one saw it crash.

Frankie's friends found themselves at the bottom of the canyon, thrown clear. The truck was near them, wheels facing skyward. Struggling to the vehicle, the boys saw Frankie pinned under it. They ran to the ranch house and notified the ranch foreman. There was no hospital anywhere near Ridgewood. The closest thing was the house of the town physician, "Doc" Babcock, who kept a few spare beds to cope with the cuts and bruises suffered by the local loggers. The foreman fetched Babcock and they rushed to the scene. Babcock climbed through the wreckage and used what little medical equipment he had to try to revive Frankie. He was too late. When the Howards arrived by special charter train from Del Monte, they were told that their son was dead, his skull and spine crushed.

Howard retreated to Ridgewood and remained secluded there for months, prostrate with grief. Doc Babcock came to console him and found the auto magnate wrestling with the question of how he could best memorialize his son. Babcock had an idea: Build a hospital in Willits. Howard embraced the idea, underwrote the entire cost, and arranged to have Ridgewood's orchards, fields, and dairy supply the hospital with food. Ground was broken by an ox-drawn plow in 1927, and in 1928, with Doc Babcock at the helm, the modern, well-equipped Frank R. Howard Memorial Hospital was open for business. Howard remained on its board of directors for the rest of his life.

He would never truly recover from Frankie's death. In his Buick office in San Francisco he kept a large painting of Frankie, kneeling beside a dog. Many years later, a teenaged job applicant named Bill Nichols casually asked Howard if he was the boy in the picture.

"Do you think it looks like me?" Charles asked.

Nichols said yes. When he looked up, tears were running down Howard's face.

In the 1920s California was not the place to be for a man in a sinning frame of mind. The temperance folks had given America Prohibition, and had thrown in a ban on gambling while they were at it. A guy couldn't cavort with women, and thanks to the ban on cabaret dancing, he couldn't even watch women cavorting by themselves. If he was discovered in a hotel room with a woman not his wife, his name would appear in the section of the newspaper reserved for public shaming. Everything was closed on Sundays. The only place to go was church. There he could hear the usual warnings about alcohol, gambling, dancing, and cavorting. When the Southern California ministers were really whipping their congregations into a froth, they would get rolling on the subject of "the Road to Hell," a byway that ran south from San Diego. At the end of it stood the town of Tijuana. "Sin City," a place where all those despicable things, and a whole lot more, were done right out in the open.

You can't buy that kind of advertising. Thousands of Americans a day were sprinting for the border.

For all the fire-and-brimstone buildup, the avenue that led down to Tijuana was a little disappointing. One might expect the Road to Hell to be well-paved. It wasn't much more than a meandering dirt lane, one car wide in spots, cutting through the blandness of sagebrush and ducking down to an anemic border river. If travelers were on foot, they could usually wade across and catch a burro taxi on the other side. If they had wheels, they could take a somewhat rickety-looking bridge, followed by a road dipping into Tijuana.

Now, *there* was some sinning. Only recently a sleepy village, Tijuana was fashioning itself into California's guilty pleasure. For every restraint in force north of the border, Tijuana offered unlimited indulgence. During Prohibition, one third of the businesses revolved around alcohol, including the longest bar in the world (241 feet), in the Mexicali Club. The minute San Diego outlawed cabaret dancing, Tijuana bristled with high-kicking girls. When boxing was illegal in California, you could find an abundance of the sweet science in Tijuana. You could get married anywhere, anytime; enterprising matchmakers tailed American couples down the streets, offering to get them hitched for cheap. Those who declined were offered quickie divorces, while single men were steered into one of the many brothels, a cottage industry in Tijuana. The town was wide open every hour, every day. In 1929, when the Depression came and poverty began to replace temperance as the narrower of American life, Tijuanan businesses kept prices at bargain-basement levels, so that northern tourists purring past the clapboard shops along the Avenida Revolución could afford to live high in every conceivable way: lobster dinners, fine spirits, salon services, dancing. The place had a state-of-nature feel to it; former jockey Wad Studley recalls seeing a truckload of Mexican soldiers pull up in the middle of the desert, force a rape suspect out onto the sand at bayonet point, send him running, then use him for target practice.

Tijuana's greatest tourist attraction was its racetrack, which benefited from the hard times afflicting the racing industry in the United States. Thoroughbred racing had a lengthy and celebrated history in America, but at the height of the temperance and antigambling reform movements in the first decade of the century, a series of race-fixing scandals involving bookmakers inspired a wave of legislation outlawing wagering. The result was catastrophic for racing. At the turn of the century, well over three hundred tracks had been operating nationwide; by 1908, only twenty-five remained, and the attrition continued until World War I. In California, the center of top-class western racing, the only track that survived the ban was San Francisco's Tanforan, which barely scraped by. Many horsemen were forced to abandon the sport and sell off their farms and horses. Most of the rest, especially in the West, retreated to a sort of racing underground, a series of leaky-roof tracks scattered through Canada and the few American states where the sport had not been banned.

For Tijuanans, the racing ban was a godsend. In 1916, shortly after California's ban on wagering, they opened the Tijuana Racecourse, which immediately became a haven for American stables and racing fans. It was a dilapidated place—one former rider compared it to an outhouse—but like everything else in Tijuana, it was innovative, offering the first primitive movable starting gates and photo finishes. When a departing Hollywood film crew forgot to pack its loudspeaker equipment, racetrackers appropriated the gear, fiddled with it, and soon fashioned the first race-calling public address system. The racing was lawless and wild and the Americans loved it.

Among the Yankees pouring down to the border was Charles Howard. He never explained why he came. Perhaps the place freed him from a straitjacket of grief. By some accounts, his marriage, already ailing before Frankie's death, was staggering, and maybe he needed to get away. Or it could have been that all that he had worked for mattered less now. The automobile, which had given him great wealth, had stolen something immeasurably more important. His interest in cars, said at least one acquaintance, withered. Howard found himself slipping down the Road to Hell and drifting into that exuberant, swaybacked little town. He avoided the girls and the booze. It was the horses that captured his attention. He tumbled along with the racetrackers, and soon found himself buying a few nondescript Mexican horses and traveling down to attend their races. They were the poorest sort of runners, racing for no more than a handful of pesos, but Howard enjoyed sitting in the stands and cheering them home.

On a summer day in 1929 Howard's eldest son, Lin, invited his father to the annual Salinas Rodeo. With Lin that day was his wife, Anita, who had talked her older sister Marcela Zabala, a local actress, into joining them for the outing. There in the stands, Charles Howard first set eyes on her dark, wavy hair, straight, slender eyebrows, easy smile. Schooled in a convent and raised on a modest horse ranch just outside of Salinas, where her father was a lawyer, she had once been named Lettuce Queen at the annual Salinas Lettuce Festival.

Charles Howard was bewitched. Not long afterward, Anita gave birth to her first child and asked Marcela to stay with her. Marcela moved into Lin and Anita's home, where she and Charles saw each other daily. Though a May-December romance must have caused a sensation, Howard fell in love with Marcela and she with him. She was twenty-five and the sister of his son's wife; he was fifty-two and married. His marriage, wounded by Frankie's death, collapsed. In the fall of 1932, at a ceremony at Lin's house, Charles and Marcela were wed.

In Marcela, Howard found his perfect complement. Like him, she was deeply empathic. Suddenly elevated into the world of the rich, she moved with an easy, charming propriety, yet had the rare grace and aplomb to make her frequent departures from convention seem amusing instead of scandalous. She dazzled the society writers. At golf, she packed such a wallop that she swung from the men's tee. In 1935, when Charles organized a five-month African safari, Marcela eagerly enlisted in the adventure. In a world in which women's roles were still highly traditional, Marcela's trip was the talk of the town, prompting the *San Francisco Examiner* to feature daily reports on her exploits in the jungle. She gave them plenty to gawk at. When a lion charged their party, it was Marcela who leveled her gun and coolly shot the animal. And when she found a tiny orphaned baby blue monkey, she smuggled him back to New York in a hatbox. She talked the Waldorf-Astoria into letting her house him in a luxury suite, posed for reporters with "Blooey" and a banana on the Waldorf's plush settee, then carried him home as a pet. She shared Howard's understanding of the importance of image and cheerfully joined him in the public eye. And like her husband, she had spent much of her life with horses.

In 1934 Charles Howard could look out from his offices and see a city shaped by his vision. The horse-drawn San Francisco he had walked into thirty years before had vanished. Only a few horses clopped down the city's streets, and they would be gone before the decade was out. Howard was worth millions, lived in supreme luxury and enjoyed the devotion of friends and the admiration of the public. But he was not content. He was ready to move on.

Howard's friend George Giannini, owner of a string of fine race-horses, thought he knew where Howard belonged. Giannini saw Howard rekindling his lost love of horses and thought he should stop dabbling and commit himself fully to Thoroughbred racing. Howard was only lukewarm. He would not enter the business on a large scale, he said, unless he could go first-class, with the very best trainer. The idea was bandied around a bit and apparently dropped.

It took a San Francisco dentist, former pro baseball player and investor named Charles "Doc" Strub, to change his mind. Five years earlier, on a Monday afternoon in the fall of 1929, Strub had sat down in his lucky chair at his barber's and settled in for a shave. He was handed a telephone. Sitting there with his face slathered in shaving cream, Strub learned that the stock market had crashed, and in a single day he had lost everything and fallen into a debt of more than $1 million. Strub put the phone down, stunned. An idea came to him. He had lost his money, but not his connections, nor his eye for opportunity. He would build a racetrack, the finest in the world, and bring horse racing back to California.

His timing turned out to be flawless, for the catastrophe that had struck him that afternoon had plowed under the entire nation. Over the next three years, as the Depression strangled the economy, state governments searched desperately for revenue. Californians hoping to relegalize racing pounced. For the first time in a quarter century, they received an audience. In 1933 California agreed to legalize wagering on two conditions. First, tracks had to use the pari-mutuel wagering machine instead of the bookmakers whose corruption had prompted the betting ban. Second, wagering would be heavily taxed. Racing was reborn.

With a ready plan for a $3-million racing Xanadu, built on the site of the vast Rancho Santa Anita at the apron of the San Gabriel Mountains just outside Los Angeles, all Strub needed was the cash. He couldn't find a bank to back him, so he went door to door in search of private investors. Strub was turned away from many homes, but when he called on Charles Howard, he was invited in. Howard, his close friend Bing Crosby, and several other wealthy Californians handed Strub a hefty sum to build his Santa Anita Park.

Strub spent the money well. He built a track like none other on earth, a cathedral to the Thoroughbred so resplendent that writer David Alexander described his first sight of it as one of the most stirring visual experiences of his life. Strub's mountain-flanked race-course opened on Christmas Day, 1934. It was an immense, immediate success with the public, and in consequence, the state, which raked in millions in new revenue. It was just as popular with horsemen, for Strub had the brilliant idea of inaugurating a signature race for the track, the Santa Anita Handicap, to be held every year in late winter, beginning in 1935. Unlike the Kentucky Derby, which was limited to three-year-old horses, the handicap would be open to any mature horse, three years old and up. But it was the purse that stopped traffic. In 1934 American marquee races carried a net value to the winner of between $6,000, and, in rare cases, $50,000. In contrast, Strub's purse was staggering: $100,000, plus a few thousand dollars in entry revenue, to the winner. It was the biggest purse in the world. Offered in a year in which the average per capita income in the United States was $432, Strub's purse caused a national sensation. The pot was so distracting that hardly anyone referred to the race by its actual name. The Santa Anita Handicap became, in the parlance of racetrackers, the hundred-grander, or "hunnert-grander."

Strub had created the race at the perfect moment. States all over the nation were relegalizing racing under the pari-mutuel system, resulting in a 70 percent increase in the number of tracks. Racing was rapidly becoming far and away America's most heavily attended sport. From 1934 on, millions of new racing fans turned their eyes to Santa Anita to see who would claim Strub's pot. The hundred-grander became an overnight classic. Everyone wanted to win it. Including Charles and Marcela Howard.

Perhaps it was Giannini's urging, perhaps the example of Bing Crosby, who was investing heavily in racehorses, or maybe the spellbinding vision of the track their money had built. Whatever the reason, the Howards, especially Marcela, hung their hearts on winning the big race. In 1935, shortly after San Francisco's new Bay Meadows Racecourse opened, Howard assembled a group of modestly talented racehorses and hired a crack young trainer named Buster Millerick to condition them. The stable was registered under Marcela's name. She designed the silks that would become legendary: crimson-and-white cap, white sleeves, and a crimson vest emblazoned with the Ridgewood cattle brand, an *H* inside a large white triangle. The horses were fairly good, but Howard had his sights on better things. That summer, he and Marcela bought fifteen yearlings at a Saratoga, New York, auction. In keeping with his love of lost causes, Howard bought only the worst-looking horses at the sale, animals who lingered in the ring, attracting few, if any, bids. Millerick was a very good young trainer, but for his new yearlings and the hundred-grander-caliber horses he planned to have soon, Howard wanted the best. In 1935 he went looking for him.

Tom Smith

CHAPTER 2

The Lone Plainsman

Several hundred miles south of Charles Howard's estate, an old horseman named Tom Smith was spending 1935 at a Mexican racetrack, living on a cot in a horse stall. He was a stark man, square-built, with a hard mouth. Ever since he had materialized at the track from somewhere on the frontier—no one knew exactly where—none of the racetrackers had known what to make of him.

As a general rule, Smith didn't talk. He had a habit of walking away when anyone asked him questions, and he avoided social gatherings because people expected him to speak. A journalist who had watched Smith for years described him thus: "He nods hello, shakes hands goodbye, and hasn't said a hundred words in all." One man swore that he had seen Smith accidentally chop off his own toe with an axe; the sum of Smith's response had been to shake the amputated digit out of his boot and say, "My toe." The men on the backstretch assumed that anyone who made such a point of saying so little had to have something to hide, something shady or, perhaps, something immodestly valiant. They filled his biographical vacuum with suitably large Wild West myths: knocked-over banks, rodeo stardom, daring exploits in the Indian wars. None of it was true, but it made for good, salty rumor, and it made Smith pleasingly terrifying. The truth about Smith was a lot more interesting, but he never let anyone in on his secrets.

He was fifty-six but he looked much older. His jaw had a recalcitrant jut to it that implied a run-in with something—an errant hoof or an ill-placed fence post—but maybe it was the only shape in which it could have been drawn. He had a colorless translucence about him that made him seem as if he were in the earliest stages of progressive invisibility. On the rare occasions when he took off his gray felt fedora, you had to look hard at his threadbare head to tell where his gray hair ended and his gray skin began. When photographed hatless, he had an unsettling tendency to blend with the sky, so that his eyes hung disembodied in space. Some photographers gave up and drew his head into the picture by hand, guessing at his outline. When they were lucky enough to catch him head-on, all his features but that big shovel of a jaw vanished in the shade of his hat brim, so that all that appeared above his mouth were his spectacles, the lenses reflecting the photographer's image back at him. Smith almost never looked at cameras anyway. He was always looking at his horses.

He appeared to have reached the end of the road. His training stable consisted of just one horse who would never be better than ordinary. The old cowboy ate his meals alone in the track kitchen and spent the rest of his time with the horse. For a time he provoked a smattering of discussion over ham-and-egg breakfasts on the backstretch benches. Eventually, the racetrackers grew accustomed to his silence, and he was forgotten.

In Tom Smith's younger days, the Indians would watch him picking his way over the open plains, skirting the mustang herds. He was always alone, even back then, in the waning days of the nineteenth century. He talked to virtually no one but his horses, and then only in their vernacular of small gestures and soft sounds. The Indians called him "Lone Plainsman." White men called him "Silent Tom." People merely brushed up against him. Only the horses seemed to know him well.

They had been the quiet study of his life. He had grown up in a world in which horsemanship was as essential as breathing. Born with a prodigy's intuitive understanding of the animals, he had devoted himself to them so wholeheartedly that he was incomplete without them. By nature or by exposure he had become like them, in their understatement, their blunt assertion of will. In the company of men, Smith was clipped and bristling. With horses, he was gracefully at ease.

His history had the ethereal quality of hoofprints in windblown snow. He came from the prairies, where he had tamed countless mustangs for the British cavalry's effort in the Boer War. Before that, his career with horses stretched back to boyhood, with stints as a deer hunter, sheep-ranch foreman, mountain-lion tracker. In childhood, he rode in the last of the great cattle drives; at thirteen, he was already a skilled horse breaker. The wheres and whens are lost, but always there were horses and empty land. He had a wife, but her presence seems to have been detected only by inference: A son named Jimmy turned up later in Smith's company, prompting his friends to conclude that the boy "must have come from somewhere."

As the century turned he rode out of the wilderness and into Grand Junction, Colorado. He was in his early twenties. The British cavalry didn't need him anymore, so he had been forced to leave the mustangs and find a new job. He and his horse strayed onto the vast continuity of Colorado's Unaweep Cattle Range. He had heard that a ranch needed a foreman.

He won the job and stayed for twenty years. He was a jack-of-all-trades, breaking the sturdy little cow ponies, treating their injuries and illnesses, trimming their hooves, and bending over an anvil to forge their shoes. He lived day and night in their company, warming himself against their skin as he wandered over the range, sleeping at their feet under the Colorado mountains.

Change was coming. As Smith passed his days in the Unaweep, the West that had formed him was making a long, painful retreat. Modernity, led by the automobile, was perforating the frontier. Horses, and all the ways of life that had grown up around them, were slowly being pushed out. Perhaps on his rare sojourns into civilization, Smith had passed the Howard Automobile Company dealerships springing up. He didn't need to see them to know that there was less and less use for skills like his. All around him, men were redefining themselves for the new world, and a vast pool of knowledge and tradition was evaporating. A myth of what the frontier had been, the Wild West legend, was taking hold in the popular imagination, and it would not be long before people defined Smith by it.

People around him moved on, but Smith stayed where he was for a little longer, quietly becoming a relic. He knew no other life, and probably could imagine none. His mind had been shaped by the prairies and ranges, and until the day he died, he would make order of the world with lessons learned from cow ponies, jagged land, and wide-open sky.

In 1921 the cattle ranch on the Unaweep was sold, leaving Smith unemployed. He drifted into a Wyoming county fair, where he found a job working for an obscure firm that supplied decrepit horses to rodeos for use in relay races. Smith was put in charge of training and shoeing six racehorses. He did a superb job, nursing the horses' ailments while honing their speed. It was strictly small-time racing, but Smith's horses were winning. A giant of a man named Irwin noticed.

"Cowboy Charlie" Irwin ran two businesses: a raucous Wild West show in summer and an even more raucous racing stable in winter. Irwin was a colossus, in form and personality. His weight, thanks to a glandular disorder and 50-pound tumors, swung from a comparatively petite 400 pounds to 540 pounds, packed mostly in a monstrous quaking belly that won him the nickname "Ten Ton" Irwin. His immediate surroundings had to be remade to accommodate his girth. He ran his business from the overburdened back of a freakishly over-sized Standardbred horse wearing a superwide saddle. Because Irwin didn't come within 200 pounds of fitting through a standard car door, he drove a customized sedan outfitted with a wide-load rear hatch through which he wiggled in and out.

Irwin was incurably newsworthy. At the hanging of his friend, con-victed killer Tom Horn, he made national headlines by stepping up to the gallows and belting out "Life's Railway to Heaven." When notori-ous fugitive Bill Carlisle robbed a train on the Union Pacific Railroad, Irwin galloped off with the posse that hunted him down, then recounted his story of how he "bagged the gamest train robber that ever pulled a hold-up in the West" in blazing prose in *The Denver Post*. As an agent for the Union Pacific, he single-handedly saved Colorado's wool trade during a blizzard by ramming locomotive plows through snowdrifts to open the tracks for trains bearing sheep feed.

Important people were always hovering around him, from General John Pershing to Will Rogers. Teddy Roosevelt once bailed out Irwin's show when it went broke and got stranded in Sheepshead Bay. Charlie paid him back with a pinto pony and a long friendship. Irwin greeted newcomers with bone-crushing handshakes and tooth-shattering back-slaps. He smothered men in broad smiles, fast talk, and wild stories. He was bold, innovative, blessed with an instinct for promotion, slick, unscrupulous, and completely magnetic. Some of his neighbors, traditional livestockers, didn't like him much, but he was the prototype of the new breed of western man. Invariably, those who knew him summed him up with the phrase used by former jockey Mike Griffin, who never forgot a brief riding audition he made for Irwin: "the biggest man I've ever seen."

Irwin saw what Smith could do with a horse, and he needed as many good horsemen as he could find. He offered Smith a job as a foreman, farrier, and training assistant. Irwin was a very hard man to refuse, and Smith had few choices. He said yes.

The Lone Plainsman had signed on to a turbulent life. In summer he clattered around the nation by rail, pulling into towns to put on the show under circus tents Irwin had bought cut-rate from the Ringling Brothers outfit when it merged with Barnum & Bailey. The acts were a curious mix of history and myth, everything from cowboy-Indian fights, Pony Express rides, cavalry rescues, and stagecoach robberies to Roman-style chariot racing, relay races, women's steer wrestling, and mounted rope tricks and gymnastics. The supporting cast was mostly disenfranchised Indians, Mexicans, and cowpunchers, all of whom possessed horsemanship and livestock skills honed on the vanishing frontier.

The headliners were Irwin's windblown daughters, Frances, Joella, and Paulene, all fearless horsewomen. As a pigtailed child, Joella had once ditched school to compete in, and win, a horse race against legendary Arapahoe riders. She came home to a whipping from her mother and a new horse from her beaming father. Smith worked mostly behind the scenes but occasionally came into the ring to hold relay horses for Irwin's daughters. Irwin oversaw it all from the back of his huge yellow horse, galloping around the center field with his feet jutting out to the sides, hat waving, booming encouragement to his cowgirls. The nation couldn't get enough of it, and the show was a sellout from coast to coast.

In the winter, the Irwin racing stable got rolling. Thanks to the wagering ban, the only places for it to go were seedy tracks, backwater ovals so small they were called "bullrings," and dirt roads, but this was Irwin's kind of racing. On this circuit, Ten Ton Irwin was king.

The Irwin racing outfit was a little city on railroad tracks. When the bigger tracks—Tijuana, nearby Agua Caliente, or Omaha's Ak-Sar-Ben (Nebraska spelled backward)—were running, Irwin's railcars would rattle into town. The workers would pull the horses and tack off the cars, throw up the Ringling Brothers tents and seats, open up "all you can eat, pitch till you win" kitchens inside horse stalls, and settle in for an assault on the racing community. Irwin's stable was probably the largest in America at the time, and may have been the largest ever, but most of the horses would have been hard-pressed to outrun Irwin himself. The vast majority were relegated to claiming races, rock-bottom events in which any competitor can be purchased for a set, low price before the race. Irwin took a shotgun approach, throwing as many horses as he could into claiming races in the hope that a few would hit pay dirt, then reloading the ones who hadn't been claimed for another go in a day or two.

When the big tracks closed, Smith and the Irwin crew piled back on the railcars and began endless loops of smaller towns, stopping off in big cities like Kansas City and crossroads like Laramie, Medicine Bow, and Sheridan, Wyoming. Indian reservations were also on the itinerary; Irwin would schedule his arrivals for the day after government checks came to be sure that everyone had betting money. Upon arrival in the town or reservation, Irwin would trot the horses off the railcars and straight to the nearest back road or bullring, where he would implement a nearly fail-safe betting system. He would talk the locals into racing their horses against his for side bets, with a forfeit fee of about $10. He would accept all comers sight unseen, but in the interim between the deal and the race, he would spy on the training of the local horses. If he thought they'd whip his runners, he'd fork over the forfeit fees and skip town, often "forgetting" to pay his hotel bill on the way out. If the local horses were clearly inferior to his, he'd talk their owners into betting all of their cash. When the cash ran out, he'd work on them until they had staked practically everything they owned, right down to their horse blankets. Irwin's horses almost always won, and Irwin would clean out the locals, pack the horses back on the trains, and leave. "Irwin would put a guy out," remembered Hall of Fame trainer Jimmy Jones, who cut his teeth running horses against Irwin's. "The minute [a man] got any money, Irwin would rob him of it. He was an old racketeer in a way."

This was a rough life for man and beast. For a wage of about $60 a month, Smith slept and ate in horse stalls and struggled to keep up with the farriery needs of fifty-four horses. And Irwin was no easy boss. He had a contract jockey named Pablo Martinez, who worked on a set salary instead of being paid per ride. To save himself the $5 fee a replacement rider would cost him, Irwin once hauled poor Martinez out of a hospital bed and made him ride a race. Though he was down with pneumonia, Martinez somehow managed both to live through the afternoon and to win the race before wheezing his way back to the hospital.

The horses fared worse. Irwin was known to pack thirty horses onto a single four-door railcar, ship them to a race, yank them off the car, and run them without giving them water or letting them warm up. His racing schedules were barbaric. In an era in which one race a week was considered a full calendar, he ran a mare named Miss Cheyenne sixteen times in twenty-one days. He ran another unfortunate horse every day for eight straight days. Rival trainers who claimed horses from Irwin sometimes found them so exhausted that they had to give them long layoffs before they were capable of running again. The hardship paid off for Irwin, who became the winningest trainer in the nation, but it took a toll on the animals. Smith patched them together, soothed their ailments, and learned.

It must have been humiliating for Smith, tending to horses run into exhaustion and watching men and women whose skills had once been so vital prancing around for an audience that had already forgotten their fading world. It is hard to imagine Tom Smith surrounded by the artificialities of show business, standing in a glitzy showring, loosing horses to run in chaotic sprints, and not think that something precious was being squandered.

But Smith adapted. He was assigned the duty of handling horses for walk-up starts in relay races and matches. In watching thousands of match races, he learned that in most cases the horse who broke from the start fastest would win. Smith began devising new ways of teaching horses to blow off the line as quickly as possible. For the time being, the knowledge helped keep the Irwin barn solvent. In the long run, it would mean much more.

The Depression upended Irwin's business. Workers, at least, were easy to find. He made annual trips through Chicago to buy horses, and to add hands to his roster he simply swung through the masses of unemployed men milling in the Chicago train stations, hauling aboard anyone who wanted a job. But attendance at his show waned, and paying his men became a problem. Eventually, his money gave out altogether. Irwin made speeches to his employees, pledging that he would pay them, but he couldn't. Irwin's horses still needed care, so Smith remained on the job. One horse had caught his eye, a hopeless wreck named Knighthood.

The horse had quite a history. In the 1920s, Knighthood had been handled by an able conditioner named Bob Rowe, one of only a handful of black horsemen training in that era. Under Rowe's handling, Knighthood was a holy terror, winning thirty races and $22,000. The horse became an icon of Tijuana's black community, which turned the horse's race days into joyful celebrations. But as Knighthood aged, his speed diminished. In 1930 he was placed in a claiming race. Rowe didn't want to part with him, but he thought that no one would claim an aged veteran of nearly 150 races. He was wrong. To add insult to injury, the claiming trainer was white. Rowe was heartbroken, and the horse's fans were outraged. After Knighthood changed hands, a rumor began circulating that someone from the horse's erstwhile rooting section had placed a curse on him. Superstition runs long and deep on the backstretch, and the trainer who had claimed the horse was unnerved enough to sell him without ever racing him. The next owner promptly dropped Knighthood into another claiming race.

Irwin was not the superstitious sort, and he put in a claim for Knighthood before the race. So did the rueful Rowe, but when a drawing was held to determine who would get the horse, Irwin came out on top. If Knighthood was running under a curse, it worked. In that very race he was badly injured and limped into Irwin's barn a seemingly ruined horse. Irwin, who was fond of the horse, refused to euthanize him. Knighthood languished in Irwin's barn, refusing to eat.

Smith wanted the horse. After two months without pay, he approached Irwin with a proposal: He would call off the debt for past wages if Irwin would give him Knighthood. Irwin at first declined, saying the horse was useless. Smith persisted and prevailed. Smith took Knighthood and disappeared. The horse was gone for so long that everyone on the backstretch assumed he had died. Ten months later Smith showed up in Tijuana with Knighthood in hand and entered him in a race. In racing, a victory by a horse older than seven, even in claiming races, is an extremely rare event; Knighthood was ten. But the horse's old fans, overjoyed to see him again, rushed the betting windows. In the time it took Knighthood to walk to the post, his betting odds plunged. Knighthood won. His comeback became legend.

Irwin knew talent when he saw it, and he offered Smith a shot at training his horses. He sent Smith out to a little bullring track in Cheyenne with a string of runners. The trainees won twenty-nine of thirty races, a feat that may be unequaled at any level of the sport. During a losing streak, Irwin shipped Smith off to Seattle to train another string. Again, Smith turned Irwin's luck around completely.

In his course from meadows and rangeland to back roads and bull-rings, Tom Smith had cultivated an almost mystical communion with horses. He knew their minds and how to sway them. He knew their bodies and how they telegraphed emotion and sensation, and his hands were a tonic for their pains. In his era, racing was a business made rigid by tradition and imitation, superstition and wives' tales. Even mainstream trainers would drop pennies in mares' water buckets to halt estrus, or exhaust themselves trying to get a mane that fell to the left—a bad omen—to fall to the right. But Smith was a radical departure from conventional trainers. He followed no formulas, no regimens, no superstitious rituals. The wisdom he harbored was frontier-tested. He approached each horse as a distinct individual and followed his own lights and experience to care for it. Horses blossomed in his care.

Perhaps Smith spoke so infrequently because he was listening so hard. Horses speak with the smallest of motions; Smith heard and saw everything. "Hotwalkers" leading horses around the shed row to cool them out after workouts would see him squatting down on the floor, staring straight ahead, turning the horses over in his mind. The grooms could circle the barn and come around again, and there he'd be, exactly as he was before. Sometimes he would become so absorbed in watching a horse that he wouldn't move for hours. At times he wouldn't leave the horses, not even to go over to the grandstand to watch the races, for weeks on end. He built ingenious training devices out of whatever was lying around, brewed up homemade liniments, prepared his horses in exactly the way they said he shouldn't. He carried a stopwatch, but left it in his pocket; he had an uncanny ability to judge a horse's pace by sight, and he resented any distraction that might make him miss a nuance of movement. "I'd rather depend on my eye than on one of those newfangled timepieces," he said. "They take your attention off your horse. I got a watch and it works, too, but the eye is better."

For Smith, training was a long, quiet conversation. He was baffled by other people's inability to grasp what he was doing. "It's easy to talk to a horse if you understand his language," he once said. "Horses stay the same from the day they are born until the day they die. . . . They are only changed by the way people treat them." He believed with complete conviction that no animal was permanently ruined. Every horse could be improved. He lived by a single maxim: "Learn your horse. Each one is an individual, and once you penetrate his mind and heart, you can often work wonders with an otherwise intractable beast."

The cow ponies, the broncs, the show horses, and the weary racers: All had helped to craft Smith into the complete horseman. He was waiting for the right horse.

An early spring sun hung in the Mexican sky on March 21, 1934, when Ten Ton Irwin shimmied his 425 pounds through the giant rear door of his sedan and pushed off for Cheyenne. The "meet" (racing session) was over at Northern Mexico's Agua Caliente Race Track and Irwin was due back in Wyoming to tend to his livestock leasing business. He drove north, making his way over the Wyoming border. On a lonely road fourteen miles outside Cheyenne, a tire blew. The car veered out of control and plunged into a ditch. Rescuers found Irwin in the wreckage with chest and head injuries. Two days later he was dead.

Irwin's barn was dissolved. Smith wound up on his own at Seattle's Longacres Racetrack. After briefly training a few of Irwin's old horses, he ended up working as a foreman for an old rodeo trick rider turned trainer named Harry Walters. That, too, was short-lived; the owner Walters trained for soon retired from the racing business. Knowing that he was putting Smith out of work again, the owner gave him a gift. It was a horse, a well-traveled $1,500 claimer named Oriley. It was a dubious present: The horse was lame.

As with Knighthood, Smith settled in to work on the horse. After a period of recuperation, he brought Oriley back on the track, sound and fit. The horse began winning. Soon Smith was bumping the horse up in class, and he kept finding the winner's circle.

Sometime in the latter half of 1934, Tom Smith brought his one-horse stable down to Agua Caliente. Oriley did passably well, but Smith was barely making it. The trainer was living out of a horse stall, sharing it with another struggling horseman. He found no clients. He was a few dollars short of flat broke and only marginally employed at the depths of the Depression.

He was saved by a remarkable coincidence. Noble Threewit, the young horseman who was sharing the horse stall with Smith, happened to be training horses for George Giannini, Charles Howard's close friend. While visiting the barn to oversee his horses, Giannini noticed how Oriley was flourishing under Smith's care. He realized that wasting away on this Mexican backstretch was a brilliant horseman. Giannini contacted Charles Howard.

"Now," he told his friend, "you can have the best trainer in the country."

Tom Smith and Charles Howard came face-to-face. The two men stood in different halves of the century. Smith was the last of the true frontiersmen; Howard was paving Smith's West under the urgent wheels of his automobiles. Howard was driven by image; Smith remained the Lone Plainsman, forbidding and solitary. But Howard was blessed with an uncanny ability to see potential in unlikely packages, and he had a cavalryman's eye for horsemen. He took one look at Smith and instincts rang in his head. He drove Smith to his barn and introduced his horses to their new trainer.

Smith and Seabiscuit

CHAPTER 3

Mean, Restive, and Ragged

Prosperity, in the form of a fat salary from Howard, had found Tom Smith. He had invested a little in the outer man. Gone were the overalls, the big plaid work shirts, the muddied boots, the chaps, the cap. He began showing up at the barn in neat gray suits, dark vests, whipcord trousers, wing tips, and on race days a restrained Republican tie. He had even purchased a camel-hair coat. Topping off the ensemble was, of course, the utterly unremarkable gray felt fedora. Head and hat were inseparable. Given that Smith was not a man of particularly noteworthy appearance, it was probably the hat, not his face, that people recognized. A couple of years later, during a stable trip to New York, Smith decided that he had just about worn the hat to death and left the barn in search of a replacement. He stomped back in, brushing past Howard, four hours later. On his head was an exact replica of the old hat. Obviously in sour spirits, he muttered that he had spent the entire morning scouring the town trying to find a hat for $2.50.

"Couldn't find one," he grumbled. "Had to get this one."

Howard asked him how much the new hat had set him back.

"Three dollars."

The new raiment fit him. Tom Smith had arrived. He had taken Howard's ill-bred yearlings, worked with them in solitude for a year, then slipped them into Barn 38 at Santa Anita and hung out his shingle. Right from the start he attracted curious glances. Someone saw him wrapping up an alarm clock in a towel and burying it in the straw of a filly's stall, letting her get used to the ticking. Then, while every-one at the track was speculating about what he was up to, Smith tacked up the horse, fished out the clock, and went to the track. He loaded the filly in the gate, set off the clock alarm, and let her rip. He brought her back and did it again and again until she was primed to jackrabbit down the track when she heard a bell.

Pretty soon, people were coming around just to watch Smith. No one had ever seen a trainer work like this. The Howards motored down and watched, too, feeding sugar cubes to their horses and surely wondering what they had gotten themselves into. But then the races began and Smith's horses started winning. Not just a little; Smith *owned* the place. The horses were almost all long shots, because no one trusted what Smith was doing, but that just made the payoffs for Howard's bets all the greater. The filly trained with the alarm clock, a 70-1 longshot, smoked a giant field right out of the gate to win the biggest juvenile race of the season, paying $143.60 for every $2 bet, a meet record. Smith won so much that he started to make the papers almost daily. The racetrackers were soon calling the winner's circle "Howard's Half Acre," and Barn 38 was the track's runaway leader in wins.

Howard and Smith came to an understanding. Howard called his trainer Tom; Smith, without fail, called his employer Mr. Howard. The Howards came to the barn almost every morning, and Charles stayed on, sometimes for fourteen hours at a stretch. He brought in a big truck of a saddle horse named Chulo so he could ride out with Smith on the track. But he knew his place. He didn't mess with Smith's business. For a hands-on executive like Howard, the urge to tinker must have been strong, but he was smart enough to recognize superior understanding, no matter how bizarre the training practices looked. "Mr. Howard pays me for results," Smith once said. "He doesn't ask questions." In turn, Smith put up with Howard's love of the spotlight, the long stream of friends and reporters he brought to the barn, his need to be in the center of things. To a point. If Howard's friends got too close to his horses, Smith would snap at them to get back. The union had its rough points, but it worked.

Howard was hungry for more winning. As the spring waned, they decided to take the show on the road. The horses would go to a little track in Michigan called the Detroit Fair Grounds. Smith was sent on alone, farther east, on a different mission. Howard wanted some mature horses to augment his fleet of juveniles. Howard had the kind of money to turn the head of any major-league owner, and he could have used it to acquire a ready-made stable of proven runners. But Howard didn't want to take the easy route. He wanted a bargain animal whose talent had been overlooked by the old-money lords of eastern racing. He knew he had the trainer who could find him. In June 1936 Smith arrived in Massachusetts. He traveled from track to track, looking at hundreds of cheap horses, but he couldn't find the one he sought. On the sweltering afternoon of June 29, at Boston's Suffolk Downs, the horse found him.

The colt was practically sneering at him. Smith was standing by the track rail, weighing the angles and gestures of low-level horses as they streamed to the post, when a weedy three-year-old bay stopped short in front of him, swung his head high, and eyed him with an arch expression completely unsuited to such a rough-hewn animal. "He looked right down his nose at me," Smith remembered later, "like he was saying, 'Who the devil are you?'" Man and horse stood on opposite sides of the rail for a long moment, sizing each other up. An image materialized in Smith's mind: the Colorado ranges, a tough little cow horse. The pony boy leading the colt to the post tugged him on his way. Smith watched the animal's rump swing around and go. Thin, yes, but he had an engine on him.

Smith flipped to the horse's profile in the track program. The colt was a descendant of the mighty Man o' War through his sire, the brilliantly fast, exceptionally handsome Hard Tack, but his stunted build reflected none of the beauty and breadth of his forebears. The colt's body, built low to the ground, had all the properties of a cinder block. Where Hard Tack had been tall, sleek, tapered, every line suggesting motion, his son was blunt, coarse, rectangular, stationary. He had a sad little tail, barely long enough to brush his hocks. His stubby legs were a study in unsound construction, with squarish, asymmetrical "baseball glove" knees that didn't quite straighten all the way, leaving him in a permanent semicrouch. Thanks to his unfortunate assembly, his walk was an odd, straddle-legged motion that was often mistaken for lameness. Asked to run, he would drop low over the track and fall into a comical version of what horsemen call an eggbeater gait, making a spastic sideways flailing motion with his left foreleg as he swung it forward, as if he were swatting at flies. His gallop was so disorganized that he had a maddening tendency to whack himself in the front ankle with his own hind hoof. One observer compared his action to a duck waddle. All of this raggedness was not helped by his racing schedule. His career had been noteworthy only in its appalling rigor. Though only three years old, he had already run forty-three races, far more than most horses contest in their entire careers.

But somehow, after throwing a fit in the starting gate and being left flat-footed at the bell, the colt won his race that day. While being unsaddled, he leveled his wide-set, intelligent eyes on Smith again. Smith liked that look, and nodded at the horse. "Darned if the little rascal didn't nod back at me," Smith said later, "kinda like he was paying me an honor to notice me." He was a horse whose quality, an admirer would write, "was mostly in his heart, and Tom Smith had been the first to recognize it." A man for whom words were encumbrances, Smith didn't take note of the horse's name, but he memorized him nonetheless. He spoke to the horse as he was led away.

"I'll see you again."

The horse's name was Seabiscuit, and for a bent-backed trainer on the other side of the backstretch, the brief exchange of glances between the horse and Tom Smith was the beginning of the end of a long, pounding headache. In 1877, when James Fitzsimmons was three, the Coney Island Jockey Club annexed his family's Brooklyn neighborhood and literally built a track around his house, leaving it standing in the infield while the racing world revolved around it. "Sunny Jim," as admirers called him, was thus entangled in the racetrack from the beginning of his conscious life. He never escaped it. "All I ever wanted to do," he once said, "was be with the horses." At age ten he worked as a dishwasher in the track kitchen. He moved on to a harrowing career as an exercise boy, then became a jockey. "I was vaccinated for jockey," he liked to say, "but it didn't take." He survived a rocky reinsman's career, then hung it up to try his hand at training. He had found his niche.

Fitzsimmons soon established himself as the most successful conditioner of Thoroughbreds in the nation. That June he was sixty-one and imprisoned in a body so ravaged by arthritis that his upper spine was slowly collapsing forward, driving his head so far downward that in time he would have to learn to identify his horses solely by their feet. He coaxed a phenomenal amount of work out of his rigid body, laboring so hard over his horses through the week that he had to sleep straight through Sunday to recover. The work paid off: Fitzsimmons had cultivated the talents of myriad champions, including Gallant Fox and Omaha, two of the first three horses to sweep the Kentucky Derby, Preakness Stakes, and Belmont Stakes—the Triple Crown. His greatness was beyond question. His was a household name across America, and trainers regarded him with profound reverence. Tom Smith was no exception. Fitzsimmons was apparently the only man whom Smith ever regarded with awe.

The events that brought the two trainers together had begun in 1928, when Fitzsimmons was entrusted with the two-year-old Hard Tack, sire of the colt Smith would see at Suffolk Downs. Owned by Gladys Phipps and her brother Ogden Mills, operators of the East's legendary Wheatley Stable, Hard Tack was a copper-colored paragon of symmetry, grace, and blinding speed. Everything about him was superlative, including his single flaw: He was uncontrollable. The characteristic had surfaced, to a greater or lesser degree, in nearly every horse to descend from his great-grandsire, Hastings, a thousand-pound misanthrope for the ages. On the track, where he won races as prestigious as the 1896 Belmont Stakes, Hastings deliberately rammed and attempted to maul his competitors. Off the track, he ripped groom after groom to ribbons. "He went to his death unreconstructed and unloved," wrote Peter Chew in *American Heritage* magazine, "having left his mark literally and figuratively on many a stablehand." Hastings passed both speed and malevolence down to his son Fair Play, who in turn bequeathed it to his incomparable son, Man o' War. Racing in 1919 and 1920, this immense red animal so devastated his competition that he won by as many as one hundred lengths and set numerous speed records. Man o' War lost only once in his career—to a colt coincidentally named Upset—a defeat that still ranks among the most shocking in sports history. Arguably the greatest runner who ever lived, Man o' War became a prolific sire, populating the racing world with beautiful man-eaters.

A typical example was War Relic. While a youngster, he acquainted the world with his jolly personality by stomping a groom to death. His trainer, Culton Utz, tracked down leading jockey Tommy Luther, famed for his fearlessness and ability to stay aboard even the most unrideable beasts, and brought him to the training farm to work with the horse. Luther was appalled at just how bad the colt was. "The horse," remembered Luther, "would do *everything* wrong." Luther and Utz put War Relic through endless hours of patient schooling until they felt he was ready to go to the track without killing anyone. At Rhode Island's Narragansett Park they entered him in a race. War Relic displayed cherubic behavior, grabbed the lead out of the gate, and never relinquished it, winning with consummate ease. "Next time he runs," Luther told his wife, Helen, "bet a hundred dollars. It will be like taking candy from a baby."

Helen did as her husband asked, then sat in the stands on race day, terrified and praying. War Relic rocketed to the lead, held it around the track, and flew into the homestretch all alone. Luther thought his $100 bet was going to cash in. But War Relic had been an angel for exactly one and three quarter races, and he was pushing his limits. As the crowd cheered him on from the grandstand, he abruptly bolted to the inside, hit the rail, and stopped dead, vaulting Luther into a spiraling dive directly toward the toothy track harrows parked in the infield. Luther was on the verge of being skewered. Throwing out his hands, he caught the rail, swooped around it like a gymnast, and made a clean dismount onto the track. Steward Tom Thorpe walked across the course and stared at Luther's uninjured body, incredulous.

"Tommy," he said, "you must have had somebody praying for you."

Praying was usually the best you could do when confronted with a son of Man o' War. Hard Tack, also a Man o' War son, inherited the fabled Hastings temper distilled to crystal purity. The colt spent three years plunging around the track in devil-possessed rages and nurturing a vendetta against the hapless assistant starters assigned to hold his head in the doorless starting gate. He terrorized them without mercy; they feared and loathed him without reserve. Hard Tack became a notorious rogue, inspiring turf writer John Hervey to dub him "the archexponent of recalcitrance." Fitzsimmons had gentled plenty of miscreants, but he had no answers for Hard Tack. By some miracle, on three occasions, he was able to coax the horse into playing the racing game. Running with an unusual gait in which one foreleg jabbed out as he swung it forward, Hard Tack channeled savagery into velocity, whipping top horses in stakes races—the highest level of racing—and breaking speed records. But these were only skirmishes. Hard Tack won the war. At the starting gate before a race in 1931, he issued his declaration of independence. When the starter banged the bell, Hard Tack rooted his hooves in the ground and stayed right where he was. Fitzsimmons packed him up and shipped him back to owner Phipps.

By the time Hard Tack entered stud in 1932, his name burned in infamy. No one was foolish enough to pay a stud fee to breed a mare to him. Poor Gladys Phipps offered him to Maryland breeders for free, but she couldn't find a single taker. She then asked Kentucky's famed Claiborne Farm, which boarded her mares, to stand him at stud. They declined. Eager to see some return on her investment, she had him vanned far down a lonely Kentucky lane, onto an obscure farm called Blue Grass Heights, and parked him in a paddock deep in a grove of mulberry trees. She sent some of her own mares over from Claiborne to be bred to him. One of them was a mealy, melon-kneed horse named Swing On. She, too, had once been in Fitzsimmons's care, but though she had shown a quick turn of foot occasionally, she hadn't trained well enough for Fitzsimmons to think she was going to be much of a racehorse. He had retired her without ever racing her. She was nicely bred, so Phipps decided to send her to Hard Tack's court, along with three other mares. Swing On and her fellow mares came back to Claiborne pregnant. Phipps crossed her fingers, hoping that these matings would re-create the perfect forms of the forebears without the tyrannical disposition.

They didn't. At New York's Aqueduct Racecourse late in 1934, Hard Tack's first two yearlings stepped off a railcar into Fitzsimmons's care. Swing On's son Seabiscuit (a synonym for his sire's name) and the other colt, Grog, could not have looked less like their sire. Noah, the foaling groom at Claiborne, had summed it up about as well as anyone when he pulled Seabiscuit into the world: "Runty little thing." Claiborne handlers had been so dismayed with the colt that they had hidden him in a back barn when Phipps came to look over her new crop of horses. A year of maturing hadn't helped much. "Seabiscuit was so small," said Fitzsimmons, "that you might mistake him for a lead pony." Curiously, Hard Tack appeared to be stamping his foals in a mold that was the polar opposite of his own. The only similarity, evident in Seabiscuit, was that swatting foreleg. Not only were these colts strange-looking, shaggy, and awkward, but aside from the slight difference in their mutually diminutive heights—Grog was a hair shorter—they were identical. Without the assistance of a halter nameplate, virtually no one could tell them apart. The colts must have liked the mirror image; they had become inseparable in the Claiborne paddocks.

Fortunately, Hard Tack's raging temper had also come out in the genetic wash. Seabiscuit floated along in a state of contented, bovine torpor. Sleeping was his favorite pastime. Horses usually sleep in numerous brief sessions scattered throughout the day and night; about 20 percent of their daytime is spent snoozing. Because of the size and configuration of their bodies, they suffer impeded breathing and circulation when recumbent, and as prey animals who have trouble getting to their feet quickly, they are instinctively disinclined to stay down. As a result, the vast majority of horses' sleeping is done standing, which they can do thanks to ligaments that lock their leg joints in the extended position. The average stabled horse spends just five minutes at a time lying down to sleep, almost always at night.

Seabiscuit was the exception. He could keel over and snooze for hours on end without suffering any negative consequences. While every other horse at the track raised hell demanding breakfast, he slept long and late, stretching out over the floor of his stall in such deep sedation that the grooms had to use every means in their power just to get him to stand up. He was so quiet that Fitzsimmons's assistant trainers once forgot all about him and left him in a van for an entire afternoon in brutal heat while they went for a beer. They found him there hours later, pitched over on his side, blissfully asleep. No one had ever seen a horse so relaxed. Fitzsimmons would remember him as "a big dog," the most easygoing horse he ever trained. The only thing Seabiscuit took seriously, aside from his beauty rest, was eating, which he did constantly, with great vigor.

He may have been an amiable little horse, but his career prospects looked dim. He was as slow as growing grass. He barely kept up with his training partners, lagging along behind with happy ineptitude. Worked over and over again, he showed no improvement whatsoever. "The boys who took care of him could do anything with him," Fitzsimmons said. "Anything, that is, except to get him to run in the mornings. . . . I thought he simply couldn't run."

But in time, something in Seabiscuit's demeanor—perhaps a conspicuous lack of sweating in the workouts, perhaps a gleam in the horse's eye that hinted at devious intelligence—made Fitzsimmons question his assumptions. "He was as wise as a little owl," Fitzsimmons remembered later. "He was almost too quiet, too docile." Fitzsimmons began to wonder if this horse might be just as obstreperous as his sire, only much more cunning in his methods. His father had raged; Seabiscuit seemed . . . amused. "He struck me," Fitzsimmons said, "as a bird that could sing but wouldn't unless we made him."

Fitzsimmons made him. "I decided to fool the Biscuit," he explained, "to prove to him he wasn't fooling me." One morning, when working all the yearlings over two furlongs—a quarter of a mile—in sets of two, he paired Seabiscuit with Faust, the fastest yearling in the barn and a future major stakes winner. He told Seabiscuit's exercise rider to find a stick to use as a whip. This was a radical departure from Fitzsimmons's regular training practices, which mandated that exercise riders never use whips on their horses. The trainer believed that racehorses were instinctively hard-trying, competitive creatures who did not need to be forced to exert themselves. During one race in his jockey days, he heard another rider cursing after dropping his whip on what he thought was an otherwise sure winner. Fitzsimmons handed the jockey his whip, then rode his own horse right past him to win, urging him with nothing but hands and voice. But Seabiscuit could not be coaxed into showing any speed at all, and to find out if the horse was hoodwinking him, Fitzsimmons opted to make an exception to his no-whip rule. To ensure that the stick would not hurt Seabiscuit, Fitzsimmons had the rider select one that was flat, so it would merely slap his flank.

"Keep this colt right up with Faust as close as you can," he later recalled telling the jockey. "Just see how many times you can hit him going a quarter of a mile." Fitzsimmons expected that, at best, Seabiscuit would be able to cling to Faust for a little while.

Faust never had a chance. Slapped over and over again with the stick, Seabiscuit blew Faust's doors off, covering a quarter mile in an impossible 22⅗ seconds. It may have been the fastest quarter ever run by a yearling. Today, on tracks that are several seconds faster than they were in the 1930s, such a workout time is considered exceptionally swift, even for a mature horse. The bird could sing.

"I found out why he wasn't running," said Fitzsimmons. "It wasn't that he couldn't. It was that he wouldn't." Fitzsimmons realized that he was confronted with a behavioral problem at least as maddening as Hard Tack's murderousness: pathological indolence. "He was lazy," marveled Fitzsimmons. "Dead lazy."

The colt had proven that Hard Tack's speed lived on in his homely little body. But the revelation didn't make him any more eager to work. Though he later denied it, Fitzsimmons evidently suspended his no-whip rule indefinitely with Seabiscuit. "We used a whip on him every time we sent him to the track, and we used it freely, too," he once conceded. "When we didn't, he loafed along." The horse performed better, but he still wasn't working hard enough to get himself fit. Fitzsimmons came to the conclusion that the only way to tap into the potential he had glimpsed was to race him hard. Very hard. His logic: Since the horse rested himself so much more than other horses, he could stand up to an unusually heavy racing schedule. And since the horse was uncommonly intelligent, he would know to back off if he became overworked.

Entrusted to assistant trainer James Fitzsimmons, Jr., while Sunny Jim manned the helm on the more precocious horses, Seabiscuit began a regimen of incredibly rigorous campaigning. Thoroughbreds are placed in age classes according to the year in which they are born, rather than their birth month. On January 1 all horses graduate to the next age class even if their birthdays fall months later. Seabiscuit had been a very late foal, born at the end of May 1933, but in January 1935, half a year short of his actual birthday, he was deemed a two-year-old, officially eligible to race. On January 19, he began his career at Florida's Hialeah Race Track. He finished fourth. It wasn't good enough for the Wheatley Stable, which was overflowing with top prospects. Three days later, Seabiscuit was put up for sale, placed in a rock-bottom claiming race for a tag of just $2,500. No one wanted him even at that price, and he lost again. James junior then put the colt on the road, touring through thirteen tracks up and down the East Coast to run in low-rent races spaced as little as two days apart. Sixteen times Seabiscuit ran; sixteen times he lost. From Florida to Rhode Island and practically everywhere in between, he was offered in the cheapest claiming races. No one took him.

Once in a while the Hard Tack speed reappeared. In the colt's seventeenth start, for no explicable reason, he finally won, clocking a sterling time. Rolled back into another claiming race just four days later, he broke a track record, an unheard-of feat for a claimer. But the brilliant form fell apart immediately, leaving him back among the dregs of racing. He plodded along for another few months, then rebounded with three moderate wins in the fall of 1935 before sinking back into failure.

By season's end, Seabiscuit had been shipped over six thousand miles and raced a staggering thirty-five times, at least triple the typical workload. Grog had fared even worse, racing thirty-seven times before being claimed for a paltry $1,500. Sooner or later, it appeared, Seabiscuit would meet the same fate.

At least the problem of how to get Seabiscuit in shape had been solved. Raced constantly, he surely no longer lacked for fitness. But his problems were predominantly mental. By the time his two-year-old season drew to a close, he was showing signs of burnout. He became edgy. He stopped sleeping, spending his nights pacing around and around his stall. On the track, he fought savagely in the starting gate and sulked his way through races, sometimes trailing the field from start to finish. A young jockey named George Woolf, aboard for one of these woeful performances, summed up the colt's mental state in four words: "mean, restive, and ragged."

Years later Fitzsimmons would argue that the intense campaign through which he and his assistants put Seabiscuit gave the horse the seasoning that enabled him to race for so long as an older horse. There may be some merit to this, as recent research suggests that steady, hard training and racing in sound horses, especially in young ones, may give bones and soft tissue the loading they need for optimal durability, and give horses the wind foundation to tackle harder racing later. But such a thing can be overdone. Thoroughbreds run because they love to, but when overraced they can become stale and uninterested, especially when repeatedly trounced and bullied by their riders, as Seabiscuit was. By the spring of 1936 he was clearly miserable, and it is hard to avoid the conclusion that his exhausting schedule was the cause. Given that he wasn't winning, or even running passably well, it's very difficult to defend it.

Seabiscuit had the misfortune of living in a stable whose managers simply didn't have the time to give his mind the painstaking attention it needed. Fitzsimmons's barn, consisting of horses owned by the Wheatley and Belair Stables, was teeming with precocious youngsters and proven, high-class older horses. As Seabiscuit plodded through his first season, Fitzsimmons was touring the nation amid a storm of publicity as Seabiscuit's stablemate, Omaha, made a successful assault on the Triple Crown. The following season Fitzsimmons turned his attention to the promising Granville, readying him for a shot at the '36 Kentucky Derby. It was often said that Fitzsimmons nearly ruined Seabiscuit by using him as a workmate for Granville, pulling him up during hot contests to bolster Granville's confidence. This is highly unlikely. Since Seabiscuit refused to exert himself in workouts, it would have made little sense to pair him with the brilliantly fast Granville, especially as Granville already had a designated workmate who traveled with him. Further, as Fitzsimmons often explained, Granville was owned by Belair Stable, Seabiscuit by Wheatley, and one of horse training's cardinal rules is that the horse of one owner is never sacrificed to benefit the horse of another. Fitzsimmons would certainly have avoided this conflict of interest.

But Granville's presence probably did work against Seabiscuit, simply by virtue of the demands that a Kentucky Derby contender makes on his trainer. Granville was a temperamental animal who needed coddling, and little time was left over for the Seabiscuits and Grogs of the stable. The Fitzsimmons barn was one in which a horse who did not display spectacular talent could slip through the cracks. That is what happened to Seabiscuit, and Fitzsimmons knew it. "He had something when he wanted to show it," the trainer later admitted, "It was like he was saving himself for something. Trouble was, I didn't have time right then to find out for what."

In the spring of '36 Fitzsimmons set off for the Triple Crown prep races with Granville, leaving Seabiscuit in the hands of assistant trainer George Tappen. The horse's campaign became a road show of athletic futility. Seabiscuit shipped all over the Northeast, never stayed more than two or three weeks in one place, averaged one race every five days, and racked up losses to inferior horses practically every time out. But just as in his freshman season, he showed glimmers of promise.

There was a decent effort at New York's Jamaica Race Track, then a modest allowance win at Narragansett Park. The decent performances were mixed with laughably bad outings—two ten-length thumpings, one of which saw him lag in twelfth from start to finish—but Fitzsimmons was becoming more and more convinced that the colt could be improved. He never stopped trying to encourage Seabiscuit to work harder in the mornings, including offering a $1 incentive—twice the standard fee—to any exercise rider who could get him to run a half mile in anything under a sleepy fifty seconds. "None of them," Fitzsimmons lamented, "ever won the dollar."

The puzzle of the horse weighed on Fitzsimmons's mind. One morning at Aqueduct, while standing by the track to watch Granville complete his preparations for the Kentucky Derby, reporters were surprised to hear Sunny Jim ruminating not on his stable star but on the unknown Seabiscuit. The colt was, said the trainer, "a pretty nice hoss, the kind that might take some time to get going, but would take a lot of beating when he did."

As Fitzsimmons was warming up to Seabiscuit, Wheatley was cooling off. Gladys Phipps was convinced that even if Fitzsimmons could make a silk purse out of this sow's ear, the horse was still much too small to make it in the more lucrative "handicap" division, in which he would have to carry heavier weights. The new crop of horses coming into the barn was a big one, and the stable string had to be culled. Seabiscuit topped the list of disposable horses, and Phipps was eager to find a buyer. Unable to do so, she tried to pawn the colt off as a polo pony. The prospective buyer took one look at the colt's crooked legs and passed. Early that spring, before she left for a tour of Europe, Phipps set a $5,000 price on Seabiscuit, hoping he would be sold before she came back.

Fitzsimmons had bigger things to worry about. In early May, a few days before Seabiscuit earned $25 for finishing fourth in a race at Jamaica Race Track, Fitzsimmons and Granville shipped off to Churchill Downs to go for the $37,725 winner's share of the purse in the Kentucky Derby. Coming into the race with an excellent shot at winning, Granville fumed, stormed, and lathered through the post parade and bounced and shimmied in the starting gate. When the bell rang, he was sideswiped by a horse named He Did and nearly went down. He dumped jockey Jimmy Stout and took off for a glorious solo gallop around the track. In Baltimore's Preakness Stakes, Stout stuck to his stirrups but finished second to Derby winner Bold Venture, foiled by the brilliant reinsmanship of Seabiscuit's onetime jockey, George Woolf. In early June, as Seabiscuit was being humiliated in a cheap stakes race in New Hampshire, Granville finally lived up to expectations by winning New York's Belmont Stakes, the final jewel in the Triple Crown. He would be named Horse of the Year for 1936. With a competitor like Granville in his barn, Fitzsimmons now had no reason to be fretting over a colt like Seabiscuit.

In June, after being whipped by a total of more than twenty-five lengths in his previous three starts, Seabiscuit appeared at Massachusetts's Suffolk Downs to compete against a lowly field vying for a $700 winner's purse. There Tom Smith bent over the track rail and exchanged looks with him for the first time. Countless horsemen had run their eyes over that plain bay body. None of them had seen what Smith saw.

In a private box above Saratoga Race Course on August 3, 1936, Marcela and Charles Howard surveyed a field of generic $6,000 claimers. In town to bid on the yearling sales on behalf of Bing Crosby, they had stopped by the track to take in a few races. Charles pointed to an especially homely colt and asked his wife what she thought of him. She offered a wager of a cool drink that the horse would lose. He accepted the bet, and they watched as the colt led wire to wire. Marcela bought her husband a lemonade. Sitting together in the clubhouse that afternoon, husband and wife felt a pull of intuition. Howard contacted Smith and told him he had a horse he wanted him to look at, stabled in the Fitzsimmons barn. Smith was probably skeptical. That spring he had been shown nearly two dozen prospects and had frowned over every one of them.

Smith walked over to the Wheatley barn and presented himself to

Fitzsimmons, asking to see the horse of whom Howard had spoken. Fitzsimmons walked the colt in question out of his stall. Smith recognized him immediately; it was Seabiscuit. Smith saw the bucked knees, the insistent pressure of ribs under skin, the weariness of the body. But he saw something else, too. He tracked down Howard.

"Better come and see him for yourself," he said.

Led out of his stall with the two men standing by, Seabiscuit head-butted Howard. Smith made his case with four sentences: "Get me that horse. He has real stuff in him. I can improve him. I'm positive."

It was a statement astounding for its audacity. Tom Smith was an obscure trainer with one year's experience with a mainstream stable. Fitzsimmons was the undisputed leader of the nation's training ranks. If Sunny Jim couldn't get a horse to win, no one could. Few trainers, even the most cocksure, were fool enough to buy a horse from the master. For Smith, walking into that barn must have been akin to entering a cathedral; telling Fitzsimmons that he could improve on his work must have felt like sacrilege. And there was another reason for worry. Howard sent veterinarians to inspect the horse. They were only lukewarm about his prospects, eyeing that iffy left foreleg and pronouncing the horse only "serviceably useful." But in this horse, Smith knew there was something lying dormant.

The bump from Seabiscuit's head took care of Howard's sentimental side. "I fell in love with him," he said later, "right then and there." Marcela was sold and urged him not to wait. But Howard's business side was still not convinced. He contacted co-owner Ogden Mills and made an offer of $8,000, with one string attached: Seabiscuit had to perform well in his next start.

The appointed day arrived with pouring rain, and Fitzsimmons considered scratching Seabiscuit. But no one else seemed to want to run in the mud either. All day long, trainers kept scratching horses from the race. By afternoon, only one other horse remained in the field. Fitzsimmons decided he had nothing to lose. Howard amused himself by putting a $100 bet on the horse, then settled in to watch. Smith was terrified. He had studied Seabiscuit's past performances and knew that the horse did not run his best in mud. The trainer stood on the track apron and fretted.

Seabiscuit broke slowly and dropped farther and farther back. By mid-race, he was trailing by at least ten lengths. Smith was dismayed. But Seabiscuit began to rally. Slogging through the slop, he lumbered up to his competitor, pushing as hard as he could, and passed him. It wasn't much of a race, but it was a win nonetheless. Howard was satisfied. The horse had grit.

"I can't describe the feeling he gave me," Howard said later, "but somehow I knew he had what it takes. Tom and I realized that we had our worries and troubles ahead. We had to rebuild him, both mentally and physically, but you don't have to rebuild the heart when it's already there, big as all outdoors."

Smith breathed a sigh of relief. Years later, he would shiver at the thought of how easily he could have lost the colt in the driving rain that day.

Howard let Mills know that the offer was still on the table. Mills mulled it over. Fitzsimmons had become deeply fond of the colt and entertained private doubts about parting with him. Seabiscuit might, he muttered dubiously, win another purse. He didn't share his reservations with Mills, an omission he would come to regret. Howard found Mills in the Saratoga paddock.

"Deal or no deal?" he asked.

"Deal," said Mills. Howard wrote out a check to Mills, then gave his new horse to Marcela.

Tom Smith had found the horse who would lift him from obscurity.

On an August day in 1936, Seabiscuit was led from the Fitzsimmons barn for the last time. No one came to see him go. Fitzsimmons hadn't been told that the sale had gone through, so he didn't come to say his good-byes. Seabiscuit was walked down the backstretch, a long canopy of trees bowing over his head. At the Howard barn, Smith waited, flanked by a cluster of stable hands. Though the trainer hardly ever said anything, there was an air to him that day that told the grooms how special the horse was to him. One kid who had not picked up on it was a teenaged apprentice jockey named Farrell Jones, who joined the others at the barn as Seabiscuit was led up. Seeing a thin, homely animal, Jones made the understandable assumption that this was no racehorse.

"Looks like they got a new saddle horse," he blurted out, loud enough for Smith to hear.

The grooms shushed him.

A few days later, Smith led Seabiscuit up onto a railcar, and the Howard barn pushed off for the Detroit Fair Grounds. Smith began thinking about finding a jockey.

Red Pollard
(KEENELAND-COOK)

CHAPTER 4

The Cougar and the Iceman

R ed Pollard was sinking downward through his life with the pendulous motion of a leaf falling through still air. In the summer of 1936 he was twenty-six and in the twelfth year of a failing career as a jockey and part-time prizefighter. He was an elegant young man, tautly muscled, with a shock of supernaturally orange hair. Whenever he got near a mirror, he wetted down a comb and slicked the hair back like Tyrone Power, but it had a way of rearing up on him again. His face had a downward-sliding quality, as if his features were just beginning to melt.

He was, statistically speaking, one of the worst riders anywhere. Lately, at least. Once, he had been one of the best, but those years were far behind him. He had no money and no home; he lived entirely on the road of the racing circuit, sleeping in empty stalls, carrying with him only a saddle, his rosary, and his books: pocket volumes of Shakespeare, Omar Khayyám's *Rubaiyat*, a little copy of Robert Service's *Songs of the Sourdough*, maybe some Emerson, whom he called "Old Waldo." The books were the closest things he had to furniture, and he lived in them the way other men live in easy chairs.

On the day Seabiscuit settled in at the Detroit Fair Grounds, Pollard was in North Randall, Ohio, sweltering through August at a middling racetrack called Thistle Down Park, which was wrapping up its summer meeting. Pollard's career had continued slipping there, as it had everywhere else. His win percentage had dropped into the single digits. The last horse he rode came to a halt right in the middle of his race. On August 16, 1936, when Thistle Down Park shuttered its doors for the season, Red Pollard appeared to be out of chances.

Back home in Edmonton, Alberta, he had been known as Johnny. Right from his boyhood, people had seen the restlessness in him. They must have known he wouldn't stay in their town for long.

Wanderlust ran in his family. Johnny's father and namesake, a refugee from poverty in his native Ireland, had spent his young adulthood rambling across the western Canadian wilderness in search of gold. In 1898, prospecting led him to a nearly vacant trail crossing that the trappers called Edmonton, where he found that the soil was the perfect medium for making brick. The Irishman staked a claim, opened a brick factory on the banks of the North Saskatchewan River, and made a fortune on the Northwest's turn-of-the-century construction boom. He bought up a huge portion of Edmonton and built the first real house in town, a vast home surrounded by sprawling acres of virgin countryside. With his wife, Edith, he raised seven whip-smart, buoyant children: Jim, Johnny, Bill, Edie, Betty, Norah, and a little girl whom, with characteristic Pollard whimsy, they called Bubbles. The elder Pollard's brother Frank and his family moved in to join the business, and the Pollard home was soon teeming with sixteen family members and a host of workers who took their meals at the house.

Born in November 1909, Johnny was the liveliest member of a clever and boisterous family. In the Pollard home, books were always open, old Irish songs sung, jigs danced, long stories spun. Johnny played on the grassy fields of his family's estate and spent his Sundays in the lap of the family Model T, competing with his siblings for a window seat. As the car swung over a high bridge that crossed the North Saskatchewan River, he could peer over the railing to see the family business at the water's edge below.

Misfortune struck suddenly and forcefully. In 1915 the river boiled up in a flash flood, ripping over the shoreline around the factory. Johnny's father rescued his family from the water by throwing them in a buggy and lugging them up the bank himself, but he couldn't save the factory machinery. The business vanished, and the tax bill arrived. Pollard traveled around Canada, trying in vain to find a bank to lend him the money. The city of Edmonton foreclosed, and the Pollards lost everything but their house. Virtually overnight, Johnny's father was bankrupt with seven children and a wife to feed. He eventually found meager income as an auto repairman. It was only by bartering gasoline for groceries that he managed to keep his family alive.

Johnny found myriad avenues of distraction from his family's penury. One was athletic. His father took him and his older brother Bill to the community boxing ring, where they were swept up in the prizefighting craze of the 1920s. Bill, a tall, powerful fighter, made it to the Golden Gloves. Johnny, smaller and leaner, became a proficient and scrappy fighter but never achieved his brother's success. He amused himself by provoking much bigger boys into fights, calling his "Golden Glove brother" to the rescue, and laughing as they ran in terror.

His other escape was intellectual. Johnny devoured great literature. He committed long passages of prose and poetry to memory and engaged in lively recitation duels with his sister Edie as they bounced over the local roads in the Model T. Graced with an agile mind, he had the makings of a man of letters. Later, when his fate became known, his boyhood friends would wish for his sake that he had gone the way of the academy. But the classroom smothered him. He desperately wanted to explore the wider world. He was impatient with his lessons, mouthed off at teachers, got poor grades, spent his hours coining witticisms and engineering elaborate practical jokes. His emotions were liquid; his anger was a wild rage, his pleasure jubilation, his humor biting, his sorrow and empathy a bottomless abyss. He was, his son John would later remember, a person who brought an uproar with him wherever he went. Johnny Pollard was a caged bird.

As he grew, his restlessness turned into aspiration. His father had somehow managed to obtain a gift for his second son, a little horse named Forest Dawn. To help make ends meet, Johnny began hitching the horse to his toboggan and using them to make deliveries for the local grocery. In long afternoons aboard the pony's back, Johnny discovered a gift for riding. His daughter, writer Norah Christianson, remembers that he had "the body of a dancer, lithe and wiry and thin, everything in balance," a physique ideally suited to the pitch and yaw of a horse's withers. Riding also suited his passion for risk. His life, from his youth onward, was a headlong rush into danger and uncertainty. Out on Edmonton's dirt roads, his legs swinging free from Forest Dawn's sides while the toboggan bobbed along behind, Johnny decided he wanted to be a jockey.

As he entered his teens, Johnny began haunting local stables, trading his labor for a chance to ride. He appealed to his parents to let him go out on the racing circuit and learn to be a jockey. His mother wanted to stop him. His father did not. Perhaps the aging prospector understood the futility of trying to contain a torrential boy within the confines of a small town. Perhaps he was proud of Johnny's aspiration to make a career of sport. Surely money played a role in the decision Pollard would make; he was barely able to feed his children. But his wife was frightened. In 1925 the Pollards made a compromise. Johnny would be allowed to go to the racetrack to pursue his career, but only on the condition that he be escorted by a trusted family friend. The Pollards swallowed their fears, kissed their son good-bye, and handed him over to his new guardian.

Sometime in 1925 Johnny and his guardian pulled into the old mining town of Butte, Montana, where the local bullring racetrack linked up with a network of other tracks, carnivals, and fairs. Featuring bottom-level Thoroughbreds and quarter horses, these tracks offered the worst of low-rent racing. Most were little more than makeshift ovals cut through hayfields. Races were begun either by walking horses away from the starter, then spinning them around when the starter said go—a method called "lap and tap"—or by lining them up behind a simple webbing that was rigged to spring upward to start the race, sometimes catching riders under the chin. Purses were often smaller than the cost of shoeing a horse—about $1.40. The tracks were only a half mile around. The turns were so tight that a horse with a head of steam on him—a top quarter horse can sprint at some fifty-five miles per hour—would go winging off into the hay if he didn't ease back as he left the straightaway. It was nothing special, but it was a start.

Johnny had only just arrived when his guardian vanished. The man never returned. Pollard was completely alone and penniless in a remote town of a foreign country. He was just fifteen years old, and his boyhood was over.

If Pollard had any way to get home, he didn't use it. Somehow, he managed to find a place to sleep and something to eat. He began wandering around the carnivals and tracks, trying to talk his way onto the backs of horses. Though he towered over other jockeys, ultimately leveling off at about five feet seven inches, he hadn't filled out his frame yet, weighing just 101 pounds, light enough to ride. The local race-trackers grew fond of the odd, bookish boy, nicknaming him Red, and a few let him ride their horses.

It was a rough place to start a career. Racing in the bush leagues was utterly lawless. "If you could survive there," remembered former jockey Joe "Mossy" Mosbacher, "you could ride anywhere." With no race cameras and only two patrol judges to oversee them, jockeys could—and would—do anything to win. Jockeys on trailing horses grabbed hold of leading horses' tails or saddlecloths so their own horses could be towed around the track, saving energy. They joined arms with other jockeys to "clothesline" riders trying to cut between horses, formed obstructive "flying wedges" to block closers, and bashed passing horses into the inside rail. They hooked their legs over other jockeys' knees, ensuring that if their rivals moved forward, they'd be scraped off their saddles. They dangled their feet in front of passing horses to intimidate them, and when less inspired, they shoved and punched one another and grabbed one another's reins. Because many of the tracks had no inner rail, some jockeys simply cut through the infield, dodging haystacks, to win. In some cases, riders toppled their opponents right off their horses.

Such tactics were, until the mid-1930s, seen at all levels of racing, but nowhere were they used with such ruthlessness as on the bush tracks where Pollard got his start. According to the great jockey Eddie Arcaro, who once rammed another rider over the rail in retribution for a bump ("I was trying to kill that Cuban S.O.B.," he told the stewards, who reformed him with a year's suspension), the desire to win wasn't the only motivation. The bush leagues contained two kinds of riders: kids like Pollard seeking to make their names and veterans in the bitter waning days of their careers, sliding down to this last and lowest place in the sport. "To succeed in those days, you had to fight for everything you got," Arcaro wrote in his autobiography, *I Ride to Win!* "You were competing with men who were aware that their own particular suns were fading, and they resented your moving into the places they would leave. They fought you, and you fought them back."

Pollard took a few licks, held his own, and learned a lot. But months passed, and still he didn't win a single race. In danger of starving, he used the only other skill he had, straying into carnival bullrings and cow-town clubs to moonlight as a prizefighter. He was no headliner. Mostly, he boxed in preliminary matches to warm up the crowd. At the time, a local kid nicknamed "the Nebraska Wildcat" was the hottest boxing property around. In imitation, Pollard took the ring name "Cougar." His skills didn't live up to the nickname. He fought a lot of matches, and lost, he said, "a lot of 'em."

Though a misnomer, his nickname proved to be the one enduring thing about Pollard's ring career. Racetrackers in that era had a peculiar animosity for given names. Among those haunting the track in Pollard's day were Lying Tex, Truthful Tex, Scratchy Balls John, Cow Shit Red, Piss-Through-the-Screen Slim, and a man the trackers called Booger. Baptist John was the nickname of a tracker famed for being run over by a police car that was chasing him, breaking his leg. He left the cast on his leg until it rotted off, so that, in the words of horseman Wad Studley, "one leg went north and the other one southwest." The given names of half the people at the track were complete mysteries. The name Cougar followed Pollard from the boxing ring to the races and stuck with him for good. He liked the name, referred to himself by it, preferred that his closest friends use it, and gave it to every dog he ever owned.

A year passed. Pollard didn't win a race. The break he needed came from a genial old former jockey named Asa C. "Acey" Smith, a traveling "gyp," or gypsy, trainer. Passing through Montana, Acey thought he saw promise in Pollard, signed him on as his rider, and brought him on a road trip to western Canada. It was at a little fair track that Pollard finally rode a winner, H. C. Basch, in a mile-and-a-half race in the fall of 1926. It was a momentous event. Once a rider logged his first win, he officially became an apprentice jockey, or "bug boy," so called because of the asterisk, or "bug," that was typed next to apprentices' names in the racing program. Then as now, all racehorses were assigned a weight, called an impost, to carry in each race. The impost consisted of the jockey, his roughly four and a half pounds of saddle, boots, pants, and silks, and, if necessary, lead pads inserted into the saddle. To help aspiring riders establish themselves in the sport, a horse ridden by a bug boy had his impost reduced by five pounds. The bug offered a substantial break: The rule of thumb is that every two to three pounds slows a horse by a length in racing's middle distances of a mile to a mile and a quarter, while in longer races every pound slows a horse by one length. Bug boys enjoyed the weight break until they rode their fortieth winner or reached the anniversary of their first win, whichever came first. After that, they were journeyman riders.

In that era virtually all jockeys were signed to stable contracts, which were clear and simple. In exchange for housing—usually a cot in a vacant horse stall—and about $5 a week for food, bug boys gave the trainer first call on their riding services, their toil in an unending stream of barn chores, and authoritarian control over their lives. Journeymen earned a slightly higher salary and usually escaped the chores. If a stable had no horses in a race, its contract jockeys were allowed to freelance for other barns. When riding for their contract stables, bug boys received nothing from the purses their horses won. Journeymen and freelancing bug boys earned $15 for a winner, $5 for every other placing, minus fees for laundry (50¢), valet ($1), and agent (10 percent) if they could afford one. Technically, freelancing jockeys were due a 10 percent cut of purses—usually about $40 at the better tracks where Pollard rode—and 50¢ for galloping horses in morning workouts, but almost no one paid it. The best journeymen negotiated for higher pay, and some tried to even things out for the struggling ones, offering to "save" or divide the winning purse among all the riders, but this was eventually made illegal as it removed the incentive for winning. In this system a tiny subset of riders became wealthy, a few lived comfortably, and the rest, the vast majority, had nothing.

The world of bug-boy jockeys was populated mostly by teenagers who had run away or been orphaned or whose families had come upon hard times, as Pollard's had. "Every one of them would have a story," recalls Mosbacher, who wound up at the track after running away from an impoverished home. Only a few had an elementary-school education, and none had made it through high school. Most had no place else to go. "I was hungry," explained child bug boy Ralph Neves, who came to the races as an orphaned runaway, "and too nervous to steal." By the rules, a boy had to be at least sixteen to ride, but no one ever asked for a birth certificate. Some riders started as young as twelve. During one 1920s season at the old Tijuana track, former rider Bill Buck remembered, the two *oldest* riders were just sixteen. Bug boys were often remarkably small; Wad Studley was so tiny when he started riding—eighty-two pounds—that he had trouble lifting his own saddle. On the day he rode his first winner, Tommy Luther weighed seventy-nine pounds. Most of these boys knew nothing of racing when they began and were completely at the mercy of their trainers.

Some trainers became surrogate parents to their bug boys. Others exploited their charges with relentless cruelty. Luther recalled that in some stables a bug boy's punishment for losing a race was a stout beating. "Father" Bill Daly, a peg-legged trainer described by one writer as "villainous," reportedly carried a barrel stave with him at all times so he could beat his jockeys. When they weighed too much, he reportedly cleaned their pockets of their pennies so they couldn't buy food or locked them up until they starved down to the right weight. To avoid train fare, Luther and his fellow bug boys were stowed away in horse cars. When the railroad police came through the train, impaling the haystacks to flush out stowaways, the trainers packed the boys into tack trunks. On another occasion, a trainer put

Luther up in a hotel, then booted him out the window when the bill came due.

On the track, bug boys were like any other commodity, to be leased, sold, swapped for horses, put up as collateral, and staked in card games. Though they earned practically nothing, they could be worth a lot, upwards of $15,000 for a good one. Many bug boys were sold without their knowledge. In 1928 jockey Johnny Longden learned of his change of ownership early one morning in Winnipeg, where his trainer had put him up in a tent. While he slept, a stranger walked up and began shaking the tent violently. "Get the hell out of here!" barked a voice from outside. "You're working for me now, and nobody on my payroll sleeps late."

Pollard was lucky. Acey treated him well. In the summer he usually raced at the cluster of tracks around Vancouver or at another western Canadian track called Glacier Park; in the fall and spring it was California's Tanforan; in the winter, Tijuana. Pollard spent his days aboard Acey's animals and his nights in a stall, sandwiched between two horses, subsisting on his books and irregular meals from the track kitchen.

Veteran horsemen were merciless to kids who wanted to be jockeys. A common prank was to send a new bug boy all over the track looking for the phantom "key to the quarter pole." One kid who came to the track in Tijuana and announced he wanted to be a jockey was told he had to take off some weight. Horsemen draped him in two horse blankets and made him run around the track in 110-degree heat. They watched him make one trip down the track, reconsider his ambition, and keep right on going into town. They never saw him or their blankets again. Pollard got much the same treatment, but he was almost impossible to discourage. "Who hit you in the butt with a saddle and told you you could ride?" a starter hissed before a race. "The same S.O.B. that hit you in the butt and told you *you* could start!" he shot back. Pollard had found the one place on earth that could hold his interest. He was broke, hungry, and, according to his sister Edie, "happy as heck."

He never lived in Edmonton again. His mother worried over his fate but hid it from her children. His father, eager to see him and furious with the man who had abandoned him, scraped together a few dollars and traveled all the way to Vancouver to stand in the crowd and watch his son ride. Thanks to the rigid rules governing bug boys, Pollard was not even allowed to turn his head to look at his father as he rode past. Never again would anyone in his family have the money to come see him.

Pollard struggled to find his place. In 1926 he had only eight mounts, winning with just one of them. But under Acey's tutelage, he began to find his niche. In his first season in Tijuana he befriended a blind trainer named Jerry Duran, who was struggling to make something of a horse named Preservator. Devoid of talent—in three years and forty-six starts he had won just five races—Preservator was also a comparatively geriatric seven years old, roughly the equivalent of a human runner in his late thirties competing against twenty somethings. Duran brought Pollard on board as Preservator's jockey. Seeing that Duran was incapable of handling many of the training duties, the seventeen-year-old took them on himself. In Pollard's care, Preservator improved dramatically, winning six races and earning a respectable $3,170. After each race Pollard would read the official chart for Preservator's performance out loud to Duran. When the horse ran poorly, Pollard skipped over the disappointing race notes and invented tales of Preservator's impressive feats, dreaming of bad-luck excuses to account for the horse's losses. His efforts heartened Duran and impressed other horsemen, who began to hire him. In 1927 he was assigned to ride more horses, and once in a while he won.

His small measure of success didn't go unnoticed. After seeing Pollard booting Acey's horses around Glacier Park, a horseman named Freddie Johnson contacted Acey and asked how much he wanted for the jockey. After a brief negotiation, a deal was struck. Pollard came cheap. For two saddles, a handful of bridles, and two sacks of oats, he became for all intents and purposes the property of Freddie Johnson. Johnson handed him over to his trainer, Russ McGirr.

McGirr soon discovered that Pollard had a rare skill. His natural empathy and experience with the horses of the bullring circuit had given him insight into the minds of ailing, nervous horses. He rode horses no one else was willing to go near. He had learned to keep his whip idle, compensating by riding with somewhat longer stirrups that allowed him to urge horses gently with his lower legs. The horses responded to his kind handling, relaxed under him and tried their hardest. Under McGirr, Pollard became known as a specialist in rogues and troubled horses and began to win regularly with them. Because a large percentage of his mounts were claimers competing for tiny purses, Pollard didn't earn much money. He mailed most of what little he did make to his father to help him hang on to the family house. The rest usually went out in "loans" to needy friends. Pollard was a pushover, and all the down-and-outers knew exactly where to go to pick up a few bucks. He never had the heart to ask for it back. "I never could," he would later say in his odd way, "throw money around like glue." But he was getting a lot of mounts and winning with almost 10 percent of them, so he got by. After two years in the saddle, it seemed that Pollard was going to make it.

On the backstretch at Lansdowne Park in the cool Vancouver summer of 1927, Red Pollard first saw George Monroe Woolf. He must have been quite a sight. Everything about Woolf spoke in the imperative. The first thing everyone noticed was the spectacular cowboy garb: ten-gallon spanking-white cowboy hats blocked porkpie style, weighty signet rings, smoked eyeglasses, fringed leather jackets, ornate breeches, gabardine shirts tailored to his powerful shoulders and dyed in a confusion of color, and hand-tooled cowboy boots embossed with animal images in real silver. Arrestingly handsome, George had dark blond hair that cruised back from a part he kept just a nudge off-center, as was the fashion. He held his chin up Mussolini-style, and the corners of his mouth turned up in a smothered smile, as if he knew something no one else did. He spoke in a slow, drizzling drawl, but his eyes were as clear and sharp as a cat's. He decorated in frontier art, pored over western magazines, listened to Gene Autry on the phonograph, and motored around town in a blindingly ostentatious hot rod

Studebaker roadster with a bug boy riding shotgun. Woolf, remembered former bug boy Sonny Greenberg, was "fabulous in everything
he done." In the summer of '27 he was seventeen, aloof, clever, and
utterly singular. He also may have been the greatest riding talent racing
ever saw.

Woolf had the ideal pedigree for a jockey. His mother, Rose, was a
mounted circus acrobat; his father, Henry, was a stagecoach driver
and rancher who, George liked to say, "never had much money but
always owned a fast horse and a fightin' bulldog"; his brothers were
both professional horse breakers. Accordingly, expectations for
Woolf's career in the saddle preceded him into the world. On May 31,
1910, in the wheat and cattle country of Cardston, Alberta, Rose was
midway through her labor with George when her husband interrupted
the doctor. How long, he asked, before he could put the child up on a
horse? If the doctor counseled patience, his words didn't leave an
impression. While growing up in Cardston and later on the similarly
broad scapes of Babb, Montana, Woolf couldn't remember a time
when his view of the world wasn't framed by a set of horse's ears.
"Must have been born on one," he mused. Riding, he said without
exaggeration, "is as natural as walking to me." He spent more of his
youth on horseback than on foot. "Horses are in my blood," he said.
"I'll be with them until I die."

Setting aside an ambition to be a Canadian Mountie, Woolf began
race riding while in his mid-teens, apparently padding his age by a
year. He cut his teeth in Montana match races, relays on unpedigreed
horses in Indian country, and contests at rough tracks with names like
Chinook and Stampede. Freddie Johnson and Russ McGirr were
quick to snatch up Woolf's contract and watched as their purchase
became a smashing overnight success in the minor leagues. In 1927
Woolf was spotted by Lemuel Tolliver "Whitey" Whitehill, a top
horseman, who soon called a meeting with Johnson. Whitey had a
good claimer named Pickpocket that caught Johnson's eye; Whitey
was equally enamored of Woolf's riding. An even swap of horse for
boy was made. Whitey brought Woolf to Vancouver, then down to
Tijuana, and turned him loose.

No one had ever seen anything like George Woolf. Right out of the box, he won every prize that wasn't nailed down. He was something to watch, pouring over his horse's back, belly flat to the withers, fingers threaded through the reins, face pressed into the mane, body curving along the ebb and flow of the animal's body. He could learn a horse's mind from the bob of the head, the tension in the reins, the coil of the hindquarters. Fifths of a second ticked off with precision in his head; Woolf timed his horses' rallies so precisely that he regularly won races with heart-stopping, last-second dives. He could, racetrackers marveled, "hold an elephant an inch away from a peanut until time to feed." He had an uncanny prescience, as if he lived twenty seconds ahead of himself, seeing the coming trap along the rail or the route to the outside. His commands had the understatement of the ancient cavalry art of dressage. He was shrewd and he was fearless, demonstrating such cold unflappability in the saddle that race caller Joe Hernandez gave him the nickname "Iceman." It stuck.

Woolf's phenomenal success came partly from God-given gifts, partly from experience, and partly from exhaustive study. He prowled the heads of his mounts and everyone else's, scouring the *Daily Racing Form* for every tidbit of information that could give him an edge, and cracked contests wide open by ruthlessly exploiting his rivals' weaknesses. His memory was a catalogue of vital notes on horses and men: *hangs in the stretch, balks in close quarters, only hits right-handed.* He also developed a race-preparation technique that was a half century ahead of its time. Sitting in the jockeys' room before a race, he would close his eyes and visualize how the race would be run. He would see the pitfalls and opportunities develop and run the race in his head until he saw how to win it. He didn't ride his races, said his archrival Eddie Arcaro, he *crafted* them.

Like all athletic greats, Woolf was a driving perfectionist. He abruptly sold his tack and announced his retirement in disgust over a ride he thought was poor. After being briefly suspended for making a mistake in a race at Tijuana in 1930, he stomped up to the jockeys' room, cleaned out his locker, lugged everything outside, heaped it into a big pile, and set the whole mass on fire. "Me, ride again?" he said.

"No sirce." He then jumped into his convertible, sped all the way to Canada, stopped at the first Mountie station he found and tried to enlist. Rejected for his diminutive stature, he sequestered himself in the Canadian wilderness, "a-huntin' and a-fishin'." Months later he reappeared in the jockeys' room and went back to riding the hide off of every jockey in town.

As Woolf matured and honed his craft, his moments of self-loathing gave way to quiet, unwavering confidence. He was greatness fully realized, and he knew it. Where other elite athletes betray their doubts about their capacities with displays of touchy egotism, Woolf was utterly insouciant. He could not be rattled. "George," remembered racing official Chick Lang, "was a guy that you could put on a street corner, and two cars would have a head-on collision right in front of him, and he would say, 'Gee, look at that,' while everybody else would be running in all directions." He seemed devoid of fear. On the track, while other riders flailed and winced and scratched their way around, the Iceman "sat chilly," as loose as water, his legs and hands supple and still. Photographers shooting races would record jockeys in various attitudes of strain; in the middle of it all would be Woolf, smiling the way a man does when he humors a child. While other riders dragged themselves to the barn to gallop horses at 4:00 A.M. seven days a week, compelled by a biting fear that their skills would wane or trainers would forget them, Woolf slept in, rarely showing up at the track before noon. "He was a better rider than most of us, and he knew it," remembered fellow jockey Mosbacher. "So he just kind of took the easier way."

Woolf was an uncensored man, in word and deed. "As a jockey," wrote Red Pollard's friend David Alexander, a columnist for the *Morning Telegraph,* "Woolf is noted for doing exactly the right thing at exactly the right time. He is also noted for saying what some persons consider the wrong thing at the wrong time." When asked a direct question, he could be counted on to say something so bald—and undeniable—that he would leave everyone around him gaping. After losing one major race on a highly regarded runner, he flatly told the national press, surely to the horror of the owner, that the horse just wasn't any good. On the night after Woolf won a top stakes race, the owner of the winning horse called to invite him to a postrace soirée with the moneyed set. "You tell 'em," Woolf replied, kicking back with a big steak, a long, cool beer, and a group of his roughneck friends, "that if the horse had got beat, they wouldn't invite us over. We got a party of our own."

"Woolf," remembered his close friend Bill Buck, "done what Woolf wanted to do." Throughout his career, if he felt like taking a day off, he'd just pack up and go, leaving his exasperated agent and jilted trainers hunting for him. On one occasion, after he failed to appear for several potentially lucrative races, his agent found him starring in a bull-riding exhibition. He once vanished without a trace a few days before the Preakness Stakes, throwing the entire Maryland racing community, including an owner who wanted him to ride one of the race favorites, into an uproar. He glided back to civilization three days later, tanned and happy. While driving through Pennsylvania he had simply happened upon a beautiful lake, pulled over, and taken an impromptu fishing vacation in perfect serenity. When he disappeared on another afternoon, horsemen eventually found him in a crowd watching a visiting Montana rodeo. A trick rider had claimed that he could jump a car while riding two horses simultaneously, "Roman" style—a foot in one stirrup of each. Woolf called his bluff and volunteered his gleaming new Cord roadster for the job. The horses nicked the car up pretty good but made it over. Woolf felt the spectacle was worth the price of new paint and a furious agent.

Only his contract trainer, Whitey, was unfazed by his jockey's behavior. This needled Woolf. To raise Whitey's blood pressure a bit, Woolf started delaying his horses' rallies until the last possible second. He would send a friend to sit nearby and watch the color drain from Whitey's face as Woolf waited, and waited, and waited before driving for the lead just when it seemed too late. Whitey surely whitened a little more with every closing kick, but the Iceman knew what he was doing. Incredibly, Woolf's timing was so good that he rode for more than a decade before he was beaten in a photo finish of a stakes race.

Woolf was fanatical about clean riding. He never initiated any rough riding tactics, and took justice into his own hands when anyone fouled him. He was known to haul off and crack offending riders right in the mouth with his whip, then frankly tell the stewards exactly what he'd done when a lie could have gotten him out of trouble. He rode claiming races with as much zeal as he rode the Santa Anita Handicap. He was also not above a little playful heckling; a few choice words from the Iceman could spook his rivals into blowing their game plans.

George Woolf, from the very beginning, stood a rung above Red Pollard. While Pollard bedded down in a horse stall at night and grazed out of the track kitchen, Woolf lived in the comfort of Whitey's house, eating home-cooked meals. Pollard would never escape Woolf's shadow, but he was not a jealous man. "I know George," he would laugh. "Big head, little ass, and roars like a lion." Pollard, famously, tried to take credit for giving Woolf the nickname Iceman, explaining it thus: "In all the smoking-car stories I have ever heard, icemen and traveling salesmen were very immoral characters. George does not have a pleasing enough personality to be a traveling salesman."

Woolf replied in the same vein. "You don't have to be an athlete to be a jockey," he told a reporter. "Why, Red Pollard is one of the smartest jockeys in the country today, and he doesn't have the strength to blow out a candle."

In those early days, Pollard and Woolf found common ground in their quick minds, cerebral riding styles, and keen senses of humor. On the backstretch of Vancouver Race Course in the summer of 1927, a friendship was forged in the crucible of the racetrack and adolescence. It would endure long into manhood and bind them together in history.

Fatally injured when his horse collided with another runner,
jockey Wallace Leischman lies on the track
at Bay Meadows Racecourse, 1939.
(*TURF AND SPORT DIGEST*)

CHAPTER 5

A Boot on One Foot, a Toe Tag on the Other

On a Saturday afternoon in July 1938, a half-starved teenager wandered into a bus station in Columbus, Ohio, appearing confused and disoriented. A policeman approached and tried to speak with him, but the boy seemed not to know his own name. In his pockets the officer found $112, a bus ticket for Petersburg, Illinois, and documents that identified him as Thomas Dowell, an obscure local jockey. Seeing that Dowell was in profound distress, the officer took him to the police station, where a police surgeon sat with him and tried to find out what was wrong. Dowell remained mute but appeared deeply shaken. Concerned that the boy might get hurt if released, the doctor sat him down in a holding cell and left to telephone his mother.

While the doctor was gone, Dowell slipped his belt off, coiled it around his neck, and hanged himself.

When word of the suicide made its way to the backstretch, no one seemed surprised. In his brief career Dowell had learned what Red Pollard, George Woolf, and countless other riders had long since known. A jockey's life was nothing short of appalling. No athletes suffered more for their sport. The jockey lived hard and lean and tended to die young, trampled under the hooves of horses or imploding from the pressures of his vocation. For three years Dowell had known the singular strain of the jockey's job, torturing his body to keep it at an inhumanly low weight, groveling for mounts in the mornings and enduring punishing violence in the afternoons, waiting in vain for the "big horse" that would bear him from poverty and peril.

Dowell was no anomaly, and everyone on the backstretch knew it. His was a life no different from that of almost every other jockey. Under its terrific weight, Dowell had come undone.

They called the scale "the Oracle," and they lived in slavery to it. In the 1920s and 1930s, the imposts, or weights horses were assigned to carry in races, generally ranged from 83 pounds to 130 or more, depending on the rank of the horse and the importance of the race. A rider could be no more than 5 pounds over the assigned weight or he would be taken off the horse. Some trainers trimmed that leeway down to just a half pound. To make weight in anything but high-class stakes races, jockeys had to keep their weight to no more than 114 pounds. Riders competing in ordinary weekday events needed to whittle themselves down another 5 pounds or so, while those in the lowest echelons of the sport couldn't weigh much more than 100. The lighter a rider was, the greater the number of horses he could ride. "Some riders," wrote Eddie Arcaro, "will all but saw their legs off to get within the limit."

A few riders were naturally tiny enough to make weight without difficulty, and they earned the burning envy of every other jockey. Most of them were young teenagers whose growth spurts lay ahead of them. To ensure that they didn't waste time and money training and supporting boys who would eventually grow out of their trade, contract trainers checked the foot size of every potential bug boy, since a large foot is a fairly good sign of a coming growth spurt. Many also inspected the height and weight of a potential bug boy's siblings. Trainer Woody Stephens, who began his racing career as a bug boy in the late 1920s, always felt he got lucky in this respect. In vetting him for the job, his trainer neglected to look at his sister, a local basketball phenom.

Virtually every adult rider, and most of the kids, naturally tended to weigh too much. Cheating, if you did it right, could help a little. One pudgy 140-pound rider earned a place in reinsman legend by fooling a profoundly myopic clerk of scales by skewing the readout to register him at 110. No one is exactly sure how he did it, but it is believed that either he positioned his feet on a nonregistering part of the scale or his valet stuck his whip under his seat and lifted up. He made it through an entire season before someone caught him.

Most jockeys took a more straightforward approach: the radical diet, consisting of six hundred calories a day. Red Pollard went as long as a year eating nothing but eggs. Sunny Jim Fitzsimmons confessed that during his riding days a typical dinner consisted of a leaf or two of lettuce, and he would eat them only after placing them on a windowsill to dry the water out of them. Water, because of its weight, was the prime enemy, and jockeys went to absurd lengths to keep it out of their systems. Most drank virtually nothing. A common practice was to have jockeys' room valets open soda cans by puncturing the top with an ice pick, making it impossible to drink more than a few drops at a time. The sight and sound of water became a torment; Fitzsimmons habitually avoided areas of the barn where horses were being washed because the spectacle of flowing water was agonizing.

But the weight maximums were so low that near fasting and water deprivation weren't enough. Even what little water and calories the body had taken in had to be eliminated. Many riders were "heavers," poking their fingers down their throats to vomit up their meals. Others chewed gum to trigger salivation; Tommy Luther could spit off as much as half a pound in a few hours. Then there were the sweating rituals, topped by "road work." This practice, used by both Red Pollard and George Woolf, involved donning heavy underwear, zipping into a rubber suit, swaddling in hooded winter gear and woolen horse blankets, then running around and around the track, preferably under a blistering summer sun. Stephens remembered seeing jockeys in full road-work attire gathering at a bowling alley, so lathered that sweat spouted from their shoes with each step. After road work, there were Turkish baths, where jockeys congregated for mornings of communal sweating. The desiccation practices of jockeys were lampooned by turf writer Joe H. Palmer in a column written on jockey Abelardo DeLara: "DeLara has to sweat off about two pounds a day to make weight. Last year, by his own estimate, he lost about 600 pounds this way. Since he weighs about 110, it is a mere matter of arithmetic that he would be a bit more than 700 pounds if he hadn't reduced so regularly."

Most jockeys ingested every manner of laxative to purge their systems of food and water. Diarrhea became the constant companion of many riders, some of whom became virtuosos of defecation. Helen Luther once watched a rider step on a scale, only to see that he was over his horse's assigned impost. He shouted to the clerk of scales to hang on, raced to the bathroom, emerged a moment later with his pants still at half mast, and made weight. Such results could be had from a variety of products, including a stomach-turning mix of Epsom salts and water—chased by two fingers of rye to stop the gagging reflex—a plant-derived purgative called jalap, or bottles of a wretched-tasting formula known as Pluto Water.

But the undisputed champ of the purgatives was born in the enterprising mind of a jockey's masseur named Frank "Frenchy" Hawley. Prowling around the Tijuana jockeys' room in reassuringly medical-looking Dr. Kildare attire, Frenchy was the self-appointed mad scientist of the racing world. Operating out of a gleaming-white training room, Frenchy stocked every manner of weight-loss facilitator, including electric blankets, infrared lamps, electric light cabinets, baking machines, "violet-rays," vibrating contraptions, and rubber sleeping bags and sheets. He also dreamed up a particularly foul-smelling recipe for self-parboiling that required riders to steep for up to thirty-five minutes (fewer if they became dizzy) in piping-hot water mixed with three to five pounds of Epsom salts, one quart of white vinegar, two ounces of household ammonia, and a mystery lather he called Hawley's Cream. He kept careful records of the weight he had stripped from riders. By 1945, it totaled 12,860 pounds—more than six tons.

One of Frenchy's cardinal rules of reducing was to "keep the contents of the bowels moving down and out steadily and regularly." To devise a mix that would bring this about, he tinkered around with God knows what until he stumbled upon a home brew that delivered a ferocious kick. The caustic laxative worked so well that Hawley marketed it commercially under the disarmingly innocuous name Slim Jim. Former jockey Bill Buck remembered it with a shiver: "It'd *kill* you." He wasn't kidding. Frenchy's bowel scourer proved to be so fabulously potent that bottles of it spontaneously exploded in the jockeys' room lavatory. Imagining their intestines going out in a similar blaze of glory, even the jockeys began to fear it, and Hawley's Slim Jim experiment went down the tubes.

For jockeys who were truly desperate, there was one last resort. Contact the right people, and you could get hold of a special capsule, a simple pill guaranteed to take off all the weight you wanted. In it was the egg of a tapeworm. Within a short while the parasite would attach to a man's intestines and slowly suck the nutrients out of him. The pounds would peel away like magic. When the host jockey became too malnourished, he could check into a hospital to have the worm removed, then return to the track and swallow a new pill. Red Pollard may have resorted to this solution.

In denying their bodies the most basic necessities, jockeys demonstrated incredible fortitude. They paid a fearsome price. Most walked around in a state of critical dehydration and malnutrition and as a result were irritable, volatile, light-headed, bleary, nauseated, gaunt, and crampy. The heavers, exposing their mouths to repeated onslaughts of stomach acid, lost the enamel on their teeth and eventually the teeth themselves. Other jockeys suffered bouts of weakness so severe that when boosted into the saddle they would fall right off the other side. Dehydration left them so prone to overheating, even in mild weather, that their valets prepared huge bins of ice cubes into which they could flop to cool off. Other riders suffered fainting spells or hallucinated.

Many jockeys' bodies could not function under the strain. To take off enough weight to ride a horse in Windsor, Canada, Sonny Greenberg steamed in a Turkish bath, guzzled Epsom salts mixed with jalap, took a boat from Detroit to Windsor—vomiting all the way—donned a rubber suit over several layers of heavy clothing, and ran around and around the track. He staggered into the woods, collapsed, and either fell asleep or fainted. He awoke in a pool of sweat, and tried to clear his disorientation by downing a half-ounce of whiskey. Dragging himself to a scale, he found that he had suffered away ten and a half pounds in one night. It was all for naught. By post time he was too weak even to sit upright in a saddle. He gave someone else the mount, and retired soon afterward.

Greenberg escaped without permanent damage, but others, including Fitzsimmons, may not have been so lucky. Severe reducing was thought to be the culprit behind an epidemic of fatal lung diseases, such as pneumonia and tuberculosis, among jockeys. Other long-term health problems may also have stemmed from reducing practices. In a single day, to make weight on a horse, Fitzsimmons endured purgatives, an entire afternoon in a Turkish bath, heavy exercise on horseback and on foot while swaddled in several sweaters and a muffler, topped off with an hour standing inches from a roaring brick kiln. He lost *thirteen* pounds. Thick-tongued and groggy, he won the race by a nose but couldn't repeat the weight-loss performance and retired from the saddle not much later. He soon experienced the first shooting pains from the severe arthritis that would grotesquely disfigure his body. He came to believe that that one terrible day of reducing may have triggered the onset of the crippling disease.

Finally, there was the mental toll. Stephens described his realization that he could no longer take the punishment of reducing as "the biggest disappointment of my life." The legendary nineteenth-century European jockey Fred Archer understood the emotion. Falling into a severe depression attributed to his taking constant doses of purgatives to fight a weight problem he could not beat, he shot himself to death at age twenty-nine.

A Thoroughbred racehorse is one of God's most impressive engines. Tipping the scales at up to 1,450 pounds, he can sustain speeds of forty miles per hour. Equipped with reflexes much faster than those of the most quick-wired man, he swoops over as much as twenty-eight feet of earth in a single stride, and corners on a dime. His body is a paradox of mass and lightness, crafted to slip through air with the ease of an arrow. His mind is impressed with a single command: *run*. He pursues speed with superlative courage, pushing beyond defeat, beyond exhaustion, sometimes beyond the structural limits of bone and sinew. In flight, he is nature's ultimate wedding of form and purpose.

To pilot a racehorse is to ride a half-ton catapult. It is without question one of the most formidable feats in sport. The extraordinary athleticism of the jockey is unparalleled: A study of the elements of athleticism conducted by Los Angeles exercise physiologists and physicians found that of all major sports competitors, jockeys may be, pound for pound, the best overall athletes. They have to be. To begin with, there are the demands on balance, coordination, and reflex. A horse's body is a constantly shifting topography, with a bobbing head and neck and roiling muscle over the shoulders, back, and rump. On a running horse, a jockey does not sit in the saddle, he crouches over it, leaning all of his weight on his toes, which rest on the thin metal bases of stirrups dangling about a foot from the horse's topline. When a horse is in full stride, the only parts of the jockey that are in continuous contact with the animal are the insides of the feet and ankles—everything else is balanced in midair. In other words, jockeys squat on the pitching backs of their mounts, a task much like perching on the grille of a car while it speeds down a twisting, potholed freeway in traffic. The stance is, in the words of University of North Carolina researchers, "a situation of dynamic imbalance and ballistic opportunity." The center of balance is so narrow that if jockeys shift only slightly rearward, they will flip right off the back. If they tip more than a few inches forward, a fall is almost inevitable. A Thoroughbred's neck, while broad from top to bottom, is surprisingly narrow in width, like the body of a fish. Pitching up and down as the horse runs, it offers little for the jockey to grab to avoid plunging to the ground and under the horse's hooves.

Race riding is exceptionally exhausting. It is common for aspiring jockeys to be so rubber-legged upon dismounting from their first circuit around the track that they are unable to walk back to the barn. Strength is not just a tool for winning, it is necessary for survival.

Jockey Johnny Longden was once rammed in midrace, knocked from his stirrups and sent flying downward in front of a pack of horses. He was saved by a jockey riding alongside him, George Taniguchi, who was so powerful that he was able to catch Longden with one hand. Taniguchi didn't know his own strength, and in attempting to push Longden back into the saddle he instead hurled him right over the back of his horse. Longden found himself in the same predicament on the other side of his mount until jockey Rogelio Trejos, whose horse was about to run Longden down, lunged forward, snagged the jockey with the ease of an outfielder and righted him in the saddle, also with one hand. Incredibly, Longden won the race. The *Daily Racing Form* called it "the ultimate impossibility."

A jockey is no mere passenger on a racehorse. His role in bringing home winners is critical and demanding. First, jockeys must have an exquisitely fine sense of pace over each furlong, or eighth of a mile. Strategy is crucial. Front-runners have the best chance of winning if they set moderate or slow fractional times, leaving themselves the energy to fend off closers, while closers have the best chance of winning if they lag behind a brisk pace, then swoop around the exhausted front-runners in the homestretch. The difference between a fast fraction and a slow fraction is often less than a second, and a jockey must be able to discriminate between the two to place his horse optimally. Great jockeys have a freakish talent for gauging pace to within two or three fifths of a second of the actual time and, if asked, can reliably gallop a horse over a distance at precisely the clip requested.

Positioning relative to the field is also critical. A racehorse is an enormous creature who needs a wide berth, and as he weighs half a ton and carries one hundred-plus pounds on his back, he cannot afford to have his momentum stopped or acceleration wasted. Running wide around turns offers the best chance of clear sailing but exacts a high price in extra distance the horse has to cover. In a big field, jockeys who opt to go wide may have to swing as many as ten "paths" out, forcing their horses to run roughly ten lengths farther than horses on the rail. The best riders take the inside route whenever possible, but this is risky. Because everyone wants to be there, horses usually bunch up by the rail, so closely that hips and shoulders rub and stirrups clink off each other, making maneuvering difficult or impossible. Tiring pacesetters generally slow down right in front of the rail-running pack, compounding the traffic jams.

To judge whether or not he's likely to get pocketed if he steers his horse to the rail, a jockey must be able to read the subtleties in the stances of horses and riders in front—the tautness in the reins, the height of the jockey over the saddle, the crispness and cadence of the stride—to gauge how much gas is left in the tank. Doing homework is imperative; some runners habitually drift in or out in the homestretch or on turns, and the jockey who can arm himself with this knowledge and position himself on the rail behind such a horse can ensure himself a clear path of escape. He must also have the instinct to judge whether or not a hole opening in front of him will stay open long enough to get through, if the space is wide enough, and if his horse has the acceleration to get to it before it slams shut. If he judges it correctly, he can save ground and win a race. If he misjudges it, he may end up fouling other horses and being disqualified, checking his horse sharply and sacrificing his momentum or even falling.

Requiring that its human competitors straddle erratic animals moving in dense groups at extremely high speed, race riding in the 1930s, as today, was fraught with extreme danger. Riders didn't even have to leave the saddle to be badly hurt. Their hands and shins were smashed and their knee ligaments ripped when horses twisted beneath them or banged into rails and walls. Their ankles were crushed when their feet became caught in the starter's webbing. With the advent of the first primitive, unpadded starting gates in the early thirties, some riders actually died in the saddle, speared into the exposed steel overhead bars by rearing horses. Riders suffered horrible injuries when dragged from their stirrups and under their horses' legs or when thrown forward, ending up clinging to the underside of the horses' necks while the animals' front legs pummeled their chests and abdomens.

The only thing more dangerous than being on the back of a racehorse was being thrown from one. Some jockeys took two hundred or more falls in their careers. Some were shot into the air when horses would "prop," or plant their front hooves and slow abruptly. Others went down when their mounts would bolt, crashing into the rail or even the grandstand. A common accident was "clipping heels," in which trailing horses tripped over leading horses' hind hooves, usually sending the trailing horse and rider into a somersault. Finally, horses could break down, racing's euphemism for incurring leg injuries. This could happen without warning, sending the victim pitching headfirst into the ground. A rider who lost touch with the saddle became a projectile moving at sixty feet per second, and whatever he hit became a potentially lethal instrument. If he was lucky enough to survive the impact with the ground and possibly his horse's falling body, he often had trailing horses, their hooves striking the ground with as much as three thousand pounds of force, bearing down on him. In the worst cases, a single faller could trigger a chain-reaction pileup onto a downed jockey.

Serious insults to the body, the kind of shattering or crushing injury seen in high-speed auto wrecks, are an absolute certainty for every single jockey. Today the Jockeys' Guild, which covers riders in the United States, receives an average of twenty-five hundred injury notifications per year, with two deaths and two and a half cases of paralysis. The Guild is currently supporting fifty riders who were permanently disabled on the job. According to a study by the Rehabilitation Institute of Chicago, each year the average jockey is injured three times and spends a total of almost eight weeks sidelined by injuries incurred on the track. Nearly one in every five injuries is to the head or neck. A 1993 survey found that 13 percent of jockeys suffered concussions over a period of just four months. Injury rates were, by all accounts, far higher in the 1920s and 1930s; between 1935 and 1939 alone, nineteen riders were killed in racing accidents. The hell-for-leather riding tactics practiced in the era, and the absence of protective gear, increased the vulnerability of race riders to mortal injury. Today races are filmed from multiple angles to ensure safe riding. Jockeys wear flak jackets, goggles, and high-tech helmets and compete at tracks equipped with safety rails and ambulances that trail the field around the track. No such luxuries were available to the jockeys of the twenties and thirties. At best, only one or two stewards monitored riding tactics. A jockey's only bodily protection was a skullcap constructed of silk-covered cardboard. Former jockey Morris Griffin, who was paralyzed in a 1938 racing fall, likened his headgear to a yarmulke. Lacking a chin strap, it usually popped off before the wearer slammed into the ground. Cutting out the lining and crown to lower their riding weight, most jockeys rendered the skullcap useless.

Once riders were down on the course, tracks had virtually no protocol for coping with their injuries. Riders were lucky if someone rounded up a car to get them to a hospital, and since virtually none of them had any money or insurance, they were likely to be turned away from any hospital to which they were taken. Track officials appeared to feel little obligation to them. In 1927 best friends Tommy Luther and Earl "Sandy" Graham were slated to ride a pair of stablemates in the same race at Winnipeg's Polo Park. Luther was assigned to a lumbering, uncoordinated colt named Vesper Lad, while Graham was up on Irish Princess II. At the last minute the trainer reversed the assignments. While Luther was hustling Irish Princess to the lead, he heard a gasp from the crowd. He finished the race, then pivoted in the saddle to see what had happened. He saw Graham lying motionless on the track. Vesper Lad had rammed into the rail, dropping Graham to the track, where he had been trampled by the field. His ribs and back were shattered.

Track officials carried Graham up to the jockeys' room and dumped him on a saddle table, where he lay moaning and incoherent. It had been decided that Graham could wait until after the races, when it was most convenient for someone to drop him by the hospital. Luther and the other jockeys were not permitted to leave the jockeys' room to take him in themselves. Had they done so, they would have lost their jobs and housing. Though Luther passed the hat to raise cabfare to send him on alone, the jockeys didn't have enough money among them. Luther spent the afternoon sitting with Graham, offering him water and pleading in vain with officials to get the boy to the hospital. Finally, after the races were over, Graham was taken to the hospital, where Luther sat by his bed. The race season soon ended, and Luther was forced to leave his friend's side to accompany his trainer to another track.

A few days later Graham died. He was only sixteen. His death was little noticed; jockey fatalities were so common that they rarely earned more than a slim paragraph in the press. The only person left in town to mourn for Graham was a woman the riders called Mother Harrison, operator of a Turkish bath that Graham and Luther had frequented. She buried the boy but couldn't afford a headstone. Luther mailed what little money he could spare to Mother Harrison to buy a grave marker. With the leftover money, she bought a small bouquet of flowers and laid it on the boy's grave. She drew a picture of the grave and mailed it to Luther. Seventy years later Luther still has the drawing.

The racetrack casualty list was full of stories of the cruel, the bizarre, and the miraculous. In 1938, leading Agua Caliente jockey Charlie Rosengarten gave up the mount on the favorite, Toro Mak, to a struggling rider named Jimmy Sullivan, who needed the money to feed his wife and newborn baby. Rosengarten watched in horror as Toro Mak, sailing toward a sure victory, inexplicably crossed his forelegs and fell, crushing Sullivan to death. After a spill that knocked him unconscious, facedown in a puddle, Eddie Arcaro would have become the first jockey in history to *drown* on the job had a photographer not rushed out from the stands and turned his head to allow him to breathe. Steve Donoghue, who rode in Europe and the United States in the interwar years, was once on a horse that clipped heels and fell, spilling him onto the track in front of a mob of onrushing horses. He was an instant from being trampled to death when an elderly woman suddenly materialized out of nowhere, grabbed hold of him, and dragged him under the rail. She left him in the safety of the infield, and vanished. Donoghue never saw her again.

But nothing tops the strange fate of Ralph Neves, a hotheaded, hard-riding teenaged jockey known as "the Portuguese Pepperpot." In the spring of 1936 Bing Crosby offered a $500 watch to the jockey who won the most races at California's Bay Meadows Racecourse. By the penultimate day of the meet, Neves was two wins in front of his nearest competitor and riding with a fury. That afternoon, rolling around the far turn aboard a horse named Flanakins, Neves was in the lead and looking like a cinch to win Crosby's prize. But without warning, Flanakins stumbled and crashed, catapulting Neves into the rail. Flipping to the track, Neves was trampled by trailing horses. Flanakins rose, uninjured—Neves had broken her fall—but the jockey lay motionless. Two physicians in the crowd sprinted out to him, joining the track doctor. They declared Neves dead on the track. The race caller made the somber announcement and asked the crowd to stand in prayer. As the sickened spectators bent their heads and reporters rushed to get word to their editors, Neves's body was carried to a mortuary. His toe was tagged, and he was parked on a table to await funeral arrangements.

Physician Horace Stevens, a friend of Neves's, got word of his death and went to view the body. When he arrived, Stevens noticed something the track doctors had missed. He prepared a syringe and injected Neves with adrenaline.

Neves woke up.

A few minutes later, he stumbled out of the mortuary and onto the street, where he caught a cab, sped back to Bay Meadows, jumped out and began rushing toward the jockeys' room. As the shirtless, blood-splattered erstwhile corpse sprinted past the grandstand, astonished fans started running after him. By the time Neves hit the wire, most of the crowd was chasing him. He shook loose from the mob, dashed past the clubhouse, and burst into the jockeys' room, a boot on one foot and, apparently, a toe tag on the other. He scared the bejesus out of everyone.

When the jockeys recovered from the shock, they took Neves, kicking and screaming, down to the first-aid room. He insisted that he was going to ride the rest of the card. The incredulous stewards refused. Neves went home, still fixated on that watch. He came back the next day loaded for bear. While San Franciscans were reading his obituary in several papers, the decidedly undead Neves rode like a man possessed and won the watch. Reports of his death were fifty-nine years premature.

A sidelined jockey was a forgotten jockey. Because of this cold reality, most jockeys would ride through virtually anything, and they shrugged off the grisliest injuries. "I got my leg broken once and my skull fractured once," said former rider Wad Studley, "but never nothin' bad." Johnny Longden once won a major race while riding with broken bones in his back and foot. When a colt named Daddy Longlegs bolted for the closed paddock gate, sailed over it upside down, and landed on top of him, Steve Donoghue simply strapped his broken wrist bones together with cloth and rode one-handed. On another occasion, his boot caught in the stirrup as he fell off, causing him to be dragged by his foot down the track. His head bumped along beside his filly's thrashing legs until his leg snapped and his foot came free. Not wanting to give up his mount in an upcoming race, Donoghue drove to the stables, had himself carried to his horse, and rode every day with a bulky plaster cast on his leg. Most incredibly, he rode for a full year with serious internal injuries incurred when another horse spiked him into the ground. Though he knew he had been critically injured, he refused treatment and grew weaker and weaker until someone finally took him to a doctor. The moment he entered the office, he fainted into his physician's arms. He was rushed to emergency surgery and barely survived. The motivation for riding through such pain soon became all too clear. While still hospitalized, he was summarily fired by his contract trainer.

Finally, jockeys would not allow themselves to admit to their injuries because that would open the door to their ultimate enemy: fear. To acknowledge pain was to acknowledge danger. In their line of work, fear had a physical presence. Once a jockey let it into his head, it would rise up over him on the track, paralyzing him. Winning jockeys are daring jockeys, capable of gunning a horse through the narrowest hole with damn-the-torpedoes bravado. Frightened jockeys take what Luther called "the married man's route," timidly detouring around the outside of the pack. No one would hire a man who hesitated in the heat of battle. Jockeys could smell fear in one of their own and would exploit it mercilessly, trying to intimidate their way past a rival. "If a jock showed even the slightest trace

86

of cowardice," wrote Arcaro, "it could get awfully rough out there."

As a result, jockeys never, ever spoke about danger, pain, or fear, even among themselves. In conversation they papered over the grim realities of their jobs with cheery euphemisms. Hideous wrecks were referred to as "spills"; jockeys hurled into the ground were "unseated." In their autobiographies, they recounted great races in intimate detail, but falls and injuries were glossed over with the most perfunctory language. Even in the grip of agonizing pain or complete debilitation, most jockeys clung to their illusion of invulnerability.

For some, fear had a way of breaking through the illusion. "You didn't talk about it," remembered Farrell Jones, a jockey tough enough to earn the nickname "Wild Horse." "I thought about it. I don't know if any of them other guys did. But I did. I was spooky." Even Arcaro, one of the most daring riders, admitted that the memory of his first spill, in which a horse stepped on his back and another kicked his skull, leaving him with a concussion, two fractured ribs, and a punctured lung, was seared into his memory and burned there for the rest of his career. It was, he wrote, "a terrifying experience that somehow cannot be blotted out."

For riders' families, the danger and injuries took their toll. In dreams, Helen Luther saw her husband's death play itself out countless times. In murky images, his horse would spiral into the ground, carrying Tommy under him, and Helen would wake into a life striated with fear.

Helen watched Tommy ride every day. She was a rarity in the sport. The vast majority of jockeys' wives couldn't stand to watch their husbands' races and rarely, if ever, came to the track. Helen missed only one ride. On that day, a horse named Brick Top speared Tommy's head into the steel overhead beam of the starting gate. He lay on the ground, his skullcap split, refusing to let the attendants take him to the hospital. "My wife will be here," he kept repeating, sure that Helen was up in the stands. Helen didn't come, and though Tommy recovered, she never ceased regretting it.

Forever after, Helen was there, her eyes trained on every move of her husband's horses. She was frightened for every minute of his career. Sometime early in her marriage, Helen began a ritual: Each time his mount left the paddock and set his first forehoof onto the track, she would pray that the horse would see him home safely.

Helen's prayers failed Tommy on a rain-drenched July afternoon at Empire City. He was a sixteenth of a mile away from winning a race when the filly he was riding abruptly tripped over her own legs and plunged headfirst into the track. Helen saw her husband ride the arc of the filly's back down into the mud and disappear under her tumbling body and the bodies of the three horses who struck her from behind. Their hooves cracked into Tommy's head as they fell.

Helen never knew how she got from the grandstand to the track. Her mind drummed: *He is under all those horses.* The next thing she recalled, she was standing over her husband. She was sure he was dead.

They carried Tommy into the first-aid room on a stretcher. His ancient valet, Johnny Mitchell, bent over him, his tears falling onto Tommy's cheeks as he gently sponged the mud and blood away. Helen stood back and stared at her husband. He didn't move. Helen was seized in violent tremors, and her teeth chattered uncontrollably. She heard someone say, "This woman is in shock" and felt someone slip a brandy into her hand. She refused it. The man who fetched it, badly shaken, drank it himself.

They loaded Tommy into an ambulance and drove him toward St. John's Hospital. Helen was left alone to find her own way there. She got into Tommy's car and drove around New York, confused by the unfamiliar streets. The fuel gauge read empty, so she pulled over at a gas station. The attendant hooked up her car to the pump and came over to chat with her.

"Isn't it too bad?" he said. "Tommy Luther was killed."

Helen whirled in panic. She didn't know what to do or where to go. She briefly thought she should go back to the track. She changed her mind and went toward the hospital. Somehow, she found it. She ran in. Tommy was still alive. Helen nearly collapsed.

Tommy survived. He would have no short-term memory for several days and no depth perception for six months. He staggered like a drunk for a good while. But he would ride for twenty more years, bearing only a single scar from a hoof.

Helen went back to their lodgings alone. It was a rental house in Yonkers, one of countless, faceless rental places she lived in for decades, like nearly all jockeys' wives. You never stayed long enough to get a pet or a houseplant or hang any paintings. The neighbors sneered at you, knowing that you were "racetrack people." Helen once found a burglar hiding beneath her bed in a rental place, but the neighbors didn't respond to her screams because they assumed that screaming was the normal mode of discourse for racetrackers. Always, on nights returning alone, there were worries about practical matters. A jockey's pay couldn't begin to cover the sky-high insurance rates his job warranted, much less the doctor's bills. Track officials viewed any effort to create funds for injured riders as unionizing, and they were ready to ban any jockey who took steps in that direction. So jockeys went without insurance and made do with what they had, passing the hat when one of their colleagues went down. Women like Helen could only hope there would be enough.

Helen ran to the front door, jammed the key in, and rushed inside. The empty house frightened her, and she nearly fainted when the landlord's parrot spoke to her in the dark. She went upstairs and locked herself in the bathroom.

"If I didn't have him," she said as her mind rolled back over that night, "I was alone."

Red Pollard and George Woolf had signed on to a life that used men up. But for all its miseries, there was an unmistakable allure to the jockey's craft, one that both found irresistible. Man is preoccupied with freedom yet laden with handicaps. The breadth of his activity and experience is narrowed by the limitations of his relatively weak, sluggish body. The racehorse, by virtue of his awesome physical gifts, freed the jockey from himself. When a horse and a jockey flew over the track together, there were moments in which the man's mind wedded itsclf to the animal's body to form something greater than the sum of both parts. The horse partook of the jockey's cunning; the jockey partook of the horse's supreme power. For the jockey, the saddle was a place of unparalleled exhilaration, of transcendence. "The horse," recalled one rider, "he *takes* you." Aboard a racehorse in full stride, wrote Steve Donoghue, "I am so completely in the race that I forget the crowds. My horse and I talk together. We don't hear anyone else." At the bottom of the Depression, when wrenching need narrowed the parameters of experience as never before, the liberation offered by the racehorse was, to young men like Pollard and Woolf, a siren song.

On the ground, the jockey was fettered and muted, moving in slow motion, the world a sensory vacuum after the tenfold high of racing speed. In the saddle, emancipated from their bodies, Pollard, Woolf, and all other reinsmen sailed eight feet over the world, emphatically free, emphatically alive. They were Hemingway's bullfighters, living "all the way up."

Red Pollard's Mexican visa, 1932
(NORAH POLLARD CHRISTIANSON)

George Woolf
(CHEERS MAGAZINE)

CHAPTER 6

Light and Shadow

S ooner or later, just about all the bug boys went up the hill. When they began the journey the first time, following the narrow dirt road that turned up from the racetrack, they probably looked very young and somewhat breathless. When they came back, they were half a dollar poorer, twenty minutes older, and decidedly more swaggering at the walk. And the stories they could tell!

"At the top of the hill," as everyone knew, stood the big cinder-block building that stared down on the track at Tijuana, or "Tee-a Joo-ana," as they called it. The building was the home of the Molino Rojo, or "red mill," a shag-carpeted shrine to the world's oldest profession. It was by far the largest house of prostitution in the world, and probably the most successful. Hovering right over the old Tijuana track, consuming half a city block, topped by an immense spinning windmill and decked out in flashing red lights that were visible clear across the border, the Molino Rojo must have been to the racetrackers what the North Star was to the magi. It took effort for the riders to avoid looking right at it every time they rode in morning workouts or circled the barn walking hots. The jockeys called it "the house of the wilted pigeons."

The Molino Rojo had no madam. The girls ran the place themselves, and they did so with the cunning of robber barons. It was no surprise to them that half the people at the racetrack were unsupervised hellraisers gripped in the ferocious throes of puberty. Surely it was more than happy coincidence that the price of admission—"fifty

93

ccnts, straight up," remembers one former bug boy—was precisely equal to the pay for galloping a horse. Any rider who made it up the hill had his beer paid for, compliments of the house. And in the unlikely event that a lad wasn't quite in the mood, he would be ushered into the house theater to be inspired by an exotic blue movie. There were so many girls to choose from, every conceivable nationality, that a kid would have to gallop three hundred horses to afford them all. He could walk down the long, narrow halls, off of which were countless fabulously appointed bedrooms, listen to the girls beckoning in soft Spanish, and simply take his pick. "You went through there," remembers one client, "like you were going through a grocery store."

The girls took customer service seriously. Velvet-Tongued Velma and Chi Chi Grande needed no introduction. A girl the riders called One Wing Annie did a brisk business despite missing one arm. One girl told a bug boy that if he could track down $5, she'd show him something he'd never forget. Five dollars was the kind of money you could live on for a week back then, but practical considerations were unlikely to occur to a bug boy in such a situation. Within moments, a herd of jockeys packed into a room at the mill and showered $5 worth of nickels and dimes on the girl in question. She promptly stripped naked, lit up a cigarette, and blew smoke rings from a place into which only a creative-minded and supple-bodied prostitute would think of placing a cigarette. It was the greatest day of the bug boys' lives. "What talent!" recalled a witness. "Of course, I had to change my brand of cigarettes after that."

The Molino Rojo set the standard for Tijuana. The jockeys lived high and hard, riding by day, roaming the town in dense, noisy scrums by night, pouring into the Molino Rojo, then the Turf Club saloon, then on to wild exploits in town, chasing giggling girls buck naked down motel corridors, stealing all the room keys to the town's biggest hotel. Among the riders were Red Pollard and George Woolf. It was to this strangely bountiful place that they came each winter, and they thought of it as home. Riding there from fall to spring every year, they defined themselves as athletes and as men.

*

In 1928, their first full season together, they took the racing world by storm. Settling into his niche as a miracle worker for tough and neurotic horses, Pollard earned assignments on nearly three hundred mounts and guided them to more than $20,000 in total purse earnings. His fifty-three winners placed him in a tie for twentieth in winning percentage among fully employed riders in North America. He was a complete success. But Woolf was supernatural. Though in the big leagues only a few months, Woolf was signed on to ride more than 550 mounts, many of whom were stakes horses of the highest quality, and won with more than 100 of them for total purse earnings of $100,000. His winning average of 19 percent ranked him in a tie for sixteenth among fully employed riders. As the weekday wonder and the money man, Pollard and Woolf established themselves in the uppermost tier of North American racing.

They also carved out their own respective roles in the social world. Pollard, with his books, his stories, and his offbeat sense of humor, earned the bewildered affection of everyone at the track. A small cadre of racetrack eccentrics gathered around him. In the jockeys' room he orchestrated a string of clever practical jokes, sequestered himself in corners to pore over literature, and mystified his fellow jocks with aphorisms from Omar Khayyám and "Old Waldo" Emerson. A passing incident might inspire him to gallop through huge sections of Shakespeare, committed to memory, leaving the bug boys furrowing their brows. His language was a patchwork of cultivated speech and blue-streak profanity. He was loved for his wicked humor, delivered with a Buster Keaton straight face, and boundless generosity. He was feared and admired for his fistfighting skills, drop-of-a-hat volatility, thundering bass voice, and daring.

He was a prolific yarn spinner. One tale featured Pollard riding racehorses for Czar Nicholas. He could slip this one past the bug boys, who hadn't gone to school long enough to know that the Bolsheviks had put an end to poor Nicholas when Pollard was only nine. Another favorite described how he inadvertently bedded down beside five hibernating bears in a Canadian cave. Hair grew on this story until the bears were wide awake and the ex-boxer was using his deadly left hook to knock all five unconscious. When he wasn't telling stories, he was smartassing racing officials. He once attended a racing banquet at which a racing starter was the keynote speaker. The starter was notorious for his profanity, specifically his trademark phrase "Put a twitch on that son of a bitch!" referring to a restraint device that was pulled over horses' upper lips to distract them while they were being loaded into the gate. As the host droned through the starter's introduction, Pollard fidgeted in the crowd, slurping up champagne and, like everyone else, stagnating in boredom. As the starter rose to speak, clearing his throat for effect, Pollard abruptly stood up. "Put a twitch on *that* son of a bitch!" he boomed.

In the rough-and-tumble world of the track, Pollard was something of a sheriff. Farrell Jones, who rode alongside Pollard, recalled a fight he got into with a veteran jockey in a dispute over a checkers match. When Jones won the match, the older jockey flipped the board across the room and promptly tackled him. Jones, who was only thirteen and weighed little more than eighty pounds, quickly found himself on the losing end of the tussle. The older jockey pounded him mercilessly and tried to jam his thumbs into his eyes. Pollard swept up to them, grabbed the attacking jockey by the back of the neck, tossed him to the ground, and pinned him. Pressing the jockey to the floor, he pinched his nose between his fingers and twisted it. The jockey howled for mercy. After letting him squirm for a while, Pollard released the rider, who had blood running from his nose and tears streaming down his face. "Don't you ever touch that kid again," Pollard hissed. He stalked off, leaving the room in silence. Nobody *ever* messed with Red.

If Pollard was the jester, Woolf was the king. The crowds adored him, shouting "Ride 'em, cowboy!" as he powered down the stretch on his good-luck piece, a battered kangaroo leather saddle once carried by Phar Lap, the greatest racehorse in Australian history. The press doted on him. The lost boys of the racetrack worshiped him. Woolf took them under his wing, letting them copilot his roadster and teaching them the fine arts of horsemanship. After winning races, he'd drive over to the backstretch and stuff cash into the pockets of his mounts' grooms. He chaperoned groups of riders on mornings of road work, but by the end of the run discipline always seemed to break down and he'd end up jogging them into a gin joint to refill their depleted systems with a tall one. To help some of them conceal their big feet— and their coming growth spurts—Woolf started up a black market in his shoes. Riders all over the backstretch balled up their toes, wadded them into Woolf's hand-me-down silver inlaid boots (which, to their misery, were pointed), and limped around in them all day. A jockey's feet might bleed, but donning Woolf's shoes was an honor. Horseman Harold Washburn's boyhood memory of his first sight of Woolf sums up the impression the Iceman left on the kids of the backstretch. "I walked out and see Georgie pull up with that big car with them superchargers on it, step out of that car with them boots with silver inlaid on it, white western hat, and I thought, 'Oh my God! I am going to be a jockey!'"

Woolf could get away with anything. In the spring of 1932, when a solar eclipse occurred just as he was scheduled to ride to the post, he carried a shaded glass out onto the horse with him, pulled up, lay his head back on his horse's rump, and sat there, gazing at the sun while the crowd stared at him. In winning another race, he rode with such supreme concentration that he didn't notice that he had torn right out of his paper-thin pants. He didn't have a stitch of clothing on underneath, nor did he have the good fortune to at least be trailing the field. By the time he was galloping out, everyone at the track knew what Woolf had not yet noticed. "Hey Woolf!" came a laughing voice from behind. "You're sticking out!" Woolf cantered the horse back to the cheering grandstand and calmly asked his valet for a saddle towel. The valet trotted up with the requisite fig leaf, and Woolf, smiling out of one side of his mouth, wrapped it around his waist, rode into the winner's circle, and posed for the photo. He hopped down and glided back to the jocks' room to a hearty round of applause.

Off the track, Woolf steered clear of the town's appeals to vice, preferring late-morning pit stops in Checks Sloan's restaurant for a complimentary beer and a bowl of turtle soup. Not even the Molino

Rojo tempted him. He had better things on his mind. In 1930, while cruising up over the border with Sonny Greenberg, he stopped at a San Ysidro train-car diner and fell head over heels in love with a gorgeous sixteen-year-old waitress named Genevieve. Woolf began coming in regularly, parking his Stetson on the table and pointing Greenberg's nose in the *Racing Form* while he romanced her. In 1931, at age twenty-one, Woolf married her.

Pollard, a more adventurous soul, probably lived a little closer to the pulse of Tijuana. A romantic, he appears to have passed up the offers from the Tijuana prostitutes. He drank a little with the boys, got into a few fistfights, and lived at the top of his game. It was the happiest time of his life. "How can I keep away from this place?" he would say on a visit ten years later. "Isn't it my first love?"

The halcyon days at the Tijuana track came to a spectacular end. On the backstretch early each morning men guided teams of horses on circuits of the barns, shoveling the mucked-out manure into wagons and driving the teams up the hill behind the backstretch, where they would dump it. The pile had been accumulating since 1917, and because the city received little rain to wash it down, it was enormous. "Oh my *gosh*," remembered trainer Jimmy Jones. "It was as big as the grandstand." Inside its percolating depths, the manure fermented, generating scalding heat.

To the locals, the mountain of manure was a steaming eyesore. To the jockeys, it was prime sauna country. Every day riders dug holes in the surface and burrowed in, Pollard and Woolf probably included. A few took the precaution of zipping into rubber suits before wiggling in, but most just wore street clothes. It was almost too hot to take, but Mother Nature's hotbox proved unbeatable for sweating off weight.

The mountain was not long for this world. Sometime in the late 1920s, after extraordinarily heavy rains, swollen streams running off the nearby mountains backed up into a ravine, then exploded over the banks. Howling through Tijuana, the wall of water crashed into the racetrack, hurling houses, barns, and bridges along with it. Grooms ran down the backstretch before the onrushing water, throwing open stall doors and chasing out the horses, who scattered in all directions.

Behind them, the irresistible force of the flood met the immovable object of the manure pile. The water won. The mound, a marvel of solidity for a decade, was uprooted whole and began to shudder along in one murderous mass. It rolled over the San Diego and Arizona railroad tracks that fed the racetrack, tearing them out. Moving as if animated with destructive desire, it gurgled down the backstretch, banked around the far turn, bore out in the homestretch, and mowed down the entire grandstand. It made a beeline for the Monte Carlo Casino, crashing straight through its walls and cracking it wide open. Then, like a mighty shit Godzilla, it slid out to sea and vanished.

For two days the track was underwater, stranding a cluster of grooms and loose horses atop a spit of land. People scurried in and out of what was left of the casino, pushing wheelbarrows brimming with silver dollars scooped up from the opened vaults. As the water subsided, grooms combed the town for the freed horses. Most had vanished in the hills, never to be reclaimed. But one man's loss was another man's gain. Impoverished mountain-dwelling Mexicans, who usually got around on wormy little burros, were soon cantering through town in high style, straddling blue-blooded Thoroughbreds worth a lifetime of their income. The Tijuana horsemen, long accustomed to calamity, wrote off the horses, picked up, and went on. They were racing again in a couple of days.

Soon afterward, a new $3 million racetrack called Agua Caliente was built just down the road. The old Tijuana track was reduced to a squatter's haven, and Pollard and Woolf set up shop across town.

Woolf immediately ruled the roost at Agua Caliente. Riding the best horse at the track, Gallant Sir, he won the 1933 Agua Caliente Handicap, one of the world's most prestigious races. In 1934 Woolf and Gallant Sir were set to defend their title. On the morning of the race, Woolf was scheduled to give the horse a light gallop. But at the appointed hour the rider was nowhere to be found. Trainer Woody Fitzgerald jumped in his car and drove to Woolf's house. He found the Iceman sprawled across his bed, too absorbed in a cowboy magazine to bother going to his job. Fitzgerald fired him on the spot. Woolf went back to reading.

Fitzgerald sped back to the track and began a frantic hunt for a last-minute replacement. Pollard didn't have a mount in the race, so Fitzgerald let him ride. Pollard rode flawlessly and won. Gallant Sir had won more than $23,000 that day, and Pollard's cut was the biggest payday of his life. It was only the third stakes win of Pollard's career, and in a backward kind of way, he owed it to Woolf. It would be four years before he was in a position to repay him.

The days of large life and uncomplicated success were fleeting. For Woolf, the longest shadow on his life surfaced a few years into his career. Its most evident manifestation seemed innocuous enough: Woolf was prone to nodding off. He would spend his days off stretched out in bed, snoozing. At parties, he was known to fall asleep in mid-conversation. His wife, Genevieve, and his friend Bill Buck were so concerned about his sudden attacks of sleep that they chauffeured him everywhere. Between races, Woolf climbed atop the jockeys' lockers and curled up in the arms of Morpheus. He took napping so seriously that he eventually staked out a secret nest on the track roof, tucked in behind a chimney. Roused as the jocks' room custodian shouted the traditional prerace call of "Jockeys! Jockeys!" Woolf would slip downstairs, wake himself with a tall Coca-Cola spiked with a couple of drops of ammonia, blot his lips, mutter, "Let's go get this money and go home," and stride into battle.

To almost everyone in the jockeys' room, Woolf's perpetual sleepiness was just another of his many eccentricities. To Woolf, Genevieve, and a few close friends, it meant something entirely different: insulin-dependent, Type I diabetes.

His disease apparently surfaced in 1931, shortly after Caliente opened. Diabetes has never been easy to live with. In the 1930s it was hellish. Insulin had only been discovered about a decade before Woolf's diagnosis. Glucose levels were monitored by testing urine, which could only measure glucose present in the blood eight hours earlier. Trial and error was the only method physicians had to figure dosage, additives had not been developed to improve the absorption of the hormone, and the proper diet for diabetes management was not yet fully understood. As a result, patients like Woolf could never truly control their illness. Giving himself repeated daily shots of canine insulin in the abdomen, arm, or leg, Woolf almost certainly spent his days boomeranging between insulin gluts and deficits. The result was frequent sickness—nausea, vomiting, extreme thirst and hunger—occasional irritability, and exhaustion.

It also created a perilous dilemma. Woolf was in a career in which staying light was of paramount importance. He was not a natural lightweight; fellow jockeys dubbed him "Old Lead Pad." This was a problem facing nearly every jockey, but with the onset of his diabetes, Woolf's problems were compounded. In most patients, Type I diabetes spurs the appetite, sometimes to extremes. Insulin injections encouraged Woolf to gain weight, and to manage his diabetes he needed to consume regular, high-protein, low-carbohydrate meals—meats were recommended—which also added pounds. Between 1931 and 1932 Woolf's weight jumped by almost 10 percent, to 115, too high to ride most horses.

He faced a wrenching conflict. To perform in the sport he was born for, he had to be very thin, but to survive his disease, he had to maintain habits that made thinness virtually impossible. He tried to find a happy medium, taking his insulin regularly, eating thick steaks, and reducing the extra weight off. Genevieve worried about the reducing and tried to stop him, but he appears to have found ways to do it anyway. He was an avid follower of Frenchy Hawley's methods. Though Frenchy's concepts of reducing were in some cases medieval, they were generally safer than those the jockeys dreamed up on their own, so Woolf probably benefited as a result. But his reducing, combined with the blunt-instrument character of diabetes treatment in the 1930s, made controlling his blood sugar extremely difficult. At times he seemed to hover on the edge of passing out. Trainer George Mohr remembered that Woolf sometimes rode while appearing strangely ashen, while Woolf's friend Sonny Greenberg recalled incidents in which he found the rider slumped in the jockeys' room, too ill to speak.

So Woolf made another concession to his disease. He began to restrict his riding to top horses assigned high imposts. Occasionally, as a favor to an old gyp trainer friend, he would agree to ride a cheap horse. Woolf weighed a lot more than the imposts assigned to most of these horses, but somehow he was able to circumvent the rule requiring riders to be within five pounds of the assignment. His skills negated the handicap; he once won on a horse carrying fifteen pounds more than his impost.

But these sojourns on cheap horses were rarities. Usually he rode only about four times a week, nearly all classy horses, rarely more than one a day. Over the course of a year, he rode one hundred and fifty to two hundred mounts, compared with as many as one thousand for other top riders. Incredibly, in spite of his small number of total mounts, his soaring win percentage invariably placed him near the top of the national jockey rankings for purse money won. In one season Eddie Arcaro nosed him out for the money-winning title, but only by riding *three times* as many horses. Woolf took to calling Arcaro "the Desperate Dude."

Woolf's habit of minimal riding for maximum purses allowed him to survive as a jockey, but he knew he was walking a very fine line. In his era, even simple lacerations often left diabetics with savage infections that necessitated limb and digit amputations, a consequence of the disease's ravaging effect on circulation and immunity. To minimize the risk of being cut in a spill, he tried to avoid very young, inexperienced horses. On the rare occasions when he rode a green horse, he used a custom-made, reinforced saddle and slip-proof girth. But Woolf knew that infection and amputation were the least of his worries. If he played the balance of diabetes management and reducing wrong, he could faint in the saddle while moving at forty miles per hour. It was probably the only thing that ever really scared him.

At roughly the same time that Woolf started his potentially deadly gamble, Pollard engaged in a gamble of his own. It began with a simple morning workout on a horse whose name has long since been forgotten. As Pollard rode the horse down the track that morning, another horse passed close by. Something—maybe a rock or a clump of dirt—flew up from under the animal's hooves and struck Pollard in the head. The object slammed into Pollard's skull over the visual center of his brain.

In the glimmer of an instant, for the price of a 50-cent galloping fee he was probably never paid, Pollard lost the sight in his right eye forever.

Had they known of Pollard's blindness, the stewards would rightly have banned him from racing. With virtually no depth perception and no ability to see horses to his outside, he was far more vulnerable to positioning errors. He could unwittingly charge straight into a wreck. It was an injury that should have ended his career.

But Pollard, like Woolf, was not willing to hang it up. If anything, he was bolder than ever in the saddle, either to conceal his blindness or simply because he couldn't see just how close he was cutting it. "Red is not one of our great riders, but the only word he knows is yes," wrote a columnist who didn't know of Pollard's blindness. "He'll try to thread a needle with a horse as the flying field turns down the last bend for home, and you must salute him for his courage, if not his judgment." Pollard took an awesome risk. He kept his blindness secret and kept on riding.

Just after Pollard rode Gallant Sir to win the 1934 Agua Caliente Handicap, Mexico banned gambling. The colorful racing world that had spun itself around Tijuana withered and blew off into the sagebrush deserts. Pollard and Woolf returned to the United States, where racing had been relegalized, and their careers began to diverge.

On Christmas Day 1934 Santa Anita Park opened for the first time. Woolf turned the place upside down, riding an out-of-the-clouds long shot named Azucar, a former steeplechaser, to a smashing victory in the first Santa Anita Handicap. It was one of the greatest rides anyone had ever seen. After Woolf dismounted, Azucar butted him out of the way, ran over a spectator, slashed the NBC Radio wire—cutting off the national broadcast—and dragged his terrified groom down the track like a toboggan. The Iceman watched him go from the winner's circle, a floral wreath wrapped around his shoulders, smiling his cool Gary Cooper smile as a mob of admirers cheered for him. The Iceman had arrived.

As Woolf ascended, Pollard began to fail. Perhaps his partial blindness was the reason. After Gallant Sir, he didn't ride another stakes winner for years. Then even his modest weekday mounts began losing. He moved around North America, through Chicago, New York, Canada, riding the tough horses, the sour ones, and the nervous ones, but his statistics continued to slip.

Somewhere along the way, Pollard crossed paths with a jockey agent named Yummy, a round, toad-eyed, linty man, built low. Yummy had a pronounced harelip that slurred his speech badly. He raised his voice to a pounding level to compensate, but this only made people cringe. He kept his cash in his shoe and lived year-round in the Turkish baths of whatever city he happened through. Like Pollard, he seemed to have lost the need to belong to any place in particular. The best Yummy could do for Pollard was chase his hopelessly beaten mounts down the grandstand rail, hollering and frightening spectators. But he was fanatically loyal, and he had a car. The two began kicking around the country together.

In August 1936 they turned up at Ohio's Thistle Down Park. Any hopes Pollard had of redeeming himself there were quickly silenced. His win percentage dropped to a lamentable 6 percent. He rode, on average, fewer than two winners a month. Around the track, people whispered that he was finished. He was drifting into the great slipstream in which many promising jockeys are lost, their talents never tried for lack of the skilled trainer, the wise owner, the "big horse."

On August 16 Pollard and Yummy climbed into Yummy's car, pulled out of the track, and hit the highway. Somewhere along the way, they smacked the car into something. Whatever it was they hit, it didn't have a lot of give to it; the car was showered all over the road.

They bailed out into blistering heat. There beside the hulk of the ruined car, countless miles from anywhere, Pollard was standing in a metaphor for his own life. At twenty-six, he was frightened and empty. The car was totaled, the money was gone, and there were no prospects ahead of him. He and Yummy picked through the wreckage for their most essential belongings, 27 cents and a half pint of a foul brandy they called "bow-wow wine." Pollard probably salvaged his books and his rosary. There was a sugar cube kicking around in his pocket. They abandoned the car and hung their thumbs in the northbound lane.

It was late afternoon when they rolled up Woodward Avenue in Detroit. The city was stacked up in a hot, close grid, and the summer lay heavy over it. The ruinous decade had scarred the city, as it had every other: poor boxes on the street, people living on railcars. Near the intersection of Woodward and Eight Mile Road there was a cemetery. Pollard and Yummy called for the driver to stop. On the other side of the avenue stood the gate to a racetrack, the Detroit Fair Grounds. Pollard and Yummy hopped down, turned their backs to the gravestones, and walked in.

Across the track, Tom Smith was leaning against the easternmost barn, turning a straw in his teeth. In the stall behind him was Seabiscuit. Smith had been sitting by the horse for two days, thinking on him, watching him, trying to inhabit him. Something rattled in the horse's mind that made him edgy and angry. He had been enjoying a reign of terror since they brought him to Detroit, trying to take big chunks out of the grooms, and no one wanted to go within a pitchfork's length of him. No man had ever understood him, and the horse now turned against anyone who tried. Smith was thinking that he needed a strong and intuitive jockey for this one.

Up the backstretch, Yummy was zigging and zagging his way through barns with his big paw out, booming his pitch—"Name's Yummy, not Dummy"—and coming out empty-handed. No one wanted Pollard. He and Pollard were dirty and tired and shaky from the wreck. Evening was falling, and it was time to start thinking about where to get their next meal and bed down for the night. The bottle of bow-wow wine was probably long dry.

A groom pointed to a gray man sitting in front of the barn where the Howard horses were kept. Agent and jockey turned east and walked toward Smith.

Yummy reloaded and made a run at him. Smith waved him off, eyeing the redhead and retrieving a name from years back: Cougar. He recalled the grave lines of the jockey's profile from the days when they had crossed paths somewhere out West. He looked at the brooding face and the boxer's physique and thought: *Maybe.* He offered his hand. Pollard took it. Smith smiled.

He gestured toward the stall behind him. Pollard leaned over Seabiscuit's half door. The horse had his back to him, a dark mass shifting in the straw. Pollard pushed his hand into his pocket and pulled it out again with his fingers closed. He extended his arm and opened his hand: the cube of sugar. From the back of the stall, there came a tentative sound of nostrils drawing the air, weighing the scent. A black muzzle materialized, licked up the sugar, and touched the jockey's shoulder.

The scattered lives of Red Pollard, Tom Smith, and Charles Howard had come to an intersection. Their crowded hour had begun.

PART II

Tom Smith and Seabiscuit

CHAPTER 7

Learn Your Horse

The grooms were walking around with their faces fixed in permanent winces. Every time they passed Seabiscuit's stall, the horse lunged at them, mouth wide open, ears flat back, eyes in a sinister pinch, and he meant business. Heaven help the poor kid who had to go in there, muck the floor, and curry the horse. Everyone was wondering what Smith possibly could have been thinking. The horse was a train wreck. He paced in his stall incessantly. He broke into a lather at the sight of a saddle. He was two hundred pounds underweight and chronically tired. He was so thin, said one observer, that his hips could have made a passable hat rack, but he refused to eat. And that left foreleg didn't look good.

As he did with every new horse, Smith pored over Seabiscuit when he was with him and mulled him over when he was not. The first thing he had to try to do, the trainer decided, was defuse the horse. Ignoring the snapping jaws and pinned ears, he showered him with affection and carrots. He then tried one of the oldest remedies for unhappy horses: animal companionship. Motley collections of stray animals have always populated racetracks, and being the social creatures they are, horses usually befriend them. All sorts of animals, from German shepherds to chickens, have become the stable companions of racehorses. A three-legged cat lived with Fitzsimmons's horse; the trainer dismantled a piece of harness and crafted a tiny wooden leg for him, then watched as the cat learned to snare mice with one paw and "blackjack" them with the other. At a track in Arizona a monkey was a popular mascot until he began turning on all the shed-row faucets and tearing the shingles off the roof.

Smith took the goat route. He dug up a nanny named Whiskers and parked her in Seabiscuit's stall. Shortly after dinnertime, the grooms found Seabiscuit walking in circles, clutching the distraught goat in his teeth and shaking her back and forth. He heaved her over his half door and plopped her down in the barn aisle. The grooms ran to her rescue.

Smith opted for a companion who could take a little more punishment. Down the shed row he kept a lead horse he called Pumpkin. As broad as a Sherman tank and yellow as a daisy, Pumpkin—or "Punkins," as the hands called him—had once been a Montana cow pony. Out on the range, the horse had experienced everything, including a bull goring that had left a gouge in his rump. He was a veteran, meeting every calamity with a cheerful steadiness. He was, in the parlance of horsemen, "bombproof." Smith recognized the value of a horse like this and brought him along with his racing string to work as a lead pony, Smith's track mount, and general stable calmer-downer. Pumpkin was amiable to every horse he met and became a surrogate parent to the flighty ones. He worked a sedative effect on the whole barn. After Seabiscuit evicted the goat, Smith hauled in Pumpkin. A brief mutual nose-sniffing produced no ill-will, so Smith decided to make Seabiscuit Pumpkin's new assignment. He housed Pumpkin in one stall, Seabiscuit in the next, and tore down the wall between. The horses conversed and developed a fast friendship. They would live and work together for the rest of their lives.

The experiment with Pumpkin worked so well that Smith began collecting other stable companions for Seabiscuit. Somewhere along the way, a little spotted stray dog fell in with the Howard barn and began to travel with it. Named Pocatell, the dog had curiously upright ears that were round as platters and roughly three times normal size. Pocatell took a liking to Seabiscuit and began sleeping in his stall at night. Jo Jo, a small spider monkey of undetermined origin, had the same preference for Seabiscuit's company. Sleeping with Pumpkin a few feet away, Jo Jo in the crook of his neck, and Pocatell on his belly, Seabiscuit began to relax.

The next hurdle was the horse's sore and underweight body. Smith mixed up a homemade liniment and painted it on Seabiscuit's legs. To keep the mixture from rubbing off when the horse lay in his straw and to protect his dinged-up legs from additional bumps and bruises, the trainer instituted a routine of keeping the horse in knee-high, inches-thick cotton bandages, once compared to World War I puttees. Smith also paid very close attention to Seabiscuit's fuel. He fed the colt a high-quality strain of timothy hay, cultivated in Northern California, which he had come across during his first days as a trainer. For oats, he ladled out carefully measured portions of a fine white variety grown in the Sacramento Valley. After reading an article describing the nutritional intake of the University of Washington crew team, Smith made sure the horse received feed with a high calcium content. For bedding, he spread out a thick mattress of dust-free rice straw.

Once Seabiscuit was settled in at Detroit, Smith took the colt to the track to stretch his legs. It was a disaster. Seabiscuit didn't run, he rampaged. When the rider asked him for speed, the horse slowed down. When he tried to rein him in, the horse bolted, thrashing around like a hooked marlin. Asked to go left, he'd dodge right; tugged right, he'd dart left. The beleaguered rider could do no better than cling to the horse's neck for dear life. Smith watched, his eyes following the colt as he careened across the track, running as a moth flies.

Smith knew what he was seeing. Seabiscuit's competitive instincts had been turned backward. Instead of directing his efforts against his opponents, he was directing them against the handlers who tried to force him to run. He habitually met every command with resistance. He was feeding off the fight, gaining satisfaction from the distress and rage of the man on his back. Smith knew how to stop it. He had to take coercion out of the equation and let the horse discover the pleasure of speed. He called out to the rider: *Let him go.*

The rider did as told, and Seabiscuit took off with him, trying once to hurdle the infield fence but meeting with no resistance from the reins. He made a complete circuit at top speed, but Smith issued no orders to stop him, so around he went again, dipping and swerving.

After galloping all-out for two miles, weaving all over the track, Seabiscuit was exhausted. He stopped himself and stood on the track, panting. The rider simply sat there, letting him choose what to do. There was nowhere to go but home. Seabiscuit turned and walked back to the barn of his own volition. Smith greeted him with a carrot. Neither Smith nor his exercise rider had raised a hand to him, but the colt had learned the lesson that would transform him from a rogue to a pliant, happy horse: He would never again be forced to do what he didn't want to do. He never again fought a rider.

After that wild ride, Smith put Pollard up on Seabiscuit for the first time to see how he would handle the horse. Pollard rode the horse around, studying him. Seabiscuit wouldn't try much for him. Pollard turned him and brought him back to the barn. Trainer and jockey conferred. Pollard told Smith that the whip, used so liberally by Fitzsimmons, had to be put away. It should be used, he said, only in times of great urgency. Pollard saw that if this horse was pushed around, all he would do was push back. Smith knew he had found the right jockey.

Smith and Pollard made a point of allowing Seabiscuit to do as he pleased. Smith issued orders that the horse never be disturbed while sleeping, for any reason. Riders and grooms would sometimes stand around for hours, waiting for the horse to wake up before they could get to work. Seabiscuit milked it for all it was worth. "He wakes up in the morning like a sly old codger," said Pollard. "Y'know, the Biscuit is like an old gentleman, and he hates to get up with the rising sun. When you go to his stall, he lays over like a limp, old rag and peeks out at you with one eye to see whether you get what he's trying to drive over—that he's sick as a dog. He'd get away with it if he could, but wise old Tom Smith knows him like a book."

Pollard and the other exercise riders were given instructions to simply lean on his neck, sitting still and leaving the reins loose, so that the horse could choose his own pace. By making sure that all workouts ended at the finish line, Smith taught Seabiscuit that he needed to be ahead of other horses by the time he crossed the wire. Racetracks are ringed with poles that tell riders what fraction of a mile remains before the finish wire. Pollard found that with every pole he passed, the horse would run harder. Pollard didn't need to hold him back, or "rate" him, in the early part of workouts; the horse knew that the home-stretch was where the real running was done. "Why rate him?" Pollard would later say. "He knows the poles better than I do."

Over the next weeks, Pollard and Smith discovered that obstrep-erousness was only one of Seabiscuit's bad traits. He amused him-self by propping in mid-workout, decelerating rapidly and vaulting his jockey up onto his neck. He also harbored a peculiar ardor for the inner rail. He refused to run at all unless he was practically on top of it, a consequence, Smith believed, of Fitzsimmons's practice of invariably working the horse along the inside. When he was guided away from the rail, Seabiscuit would slow down and do just about anything to get back over to it, including abruptly ducking inside. This created two problems. First, the area by the inner rail was the lowest part of the slightly banked oval, so it tended to hold the most water, making it the slowest, most tiring part of the track during and after rainstorms. Second, he was most likely to get caught in traffic jams on the rail. Any horse who refused to swing wide could get into serious trouble.

Hoping to focus the horse's mind on his job and reduce the distrac-tions of the rail, Smith fitted Seabiscuit with a set of blinkers that restricted his vision to the track straight ahead of him. He took the horse out to gallop on a morning when track officials, trying to protect the overused inside of the course, had put out "dogs," sawhorses lin-ing the rail path to keep exercising horses to the outside. By galloping the horse to the outside of the dogs, Smith hoped to wean him from the rail. Seabiscuit thwarted his efforts, ducking into the rail in the gaps between dogs, swerving out to avoid them, then cutting in again. Smith kept at it, eventually making progress. Unable to eliminate the rail obsession completely, the trainer made use of it. As Seabiscuit was apt to fight any direct attempts to rate him, Smith told his riders to adjust the horse's speed with steering. When a rider wanted Seabiscuit to speed up, he would swing him toward the rail; when he wanted him to ease off, he'd nudge him to the outside.

The most difficult quirk was Seabiscuit's behavior in the starting gate. Within its metal confines he raised holy hell, throwing himself around, exhausting the assistant starters, and reminding everyone of Hard Tack. To stop the colt's gate rages, Smith used a daring method. He led him out to the gate each morning, walked him inside it, and asked him to halt. Risking life and limb, Smith positioned himself directly in front of the horse, facing him. When Seabiscuit began banging around to get out, Smith held his ground, raised his hand, and tapped the horse firmly on the chest and shoulders until he stood still. When the horse stopped, so did Smith. When the horse moved, Smith tapped him again. Morning after morning, he was out at the gate with the horse, repeating the lesson. "You got to go at a horse slowly teaching him most anything," Smith explained later. "Easy, firm repetition does it." The effect was mesmerizing. The horse began to relax in the gate. "He caught on quick enough," said Smith. "He's wise as an old owl." Eventually, Smith was able to leave Seabiscuit standing in there for as long as ten minutes without the horse turning a hair.

Smith also made a point of giving Seabiscuit a structured life. The horse got breakfast when he woke up, usually at four-thirty, followed by stall mucking and grooming at five, and a lengthy gallop with Pumpkin at eight. For horses, "downshifting" from strenuous exercise is risky. If they are brought to idleness too soon after running all-out—in old cowboy parlance, being "rid hard and put away wet"—their major muscle groups can seize up in an agonizing spasm called "tying up." In addition, they can develop colic, a potentially fatal digestive crisis. Because of this, horses must be brought down from exercise gradually, slowly decelerating over about a half mile after a race and then undergoing a long walk. For Seabiscuit, this meant that after each workout he was covered in a blanket and hotwalked for about half an hour, until he was cool and dry. Then he was given a warm bath, dried, and led back into his stall, where his legs were painted in liniment and wrapped in protective bandages. He had lunch at eleven, hay snacks all afternoon, dinner at five. After that, the horse went to sleep, with his groom, Ollie, on a pallet in the stall with him. Seabiscuit fell into the schedule completely. Rain or shine, Smith was there to check on him at about eight every night before turning in.

Smith gave Seabiscuit time to learn to trust him and Pollard. Seabiscuit learned. When he heard Pollard's deep voice coming down the shed row, he would poke his head over the half door to greet him. When Pollard, who called the horse Pops, sat outside the stall, reading the paper while Seabiscuit was cooled out, the horse would tug his hot walker off course to snuffle his jockey's hands. When Smith led him out of the stall, he didn't even need a lead rope; the horse would follow his trainer wherever he went, nuzzling his pockets. Smith spoke to the horse in nearly inaudible tones, calling him Son and touching him lightly when he needed him to turn. Seabiscuit understood him and always did as asked. In moments of uncertainty, the horse would pause and look for Smith. When he found his trainer, the horse would relax. Smith taught him that he could trust his trainer and rider, and this became the foundation for the trials the three would share over the next five years. "[Smith] let horses get confidence in him," remembered Keith Stucki, one of the horse's exercise riders. "He was the best horseman I've ever seen."

With long, careful schooling, Seabiscuit began to figure things out. Once he was no longer being coerced, his instincts bubbled back to the surface. His innate love of running returned. Pollard used the whip not as an implement of force, but as a signal: one glancing swat on the rump at the eighth pole, another a few feet from home, a cue that it was time to hustle. Seabiscuit began to wait for it and respond with lightning quickness. "So long as you treat him like a gentleman," said Pollard, "he'll run his heart out for you." Though the horse was still goofing off and pulling tricks in his workouts, his speed was excellent.

After two weeks, Smith was ready to send him to the races. Howard agreed.

In late August they tried him in a good stakes race in Detroit. He had the bad luck of drawing into an event that featured the best filly in the country, Myrtlewood. Green to the core, Seabiscuit was all over the track, streaking out with the early leaders as they tried to keep up with Myrtlewood. On the backstretch, he was going along smoothly when, without warning, he threw his forelegs forward and propped, decelerating rapidly and dropping back through the field. Ahead of him, Myrtlewood drove to an insurmountable lead, with local star Professor Paul rallying in vain to catch her.

Seabiscuit's temperamental outburst had left him hopelessly beaten, but as Pollard angled him into the stretch and asked him to get his mind back on running, Smith witnessed something he would never forget. Seabiscuit began to rip over the track, cutting into Myrtlewood's lead even as she flew through fractions faster than any ever run at the Detroit Fair Grounds. He was much too late to overtake the filly or Professor Paul, but his rally carried him to fourth place, just four lengths behind Myrtlewood, who had broken the track record. Even more encouraging, in the homestretch, Seabiscuit's ears were up, a signal that the horse was running within himself. "He showed me two great qualifications that day," Smith remembered later. "He showed me speed, and he showed me courage. He was in trouble, and the way he pricked his ears, I knew if I could get the true speed out of him, I would have a champion."

Pollard knew it too. Leaping off of Seabiscuit's back, he ran over to Howard.

"Mr. Howard," he sang out, "that horse can win the Santa Anita!"

Howard laughed.

In his next start, on September 2 in the Roamer Handicap, Seabiscuit had nothing but bad luck. He took the early lead, then swung very wide on the far turn, falling behind into fourth. Pollard tried to rally him, but he was blocked by traffic until deep in the stretch, when he shook loose and flew up, almost catching Professor Paul for the win. Smith was pleased. The horse, he thought, was ready for sterner stuff.

On September 7 Smith led Seabiscuit out for the Governor's Handicap. The race had no national importance, but in Detroit it was the big event of the racing season. Seabiscuit was sent off at long odds, for good reason: Also entered in the race were Professor Paul and Azucar, George Woolf's Santa Anita Handicap winner, under a new rider and not quite his old self. Twenty-eight thousand fans, the biggest throng in Michigan racing history, showed up to see it, among them Charles and Marcela Howard.

They were treated to a spellbinder. Just after the start, Pollard tucked Seabiscuit in behind early leader Biography, who cut a brisk pace. Around the first turn and down the long backstretch, Pollard held Seabiscuit just behind Biography. Leaning into the far turn, Pollard saw a hole along the rail. He threaded Seabiscuit through, and in a few strides he had seized the lead. As Biography accelerated to stay with him, Professor Paul swept up on the grandstand side. In the center of the track, Azucar began to uncurl his long legs and accelerate, grinding away at the lead. In that position, the four horses bent around the turn and hit the homestretch. Pollard, in the lingo of jockeys, asked Seabiscuit the question.

Seabiscuit, for the first time in his life, answered. Pollard dropped his belly down in the saddle and rode as hard as he could. The quartet of horses blazed down the stretch at a terrific clip, with Seabiscuit a half length in front. Biography was the first to crack. Professor Paul, carrying just ninety-nine pounds, ten fewer than Seabiscuit, was skipping along under the light load, inching in on the lead, while Azucar, on the far outside, was driving at them. In midstretch, Professor Paul's blinkered head was at Pollard's hip with Azucar just behind them. A few feet later, Professor Paul was past Pollard's elbow and still gaining. Then Azucar gave way. It was down to Seabiscuit and Professor Paul. The latter was cutting the lead down with every lunge. With the crowd on its feet, Pollard spread himself flat over Seabiscuit's withers, reins clutched in his left hand, right hand pressed flat to Seabiscuit's neck, head turned and eyes fixed on Professor Paul's broad blaze. A few feet from the wire, Professor Paul reached Seabiscuit's throat. He was too late. Seabiscuit had won.

Red Pollard had won just his fourth stakes race in eleven long years in the saddle. He was radiant. He galloped Seabiscuit out to the cheers from the crowd, then turned him back toward the grandstand.

Beneath him, Seabiscuit bounced along with his tail fanned out high in the air. He played with the bit and wagged an ear at the photographers who stood by the rail, snapping his picture for the morning papers. Pollard steered him back to the winner's stand, leapt off, and ran to Howard, who beamed like a schoolboy. It was only a good stakes race at a minor-league track, but it might as well have been the hundred-grander.

The ceremonies began. On the winner's stand, which was swathed in a huge American flag and crammed with suited dignitaries, Marcela smiled demurely for the lieutenant governor, who extended a huge silver loving cup. Pollard, his skullcap off, his hair dark with sweat and his head tilted so his good eye focused on the camera, stood behind her, dwarfed by the cup. Smith, grim and spectral, stood alongside him. His mouth was set in its habitual glower, the corners bent downward in perfect convexity, and his ashen head blended seamlessly into the white clouds overhead. Howard, giddy and grinning, was nearly crowded right off the stand. The photo opportunity over, they smoothed a new blanket, emblazoned with the words GOVERNOR'S HANDICAP DETROIT, over Seabiscuit's back, and Howard held Seabiscuit's nose in his hands as a new set of photographs was snapped. Smith stood with them, ignoring the popping flashbulbs to let his eyes comb over his horse. Seabiscuit stood square under his head-to-toe blanket, posed in the stance of the conqueror, head high, ears pricked, eyes roaming the horizon, nostrils flexing with each breath, jaw rolling the bit around with cool confidence.

He was a new horse.

In the fiftieth start of his life, Seabiscuit finally understood the game. Smith and Pollard had unearthed in him, in Smith's words, "more natural inclination to run than any horse I have ever seen." Behind his frown, Smith was pleased.

The colt was transformed. In the barn he became a disarmingly affectionate glutton, "as gentlemanly a horse," marveled Smith, "as I ever handled." On the track, once the forum for rebellion, he displayed blistering speed and bulldog tenacity. Smith wasn't ready to put the screws to him just yet. He was beginning to think that Pollard was right about the horse's chances in the Santa Anita Handicap. Because track handicappers assign higher imposts to faster and more accomplished horses, Smith wanted to keep his horse a secret for as long as he could. Smith kept the horse in the small pond of Detroit, where Seabiscuit followed the Governor's Handicap win with an impressive score in the Hendrie Handicap. Smith then shipped him down to Cincinnati's River Downs, where the horse narrowly missed winning two more minor stakes.

It was at Cincinnati that Seabiscuit's handlers first realized how fanatically competitive the horse was. Those unfamiliar with horses might scoff at the notion of equine pride as a silly anthropomorphism, but the behavior is unmistakable. Those who make their lives among horses see it every day. Horses who lose their riders during races almost always try to win anyway, charging to the lead and sometimes bucking with pleasure as they pass the last opponent. Weanling herds stampede around their paddocks several times a day, running all-out to beat one another. Even old stallions, decades away from the track, still duel with one another up and down the fences of breeding farms. As George Woolf noted, losers show clear signs of dejection and frustration, even shame; winners prick their ears and swagger. "You don't have to tell good horses when they win or lose," he said. "They know. I guess they come by it kinda natural." Humans aren't the only creatures to seek mastery and rebel at being mastered. The fire that had kept Seabiscuit frustrated and unruly now fueled a bounding will to win.

It first surfaced in the midst of a scorching workout alongside Howard's excellent sprinter, Exhibit. Seabiscuit had him beaten, but instead of pulling away, he eased himself up and galloped alongside, going just fast enough to keep Exhibit a notch behind. Exhibit tried his hardest, but Seabiscuit kept adjusting his speed to maintain the short advantage. He appeared to be taunting Exhibit. The two kept it up for a few furlongs before Exhibit abruptly pulled himself up. From that day forward, he refused to work with Seabiscuit.

The scene would be reenacted countless times on the racetrack in the next few years, and it would become Seabiscuit's trademark. The horse seemed to take sadistic pleasure in harassing and humiliating his rivals, slowing down to mock them as he passed, snorting in their faces, and pulling up when in front so other horses could draw alongside, then dashing their hopes with a killing burst of speed. Where other horses relied solely on speed to win, Seabiscuit used intimidation.

Finding workmates was immediately problematic. One by one, Seabiscuit disposed of the Howard horses in morning workouts, merrily abusing them as he ran. Horses all over the barn became his mortal enemies. Others were heartbroken; Seabiscuit could suck the joy out of any good racehorse's career. A typical example was a fine Argentine import named Sabueso. He managed to beat Seabiscuit in a short blowout one morning and returned to the barn cocky and full of himself. Pollard vowed revenge. In another meeting a short while later, he boasted, "I *poured* Seabiscuit at him." Seabiscuit humiliated Sabueso.

Sabueso refused to eat and didn't sleep for several days. "We had a terrible time straightening him out," Pollard remembered. "He sulked and pouted as if to say, 'I wish I was back in the Argentine.'" Smith finally resorted to convincing Sabueso that Seabiscuit had left the string. He housed the two horses as far apart as possible, and whenever Seabiscuit was led down Sabueso's shed row, Pollard or Smith would shut the stall doors so Sabueso wouldn't see him. "I guess the Argentine must think the big horse has gone away," said Pollard. "At any rate, he's all right now. A good horse, too. A little chunk of granite. But make no mistakes—he ain't no Seabiscuit."

Seabiscuit's psychological warfare raised more problems than simple wounded pride. If he became too absorbed in rubbing a particular horse's nose in his defeat, he risked being unable to regain his momentum when the closers came after him. Fortunately, though taunting was one of Seabiscuit's greatest pleasures, once he was challenged, the games ended. In a fight he was all business. As Smith watched him in racing combat, images from his mustang days assembled in his head. "Did you ever see two stallions fight?" he would later ask. "They look about evenly matched—most times they are—but one of 'em has that last reserve of courage and energy which licks the other. Seabiscuit has it."

After the performance against Exhibit, Smith thought Seabiscuit was ready to move up a notch. The upstart West had the new Santa Anita Handicap, but the East, seat of racing's elite governing bodies and home to all of America's venerable old races and stables, had prestige. In October 1936 Seabiscuit climbed down from a railcar and stepped onto Empire City Racetrack in New York. He was not yet good enough to shoot for the East's great races, so Smith entered him in the Scarsdale Handicap, a midlevel stakes race. Few spectators cared that Seabiscuit, the second-longest shot on the board, was in the field.

The horse needed just a minute and forty-four seconds to change their minds. Fighting his way through one of the wildest contests of the season, Pollard swung Seabiscuit clear of a set of chain-reaction collisions on the far turn, circled the field, and sent his mount running in a frantic effort to catch the leaders. In a hub-scraping finish Seabiscuit dropped his head and won by inches. The finish photo captured the scene: A dense cluster of horses stretched out for the wire, ears flat and lips peeled back in extreme effort. Ahead of them all, ears tipped forward with a jaunty expression, was Seabiscuit's heavy, homely head. Easy.

One week later, Howard met with Smith. "Let's head for California," he said. "A little wind off San Francisco Bay would do us good." Smith agreed, thinking Seabiscuit could use a rest.

The trick was getting the horse there. In the 1930s, long-distance horse-shipping could only be done via railcar. A cross-country journey was a harrowing ordeal, five days of clanging, rocking, and bumping in a confined space. Train travel was so exhausting and upsetting to most Thoroughbreds that few could be taken outside their region. With Seabiscuit, Smith had reason to worry. Back at Saratoga, when he caught sight of the train to Detroit, the colt had panicked so badly that sweat had streamed from his belly.

While the other Howard horses filed onto standard horse-class cars, Seabiscuit had earned himself a luxury berth: a full end of an eighty-foot Pullman car. Half of the car was knee-deep in straw, half was left unbedded so he could stretch his legs. Smith watched to see how Seabiscuit would behave. The horse stepped in and lay down. He would sleep during most of the journey. Smith climbed into the caboose, coming forward at each whistle-stop to check on his horse.

They were retracing Charles Howard's youthful journey, thirty years later.

"We're coming back," the old bicycle man told his friends. "And when we do, hang on to your hats."

*Seabiscuit and Rosemont drive toward the wire together
in the 1937 hundred-grander.*
(© BETTMANN/CORBIS)

CHAPTER 8

Fifteen Strides

The *Overland Limited* sighed into Tanforan on a cool Wednesday morning in November 1936. Seabiscuit clopped onto the unloading ramp and paused halfway down, looking over his new home state. There wasn't much to see. The California sunlight had the pewter cast of a declining season. One or two stable hands crisscrossed the tamped-down earth before the siding. Horses murmured over the grounds.

A couple of reporters stood around, looking indifferently at Howard's new horse. They knew that the colt was aiming for the February 27 Santa Anita Handicap, but he hadn't done enough to merit serious consideration. Their thoughts were occupied by weightier names: world-record holder Indian Broom; speed demon Special Agent; and above them all, the magnificent Rosemont, king of the East and conqueror of 1935 Triple Crown winner Omaha. Eastern horses rarely came to the West in those days, but the size of the purse had brought Rosemont over the Rockies. With Rosemont in the race, no one had any reason to believe that the horse Tom Smith was leading down the platform would be anything more than an also-ran.

The reporters jotted down a word or two on Seabiscuit's arrival and moved off. Smith settled the horse in a comfortable stall and retired to his own little room right above it.

Smith liked the anonymity. The New York trip had told him that he had a very good horse in his barn, and until the weights were assigned for the hundred-grander, he intended to keep him hidden. So the trainer tucked Seabiscuit away on the Tanforan backstretch. He didn't even let his stable hands know how good he thought the horse was. Quietly, slowly, he schooled the horse, fed him well, built his trust. Seabiscuit's ribs filled out—he had put on two hundred pounds in the three months since he had joined Smith—and his manners had improved. When he came out on the track, he bounced up and down in eagerness to get going. Smith knew Seabiscuit was improving rapidly, but when he sent him out for workouts before the track clockers, he gave him only easy gallops that veiled his speed. No one took much notice of him.

One afternoon when the track was deserted, Smith snuck him out. Smith and Pollard had stripped away the temperamental barriers. It was time to see how fast the colt could go. Smith loaded weight onto his back, boosted an exercise rider aboard, and turned him loose.

He watched as Seabiscuit's body flattened down, his speed building, humming over the rail. Smith ticked off the seconds in his head. *Something is happening.* Lacking competition, racehorses in workouts rarely approach the speeds they achieve in races. But Smith had never seen a horse—*any horse*—flash this kind of speed, not in a workout, not in a race. Perhaps Smith thought his eyes were failing him, the clock in his head winding out of time. *Coming up, a mile to go.* He pulled his stopwatch out and pumped the trigger as the horse ripped past the marker. Seabiscuit kept rolling, faster and faster, covering more than fifty feet per second. His trainer watched intently, the surprise of it pushing up through him. Seabiscuit's speed was not flagging. A thought drummed in Smith's mind: *He's burning the top right off the racetrack.* Seabiscuit banked into the turn. There was a supple geometry to his arc, a fish bending through a current. Where virtually all horses decelerate and often drift out as they try to negotiate corners, Seabiscuit was capable of holding a tight line while accelerating dramatically. *No horse has ever run a turn like this one.*

When the colt flashed under the wire, Smith looked down at his hand. Seabiscuit had worked a mile in 1:36. The track record was 1:38.

At that speed, Seabiscuit would have trounced the track record holder by more than a dozen lengths.

Tom Smith was wide awake. In sixty years lived alongside thousands of horses, he had never seen anything like this. It was no fluke: in another clandestine workout not long after, the colt would tie a thirty-year-old world record for seven eighths of a mile, running it in 1:22.

Smith took Seabiscuit back to the barn, his secret seething in his head. For the first time, he grasped the awesome responsibility that lay in his hands.

The old cowpuncher was scared to death.

Smith wasn't about to let anyone know what he had seen in that workout. Not yet. The weights weren't out for the hundred-grander. He would keep Seabiscuit in San Francisco, where he could work in peace until he was ready for Santa Anita. Howard wanted to show his colt off to his hometown anyway.

On November 28, 1936, after nearly a month of legging up at Tanforan, Seabiscuit was trucked ten miles down the pike to run in Bay Meadows' mile-long Bay Bridge Handicap. The field was the best San Francisco had to offer, including Velociter, the former track record holder for the race's mile distance, and the terrific mare Uppermost, the only horse to better Velociter's time. Though his two main rivals had established themselves over the Bay Meadows course, Seabiscuit, by virtue of his Scarsdale Handicap win, was given the high weight of 116 pounds, 2 more than Uppermost and 9 more than Velociter.

Seabiscuit, a little stir-crazy after a full month on the sidelines, pushed off so hard at the starting bell's ring that he shoveled a big hunk of ground right out from under his hind hooves, dropping nearly to his knees. At the same moment he was bumped hard by the horse to his left. Pollard somehow managed to stay aboard while his colt regained his footing. By then, the field was six lengths up the track.

Starting his race all alone, Pollard tried to turn the incident to his advantage, cutting in to the rail for a ground-saving trip while far ahead of him, Velociter and Uppermost cruised to the lead. Pollard unleashed Seabiscuit's rally immediately, rushing up behind the field in hopes of finding an avenue through the pack. As the first turn approached, the horses farther out from the rail hustled inward and cut Seabiscuit off. With nowhere to go, Pollard waited. They pulled toward the backstretch, and Pollard saw a narrow hole open between horses and tried to send Seabiscuit through it. He didn't make it, and had to snatch up the reins and yank Seabiscuit back to prevent him from clipping the heels of the horses coming together in front of him. Trapped again, Pollard waited until the field straightened out. A hole opened. Pollard told Seabiscuit to take it, and the horse darted in.

Seabiscuit shot through the pack, swung out, and drew ahead of Uppermost, claiming second on the outside. Only front-running Velociter remained to be caught. Tugging his right rein, Pollard fanned his colt out and hung on as Seabiscuit gunned Velociter down. All alone again, but this time in front, Pollard leaned back and slowed Seabiscuit for the last fifty yards. They cantered down the lane and hit the wire, winners by five lengths.

A thrill went through the crowd. Seabiscuit had equaled his Tanforan workout time of 1:36 for the mile, breaking the track record. Two clockers who had started their watches when Seabiscuit actually left the gate stared at their watch hands in disbelief. When his time was adjusted for his late start, Seabiscuit had clocked the fifth-fastest mile ever run, just three fifths of a second off the world record.

Back at the barn, the stable hands were shocked. They had no idea that the horse was so fast. Only Smith was unsurprised, but he was not happy that the news was out.

On Sunday, December 12, Team Seabiscuit re-assembled in the Bay Meadows paddock for the mile-and-three-sixteenths World's Fair Handicap, the crowning stakes race of the track meeting. The field, including two major stakes winners, was the most formidable Seabiscuit had ever faced. Just after Pollard swung aboard, a paddock official waved him back so another horse could precede him in the post parade. Howard yelled across the paddock to the horse's owner,

"This is your last chance to be in front!" The crowd gave Howard a hearty round of applause.

Determined not to be left behind as they had been in the Bay Bridge Handicap, Pollard shot Seabiscuit from the starting gate and sent him blowing past the field. Seabiscuit streaked out to a twelve-length lead. The panicked jockeys behind him launched frantic rallies to catch him, but they could only cut the lead down to eight lengths. To wild cheering, Seabiscuit jogged down the homestretch all by himself. Pollard, laughing as he stood in the stirrups and leaned his full weight against the reins, did just about everything he could to slow Seabiscuit down. He wasn't much of a match for his colt, who tugged away at the bridle, begging to run.

When they returned to the scales, Seabiscuit wasn't even breathing hard. He had eclipsed another track record, running less than a second off the world record. His time was so fast that in the following year, no horse at Bay Meadows would come within three seconds of it. Pollard suddenly found himself in a sea of reporters. If he met the same field again, he sang out, he'd have time to ride Seabiscuit right off the track, canter him down to San Mateo for some Christmas shopping, swing by the post office for their fan mail, and still trot back in time to win the race.

The Bay Meadows operators got the point: Seabiscuit was far too good for anything at their track. The message was underscored when the West Coast's most prominent "future book" wagering operator, who was based in San Francisco, rated Seabiscuit above Rosemont for the hundred-grander. Hoping to keep Seabiscuit around for another race, the Bay Meadows racing secretary made an emergency trip out of town, hoping to scare up some of the Handicap favorites to face him at Bay Meadows.

Rosemont and the other big boys weren't coming. Seabiscuit was going to have to go get them.

On December 18, Seabiscuit stepped onto the russet soil of Santa Anita for the first time. In Barn 38 Smith kicked down the wall between two stalls to create a palatial home for Seabiscuit and Pumpkin. The stable boys dubbed it the Kaiser Suite.

The locals at Santa Anita and the press outside the Bay Area greeted the raving headlines from San Francisco with incredulity. A prominent eastern handicapper called him "the most overrated horse in California." The phrase "who did he beat?" appeared over and over in the press. "It is difficult to give him a rating above a $5,000 plater," wrote one journalist, using the synonym for claimer. Seabiscuit was a horse who had to be seen to be believed.

Trouble dogged him from the moment he was vanned into Santa Anita. Smith had initially planned on running him Christmas Day, but the trainer thought the horse seemed slightly weary and decided to back off for a while. He found a replacement race in the New Year's Stakes, but the track came up muddy. Smith didn't want to risk Seabiscuit's soundness by running on a slippery track, so he scratched him and moved his scheduled Santa Anita debut to January 16, 1937. On the appointed day, an ominous hive of an inch or so square popped up on the colt's coat. Smith withdrew him again.

One hive became two, then three, then an army of angry lumps. Driven mad by itching, Seabiscuit began to lose his newfound calm. Unable to train, he began pacing in the stall again. Smith tried every remedy he knew, but the rash kept marching onward. Finally, after more than a week, the rash began to retreat. "Don't tell me about bad breaks," Howard grumbled. "Seabiscuit certainly gets them."

The long layoff from racing, culminating in a week stuck itching in the barn, took its toll. Seabiscuit, already inclined toward portliness, was turning into one thousand pounds of flab. Smith looked the horse over and frowned. "Butterball," he called him. Idleness wasn't the only reason for the added weight. Seabiscuit's groom, Ollie, had been feeding the horse enough rations to fatten up an elephant. Smith had asked him to limit the horse to dry mash, but Ollie had begun sneaking in warm oat-mash snacks when he thought Smith wasn't looking. Smith considered firing Ollie, but the horse was so enamored of the groom that Smith decided otherwise. It was the beginning of a chronic problem for Seabiscuit, who loved eating so much that he often followed up his regular meals by consuming his own bedding.

Burning the flab off was going to be difficult. Smith was concerned that he'd have to work the horse to death to get the weight off. To get as much weight off as he could with each workout, he took a cue from the jockeys' room and began zipping the horse into rubber-lined sweating hoods during the gallops, then wrapping him in hot blankets afterward. He strapped him into a muzzle to stop his snacking. But the biggest problem was Ollie. The groom simply wouldn't do as asked.

Smith appealed to the highest court: Marcela Howard. She was the kind of woman who had a certain unspoken authority. She never had to raise her voice; she had a certain expression that communicated things well enough. Smith had seen it himself. She had once come into his barn and discovered jockey Farrell Jones lying on a cot in the cold, drafty tack room, desperately ill with an infection. Smith, who never missed a pimple on a horse but tended to be oblivious to the plight of his fellow man, hadn't taken the slightest notice of the boy and whatever ominous hacking noises must have been coming from the tack room. Marcela was appalled. She fired that look around, Farrell got his medicine and blankets, and everyone felt ashamed of themselves. No one ever forgot it.

Smith asked Marcela to see what she could do about Seabiscuit's clandestine munching. Marcela called on Ollie, and they had a talk. The gift snacks disappeared. Smith started conditioning his horse all over again.

By the time Smith was able to get Seabiscuit in racing shape, two months had passed since the World's Fair Handicap. It was already the second week of February, the Santa Anita Handicap was a little more than two weeks away, and Seabiscuit was far behind in his preparation. If Smith could get the horse into a race on the weekend of February 9, he would have time enough to run him once more before the hundred-grander. The only suitable race that weekend was the seven-furlong Huntington Beach Handicap, in which

Rosemont was set to run. Smith had avoided Rosemont earlier in the season not because he feared Seabiscuit would lose, but because he feared his horse would win, prompting the racing secretary to assign him heavy weight for the hundred-grander. That problem no longer existed; weights had finally been posted. Seabiscuit would carry 114 pounds, probably not as few as Smith had hoped for, but no back-breaker either. On February 9, Smith sent his horse out for the Huntington.

Without any urging from Pollard, Seabiscuit bolted from the gate as he had in the World's Fair, but this time there was a horse to go with him, Cloud D'Or. Pollard clucked once in Seabiscuit's ear, and his colt hooked up with his rival on a dizzying pace, with Seabiscuit down on the deep, slow rail and Cloud D'Or on the outside. After half a mile, they had lopped two and two-fifths seconds from the track record. At three quarters of a mile, they were just one second off the world record. They left the field far behind them, never to catch up.

In the homestretch, with a sixteenth of a mile to go, Seabiscuit had had enough fooling around and abruptly burst away from Cloud D'Or. Once safely in the lead, Pollard slowed him down, and Seabiscuit galloped in ahead by four and a half lengths. Rosemont labored in far behind. After they passed the wire, Pollard let Seabiscuit keep running to get more of a workout from the race. The horse galloped until he had completed a mile in 1:36, more than a second faster than any horse would run that distance at Santa Anita in the entire year. Again, Seabiscuit wasn't even breathing hard in the winner's circle.

"Heck, I've never let Seabiscuit out yet," Pollard boasted after the race. "You'll really see Seabiscuit do some running when I cut him loose in the big race."

Smith knew he had the best horse in America.

Horsemen in the East didn't know it yet. In the eastern race books, the horse was still a long shot for the hundred-grander. Seabiscuit's final prep race, the San Antonio Handicap, seemed to confirm the easterners' wisdom. Hung out in post position eleven—eleven positions out from the rail—Seabiscuit was bumped at the break, dropped back to fourteenth, then drifted extremely wide down the backstretch as Rosemont cruised ahead of him. Seabiscuit ran up on the heels of a group of horses and was forced to check sharply, then ran hopelessly wide again on the final turn. Finally loose in the stretch, Seabiscuit cut Rosemont's eight-length lead in half but couldn't catch him, finishing fifth. Rosemont won.

Quiet trepidation settled over the Howard barn in the week before the Santa Anita Handicap. Late in the week, a long, soaking shower doused the racing oval. When the rain stopped, asphalt-baking machines droned over the course, licking flames over the surface to dry the soil. Rosemont emerged from the barn three days before the race and scorched the track in his final workout. Reporters waited for Smith to give his horse a similar workout, but they never saw Seabiscuit doing anything more than stretching his legs. Rumors swirled around the track that Seabiscuit was lame. Rosemont's stock rose; Seabiscuit's dropped.

Smith had fooled them. At three o'clock one morning shortly before the race, he led Seabiscuit out to the track and gave him one last workout in peace and isolation. The horse ran beautifully.

On February 27, 1937, Charles and Marcela Howard arrived at Santa Anita to watch their pride and joy go for the hundred-grander. They were giddy with anticipation. "If Seabiscuit loses," mused a friend, "Mrs. Howard is going to be so heartbroken that I'll have to carry her out. If he wins, Charley'll be so excited that I'll have to carry him." Howard couldn't keep still. He trotted up to the press box and made the wildly popular announcement that if his horse won, he'd send up a barrel of champagne for the reporters. He went down to the betting area, and seeing that the line was too long to wait, he grabbed a bettor and jammed five $1,000 bills into his hand. "Put it all on Seabiscuit's nose, please," he told the bewildered wagerer before trotting off again.

At a little past 4:00 P.M. Pollard and Seabiscuit parted from Smith at the paddock gate and walked out onto the track for the Santa Anita Handicap. A record crowd of sixty thousand fans had come to see eighteen horses try for the richest purse in the world. Millions more listened on radio.

As Pollard felt Seabiscuit's hooves sink into the russet soil, he had reason to worry. The baking machines had not completely dried the surface. Rain and dirt had blended into a heavy goo along the rail; breaking from the three post, Seabiscuit would be right down in it. Far behind him in the post parade, jockey Harry Richards was contemplating a different set of obstacles for Rosemont. He had drawn the seventeenth post position. He was going to have the luxury of a hard, fast track, but his problem would be traffic. As a late runner, Rosemont would have to pick his way through the cluttered field.

The two jockeys virtually bookended the field as they moved to the post. Pollard feared nothing but Richards and Rosemont. Richards feared nothing but Pollard and Seabiscuit. The two horses stood motionless while the field was loaded around them.

At the sound of the bell, Seabiscuit bounded forward. To his outside, a crowd of horses rushed inward to gain optimal position. The field doubled over on itself, and the hinge was Seabiscuit, who was pinched back to ninth. In a cloud of horses, Pollard spotted daylight five feet or so off the rail. He banked Seabiscuit out into it, holding him out of the deep part of the track. He slipped up to fourth position, just off of front-running Special Agent. On the first turn Seabiscuit was crowded back down to the rail. As the field straightened into the backstretch, Pollard found another avenue and eased him outward again, to firmer ground. Ahead, Special Agent was setting a suicidal pace, but Pollard sensed how fast it was and was not going to be lured into it. He sat back and waited. Behind him, Rosemont was tugging along toward the back of the field, waiting for the speed horses to crumble.

With a half mile to go, Pollard positioned Seabiscuit in the clear and readied for his move. Behind him, Richards sensed that the moment had come to shoot for Seabiscuit. He began threading

Rosemont through the field, cutting in and out, picking off horses one by one, talking in his horse's ear as clumps of dirt cracked into his face. His luck was holding; every hole toward which he guided his horse held open just long enough for him to gallop through. On the far turn he reached Seabiscuit's heels and began looking for a way around him. Ahead of him, Pollard crouched and watched Special Agent's churning hindquarters, waiting for him to fold.

At the top of the stretch Special Agent faltered. Pollard pulled Seabiscuit's nose to the outside and slapped him on the rump. Seabiscuit pounced. Richards saw him go and gunned Rosemont through the hole after him, but Seabiscuit had stolen a three-length advantage. Special Agent gave way grudgingly along the inside as Indian Broom rallied up the outside, not quite quick enough to keep up.

Lengthening stride for the long run to the wire, Seabiscuit was alone on the lead in the dry, hard center of the track. Pollard had delivered a masterpiece of reinsmanship, avoiding the traps and saving ground while minimizing his run along the boggy rail. He had won the tactical battle with Richards. He was coming into the homestretch of the richest race in the world with a strong horse beneath him. Behind them were seventeen of the best horses in the nation. To the left and right, sixty thousand voices roared. Ahead was nothing but a long strip of red soil.

The rest of the field peeled away, scattered across thirty-two lengths of track behind them. It was down to Rosemont and Seabiscuit.

Seabiscuit was moving fastest. He charged down the stretch in front with Pollard up over his neck, moving with him, driving him on. Rosemont was obscured behind him. He was gaining only by increments. Seabiscuit sailed through midstretch a full length ahead of Rosemont. Up in the stands, the Howards and Smith were thinking the same thing: Rosemont is too far behind. Seabiscuit is going to win.

Without warning, horse and rider lost focus. Abruptly, inexplicably, Pollard wavered. He lay his whip down on Seabiscuit's shoulder and left it there.

Seabiscuit paused. Perhaps he slowed in hopes of finding an

opponent to toy with. Or maybe he sensed Pollard's hesitation. His composure, which Smith had patiently schooled into him over six months, began to unravel. Seabiscuit suddenly took a sharp left turn, veering ten feet across the track and back down into the deep going, straightening himself out just before hitting the rail. He had given away several feet of his lead. The cadence of his stride dropped. What had been a seamless union was now only a man and a horse, jangling against each other.

From between Rosemont's ears, Richards saw Seabiscuit's form disintegrate. He looked toward the wire. It seemed close enough to touch, but Rosemont still wasn't past Seabiscuit's saddlecloth. He had been riding on instinct, reflex, but now his heart caught in his throat: *I am too late.* Desperate, he flung himself over Rosemont's neck, booting and whipping and screaming, "Faster, baby, faster!" Striding high in the center of the track, Rosemont was suddenly animated by Richards's raging desire. He dropped his head and dug in. Seabiscuit's lead, stride by stride, slipped away.

For a few seconds at the most critical moment of their careers, Pollard and Seabiscuit faltered. For fifteen strides, more than the length of a football field, Pollard remained virtually motionless. Rosemont was some ten feet to his outside, leaving plenty of room for Pollard to swing Seabiscuit out of the rail-path's slow going, but Pollard didn't take the opportunity. From behind his half-moon blinker cups, Seabiscuit could see nothing but an empty track ahead of him, nor is it likely that he could hear Rosemont over the roar from the grandstand. Or perhaps he was waiting for him. His left ear swung around lazily, as if he were paying attention to something in the infield. His stride slowed. His mind seemed scattered. The lead was vanishing. A length. Six feet. A neck. The wire was rushing at them. The crowd was shrieking.

With just a few yards to go, Pollard broke out of his limbo. He burst into frenzied motion. Seabiscuit's ears snapped back and he dived forward. But Rosemont had momentum. The lead shrank to nothing. Rosemont caught Seabiscuit, then took a lead of inches. Seabiscuit was accelerating, his rhythm building, his mind narrowed down to his task at the urgent call of his rider. But Richards was driving harder, scratching and yelling and pleading for Rosemont to run. Seabiscuit cut the advantage away. They drew even again.

Rosemont and Seabiscuit flew under the wire together.

Up in their box, the Howards leapt up. Charles ran to the Turf Club bar, calling for champagne for everyone. Voices sang out and corks popped and a wild celebration began.

Gradually, the revelers went silent. The crowd had stopped cheering. The stewards posted no winner. They were waiting for the photo. The exhausted horses returned to be unsaddled, and the fans sat in agonized anticipation. Two minutes passed. In the hush, a sibilant sound attended the finish photo as it slid down to the stewards. There was a terrible pause. The numbers blinked up on the board.

Rosemont had won.

A howl went up from the grandstand. Thousands of spectators were certain that the stewards had it wrong, that Seabiscuit had been robbed. But the photo was unequivocal: Rosemont's long bay muzzle hung there in the picture, just a wink ahead of Seabiscuit's. "Dame Fortune," wrote announcer Joe Hernandez, "made a mistake and kissed the wrong horse—Rosemont—in the glorious end of the Santa Anita Handicap."

Charles and Marcela collected themselves. The length of Rosemont's nose had cost them $70,700. They continued passing out the champagne, brave smiles on their faces.

Pollard didn't need to look at the tote board. He knew he had lost from the instant the noses hit the line. Wrung to exhaustion and deathly pale, he slid from Seabiscuit's back. He walked over to Richards, who was being smothered in kisses by his tearful wife. Pollard's face was blank, his voice barely above a whisper. All around him, people regarded him with expressions of cool accusation.

"Congratulations, Harry, you rode a swell race," Pollard said.

"Thanks," said Richards, his face covered in lipstick and his voice breaking; he had shouted it away urging Rosemont on. "But it was very close."

"Close, yes," said Pollard almost inaudibly, "but you won."

Pollard saw Howard hovering nearby, waiting for him. The jockey went to him.

"What happened?" Howard asked gently. Ashen and spent, Pollard said that the rail had been slow, and that he had been unable to get outside without fouling Rosemont. If he and Rosemont had switched positions, he was sure Seabiscuit would have won.

It was a thin excuse. Pollard must have known that to save his professional standing, he would have to offer more than that, say something that would explain how he had allowed Rosemont to come to him without fighting back until the last moment. Already, harsh words were being hung on him: *arrogant, inept, overconfident.* He could not have mistaken the reproach on the faces of those around him. His reputation was tumbling. But Pollard gave the public nothing to make them reconsider.

Perhaps he couldn't. He had a secret to keep, a gamble he had made years earlier and remade with each race. But he could no longer think that its risks affected only himself.

Perhaps Pollard didn't see Rosemont coming because of the blindness of his right eye.

It is unlikely that he could have heard Rosemont over the din from the crowd. Rosemont's surge, unexpected and sudden, may have eluded Pollard until very late in the race. Pollard did not begin urging Seabiscuit in earnest until Rosemont was alongside him, just forward enough for Pollard to see him with his left eye, upon turning his head. One good eye offers little depth perception, so he may not have been able to judge whether Rosemont was far enough to his right to allow Seabiscuit to move outward.

If this explanation is correct, then Pollard was trapped. He was publicly accused of inexcusable failure in the most important race of his career, but he could not defend himself. Had he let on that he was blind in one eye, his career would have been over. Like most jockeys in the 1930s, he had nowhere else to go, nothing else to live on, nothing else he loved. For Red Pollard, there was no road back to Edmonton. If his blindness was the cause of the loss, his frustration and guilt must have been consuming.

Howard accepted Pollard's explanation without criticism. Neither he nor Smith blamed him.

Almost everyone else did.

(AP/WIDE WORLD PHOTOS)

CHAPTER 9

Gravity

For six months Tom Smith had been holding Seabiscuit in his closed fist. He had inched him up through back alleys and smaller races, bypassing the nationally spotlighted races in favor of slow cultivation and parochial seclusion. It wasn't until the Santa Anita Handicap, with the whole world watching, that Smith had opened his hand.

The world had been waiting for him. In the winter of 1937, America was in the seventh year of the most catastrophic decade in its history. The economy had come crashing down, and millions upon millions of people had been torn loose from their jobs, their savings, their homes. A nation that drew its audacity from the quintessentially American belief that success is open to anyone willing to work for it was disillusioned by seemingly intractable poverty. The most brash of peoples was seized by despair, fatalism, and fear.

The sweeping devastation was giving rise to powerful new social forces. The first was a burgeoning industry of escapism. America was desperate to lose itself in anything that offered affirmation. The nation's corner theaters hosted 85 million people a week for 25-cent viewings of an endless array of cheery musicals and screwball comedies. On the radio, the idealized world of *One Man's Family* and the just and reassuring tales of *The Lone Ranger* were runaway hits. Downtrodden Americans gravitated strongly toward the Horatio Alger protagonist, the lowly bred Everyman who rises from anonymity and hopelessness. They looked for him in spectator sports, which were enjoying explosive growth. With the relegalization of wagering, no sport was growing faster than Thoroughbred racing.

Necessity spurred technological innovations that offered the public unprecedented access to its heroes. People accustomed to reading comparatively dry rehashes of events were now enthralled by vivid scenes rolling across the new Movietone newsreels. A public that had grown up with news illustrations and hazy photo layouts was now treated to breathtaking action shots facilitated by vastly improved photographic equipment. These images were now rapidly available thanks to wirephoto services, which had debuted in *Life* in the month that Pollard, Howard, and Smith formed their partnership.

But it was radio that had the greatest impact. In the 1920s the cost of a radio had been prohibitive—$120 or more—and all that bought was a box of unassembled parts. In unelectrified rural areas, radios ran on pricey, short-lived batteries. But with the 1930s came the advent of factory-built console, tabletop, and automobile radio sets, available for as little as $5. Thanks to President Roosevelt's Rural Electrification Administration, begun in 1936, electricity came to the quarter of the population that lived on farmlands. Rural families typically made the radio their second electric purchase, after the clothes iron. By 1935, when Seabiscuit began racing, two thirds of the nation's homes had radio. At the pinnacle of his career, that figure had jumped to 90 percent, plus eight million sets in cars. Enabling virtually all citizens to experience noteworthy events simultaneously and in entertaining form, radio created a vast common culture in America, arguably the first true mass culture the world had ever seen. Racing, a sport whose sustained dramatic action was ideally suited to narration, became a staple of the airwave. The Santa Anita Handicap, with its giant purse and world-class athletes, competing in what was rapidly becoming the nation's most heavily attended sport, became one of the premier radio events of the year.

In February 1937, all of these new social and technological forces were converging. The modern age of celebrity was dawning. The new machine of fame stood waiting. All it needed was the subject himself.

At that singular hour, Seabiscuit, the Cinderella horse, flew over the line in the Santa Anita Handicap. Something clicked: Here he was.

Immediately, the reporters infested everything. Smith swatted at them. They staked out the barn, constantly asking Smith to pull the horse out of his stall for photo sessions and even to let them sit on his back, as if he were a carnival pony. They stood by the rail in noisy clumps during morning workouts, snapping pictures and buzzing in Smith's ear. They photographed the Howards everywhere they went, at the betting windows, at dinner, getting in and out of their Buick. One paper ran a large shot of Marcela in the act of blowing her nose. Smith, Pollard, and the Howards were soon intimately familiar with the strange gravity of celebrity. The earth seemed to dip under Seabiscuit's hoof-falls, pulling the world in toward him and everyone around him.

The paradox of all this attention was that many of the turf writers who covered Seabiscuit knew next to nothing about horses and racing. Pari-mutuel racing was spanking new in California and many other places, so there were few established racing writers. Much of the coverage was left to complete novices on loan from other beats. Because Seabiscuit's popularity was so broad-based, reporters from publications that had nothing whatsoever to do with sports covered him. Many newsmen were completely ignorant of standard training practices. Some were in so far over their heads that they resorted to invention, fabricating preposterous stories or quotations out of thin air. One columnist wrote that Tom Smith fed Seabiscuit two quarts of Golden Rod beer before each race; if the horse doesn't get his beer, he wrote, he "whinnies and stomps to indicate displeasure." Worse, there were more than a few conspiracy theorists in the bunch. Racing had recently emerged from an era of corruption, and though incidents of foul play were now extremely rare, reporters tended to be overly suspicious of horsemen, accepted rumors of wrongdoing with credulity, and adopted a studied cynicism.

Pair an intrusive, usually ignorant, and often suspicious press corps with an intensely private trainer, and you have a volatile mix. Smith viewed the press as parasitic. To foil it, he elevated obstruction to an art form. His first line of defense was frowning terseness. Once, when asked to describe Seabiscuit at length, he replied, "He's a horse," and walked away. It was typical of Smith to stroll off in silence while reporters were in mid-question. At other times he would respond to a question by staring straight at a reporter with a blank expression for as long as three minutes, saying nothing. "Tom Smith," lamented a reporter, "is by no means a long distance conversationalist. Ten words in a row for him would constitute a course record." Talking to Smith, remembered one racetracker, "was like talking to a post." His stable agent, Sonny Greenberg, compared him to a mummy. The smart ones learned to keep quiet and let Smith initiate a conversation, which he did every once in a while. The dumb ones pecked at him and got nothing but ulcers.

Smith also went to great lengths to keep Seabiscuit's training private. To mollify reporters, he would take Seabiscuit out onto the track during the heavily attended morning hours, but only for slow workouts or jogs. In the afternoons, when the reporters were watching the races, he would sneak the horse out for his real workouts on the training track or another track altogether. If anyone happened to be standing around, he'd do his best to keep them from learning anything interesting. Once, when a man wandered up to the rail of the otherwise deserted track and pulled out a stopwatch to time the horse's workout, Smith asked to borrow the watch, held it while the horse galloped, reset it, and handed it back.

"How did it go?" asked the man.

"Looked all right to me—it seems to be a nice watch," said Smith.

"Not the watch," said the man, "Seabiscuit's work. How fast did he go?"

"Damned if I know."

The secret workouts had three purposes. First, they concealed the horse's superb form from track racing secretaries, who assigned imposts. Second, through an ingenious method devised by Smith, they helped the horse stay in racing trim. Seabiscuit was more prone to weight gain than any horse Smith had ever handled. Because he believed that the quickest way to ruin a horse was to overwork him, Smith resorted to creative solutions to overcome Seabiscuit's weight problem. On mornings when an afternoon workout was planned, he would set the horse's bridle and saddle out where he could see them, withhold breakfast, skip his normal morning workout, and do everything else that was typical of a race day. Seeing the tack and thinking he was racing that day, Seabiscuit would become keyed up, lose interest in eating, and fret weight off. Smith would then take him out to work in the afternoon, just as if he were racing. The method worked, and Seabiscuit kept his weight down.

The final benefit of the secret workouts was sadistic pleasure. Smith took immense satisfaction in making reporters and clockers miserable. The old man had an offbeat sense of humor. He once electrified a park bench with wires and tacks, ran a trigger wire down the shed row, hid himself in a stall, and spent the day shocking the hell out of every weary hot-walker who tried to sit down and rest. Once he became a major subject for the press, nothing was more amusing to him than creating situations that left his pursuers confused and frustrated. They gave him limitless opportunity; Seabiscuit was one of the biggest stories in the country, so they just kept coming back for more punishment. For people trying to make a living covering him, Smith was thoroughly maddening. "Turf writers and clockers swear by Tom Smith," moaned a reporter, "and very often they just swear."

The secret workouts worked for Seabiscuit, but because Smith refused to explain himself to the press, they created a serious misapprehension. The rarity of Seabiscuit's public appearances fueled rumors that the horse was unsound, rumors that were reinforced by the horse's choppy gait. Smith did little to correct them. "That horse of yours can't walk," said one spectator as Seabiscuit bumped past. "Runs, though," Smith replied. Though the horse was dollar sound at this stage of his career, reporters given to hyperbole began regularly referring to him as a "cripple." The stories were accepted as fact, and soon the word attached to Seabiscuit for good. It was a misconception that would create serious headaches for Smith later.

And Smith couldn't fool everyone. *Los Angeles Times* and *San Francisco Chronicle* columnist Oscar Otis was one of the few truly knowledgeable turf scribes and dean of the western racing writers. Almost immediately, Otis was onto Smith. Shortly before the Santa Anita Handicap, Otis discovered Smith working Seabiscuit at three o'clock in the morning. "Seabiscuit and Greta Garbo can be coupled in the betting from now on," he wrote in the *Times*. "Both want to be let alone." The reporters and clockers now knew Smith was up to something. Most of them didn't like Smith any better than he liked them, and they resolved to catch him in the act. Smith was determined to thwart them. The battle was joined.

Unlike Smith, Howard relished the attention. Celebrity was his natural habitat. He was not content with mere greatness for his horse. For Seabiscuit, he wanted superstardom, in his own age and in history. He understood that this could not be achieved through racing exploits alone. He had to win over the public. After the 1937 Santa Anita Handicap, Howard began a conquest of the popular imagination.

His first effort was to maximize his horse's exposure, plotting an exhaustive cross-country racing campaign that was probably unprecedented in scope, adopting a take-all-comers attitude in choosing Seabiscuit's races and opponents, and even running full-page ads celebrating Seabiscuit's wins. Understanding that the press, as the public's proxy, was the most important agent in his campaign, Howard wouldn't leave the reporters alone. He practically lived with them, bounding up the press-box stairs before and after races to make himself available for questions and photo ops, dashing down to the press pool when the horse's train pulled into a station. He made sure that every journalist was aware of Seabiscuit's itinerary. He and his wife indulged every photographer and cheerfully fielded calls from reporters at any time, day or night. Howard went to great lengths to manipulate those covering his horse. He read every word written about Seabiscuit and wrote long letters to reporters. He kept all their phone numbers on hand and called them personally to sway their opinions and make each one feel like a privileged insider with a sensational scoop. He used them to put pressure on racing officials and owners he couldn't influence with charm alone. He offered Seabiscuit mementoes for newspaper raffles and sent oversized Seabiscuit Christmas cards to scores of reporters. He even presented members of the press with valuable gifts, including Seabiscuit's shoes cast in silver. It became a little unclear who was stalking whom.

Even as he sought mastery over the press, Howard was its servant. He understood that his influence was not limitless, and if he made a move that failed to conform to journalistic expectations, the image that he had painstakingly cultivated could be ruined. In the years ahead, there would be critical moments in which his pursuit of image conflicted with his horse's interests. For Howard, they would present some of the most difficult quandaries of his public life.

Howard started marketing his horse in earnest on the morning after the hundred-grander. He made things easy for the reporters, posing questions out loud to himself, then answering them. "Are we downhearted over getting licked by Rosemont in that hundred-grander?" he asked. "No!" To underscore his point, he sent a gigantic barrel of ice-packed champagne to the press box, complete with a card. "To the good health of the press box," it read. "We tried our best. —Seabiscuit." He had promised to send up the champagne only if the horse won, but "it was so close," he said, "I thought I'd send it up anyway." The reporters had a grand afternoon sipping bubbly and raising enthusiastic toasts to Seabiscuit.

The newsmen may have been drinking to the health of Howard and Seabiscuit, but no one was toasting Pollard. Up until the Santa Anita Handicap the redhead had been basking in the attention, boasting of his horse's infallibility and entertaining the reporters with his quick wit. He would later say, quoting Henry Austin Dobson, that "fame is a food that dead men eat / I have no stomach for such meat." In truth, he was delighted with his newfound celebrity. The reporters returned his affection. In a discipline in which athletes bored newsmen to death with clichés and blandly politic statements, Pollard was a singularly fresh interview, articulate, irreverent, and self-deprecating. "He'll probably win if I don't fall off," he told them before a major race. "I fall off a lot of horses, though, you know."

But no one was ready to overlook Pollard's ride, the biggest story to emerge from the hundred-grander. When Pollard returned to the jockeys' room following the loss to Rosemont, he confronted the other side of fame. With Richards a few feet away, happily fielding his invitation to the Santa Anita Turf Club Ball, the traditional party held to honor hundred-grander winners, Pollard was bombarded with harsh questions. Why hadn't he used the whip late in the race? Had he thought the race was won? He tried to defend his ride, protesting in vain that he had indeed used his whip and that he was stuck on the slow part of the track, but no one seemed to be listening.

The next morning the excoriation continued. On the track there were whispers that Pollard had been drunk during the race. The papers hyped his seeming lapse of concentration. Grantland Rice, the preeminent sportswriter in the country, accused him of gross overconfidence. But it was Oscar Otis whose criticism cut the deepest. Though he praised Pollard's riding early in the race and his courage in handling the defeat, Otis, who knew Pollard as Jack, was unequivocal in his assessment of blame. "Jockey Harry Richards outrode Jack Pollard at the wire, otherwise Seabiscuit, streaking along in midstretch with a length lead, must surely have won," he wrote in the *Los Angeles Times*. "With riders reversed, Seabiscuit would have won by half a length. Jack Pollard did not go to the whip near the wire until too late. The defeat may be chalked up to Mr. Pollard."

The criticism infuriated Smith, who thought that the horse's swerve down into the rail was the real reason for the loss, a factor unremarked in the press. Smith took Pollard aside and assured him that his critics were wrong. Few things could inspire Smith to actually speak at length. Unjust sniping at Pollard was one of them. He startled reporters with several complete sentences. "Pollard deserves at least half the credit for the brilliant showing of Seabiscuit in the Santa Anita Handicap. He is the only boy who knows his peculiarities, his idiosyncrasies, who knows how to get the best of him. Criticism of Pollard is unjust. He rode the horse perfectly."

It didn't do any good.

A pall hung over Barn 38. Ollie, the groom, was openly miserable. Howard's usual cheer was forced. Smith was even less friendly than usual. Mulling over the loss to Rosemont, he took out Seabiscuit's blinkers and a pocketknife and cut small holes in the back of each eye cup, giving the horse two rearview windows. No horse was going to sneak up on him again.

Only Seabiscuit was buoyant. He came out of the race full of fight. Pollard took him out for a spin two days after the race, and the horse pulled so hard that the jockey returned with angry blisters on his hands. Seabiscuit was screaming to run, and the $10,000 San Juan Capistrano, the stakes finale of the Santa Anita winter meeting, was the perfect spot.

On March 6, 1937, Pollard and Seabiscuit walked onto the course for the race. Smith and the Howards looked out over the crowd and saw for the first time how famous Seabiscuit had become. Forty-five thousand rowdy fans had packed the track to see him run, and they had made him the heavy favorite. Though Rosemont had passed on the race in favor of a journey east, it was still a formidable field. Indian Broom, who had been running beyond his ideal distance when he finished third in the mile-and-a-quarter Santa Anita Handicap, was the world record holder at the San Juan Capistrano distance of a mile and an eighth. Special Agent, who like Indian Broom was owned by the ACT Stock Farm, was the track record holder at a mile and a sixteenth.

The ACT riders were in cahoots to beat Seabiscuit. Special Agent's rider planned to slip away to an insurmountable lead early in the race, while George Woolf, on Indian Broom, would lay behind Seabiscuit, hoping that Pollard's colt would wear himself out chasing Special Agent and leave him free to pounce on him late, as Rosemont had. Pollard was in a tricky spot. Hot pursuit would be Seabiscuit's downfall, but holding back might hand the race to Special Agent.

Pollard wrapped the reins in loops around his fingers and waited in the gate. At the break, Special Agent bolted out ahead of him, while Woolf dropped Indian Broom behind. Pollard could feel that the pace Special Agent was setting was too fast, so he held Seabiscuit right behind him, just close enough to keep him from stealing away but just far enough behind to keep Seabiscuit's speed in reserve. Special Agent's rider hustled him furiously; Pollard tracked him like a tiger. Rounding into the bend for home, Pollard let a loop of the reins slip through his fingers. Seabiscuit ate up the length of rein, bounding past Special Agent and leaving Woolf and Indian Broom flat-footed. The race caller yelled, "Here comes Seabiscuit!" and a joyful shout rose over the track. Seabiscuit buried the field. With Pollard standing on his back, pulling him in, he flew down the lane to win by seven lengths, smashing the track record.

Cheering swept down in waves from the stands. A spontaneous call was echoing over the sea of heads: "Bring on Rosemont!"

Rosemont had returned east. Smith wanted to go get him, but Howard wasn't ready yet. He was working out a glory tour in his head, and he wanted his hometown of San Francisco to see his horse once more. Rosemont could wait. They returned north, to Tanforan.

Smith was getting wound up. He had tucked Seabiscuit into a steel-doored stall and cordoned off the barn area, but the reporters were driving him to distraction. And he was worried about the weight assignments his horse's success would bring. On April 3, he swung Pollard onto Seabiscuit and secured enough lead pads under the saddle to bring the horse's impost to a whopping 130 pounds. As dusk fell, he led the two out onto the emptiness of Tanforan. Smith stood at the finish line as Pollard turned Seabiscuit loose for a nine-furlong workout. Seabiscuit inhaled the track. As he flashed under the wire in the darkness, Smith waved him down.

Smith thought he had pulled off the workout in secret. But

somewhere on the oval's apron, a *San Francisco Examiner* photographer had stepped out of the darkness and snapped the horse's picture. Worse, an owner who happened to be passing by saw the horse working and pulled out his stopwatch. Seabiscuit had worked faster than any horse had raced the entire season. The story was all over the sports pages.

Foiled by the press once again, Smith was ready to crank things up another notch. A coincidence gave him a new way to thwart his pursuers. One afternoon in early April, Smith and Howard discovered Grog, Seabiscuit's old stable pal in the Fitzsimmons barn, doddering along in a claiming race at Tanforan. He had changed hands as often as a dollar bill and was now running under the colors of a Hollywood screenwriter. Howard had become fiercely sentimental about all sons of Hard Tack. "Never sell a Hard Tack short" he liked to say. He had nearly achieved his goal of buying every single Hard Tack yearling on the market. He wanted to take Grog in. Smith agreed, and they claimed the horse and moved him in next to Seabiscuit. Within two weeks Smith had Grog and Pollard back in the winner's circle.

It is possible that Smith saw something promising in the $4,000 claimer. But the trainer's interest probably had less to do with Grog's speed than with his appearance. Grog and Seabiscuit were practically identical, as they had been as youngsters. Only Smith and his grooms could distinguish one from the other. Grog gave Smith another weapon in his war with the press.

One morning shortly after buying Grog, Smith logged the colt's name on the work tab, then sent Seabiscuit out to work in his place. With no one on the grounds the least bit interested in watching a claimer, the horse proceeded to work six furlongs in an unbelievably fast 1:11⅗. Someone told the reporters about the workout time, and they were puzzled. With a rocket in his saddle and wings on his sides Grog couldn't possibly have clocked such a time, but the reporters weren't sure of that, given what Smith had done for Seabiscuit. Someone suggested that the working horse was really Seabiscuit. Smith was, as usual, mum. "If that was Grog the boys took for Seabiscuit the other morning then let me caution you thus," wrote the turf reporter known as Jolly Roger, who wrote for the *San Francisco Chronicle.* "Look out for Grog."

Smith had a field day. On some mornings, he sent Grog out to gallop in Seabiscuit's name at standard morning workout periods, then snuck the real Seabiscuit out to exercise at night. On other days, just to mix things up, he worked Seabiscuit in the morning under his own name. The reporters were immediately and thoroughly confused, and some took to spying on Smith. Jolly Roger, for one, began climbing up to the attic window of the track cook's house to try to catch Seabiscuit working at night.

Smith carried the deception to the stable area. When the newsmen asked him to produce Seabiscuit for photo shoots, he would turn to his new groom, Whitey Allison—so called because of his unnerving white eye—and ask him to "bring the old Biscuit out." Whitey would trot out Grog, who was sometimes housed in Seabiscuit's stall to make the ruse more convincing. Hoodwinked onlookers invariably asked to climb on the horse, and Smith, with hospitality that should have aroused suspicion, always agreed. Newsmen, bragging that they had ridden the great Seabiscuit, unwittingly printed images of the lowly Grog in countless magazines and newspapers. Even Howard became one of Smith's victims. One unfortunate artist whom Howard sent to paint Seabiscuit's portrait never learned that the horse he immortalized was actually Grog.

The stable hands got into the spirit of things. They found that as easy as it was to convince people that Grog was Seabiscuit, it was even easier to convince them that the real Seabiscuit was not Seabiscuit. The horse's bad-legged, cow-pony appearance made fooling people a cinch. Once, while Whitey and exercise rider Keith Stucki were rubbing Seabiscuit down after a workout, Whitey noticed a man eyeing the horse. The man stepped up, looked the horse over without recognition, and frowned at his knees.

"When a horse is broke down like that, what do you do with him?" he asked.

"Well," replied Whitey, "we usually sell him to somebody that comes along and wants to buy him."

"And what would a horse like this bring?"

"Oh, five or six hundred dollars," said Whitey. "He ought to be worth that." At the time, Seabiscuit was insured for $100,000, more than any other horse in America.

Intrigued at the cheap price, the man walked around to the other side of the horse. He saw the horse's halter plate, engraved with Seabiscuit's name.

"Sure," said the man dismissively, "with Seabiscuit's halter on."

San Francisco was overjoyed to see Seabiscuit again. Responding to banner headlines that read, SEABISCUIT GOES TODAY!, the largest crowd in the history of Northern California racing packed into Tanforan to witness the Marchbank Handicap, Seabiscuit's rematch with Indian Broom and Special Agent. Pollard was again spectacular. Instructed by Smith to wait behind Special Agent's lead, he quickly saw that the pacesetter was blocked and was not going to be able to get to the front. Pollard dove for it himself, took control of the race, then eased Seabiscuit back. Hauling a load of 124 pounds, Seabiscuit clipped past the quarter-mile mark in 22⅖ seconds, six furlongs in a breathtaking 1:10⅗, then a mile in 1:36, each fraction well below the track record for those distances. Then he slowed down dramatically. The crowd gasped. When the field caught him, Seabiscuit bounced away again, winning by three lengths under a stranglehold. As the newsmen wondered aloud if Man o' War himself could have beaten Seabiscuit, Howard clattered in. Everyone looked up.

"Say!" Howard panted, winded from bounding up the stairs. "Who finished second and third?"

Trouble surfaced at Bay Meadows a few weeks later. Seabiscuit was entered in the prestigious Bay Meadows Handicap, but the track handicapper delivered bad news: Seabiscuit received a 127-pound impost. Smith dug his heels in. Knowing that they would soon be off to the East, he didn't want to demonstrate to handicappers that his horse was a terrific weight carrier. But Howard insisted, and prevailed.

Race day dawned with gale force winds. With the gusts swirling around him, Pollard arrived at the track. He was in shocking condition. He had been reducing drastically to make weight for another horse, and was barely able to stand. Once in the jockeys' room, he collapsed. He was unconscious through most of the afternoon. When he was still out cold half an hour before the race, the stewards debated whether or not to call Howard in and get him to choose another rider. A few minutes before post time, Pollard finally rose. He insisted, adamantly, that he was strong enough to ride. The stewards reluctantly let him go.

Seabiscuit seemed to sense Pollard's weakness. At the starting gate he broke through over and over again, delaying the start for three minutes. He raced tentatively, and with the winds buffeting him through the homestretch, won by a modest margin over his stablemate Exhibit. In the final sixteenth of a mile Pollard seemed as if he was about to pass out again, but he hung on for the win.

Pollard rode back to the winner's circle and somehow managed to complete the ceremonies. Since the Santa Anita Handicap, his riding on Seabiscuit had been impeccable. But he had not gotten past the loss in the hundred-grander. The public condemnation was corrosive. The press would not let go of it.

At Bay Meadows his anger boiled over. While walking on the track, Pollard saw Oscar Otis making his way across the parking lot. Otis had praised Pollard in print since his initial condemnation of his ride in the Santa Anita Handicap, even suggesting that he may have been wrong in attributing the loss to the jockey. But Pollard's animosity still burned. He turned off the track and into the parking lot, where he stopped Otis and confronted him. They traded angry words.

Pollard, surely overwrought from the reducing, lost control. He picked up a newspaper, folded it into a rigid baton, and clubbed Otis once across the face. Otis, a much larger man, dropped to the ground under the tremendous force of Pollard's arm. His face injured, he lay on the pavement, stunned. Pollard turned and walked away.

Seabiscuit may have been a public and media darling in the West, but in the prestigious eastern racing circles he still wasn't taken seriously.

Smith was itching to go east and teach the old guard a thing or two. Howard conceded that now was the time. There wasn't anything left to beat in California anyway. Pollard, too, needed a change of scenery and a chance to redeem himself. A week after the Bay Meadows Handicap, Seabiscuit and Pumpkin walked up the ramp of the Pullman car and settled into the straw to sleep. Smith stocked a rear car with all the oats, hay, and straw Seabiscuit would need—he didn't trust eastern feed—then climbed in with his horse, unfolding a cot at Seabiscuit's feet.

There were giants to slay in the East that summer. Rosemont was there, waiting to meet Seabiscuit in the venerable Brooklyn Handicap. So was Aneroid, rawhide-tough king of the eastern handicap ranks. And there was someone else, a horse greater than the others.

His name was War Admiral.

War Admiral and jockey Charley Kurtsinger
(© BETTMANN/CORBIS)

CHAPTER 10

War Admiral

Samuel Riddle bore a startling resemblance to the illustrated figure on a Monopoly board. He had all the appurtenances—the black hat, the white moustache, heaps of old eastern money. Everything but the smile. Riddle was a dyspeptic man. In the summer of 1937 he was seventy-five years old, and his unsmiling face was arguably the most famous in racing. Riddle *was* the eastern racing establishment.

In 1918 he had plunked down $5,000 at an auction and walked away with the most extraordinary creature the sport had ever seen, Man o' War. The horse proceeded to run the legs off everything that came near him. To some observers, the only sour note in Man o' War's career was Riddle himself. In their view, the man had campaigned his horse too conservatively. When racing officials offered a fantastic pot of $50,000 for Riddle to pit his colt against Exterminator, the only horse who might have made Man o' War work for his winnings, Riddle declined. He held his horse out of the Kentucky Derby, in part because of a disdain for "western" tracks and in part because he felt that early May was too soon to send a horse over a grueling mile and a quarter. In 1920, Riddle retired the colt at only three years of age. Man o' War had run just twenty-one races—winning twenty—and faced only forty-eight opponents. Riddle did not want to subject the horse to the extremely high imposts he was slated to carry.

Man o' War had made Riddle world famous, but the owner disliked the press as much as Charles Howard loved it. Some of the newsroom boys returned Riddle's animosity, but the fact that he owned some of the fastest and most noteworthy horses on earth led to a certain uneasy détente. The owner didn't help things when he stood up before a throng of people, reporters included, and told them that when it came to horses, the press knew just two things: "One end bites and the other end kicks."

Man o' War became a franchise of sorts for his owner, producing a long string of gifted runners whose winner's circle visits made Riddle one of the most photographed men in sport. But while many of Man o' War's get were the best of their generations, none compared to their sire. Then, in the spring of 1934, horsemen started gathering by a fence at Riddle's breeding farm, gazing into a paddock and making the kind of awed noises that people make when a flaming meteor plunges out of the heavens and plows into someone's backyard. A regally bred mare named Brushup had foaled a near-black colt, a son of Man o' War, and they couldn't take their eyes off of him. It was just the *look* of him. Even at a standstill, he was a glittering thing. He was the picture of exquisite, streamlined elegance, light and fine and quick. He moved like a bird: flickering, darting, fluttering. The horsemen gaped. Someone mused that when this one was done with racing, no one would remember Man o' War. It was the kind of statement horsemen usually snort at, but no one who looked in at this colt was laughing.

The foal grew up and Riddle named him War Admiral. He had the same imperious, lordly way of his father. He would not tolerate stillness. He was so keyed to go that if a paddock official rang the saddling bell, he would lunge from his stall and drag his handlers toward the track. Once at the gate, he spun and fought, tossed the starters aside, lunged through false starts.

But then the starter would set the field off, War Admiral would drop down and skim over the track, and everyone would forgive him for his imperiousness. Function followed form. War Admiral had awesome, frightening speed. Once under way, he was too fast for his rivals, too fast even for strategy. He dashed his opponents against their limitations the instant they left the starting gate, leaving them to ebb out like spilling water behind him. In the spring of 1937, he displayed such overwhelming acceleration and stamina that he was never off the lead at any stage of any race. No horse could touch him.

After War Admiral, fuming and frustrated, held up the start for eight minutes, victory in the Kentucky Derby came easily to him. The Preakness followed. The Belmont, the final conquest of the Triple Crown, set his name in stone. He repeatedly crashed through the gate, delaying the start for nearly nine minutes. When for one brief second the colt was motionless, the starter hit the bell. War Admiral burst out with such power that his hindquarters overran his forequarters. He couldn't get his front hooves out of the way in time, and the toe of his hind shoe gouged into his right forehoof. He reared upward, yanking his hoof free. In doing so, he sheared off an inch-square hunk of his forehoof, leaving it lying on the track by the gate. His jockey, Charley Kurtsinger, had no idea what had happened; War Admiral gave no indication. He lunged forward on the bleeding leg, blew past the entire field in ten leaps, and charged on, a lurid spray of blood flying out behind him as he ran.

No one could catch him. He took the victory, the Triple Crown, his father's track record, and an American speed record. When Kurtsinger slid off in the winner's circle and reached down to unlatch the girth, he was horrified to discover his colt's belly and hoof dripping with blood. The onlookers shivered.

Samuel Riddle held lightning in his hands again. By the summer of 1937, as War Admiral sat on the sidelines waiting for his hoof to grow back, it was clear that nothing in his age group could stay with him. War Admiral, like Man o' War, awaited a horse who would take the true measure of his greatness.

It never would have occurred to anyone in the East that this horse would be Seabiscuit. When they had last seen him, he was a midlevel stakes winner in the hands of a trainer no one had heard of and a jockey no one remembered. The horse had spent most of his career in the claiming or cheap allowance ranks, and the most accomplished trainer in America had given up on him. His winter victories said little of his quality, as they had been achieved on the suspect terrain of the West. On the morning of June 26, 1937, the day Seabiscuit was to begin his assault on the East's prestigious races by running in the Brooklyn Handicap, a New York columnist summed up eastern opinion of him with two words: "Glorified plater."

A record crowd of twenty thousand jammed in to see Seabiscuit meet Rosemont and local hero Aneroid in the Brooklyn. As Seabiscuit came to the paddock, Smith looked over the mass of noisy humanity and frowned. He called over to Seabiscuit's exercise rider, Keith Stucki, and asked him to position Pumpkin between Seabiscuit and the fans. Stucki did as asked, and Pumpkin's enormous frame sidled over to create an artificial paddock wall. Smith saddled the horse in peace and sent him off.

At the bell, Seabiscuit shot straight to the front and set a blistering pace around the first turn and down the backstretch. As the far turn neared, Rosemont began to roll toward him, and the crowd shouted its approval. Entering the far turn, Rosemont caught him, and for a moment they ran together. After a few strides, Rosemont faltered. Seabiscuit bounded away, but the race wasn't won yet. From the outside came Aneroid, swooping around the turn. He collared Seabiscuit with a quarter mile to go. Neither horse would give. Seabiscuit and Aneroid matched strides down the homestretch, with Aneroid whittling away at Seabiscuit's lead, inch by inch. With a furlong to go, Aneroid's head bobbed in front, just as Rosemont's had done a few months before. Through the reins, Pollard felt Seabiscuit's mouth harden down on the bit: resolution. With a second to go, Seabiscuit burst ahead and thrust his nose over the line. The wreckage of the field was strewn out behind them. Rosemont was among them, ten lengths back.

Pollard cantered Seabiscuit back to the grandstand, posed for the win photos, then slid the saddle off and handed the horse to Stucki, who was up on Pumpkin. Smith asked Stucki to take Seabiscuit back to the barns, keeping him at a trot the whole way. Stucki led the horse past the shouting fans and up through the shed rows. The cheering died out, and they were alone, trotting past row after row of barns.

They drew near the Fitzsimmons barn, Seabiscuit's old home. A silent procession of stable hands came out and solemnly gazed at the horse they had let slip away. Regret was evident on every face. Stucki said nothing and kept going.

In New York, the trees swayed. Seabiscuit's eastern critics were, in the words of Jolly Roger, "numbed to quietude." Their respect was grudging. Back in California, they had known it all along. The Western Union office in San Francisco was overwhelmed with hundreds of congratulatory telegrams for the Howards, including those from Bing Crosby, Al Jolson, and Fred Astaire. The papers were full of Seabiscuit, proclaimed on that coast to be the best horse in America. Back East, they weren't ready to grant him that much. The easterners believed they still had one horse that could whip the Howards' "plater." Around the backstretch, the murmurs began. "A single steed rests between him and the full championship," continued Jolly Roger. "War Admiral."

July arrived and on Seabiscuit went, back to Empire City, where he won the mile-and-three-sixteenths Butler Handicap while conceding between seven and twenty-two pounds to the rest of the field. Two weeks later, he humiliated his opponents down in the Yonkers Handicap under a staggering 129 pounds, breaking a mile-and-one-sixteenth track record that had stood for twenty-three years.

In August, Seabiscuit went to Suffolk Downs to run in the prestigious Massachusetts Handicap. There, he hooked up in a murderous head-to-head duel with a filly named Fair Knightness, who was carrying 108 pounds to Seabiscuit's 130. Screaming around the track side by side, she and Seabiscuit disposed of Aneroid, then left the field far behind. Deep in the homestretch, Fair Knightness finally began to weaken. Seabiscuit shook loose to win, clipping two fifths of a second off the track record. Fair Knightness finished just two lengths behind him, fighting to the last. Seabiscuit cantered back to wild applause. Pollard leapt from his back and ran up the jockeys' room stairs, shouting, "Hail the conquerin' hero comes! Well, boys, I finally got my picture took!"

The festivities moved from the track to the New England Turf

Writers Association's annual dinner. Howard received a trophy, then Pollard came up to the stage to receive a commemorative whip. "I'll raise high and hit hard with it," he quipped. The audience, anesthetized by highballs, made no response. Pollard started clapping loudly, and the crowd looked up. "Hell!" he shouted. "Let's have some applause in this place!"

The Howards couldn't stop thinking about Fair Knightess's dazzling performance. Sometime after the dinner, Howard contacted the filly's owner and offered an exorbitant sum for her. Shortly after, Fair Knightess was led over to the Howard barn and moved into a stall down the row from Seabiscuit. She proved to be one of the few horses who could keep up with Seabiscuit in morning workouts, and unlike the colts, she didn't get demoralized when he taunted her, giving it right back to him. When Fair Knightess's racing days were over, Howard wanted to breed her to Seabiscuit.

A single thought occupied the minds of everyone in racing. Seabiscuit and War Admiral had to meet. Seabiscuit had beaten everything else the East had to offer. What's more, a heated money-earning race had developed. Seabiscuit's 1937 earnings were now $142,030, about $2,000 behind War Admiral, who was the leading money winner for the season. Both horses were chasing the all-time career mark of $376,744, set by Sun Beau in 1931. War Admiral's hoof had grown back, and he was back in training. All of the sport began talking of a match race. Even Bing Crosby, owner of a promising colt named High Strike, began goading Howard. CONGRATULATIONS, he wrote in a telegram to Howard after the Massachusetts Handicap. PACIFIC COAST CLAMORING FOR MATCH RACE HIGH STRIKE WAR ADMIRAL SEA BISCUIT IN THAT ORDER. Howard loved the idea.

Across the country, turf writers began agitating for the match. The *Los Angeles Daily News* began a running poll on who would win. Seabiscuit held a slight edge. Racetracks all over the nation began bidding for the race. Down in Florida, Hialeah officials began talking of $100,000 for a match on George Washington's birthday. Arlington

Park in Chicago also bandied around the idea. Then, in late August, Bay Meadows wired a formal proposal to Howard and Samuel Riddle, offering $40,000 for a fall match, with Seabiscuit weighted at 126 pounds to 120 for the year-younger War Admiral. Howard accepted. Riddle would not commit. The match-race idea withered on the vine.

Then Riddle surprised everyone. After strong urging from Santa Anita founder Doc Strub, he agreed to enter War Admiral in the 1938 hundred-grander, Seabiscuit's career objective. The press jumped on it.

Smith was skeptical. He knew enough about Riddle to believe that the old owner would never subject his skittish colt to a five-day rail journey to race in what he viewed as the sport's minor leagues. Smith believed they were going to have to hunt War Admiral on his own turf.

Seabiscuit had won seven consecutive stakes races. The all-time record was eight. Howard wanted to break the record, but he had a tough choice to make. As Smith had foreseen, since his stellar performance in the 1937 Santa Anita Handicap Seabiscuit had been assigned the highest weight in virtually every race, at times carrying over twenty pounds more than his rivals. By the rule of thumb that every two to three pounds slows a horse by a length at eight to ten furlongs (a mile to a mile and a quarter), and every pound costs him a length at ten furlongs or more, Seabiscuit was running with massive handicaps. The highter the impost, the greater the risk of injury, a significant concern for Seabiscuit, who had a history of leg trouble. Many top horses before him, such as his grandsire, Man o' War, had been retired prematurely to avoid high imposts. Others who had continued to campaign under high weight, such as Equipoise and Discovery, had lost repeatedly.

Howard was willing to accept higher weight, to a point. "Seabiscuit," he said, "is not a truck." He set a limit of 130 pounds, choosing that weight because it was the most the racing secretary would be permitted to assign in the 1938 Santa Anita Handicap. Should Seabiscuit win that event, Howard stated, he would be willing to accept higher imposts. One hundred and thirty was an enormous impost—many of history's greatest horses had failed to win under it—but Howard's statement was not well received. Several columnists accused him of lacking the courage and sportsmanship to truly test his horse. The charge cut deep.

The issue came to a head that September. Seabiscuit had been entered in both the Hawthorne Gold Cup in Chicago and the Narragansett Special in Rhode Island. The races were both scheduled for September 11. Narragansett assigned Seabiscuit a leaden 132 pounds, while Hawthorne gave him 128. Howard agonized over the decision. He didn't want to burden Seabiscuit with 132 pounds, but he knew that going the way of the lighter weight would draw criticism. Howard opted to break his 130-maximum rule and promised that Seabiscuit would run at Narragansett under 132 pounds.

On the race's eve, a downpour rendered the track at Narragansett a quagmire. Seabiscuit had a reputation for being a terrible mudder. The charge was an exaggeration, but his performances were compromised by a wet surface. According to Pollard, Seabiscuit ran with a nervous, quick, belly-down stride that made mud-running difficult. "You know how Jack Dempsey used to punch, short, snappy jolts?" Pollard asked. "This is exactly how the Biscuit runs. On a muddy track Biscuit can't use those short steps. In mud, a horse has to leap, and that's not the Biscuit's style. It would get him utterly untracked and he could do nothing." Pollard, in his odd way, urged others to forgive the horse this one flaw. "We have to give him a break," he said to journalist David Alexander, his close friend. "There's more than one thing I can't do and there are a lot more things than that that you can't do or you wouldn't be in the newspaper business. You'd be a jockey and a scholar and a connoisseur of femininity, like I am."

Psychological reasons also played a role. Seabiscuit hated to be pelted in the face with mud thrown up by other horses. "He just made up his mind that he didn't like it," Smith explained, "and he's got a pretty definite mind. Alone, he could work well on the worst kind of a track, but when it splattered in his face, and particularly in his ears, he wanted no part of it. Oh, he'd go on, try—he wouldn't have quit in a Wyoming hail storm where they come down as big as golf balls—but he couldn't, somehow, give his best. And why punish him unnecessarily?"

Smith was also concerned about soundness. At Santa Anita the horse had slipped and kicked himself during a mud workout. Knowing that his colt had had some leg trouble in the past, Smith wanted to avoid mud whenever possible.

But Howard had made a promise to run at Narragansett, and had he scratched the horse so late, it would have looked as if he had never intended to run. He was again forced to choose between his image and his trainer's wishes, and Howard was a man who had great difficulty compromising his image. So, swimming in fetlock-deep slop and conceding as many as twenty-four pounds to his adversaries, Seabiscuit finished third, snapping his historic win streak.

Howard couldn't win. "The consensus was that Seabiscuit should not have been started in the mud," wrote Oscar Otis, echoing the words of many columnists. "Why he was started anyway is not known, but it seems a shame that his unbeaten record for the eastern invasion was not kept unsullied."

Gradually, the sniping died off. But they hadn't seen the last of muddy tracks or hard choices.

On October 12, 1937, after a month's rest, Seabiscuit resumed his winning ways in smashing style, bounding home first under 130 pounds in the rich Continental Handicap at New York's Jamaica Race Track. The victory bumped him up to the top spot in the 1937 earnings race. With $152,780, he was now some $8,000 ahead of War Admiral. As he streaked under the wire, the fans began chanting, "Bring on your War Admiral!"

Smith and the Howards knew that War Admiral was not going to come to them. They shipped down to Maryland, where War Admiral was completing his training for his return to racing, and prepared to meet him there. There were three possibilities for a meeting: Laurel Racecourse's Washington Handicap on October 30, Pimlico Racecourse's Pimlico Special on November 3, and Pimlico's Riggs

Handicap on November 5. Both horses were entered in all three. A meeting now seemed certain.

For Smith, the trip to Maryland was gratifying. His accomplishments with Seabiscuit were the wonder of the racing world, and the man who had been considered an obscure oddball a year before now enjoyed cult status among his peers. Across the backstretch, other trainers began to mix up homemade liniments, trying to brew what they called Smith's "magic salves." Everyone wanted to know what sort of shoes he was putting on his horses. They began to watch everything he did and query him about his training practices, from feed to workouts. One enterprising promoter even offered to pay Smith to hold training tutorials.

Smith was incredulous. He insisted that the training community was missing the point. It wasn't the shoes or the liniments. "We have a great horse," he said. "That's all there is to it. And we tried to use common sense in training him and in racing him."

There was one admirer whom Smith didn't brush off. On October 16 he led a blanketed Seabiscuit into the paddock for the Laurel Handicap. Twenty thousand people crammed into the track to see him. As Smith walked Seabiscuit into the paddock stall, a stooped man emerged from the crowd and approached him.

"I'm Fitzsimmons," he said, as if Smith didn't know. "I want to ask you a favor."

Smith, a little starstruck, listened.

"Mr. Smith, I am very fond of Seabiscuit, and I would consider it an honor if you would permit me to hold him while he is being saddled."

Smith's eyes shone as he handed Fitzsimmons the reins. He quietly saddled Seabiscuit while Fitzsimmons stood at the head of the horse he had lost. In a few moments the horse was ready, and Fitzsimmons passed the reins back and stepped away. Smith turned back to his horse and collected himself. It was, he would say later, the greatest moment of his life.

Ten minutes later Seabiscuit finished in a dead heat for first with a horse named Heelfly, who carried fifteen fewer pounds. In the jockeys' room, Pollard surely never heard the end of it: George Woolf had ridden Heelfly.

The meeting with War Admiral, slated for the Washington Handicap, was just two weeks away.

A storm front rolled in and stalled over Maryland, drenching the track day after day. Smith urged Howard to pass on the entry in the Washington Handicap. Howard, ever the optimist, insisted that the track would be dry, and entered the horse. He was wrong. The morning of the race, an inspection of the track revealed a boggy surface, especially along the rail, where Seabiscuit preferred to run. This time they would not be pressured into starting. Seabiscuit was scratched. With Smith watching from the track apron, War Admiral led from wire to wire, winning easily.

After the race, Howard learned that members of the Riddle barn were publicly mocking him for being afraid of War Admiral. He was furious. Though both horses were still entered in the Pimlico Special and Riggs Handicaps, each race would feature a full field. Howard and Smith much preferred that the horses meet in a definitive one-on-one match, in which no other horses could cause interference or otherwise affect the outcome. Howard again tried to arrange a match race.

The man he approached was Alfred Gwynne Vanderbilt, Jr. A dead ringer for actor Jimmy Stewart, Vanderbilt was a gangly twenty-five-year-old whose gentle, self-effacing manner belied his fabulous wealth. His father was heir to the Vanderbilt railroad and oceanic shipping fortune; his mother's father had invented the fantastically lucrative Bromo-Seltzer. In May 1915, when a German submarine torpedoed the *Lusitania* and sent the liner and Alfred's father to the bottom of the Atlantic, two-year-old Alfred had inherited $5.8 million in government bonds, a fortune augmented by $2 million more and a sprawling Maryland property when he turned twenty-one in 1933. Dubbed the nation's most eligible bachelor, Vanderbilt eschewed the debauchery that would have tempted other men fresh out of their teens and into a bottomless bank account. He had fallen madly and intractably in love with horse racing from the moment he saw his first race as a child, and knew where he wanted his money to go. He bought controlling interest in Baltimore's legendary but struggling Pimlico Racecourse and set out to restore its glory. In spite of his youth, he proved to be an imaginative and effective businessman. He revolutionized Pimlico, installing a public-address system and a modern starting gate and leveling out the large hill in the infield that had given the track its nickname—"Old Hilltop"—but obstructed the view of the races. By the fall of 1937 Pimlico was beginning to make a comeback, but progress was slow. Vanderbilt wanted a headliner.

Howard recognized Vanderbilt's tremendous influence and powers of persuasion, and knew that Pimlico needed his horse. He proposed that Vanderbilt try to host a meeting between Seabiscuit and War Admiral. He told him that he'd take a match at any distance from a mile to a mile and a quarter, anytime the track was fast. He offered to run against the colt for a small purse or simply for a winner's cup. "I believe Seabiscuit can beat War Admiral," he said. "Maybe I'm wrong, but I'm willing to run against him to test the theory. It is all up to Mr. Riddle." Vanderbilt approached the elder horseman with an offer for a match race for $50,000. Riddle declined.

Howard was left with either the Pimlico Special or the Riggs. At first, it appeared that both horses would run in the former, and Maryland geared up for the meeting of the two titans. Again, the weather intervened. Ten straight days of downpour kept Seabiscuit in the barn, taking the edge off of his form. Smith again scratched him.

On race day, Smith walked out to the track to see War Admiral run. The Triple Crown winner was a hellion, repeatedly barging through the gate and dragging the assistant starter with him. War Admiral was growing so violent that he was endangering himself and everyone nearby. Head starter Jim Milton tried a new tack. He brought the colt around to the front of the gate, had the assistant place a pair of tongs on the horse's lips to distract him, then had him backed into the stall. It worked. War Admiral quieted down and Milton was finally able to break the field in good order.

Across the track, Smith lifted his binoculars and watched as War Admiral pulled around the far turn, meeting with unexpected pressure from Masked General, who carried twenty-eight fewer pounds. Smith saw Masked General level his eye right at War Admiral. It lasted only a moment, but that was all Smith needed to notice something unusual. For the first time in his career, War Admiral hesitated. Smith thought: *He is befuddled.* War Admiral's jockey, Charley Kurtsinger, also seemed confused. An instant later, War Admiral pulled himself together and won, regaining the lead in the money-winning race. But Smith took note. He believed he had found a way to beat War Admiral. After the race, he was smiling.

"Seabiscuit," someone heard him saying, "will lick him sure."

Riddle was furious with Milton for using the tongs on War Admiral, despite the fact that one of his own employees had reportedly given them to Milton to be used on the colt if he acted up. Riddle had been harboring a grudge against Pimlico since 1926, when the track's racing secretary had assigned his colt Crusader 126 pounds in a major race—Crusader lost to a horse carrying 93 pounds. The tongs incident was the last straw. Riddle didn't want Milton going anywhere near his horse again, and vowed never to run another horse at Pimlico. He had Conway shelve War Admiral for the season.

Two days later, Seabiscuit ran in the Riggs Handicap, over the same distance as the Pimlico Special. Members of the Riddle barn came out to the track to watch him. They were treated to quite a spectacle. Seabiscuit annihilated the field, breaking the track record while carrying 130 pounds, two more than War Admiral had lugged in the Pimlico Special. With the victory, Seabiscuit took back the lead in the earnings race, amassing about $9,000 more than War Admiral.

Vanderbilt worked on Riddle for a few days to get the owner to rescind his boycott of Pimlico and bring his colt back to meet Seabiscuit. Howard kept his horses in town in case something came of it. For a few days, Vanderbilt thought Riddle would reconsider and run War Admiral in the Bowie Handicap. He talked Howard into committing to the race, even though it was at the marathon distance of one-and-five-eighths miles, farther than Smith wanted to send Seabiscuit.

But by race day, it was clear that War Admiral wasn't coming. Train-loads of fans were pouring in for the race, and Howard didn't want to disappoint them, so he agreed to send Seabiscuit out anyway. Carry-ing 130 pounds, Seabiscuit endured a rough trip and lost by a nose to the brilliant race mare Esposa, who carried fifteen fewer pounds and set a track record. With that, the Pimlico season ended.

In mid-November Smith loaded Seabiscuit and the rest of his stable, blanketed in red and white stable colors, into three cars of the *Overland Limited*, bound for California. The train rolled up the East Coast. It paused at Belmont Park in New York while Howard com-pleted a transaction. Bing Crosby had long been deeply impressed with Howard's racing success—he once suggested to his wife that they name their son Seabiscuit—but every attempt to emulate his friend ended in spectacular failure. In 1937 Bing joined forces with Howard's polo-playing son Lin to form the Binglin Stock Farm, hoping that Lin's considerable horsemanship could turn his luck around. That fall, while in Argentina for a polo tournament, Lin had stumbled upon some promising racehorses. He had purchased several, shipping them by sea to New York. Charles Howard had agreed to pick them up and bring them to California with his own horses. Lin and Bing told the elder Howard that he could pick out one that he liked and buy him.

Howard and Smith came down to the docks to see the horses. Two stood out from the rest. One was Kajak, later renamed Kayak II. Big, black, and gorgeous, he was barely halter broken and fought every attempt to handle him. The other was a mature horse, Ligaroti, Argentina's champion miler. Smith was particularly enamored of Ligaroti. Howard liked both horses. He chose to buy Kayak.

After tacking on additional railcars to bear the Binglin horses west, the Seabiscuit train rolled out of the East, across the plains and over the Rockies, desolate and white and still in their early, deep winter. When the train paused at little towns along the route, fans gathered in the cold to peer in the windows and catch a glimpse of Seabiscuit.

Ahead, a celebration awaited the travelers. Howard had telephoned

Oscar Otis to tell him that Seabiscuit was coming back, and Otis had printed the news. Five hundred enthusiastic fans were preparing to rise early and come to the track to give the hometown hero a noisy welcome. City and state dignitaries would be there to pair their images with the hottest celebrity in the nation. Even the jaded horsemen would take a respite from their labors to see him, eating their breakfasts outdoors on the benches near the siding. To joyful applause and popping flashbulbs, the horse would draw up in his railcar. He would step from his three-foot-deep bed of straw, give Smith an affectionate bump with his nose, and leave the train bucking. The men around him would be triumphant and relieved. Even Smith would be in an optimistic, relatively chatty mood, stringing several hundred words together in what the papers would call "a great moral victory for the reporters present."

But there were long, cold miles to go before they were home. The train rolled through country where the temperature was fourteen degrees below zero. Storm after storm buffeted the train and buried the landscape in snow. The going was treacherous and frightening.

When the train's water pipes froze, Howard left Marcela in the sleeper car to join Seabiscuit. It was a habit he had learned, looking to the horse to steady himself. He found Seabiscuit warm and drowsy under a double layer of blankets, swaying on his feet as the cars snaked over the mountains. In the icy, rocking train, Howard sat with his horse over the journey home.

It was going to be a long, cold winter.

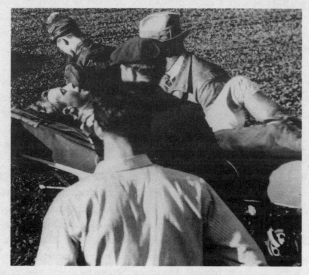

*Critically injured, Red Pollard is carried off the track
at Santa Anita, February 19, 1938.*
(LOS ANGELES EXAMINER)

CHAPTER 11

No Pollard,
No Seabiscuit

It was December 7, 1937, and Red Pollard was winging around
the far turn at Tanforan. He was riding Howard's colt Exhibit,
circling the field in a weekday sprint race. He was ticking past
horses one by one, watching them waver and fail as his colt powered
by. At the juncture between turn and homestretch, he collared the last
of the front-runners, Half Time, who was laboring along the rail.
Ripping down the center of the track, Pollard saw a wide-open lane in
front of him. He knew he had more than enough horse under him to
last to the wire.

Suddenly, Exhibit bolted inward, shying from something to his
right. Pollard's weight sank hard into his right stirrup, and he pushed
off against it, trying to avoid falling over Exhibit's shoulder and down
into the dirt. Exhibit veered toward Half Time. As he careened left,
Pollard must have heard the hard irregular pounding of Half Time's
forehooves as his jockey, standing bolt upright in panic, sawed on the
reins, trying to back his horse out of the way before Exhibit crashed
into him. Half Time's head came up, and he dropped out of the pocket
an instant before Exhibit's broad rump bulled into it. Pollard got his
weight back under him, straightened the horse's course, and galloped
him under the wire first.

Half Time's jockey was off his horse and up to the stewards in seconds. Exhibit was promptly disqualified, and the stewards scheduled
a meeting to determine if Pollard would have to serve a suspension for
the incident. Pollard must have expected to be taken off his weekday

mounts for a few days. Though the jockey was probably not at fault for Exhibit's change of course, it was common for stewards to briefly suspend riders caught in his situation to guard against foul play.

But no one expected the Tanforan stewards to do what they did. Perhaps they were erring on the side of overpunishment out of concern for the sport's image. Or maybe they wanted to take a strike against Pollard, who delighted in sassing them. He had nicknamed a particularly tyrannical, humorless, and rosy steward "Pink Whiskers," a sobriquet that was soon used by all the jockeys. Whatever their motivation, the stewards buried him. Handing out the toughest sentence of the season, they not only suspended Pollard from riding for the rest of the Tanforan meeting, they asked the state racing board, which usually followed their recommendations, to suspend him from riding at *any* California track for the rest of 1937. Nor was that all. It was customary for stewards to allow suspended jockeys to ride in stakes races except in cases of fraud, of which Pollard was not accused, but the Tanforan stewards scheduled a later meeting to consider taking this privilege away from him as well.

The news stunned the Howard barn. Seabiscuit was set to meet War Admiral in the Santa Anita Handicap on March 5, and his preparations were just getting into high gear. His first prep race was the San Francisco Handicap, to be run on December 15, during Pollard's suspension. Howard was livid. For the Howards, the jockey had long ago ceased being a mere employee. He was more like a son. For Charles, Pollard may have become a surrogate for little Frankie, the boy he had lost. Both Charles and Marcela fretted like nervous parents over the jockey's welfare. Marcela called the jockey by his childhood name, Johnny; though Pollard was approaching thirty, Charles hadn't been able to break his habit of referring to him as a boy. Any insult to Pollard was received by the Howards as a slight to themselves.

Howard's anger over the suspension went beyond loyalty. Riding Seabiscuit was a nuanced task. No other jockey had ever ridden him successfully, and Howard believed no one else could. More important, he knew that Pollard was the jockey best able to protect his horse's idiosyncratic body from injury. "If Pollard rides Seabiscuit," he explained to the press, "I know he will bring the horse back intact, and that is my chief concern."

"Nobody," he said, "fits my horse better than that boy."

When Pollard returned from his meeting with the stewards that night, there was more bad news. The *Turf and Sport Digest* sportswriter poll had named War Admiral Horse of the Year, outballoting Seabiscuit 621 to 602. *Horse and Horseman* magazine, which polled horsemen, not sportswriters, had named Seabiscuit Horse of the Year, but the *Turf and Sport* vote was regarded as the deciding one. There were consolation prizes—*Turf and Sport* was going to present Seabiscuit with a special plaque commending his performances, and by unanimous vote, they had named him Handicap Champion—but these weren't the honors the Howard barn craved. And Smith had been right about War Admiral: Riddle's camp announced that the horse would not be coming to the Santa Anita Handicap after all. He was off to Florida's Hialeah Race Track, where he was greeted with near hysteria, generating a bigger stir than any Florida visitor save President Roosevelt. Instead of meeting Seabiscuit, War Admiral would face a soft field in Hialeah's Widener Handicap.

The next morning, Howard issued his response to Pollard's suspension.

"No Pollard, no Seabiscuit."

The stewards did not like being threatened. After leaning toward allowing Pollard to ride in his stakes engagements, they changed their minds. He was suspended from all mounts. Howard struck back. As the state racing board prepared to decide whether or not Pollard's suspension would be extended to year's end, Howard scratched Seabiscuit and Fair Knightess from the San Francisco Handicap. Seabiscuit's next scheduled start was in the Christmas Day Handicap, but Howard made it clear that he would pull Seabiscuit from that race, and any other, if Pollard's suspension were extended. The crisis was escalating rapidly, and Pollard was getting alarmed. He didn't want the horse to miss any races on his account. He approached Howard with a compromise: Get George Woolf to ride Seabiscuit. Howard wouldn't consider it. He trusted no other rider on his horse. He was going to take the state officials to the mat.

On December 22 the chairman of the California Horse Racing Commission gathered reporters together and issued the board's decree: Red Pollard was banned from riding all horses, including stakes mounts, until January 1, 1938. Five minutes later Charles Howard stormed into the racing secretary's office at Santa Anita and announced that Seabiscuit would not run on Christmas.

Seabiscuit idled. He was entered in the New Year's Handicap, held on the day Pollard's suspension would end, but that was more than a week away. Smith had to keep him fit through workouts. Every reporter and clocker on the West Coast wanted to sit in on them, and Smith was determined to keep them away. His war with the press resumed.

The enemy, Smith discovered, was getting smarter. Knowing that Smith had a history of giving his horse moonlight workouts, the newsmen first tried showing up at ungodly hours of the morning. When he led Seabiscuit and Fair Knightess out for what was supposed to be a secret predawn workout veiled in thick fog, Smith discovered a thicket of clockers and reporters waiting for him. Because visibility was so low, they had formed a human chain stretching all the way around the track, each man clocking a portion of Seabiscuit's workout. In spite of the pea-soup fog, they caught the Biscuit spinning six furlongs in 1:14, a solid workout.

Smith tried plan b: working Seabiscuit in the afternoons on Mondays, when Santa Anita was closed to racing and the clockers and reporters had gone home. His adversaries guessed his tactic and hung around Santa Anita hour after hour on the following Monday. Seabiscuit didn't show. One by one, the reporters bailed out. As dusk fell, the last one drove away. Seconds later Smith and Seabiscuit trotted out onto the track. The horse worked in solitude. The next day the clockers and press got word that they had been duped.

The Howards blew time any way they could. They showed up at the barn every morning at seven sharp, Howard with sugar cubes, Marcela with Wee Biscuit, a toy Scottish terrier given to her during a visit to

Bing Crosby's house. The reporters were almost always in tow, and Howard usually created some amusement for them to write up or photograph, including talking Smith into dipping Seabiscuit's hoof in ink and stamping their Christmas cards. In the afternoons, the Howards would walk up to their box for the races. Howard made sport of cornering journalists who had criticized Seabiscuit. Summoning them to the box, he and his whole family would rise together and ask in unison, "Tell us what you have against Seabiscuit." On one of those afternoons, Marcela brought Alfred Vanderbilt up to join them. She introduced him to her niece, a gorgeous young woman named Manuela Hudson. Vanderbilt was dazzled. A romance began, and Alfred and Manuela were soon engaged. Vanderbilt owed the Howards a favor.

Everyone was waiting for the impost announcement for the New Year's Handicap. They had reason to worry. Howard's insistence that his horse would not run under more than 130 pounds had put track handicappers in a bind. California racing rules mandated that no horse carry fewer than 100 pounds, and Seabiscuit was clearly more than 30 pounds better than most horses on the West Coast. But Seabiscuit was a fail-safe moneymaker, drawing record crowds and wagering virtually everywhere he showed his face. If tracks wanted the attendance, revenue, and exposure that a superstar like Seabiscuit brought, they had to obey Howard's wishes. But if they gave him 130 or fewer pounds, they risked the ire of rival horsemen and the excoriation of journalists.

All week before the weights for the New Year's Handicap were announced, Howard made warning noises about his 130-pound limit. On the Tuesday before the race, the weights were released. Smith and Howard groaned. Seabiscuit was weighted at 132 pounds. Seabiscuit was getting heavy and stall-crazy and desperately needed a race. That night, while playing in his stall, he reared up and smacked his head against the stall door. He came down with a nasty gash a millimeter above his right eye. Smith stitched him up, installed a safety door, and damned the racing secretary. Unable to stomach running with 132 pounds, he scratched the horse. Next among race possibilities was the

San Pasqual Handicap, but again, the secretary assigned him 132 pounds. Howard and Smith again scratched him. Howard started referring to the racing secretary as "public enemy number one." Only two races remained on Seabiscuit's schedule before the Santa Anita Handicap, the San Carlos on February 19 and the San Antonio on February 26. Seabiscuit was very, very late in his preparation.

A peculiar madness was seizing the press box and clockers' stand. There were more than a dozen clockers at the track, yet not one had seen Seabiscuit in a single workout since Santa Anita opened in December. Unable to catch him on their stopwatches, some of them began to circulate old rumors that Seabiscuit was lame. The rumors were quickly picked up by the press, which set out to investigate. While leading Seabiscuit out for walks, Smith stared in amazement as newsmen got down on their hands and knees to see if the horse had a game leg. Howard watched and laughed. Other journalists began seeing ghosts, reporting imaginary sightings of Seabiscuit working late at night. "The 'mystery' of Seabiscuit," wrote David Alexander, "seems to have been bothering a lot of the boys here to the point of a nervous breakdown."

January 31 started out as an ordinary Monday for the clockers. They watched the waves of horses coming and going from the track at their usual early-morning times. As Santa Anita was closed on Mondays, they would normally have gone home in midmorning, when the workouts were over. But they still hadn't timed a single workout for Seabiscuit since he arrived at Santa Anita a month before. They settled in to wait him out. Gradually, attrition thinned the ranks. By lunchtime, only two hardy clockers remained. A handful of reporters gutted out the wait with them. Their hopes dimmed as they watched a rainstorm approaching. They knew that Seabiscuit didn't work on wet tracks.

Shortly after lunch, just before the rains hit, the clockers were startled by an improbable spectacle. Two men and two horses materialized from under the purple storm clouds, walked up the track, and reigned up in front of the press box. It was Tom Smith, on a broad yellow horse. Alongside him, Red Pollard sat in his customary seat atop the familiar little bay horse. The clockers gaped: Smith was *waving* at them.

They lunged for their stopwatches. Smith, seeing that the track was standing at attention, cantered the horses once around, then pulled up at the finish line while Pollard and his mount peeled off for a workout. With Pollard sitting motionless in the saddle, they reeled off rapid fractions, clipping under the wire after six furlongs. Smith took the horse back to the barn. The reporters bounced along behind, teasing Smith for letting himself get caught. Smith, for some reason not his usual surly self, laughed with them, saying he hadn't been aware that the clockers and reporters were still there. "I figured I'd just steal the march on everybody," he said. "Doggone those clockers. I'll fool them yet." The next morning the papers were full of the news.

But a year of dealing with Tom Smith had gotten to some of the reporters. Paranoia was setting in. Something wasn't right. Wasn't it suspicious that Smith had waved at them? Didn't Seabiscuit seem to be blowing a little too hard after the work? Wasn't it odd that Smith was so amiable about having been caught? Had anyone *ever* seen him smile before? Could it be that the horse was not Seabiscuit after all? In the press corps only the *Los Angeles Evening Herald*'s Jack McDonald was willing to speculate publicly, and only in his headline: HOWARD HORSE PULLED UP "GROGGY" AFTER FAST WORK.

Back in Barn 38, Smith must have read that headline and smiled.

The laughter subsided immediately. A few days after Seabiscuit's six-furlong workout, a tipster contacted the local district attorney's office with a startling claim: On the backstretch at Santa Anita a man was preparing to harm Seabiscuit. His name was James Manning, and he had infiltrated the barn area with plans to break into Seabiscuit's stall and shove a sponge up his nostril, impeding his breathing. Manning had been sent by a group of men from the East Coast who wanted to ensure that Seabiscuit would lose the Santa Anita Handicap. Because Seabiscuit's fans had made him the prohibitive favorite in the race, his rivals had become relative long shots. If the race-fixing conspirators could stop Seabiscuit, they could take advantage of the other horses' long odds, cash in huge bets, and disappear.

The district attorney took the tip seriously. Manning was quickly hunted down and arrested before he could reach Seabiscuit's stall. In interrogation, he confessed. Because the police had caught him before he could carry out his crime, prosecutors didn't have much to charge him with. They settled for a charge of vagrancy and gave him the option of being expelled from the state or serving jail time. Manning chose the former. Police escorted him to the border and booted him across.

The news broke on February 1 with front-page banner headlines. A ripple of horror spread across the backstretch. "Sponging," an old race-fixing technique from racing's corrupt days, threatened horses' lives. The ensuing partial strangulation frequently triggered systemic, stress-related diseases that were often fatal. And unless a horseman was actively looking for the sponge, it could go undetected for weeks.

Smith put Manning out of his mind and went back to tormenting the clockers. By mid-February the reporters had figured out that when Howard went to the training track Seabiscuit was soon to follow, and they had taken to trailing the owner around. Smith used this to his advantage. During the races he sent Howard over to his box at the main Santa Anita track as a decoy while he led Seabiscuit over to the training track nearby. Just before Seabiscuit worked out, Howard excused himself from his box for a moment. Sprinting to the training track, he stayed for the one and a half minutes necessary for Seabiscuit to blaze through a mile workout. A moment later he was back in his box. He'd been gone so briefly that no one suspected he'd done anything more interesting than visit the men's room.

The workout demonstrated that the horse was ready for the February 19 San Carlos Handicap, and for once the track secretary relented, assigning him 130 pounds. Pollard, finally released from his suspension, was itching to ride him. On the day before the race, everything seemed to be coming together.

But again, luck ran out. All night long, rain pounded the track. The next morning the course was a swamp, and Smith scratched his horse for the fourth straight time. Fair Knightess, a better mudder, was left in the race, and Pollard opted to ride her instead. The decision was the pivot point of his life.

As the San Carlos field leaned around the far turn, Pollard was bent over the back of Fair Knightess, who was racing along the rail in fourth. Around him, close enough to touch, was a dense phalanx of horses moving at terrific speed: Indian Broom on the rail, Pompoon on the outside, Mandingham right on Fair Knightess's tail. Just inches ahead of Fair Knightess was He Did, whose main claim to fame was having sideswiped Seabiscuit's old stablemate Granville at the start of the 1936 Kentucky Derby, knocking his jockey off. Midway around the far turn at Santa Anita, He Did did it again.

Leading the dense pack of horses around the turn, He Did took an awkward, sagging step. For an instant, he lost his momentum. The formation of runners collapsed, and horses began to rack up behind him. With nowhere to go and no time to stop herself, Fair Knightess charged straight into the bottleneck. Pollard must have seen He Did's dark hindquarters suddenly in his face, too close. He had no time to react. Fair Knightess reached forward just as He Did kicked out with his heels.

Jockeys say there is a small, bright sound when hooves clip against each other, a cheery portent of the wreck that is likely to follow. Pollard must have heard it. Fair Knightess's forelegs were kicked out from under her. Unable to catch herself, she pitched into a somersault at forty miles per hour. Under Pollard her head and neck dropped away as the ground heaved up. Pollard went down with her, his helpless form following the line of her fall, over her back and neck and vanishing under her crashing body. She came down onto him with terrific force and skidded to a stop.

Behind her, jockey Maurice Peters, aboard Mandingham, saw her plow into the track and knew he could not avoid her. Mandingham saw her too, and gathered himself up to make a desperate leap over her as she lay on the track. Perhaps, for an instant, it seemed as if he would make it. But just as he reared up and launched himself into the air, Fair Knightess thrust her forelegs out in front of her and lifted herself up directly into Mandingham's path. Mandingham slammed into her. The force of the collision knocked Fair Knightess down the track and flipped her upside down. Pollard, lying just beyond her, couldn't get out of her way. Her full weight came down on his chest. Mandingham flew over Fair Knightess, his legs tangling with hers. He bent in the air like a thrashing fish and spun into the ground shoulder first. Peters rode him down.

From the grandstand came a heavy sound. Then all fell silent. Peters, his ankle sprained, lifted himself up. Mandingham rose, his shoulder bruised and his foreleg gashed by Fair Knightess's hoof but otherwise uninjured. Fair Knightess lay where she was. Peters limped over to Pollard and looked down.

The left side of Pollard's chest was crushed.

Charles Howard saw Pollard go down, staring in horror as Fair Knightess's flailing legs rolled skyward over him. He stared at the crumpled form, the great overturned animal—in an instant he and Marcela were running blindly, pushing through the crowd. They sprinted through the mud to Pollard's side. The jockey was barely conscious, his mouth wide open. He was carried to the track infirmary. An ambulance arrived. The Howards climbed in and rode with Pollard to St. Luke's Hospital in Pasadena.

Behind them, Smith sank down into the dirt beside Fair Knightess, who did not rise. Her back had been horribly wrenched. Her hind end was paralyzed. Smith somehow got her pulled into a van and taken back to the barn, where she lay helpless. Smith ordered X rays. If her back was broken, it was over. He stayed at the barn and worked over her to save her life.

At the hospital, the news was grim. Pollard's chest had virtually caved in. He had several broken ribs, a collarbone shattered into countless fragments, severe internal injuries, a broken shoulder, and a concussion. For several hours, he barely clung to life. Newspapers all over the country shouted the news. Some reported that Pollard had been killed. Up in Edmonton, his father stumbled into his house before his children, clutching a newspaper. Pollard's sister Edie saw the headline: SEABISCUIT'S JOCKEY NEAR DEATH.

Three days passed. Pollard hovered. Smith and Howard sat by his bed. Finally, the jockey stabilized. The reporters slipped into his hospital room. Flashbulbs popped in his pale, unshaven face. His arm hung up in traction. Pollard didn't look at the reporters. He stared without expression at the half-page newspaper photos of himself, taken an instant before the wreck, showing him coiled over Fair Knightness's withers.

Doctors told him he wouldn't ride again for at least a year.

In the jockey's risky universe, everyone understood that some rider was going to profit from Pollard's loss. The redhead was not even out of danger before Howard and Smith were tailed by jockeys and agents seeking the mount. Howard couldn't think about them. All he could think of was Pollard's injuries, incurred on his horse. He couldn't bring himself to run Seabiscuit in the Santa Anita Handicap.

Howard and Smith went to the hospital, and Pollard made himself clear. The horse had to run without him. After some consideration, Howard agreed. They had to find a new jockey. Again, Pollard asked Howard to hire George Woolf. Smith thought it was a good idea. Woolf had already committed to ride a horse named Today in the hundred-grander and its final prep race, the San Antonio Handicap, but there was a chance they could get him out of the contract. Howard favored eastern rider Sonny Workman, but Lin and Bing had already signed him on to ride Ligaroti. Smith, who operated under the assumption that all easterners were up to no good, didn't trust Workman anyway. With the decision up in the air and the San Antonio less than a week away, Howard, Smith, and Pollard parted. Howard made his announcement. "Seabiscuit will run if I have to ride him myself," he said. "Of course, that might put a little too much weight on Seabiscuit."

With that, the flood began. Howard and Smith were besieged with telegrams and calls from jockeys all over the country. As Howard walked through the track, riders swirled around him like snowflurries. He and Smith conducted interviews in the tack room. Smith decided that if he couldn't have Woolf, he wanted a rough-and-tumble, bespectacled western rider named Noel "Spec" Richardson, a close friend of Pollard and Woolf. Howard couldn't make up his mind.

Meanwhile, Smith honed Seabiscuit. The fact that the trainer was working the horse on Mondays was now the worst-kept secret in racing; when he led the horse onto the track on the Monday after Pollard's accident, two thousand cheering fans greeted him. Smith asked Farrell Jones, who would be up for the workout, to wear his bulkiest leather jacket and use an extra-heavy saddle. All told, Jones, the saddle, and the jacket tipped the scales at 127 pounds. Smith then drilled Seabiscuit in tag-team fashion. Sending him off alongside sprinter Limpio, he stationed the other two stablemates, Advocator and Chanceview, at preassigned places around the track. Limpio took off with Seabiscuit, and the two dueled through sprinter fractions. After half a mile, Advocator hooked up with Seabiscuit as Limpio dropped away, exhausted. In another half mile, Chanceview relieved Advocator, gunning alongside Seabiscuit for a final eighth of a mile. The final time was superb. It was a solid, taxing workout, whittling ten pounds off of Seabiscuit's frame. Howard was buoyant. He began making side bets with friends that Seabiscuit would smash the track record in the San Antonio. Smith agreed that the horse was better than ever. "I have the big horse as good as hands can make him," he said. "Now it's up to the rider to get him home in front."

Who that rider would be was still undecided. On the day before the San Antonio, Smith and Howard put Sonny Workman up on their colt Ariel Cross for a race. He rode beautifully, and Ariel Cross won. There had been a rider switch on Ligaroti—perhaps Howard had talked his son into going with another jockey—and Workman was suddenly available for the San Antonio and Santa Anita Handicaps. Smith still didn't want him going anywhere near Seabiscuit, but it wasn't up to him. The next morning Howard hired Workman, but only for the San Antonio. If he rode well in the race, it was implied, Workman had the mount on Seabiscuit in the hundred-grander. Smith took Workman to Pollard's hospital bed for a tutorial on the subtleties of riding Seabiscuit.

It was there that the confusion began. Pollard told Workman all about Seabiscuit's oddities. The redhead stressed one point: Do not use the whip. It is not clear why he gave this advice, since he usually gave the horse two taps during races. He was probably concerned that Workman, being unfamiliar with Seabiscuit, would overdo it and antagonize the horse. Knowing that the horse, when forced, tended to become obstreperous, Pollard may have decided to err on the side of caution and advise Workman to withhold the whip.

The next afternoon Smith and Howard stood on the grass in the infield and gave Workman their own instructions. They told him to use his judgment on strategy, but to give Seabiscuit two swats with his whip, once at the top of the stretch and once seventy yards from the wire. Smith was apparently unaware that his advice conflicted with Pollard's. Workman opted to follow the rider's instructions.

The San Antonio was a terrible place to make a season debut after a long layoff. The track, though fast, was thick. The field was formidable, featuring Seabiscuit's old rivals Aneroid and Indian Broom, plus Today, with Woolf up. Scabiscuit was carrying 130 pounds, 12 more than second-high weight Aneroid and as much as 20 more than other horses in the field. The man on his back was a stranger, unfamiliar with his quirks, with only a few hours of preparation and conflicting advice on how to ride him. It was a formula for disaster.

As Seabiscuit cantered to the post for the San Antonio, Pollard lay on his hospital cot at St. Luke's. He was in severe pain. Nurses had stacked sandbags all along his left side to prevent him from turning over on his broken chest. His left arm was in traction, a pulley slung to his wrist. His right, pinching a cigarette, was stretched out for the knob on a radio, which the nurses had perched on a stack of magazines. He fiddled with the tuning knob, trying to find the station that would air the race. Turf writer Sid Ziff, from the *Los Angeles Evening*

Herald, slipped into the room. Pollard greeted him with a pained smile. "Good old Biscuit," he said, "he'll break the world record today." He surveyed his arm and winced. "It doesn't matter that I'm here, Sonny Workman's up out there. Sonny's a great jockey." He lay back and fell silent, listening to radio caller Clem McCarthy tell his audience about the crash of Fair Knightess. He stubbed out his cigarette. He was agitated and unhappy. He was out of place, here on the cot while his horse ran without him.

Miles away, Seabiscuit was coming unwound. Workman couldn't get him settled down. The horse reverted to his rebellious habits in the starting gate, bulling forward and raising a fuss. He reared, flung the starter aside, and broke through the front of the gate. They loaded him again, but Workman couldn't quiet him. The frustrated assistant starter began waving a rope back and forth in front of the horse's face to distract him. Just before the bell rang, Seabiscuit lunged. The assistant starter caught him and shoved him backward at the same instant that the field sprang away. Seabiscuit came out late, only to be bumped by a straggling horse to his outside. By the time he recovered, he was in seventh, four lengths behind Aneroid and Indian Broom.

Pollard jerked partially upright, his hair mussed from the pillow. "Biscuit!" he shouted. "Get going, Biscuit!" He wiggled closer to the radio. Word came that Seabiscuit was inching forward, and he relaxed a little.

Workman held Seabiscuit back, around the first turn and down the long backstretch. On the far turn, he began sweeping around the field. As Seabiscuit pulled into the stretch, only Indian Broom and Aneroid remained to be caught. "Here comes Seabiscuit!" shouted McCarthy, and the crowd noise echoed into Pollard's hospital room. "Go get those bums, Seabiscuit!" Pollard sang out. "Get 'em, you old devil!"

In the stands, Smith was focusing on Workman's hands. The jockey was not cocking his whip. He thought he didn't need to. Seabiscuit was picking off horses and running freely beneath him. In midstretch he collared Indian Broom, then took aim at Aneroid, who was alone on the lead but weakening. They clipped past the seventy-yard pole. Seabiscuit was lopping a foot off of Aneroid's lead with every stride, but room was running out. Workman thought he would get there. Smith felt the anger rising in him. He could see that the horse was fooling around, playing with Aneroid. Workman didn't seem to notice. He just *sat* there. The whip lay flat on Seabiscuit's neck.

"Aneroid is leading, still leading," chanted McCarthy. Pollard rose up as if in the saddle, yanking at the pulley holding his arm. The sheets slid from his body and the sandbags tumbled free as he bent before the radio. "Go get him, Biscuit!" he pleaded. "You broke his heart once. Break it again." He crouched over the bed, as if moving over his horse. His forehead was puckered in sweat.

Smith was livid. The whip was sitting there in Workman's hand. Seabiscuit's ears were flicking around; the horse seemed to be waiting for the signal to go for the kill. It never came. Aneroid was driving with everything he had, and Seabiscuit was just jogging with him, a cat batting a stunned mouse. He was having a fine time. His head was still behind. He edged up a little as the wire came, but he was too late. Aneroid won by a short neck.

Pollard wilted into his pillows, drenched in sweat. "It isn't right," he said.

A nurse rushed in and began hoisting the sandbags back on the bed. "Who finished second?" she asked.

"Biscuit did."

"I told you you should have been on him," she replied.

"Maybe," said Pollard. "Only Workman gave him a good ride. . . . It wasn't his fault."

A moment later Pollard was tense again. "By God, maybe there is some way I can get this shoulder fixed up for next Saturday. [Do] you think so? If only I could. I can try." He smiled. "That's talking like a child, isn't it?" he said.

The nurse left. Pollard's shoulder began to throb. He realized that he had wrenched it during the race. He reached for a black cord pinned to his sheet and buzzed the nurse's station. When the nurse returned, he pleaded with her to sneak him a beer. "Just one, nursie," he said. "I sure desire one. I just went through hell."

Pollard had always been, like virtually everyone else at the track, a social drinker, imbibing just enough to be happy and noisy on week-end outings with other jockeys but not enough to become dependent. But analgesia was in its infancy in the 1930s. Pollard's injuries, involving fragmented bones that ground together each time he moved, were agonizing, and medicine offered few practical solutions. He must have been suffering just as much emotionally. For the first time since he was fifteen, Pollard was deprived of the intoxicating rush of riding.

Alcohol brought relief. Pollard began drinking more regularly and heavily. He was on the road to alcoholism.

At Santa Anita the press came down hard on Workman. He admitted his mistake. Pollard supported him publicly. Howard announced that he was satisfied with Workman and that the jockey would retain the mount for the Santa Anita Handicap.

He spoke too soon. Smith was hopping mad. He couldn't believe that Workman hadn't noticed Seabiscuit pricking his ears, an unmistakable sign that a horse is not concentrating. And he was furious that the jockey had disobeyed his instructions. Sitting in his tack room two days after the race, he vented his frustrations. "Workman must have ridden according to other orders. He didn't obey mine," he sniped. "Seabiscuit will win the Santa Anita Handicap. He is the best horse. He is fit and he is ready. All I want is a jockey who will obey my orders." Howard, uncomfortable with Smith's excoriation of Workman, made a point of praising the jockey to reporters. He wanted to stay with Workman, arguing that the rider wouldn't make the same mistake twice. Smith dug in: Workman had to go. Workman went, bitterly complaining that he had ridden the horse exactly as Pollard had told him to.

On February 28 Smith tacked up Seabiscuit and guided him to the track before a Monday crowd. Howard and Alfred Vanderbilt joined them. Vanderbilt was presenting Seabiscuit with the *Horse and Horseman* plaque for Horse of the Year. They had no jockey to complete the picture, so Smith boosted Farrell Jones up on Seabiscuit. After a parade before the crowd and a brief, somewhat subdued ceremony in which Vanderbilt called Seabiscuit "the greatest horse of the year in America," they took Seabiscuit back to his stall. Everybody knew that the *Horse and Horseman* award wasn't the one that counted.

One good thing had happened to Seabiscuit in the San Antonio. Today, with George Woolf aboard, had run a miserable race. Knowing that Pollard was going to bat for him with Seabiscuit's connections, Woolf had been trying everything he could think of to get out of his contract to ride Today in the hundred-grander, including offering $1,000 to the horse's owner. The skill of a man like Woolf was worth a lot more than $1,000 in a $100,000 race, and the owner turned down the offer. But in the San Antonio Today ran so abysmally that his trainer concluded he had no chance in the Santa Anita Handicap. He released Woolf from his obligations. Smith and Pollard were positive that Woolf was the right man for Seabiscuit. Howard wanted proof.

Woolf gave him just that. In a meeting a few hours after the *Horse and Horseman* award presentation, the Iceman offered Smith and Howard a glimpse into the mind of a riding genius. He laid out all of Seabiscuit's predilections and weaknesses in great detail. Howard was dumbfounded. Woolf knew more about his horse than he did. Howard asked him how he could possibly have known so much. Woolf replied that his seat to the rear of Seabiscuit in several of his winning races had given him a good spot from which to study the horse and he had simply taken the opportunity. He also recalled in surprising detail his one unpleasant ride on Seabiscuit three years earlier, when the horse was still with Fitzsimmons. He described how he would ride the horse if given the chance. Howard and Smith were speechless. Woolf had just told them exactly what they were about to tell him. Woolf had the job.

Woolf left his new employers with a prediction. If the track was fast in the Santa Anita Handicap, he'd win it.

Woolf stopped off at a betting venue and bought a ticket on Seabiscuit, to win. Then he drove over to St. Luke's Hospital and gave the ticket to Pollard. The two old friends sat together, talking of Seabiscuit. Woolf was deeply grateful for Pollard's help in getting him the mount.

He made Pollard a promise. If Seabiscuit won, he'd split the riding fee with him; 10 percent of the $100,000 purse.

*With a quarter of a mile to go, Seabiscuit (left) takes the lead
in the 1938 Santa Anita Handicap. Stagehand
(second from left) is directly behind him.*
(© BETTMANN/CORBIS)

CHAPTER 12

All I Need Is Luck

I t was raining again. Through the week before the 1938 Santa Anita Handicap, the barn roof hummed with the downpour. Los Angeles flooded. The city and track were completely cut off from all wire service. Smith sat on the damp shed row day and night, hovering around Seabiscuit, and slowly grew ill. Howard found him there, nursing a frightening cough. He urged him to see a doctor. Smith waved him away and stayed at work. As the days passed, the cough grew worse until Howard arrived one day and found Smith barely able to stand. Howard rushed to a telephone to summon an ambulance. But when it arrived, Smith refused to leave his horses. No amount of encouragement from Howard could get him to budge. The ambulance crew left, and Smith went back to work. Gradually, the cough quieted.

Everyone was jumpy. Seabiscuit snoozed behind an impenetrable wall of security. A man slept inside his stall at night. Howard hired three guards to stand by the stall, one in the daytime, two at night. The second nighttime guard was under orders to keep the first one talking so neither of them would doze off. Smith had them all on a password system, and anyone who came near was aggressively questioned. A police dog named Silver, trained to pace up and down the shed row, stood patrol. Seabiscuit lived behind an electric stall door that Smith had designed and built himself. Consisting of wire mesh stretching from floor to ceiling, it was rigged to set off a siren if anyone tampered with it. "A brigade of Chicago gorillas armed with Tommy guns might be able to get to Seabiscuit—after shooting down everybody on the lot," said Howard. "But one man trying to sponge Seabiscuit would have about as much chance as a kindergarten kid trying to jimmy his way into the United States mint with a fountain pen."

Seabiscuit was safe, but Woolf was not. Two days before the race, the police informed him that someone was trying to kidnap him. The unidentified perpetrators planned to injure him, drug him, or hold him hostage on the day of the race, preventing him from riding and leaving Howard and Smith little time to find a qualified jockey. Their hope was that without Woolf, Seabiscuit would lose, enabling wagers on long shots to pay off.

The frightening thing was that the kidnappers had not been identified. Anyone with whom Woolf came into contact could be after him. Woolf promptly hired two burly bodyguards. For two days they tailed him everywhere.

Friday morning the rains broke. The track was an oval of standing water. The superintendent dragged out the asphalt-baking machines and slowly dried the course. The post positions were drawn. Seabiscuit was again unlucky. He drew post thirteen, well outside in the nineteen-horse field.

On the night before the race, Woolf and his bodyguards joined Smith at Pollard's bedside. The three talked long and late of the race, the most formidable of Seabiscuit's life. Every single top horse in training, save War Admiral, was in the field. Seabiscuit's 130-pound assignment was by far the highest weight. A colt named Stagehand, the early favorite for the 1938 Kentucky Derby, had been assigned just 100 pounds, the lowest possible impost. He had slipped into the race with such a light assignment by virtue of a peculiarity in the race's weight system. To make it easier for the handlers of top horses to plan for their race, Santa Anita officials had assigned the weights two months before, on December 15. On that date, Stagehand's 100-pound impost was justified; he was only two years old, had never won or even run particularly well in any race, and he was about to begin 1938 as a claimer. His opening odds were 150 to 1. But since December he had turned three and reeled off four sensational victories, including one in the $50,000 Santa Anita Derby, making his hundred-grander weight assignment grossly unfair. The impost was so low that trainer Earl Sande had to send all the way to Miami to get a tiny smudge of a man named Nick Wall, the only top rider in the country who could make the weight.

A thirty-pound weight concession to Stagehand might be insurmountable, and Woolf knew it. Stagehand was the horse to beat.

On the morning of the 1938 Santa Anita Handicap, the Howards drove over to St. Luke's Hospital. Pollard, wan and frail, sat in a wheelchair and waited for them. In what must have been an excruciating effort, he had pulled a neat white dress shirt and tie over his ravaged chest. He had combed his hair, shaved, and slid a dark suit jacket over one arm, leaving the other jacket arm to hang free over his sling. Two weeks before, as he swung his leg over Fair Knightess's back, he had looked boyish for his twenty-eight years. Now he was suddenly and permanently old. The Howards brought him to their car and saw him inside. Pollard had no business being out of bed at all, but he had talked his doctors into letting him attend the race on the condition that two of them, plus a nurse, go with him.

They rolled him into Santa Anita. Seventy thousand fans swarmed the plant. Marcela accompanied Pollard up through the grandstand. At the top they stopped. A long catwalk, arching over the crowd, stood between them and the announcer's booth. The chair would not fit on it. Slowly, painfully, Pollard rose from the chair and limped along the catwalk, pursued by his doctors and nurse.

Someone in the crowd below looked up and recognized him. He nudged another fan and pointed to the jockey, and suddenly the whole crowd was gazing up at him. Someone yelled his name and began to clap. One clapper became two, then three. Soon the whole grandstand was cheering wildly. Pollard straightened himself up and bowed.

Pollard and Marcela arrived at the end of the catwalk, and the cheering subsided. Everyone must have expected Marcela to drop the redhead off there; ahead of her was the press box, den of the exclusively male radio and newspaper corps. No woman had ever entered it without being summarily booted out.

To general surprise, Marcela strode right in. As usual, she pulled it off. If anyone objected to her presence, no one said so; one admiring reporter proposed giving her a medal for bravery. But she didn't stay long. She had planned to watch the race with Pollard in the announcer's booth, where Clem McCarthy would call the race for national radio. But she was losing her nerve. The booth was on the roof of the track, up a twelve-foot ladder, but it wasn't the climb that worried her. She was terrified that in the excitement of the race she would scream into the caller's microphone.

"I can't stand this," she said. Her hands were shaking. "It's not the race that's got me at the moment. Waiting for the start is going to be bad enough, but that microphone in there is worse."

She turned and fled toward the catwalk. Gliding up ahead of her was Bing Crosby, decked out to see his Ligaroti contest the race. The Seabiscuit and Ligaroti camps had developed a lively, good-natured rivalry; Lin Howard had placed a bank-breaking side bet with his father over which horse would finish ahead of the other. Bing snagged Marcela's arm.

"Marcela," he cooed, "you come right in here and tell the people how far Seabiscuit is going to beat Ligaroti."

"That'll be easy," she replied, relaxing some and turning back to the reporters. "By about a quarter of a mile." Crosby led her back in and she started up the ladder, the wind snapping her dress around her legs. Somehow, they hoisted Pollard up the ladder. Marcela sat down with him. They tried to distract each other from their trepidation.

At the door of the jockeys' room, Woolf shed his bodyguards. His mind was full of Stagehand. He made a mental note. Stagehand would carry the same colors as his nearly identical full brother, Sceneshifter, but to enable the race caller to discriminate between them, Stagehand's jockey was to wear a white cap, Sceneshifter's a red one. Woolf walked down to the paddock, where Clem McCarthy awaited him, microphone in hand for a live interview. All I need is luck, Woolf told a rapt audience. Seabiscuit will do the rest.

Howard and Smith saw Seabiscuit and Woolf onto the track, then filed up into Howard's private box. They would say nothing to each other for the next 121 seconds.

As Seabiscuit broke from the gate, he was immediately bashed inward by Count Atlas, a hopeless long shot emerging from the stall to his right. Seabiscuit was knocked nearly to the ground. As he staggered sideways, Count Atlas sped up in front of him, then abruptly cut left and slowed down, pushing back into him again. Seabiscuit stumbled badly, his head ducking, and Woolf was vaulted up onto his neck. For a terrible moment, Woolf clung to Seabiscuit's neck, a millimeter from falling off, then regained his balance. As he shinnied back in the saddle, Count Atlas leaned hard into Seabiscuit, buffeting his right side as the field bounded away from them. For a sixteenth of a mile, Count Atlas lay over on Seabiscuit's shoulder, his head and neck thrust to the left, preventing Seabiscuit from moving up. Woolf was enraged. Seabiscuit was struggling to push Count Atlas off of him, the front-runners were disappearing in the distance, and his chances of winning were all but dashed.

Swinging his whip high in the air, he walloped it down as hard as he could on the buttocks of Count Atlas's jockey, Johnny Adams, then lifted it up and smacked it down again. Down on the rail, obscured by the pack of horses, he could not be seen by the stewards or the crowd. But Adams, who would ride back to the scales sporting angry welts, certainly felt it. He jerked Count Atlas's head to the right. Seabiscuit broke free.

Finally back in his stirrups and straightened out, Woolf despaired over his position. Seabiscuit was in twelfth place, eight lengths behind the leaders. He was trapped in a pack of stragglers. Woolf had no option but to wait for a hole to break ahead of him. He sat still, his eyes pinned on the white cap bobbing ahead.

On the backstretch, a slender, jagged avenue through a cluster of horses opened before him. Woolf saw the white cap slipping out of reach and feared that this narrow path would be his only chance to break loose. With horses surging in and out, it was likely to vanish in an instant. To seize this opportunity, Woolf would have to reach for everything Seabiscuit had. Accelerating hard under high weight burns vast reserves of energy. Horses carrying the kind of weight Seabiscuit was packing cannot afford to lose momentum. If Woolf sent his mount to top speed, he knew he was going to have to keep him going until the end of the race. A general rule of racing is that virtually no horse can sustain his maximum speed for more than three eighths of a mile. The Santa Anita Handicap was a grueling mile and a quarter, and Seabiscuit still had more than three quarters of a mile to go. Woolf faced a critical decision. If he took the lane opening ahead of him, Seabiscuit would almost certainly become exhausted in the home-stretch, leaving himself vulnerable to closers. If he waited, Stagehand might be long gone by the time he launched his bid. Woolf made his choice. He pointed Seabiscuit's nose at the gap and asked him to go through.

The response was explosive. Pent up from trailing the field, Sea-biscuit spun through the gap like a bullet rifling down a barrel. Woolf balanced over his neck and steered him deftly through the pack, on the hunt for the white cap. The quarters were so close and the speed so high that the jockey had to cut sharply in and out to avoid running up into the hind legs of horses. As Seabiscuit streaked past the three-quarter pole, several clockers saw what was happening and jammed their thumbs down on their stopwatches. In the announcer's booth, McCarthy caught sight of the horse. "Seabiscuit! He's coming through! He's cutting the others down like a whirlwind!"

Woolf rolled up alongside the jockey in the white cap. He didn't have a chance to look at him. Seabiscuit was moving so fast that the jockey and his mount were behind him in an instant. Seabiscuit over-took a pack of horses and stretched out for front-running Aneroid, his last obstacle. The two ran side by side. They flew to the quarter pole, still sustaining a fearsome clip. The clockers banged their thumbs down on their stopwatches. The hands stared back at them: $44\frac{1}{5}$.

In the middle stage of a grueling distance race, Seabiscuit had broken the half-mile world record by two seconds, the equivalent of more than thirteen lengths. It may be the greatest display of raw speed ever seen in Thoroughbred racing.

Scorching around the far turn, Seabiscuit had the lead. The crowd was on its feet. Woolf had gambled everything, and it seemed to have worked. The field was in disarray behind him, dropping back in an undulating mass.

From the far outside, Woolf felt something coming. He turned in the saddle and looked back. It was a lone horse, shaking loose from the pack and driving toward Seabiscuit as Rosemont had done a year before. Woolf studied the horse's head, then straightened out. He knew that face: a long aristocratic nose, mahogany deepening to black at the muzzle. But the silks on the rider didn't match. He had to be wrong. He swung his head back and looked again. There was no mistake.

It was Stagehand.

The realization shivered through Woolf: The caps of Stagehand and Sceneshifter had been switched. All the way around the track, the horse Woolf thought he had been chasing had in fact been behind him, stalking him. Woolf had spent Seabiscuit's rally much too early, in pursuit of the wrong horse.

Up in the grandstand, Stagehand's trainer, Earl Sande, realized what was happening. "We've got the race!" he shouted. Nick Wall, aboard Stagehand, thought he had it too. He had sat behind Seabiscuit, watched him dash off on the backstretch, and thought that Woolf had lost his head. He was sure that Seabiscuit was finished. Wall was sitting on a fresh, perfectly conditioned horse, under a feather impost, just dropping down into his run. He thought: *I am going to gallop by him and win as I please.*

Streaking down the homestretch, Woolf was a crimson blur on Seabiscuit's back, lifting him, holding him together, begging him for more, dropping flat to lie under the wind. Wall wound Stagehand up to top speed, his eyes fixed on Woolf's back. He couldn't understand it: His horse was tearing over the track, but he was barely gaining. Gradually, he snipped away at the distance between them. They drew even. Seabiscuit disappeared, his compact body eclipsed from the crowd's view by Stagehand's long, dark form. It seemed that Stagehand would surely rush right by and that Seabiscuit would reappear in his wake. Up in the stands, Pollard thought it was over.

But Seabiscuit did not appear. For as long as they lived, spectators would regard what they saw next as the most extraordinary feat they ever witnessed in sport. They recognized it all at once: Seabiscuit, under a tremendous load, having already run at world-record speed for most of the race, *accelerated*. He surged forward with such power that it was as if, said one witness, "he were breaking from the gate again." Stagehand could not shake him.

The crowd was in a frenzy. McCarthy, one of the few commentators who had not mistaken Stagehand for Sceneshifter, was screaming himself hoarse. "It's Seabiscuit and Stagehand! They're coming away! It's all between them! . . . They're almost here! Stagehand is running stronger. . . . But Seabiscuit won't yield! How he tries!"

It was too much for Pollard. He twisted in his chair and gasped for air, terrified, overjoyed. He was choking on it. His heart was thumping so hard in his chest that for a moment he wondered if it would fail, if he would die right there in the announcer's booth, the race still playing out beneath him. Marcela went white and shrieked. Someone behind her, remembering the microphone, clapped a hand over her mouth. Below them, Howard stood absolutely still. His binoculars had fallen from his hands.

The rest of the field dropped into the distance. Stagehand and Seabiscuit drove side by side, blazing through a final quarter in 24⅕ seconds, astounding for a distance race. Wall was hammering Stagehand at Seabiscuit, but Seabiscuit was hanging up against him and giving it right back, ferocious, head down, ears pinned. Woolf was strung flat over Seabiscuit's back, driving for all his worth. As the wire neared, the horses' heads bobbed out of time, so that the lead was traded every few feet. They hit the line together.

Again, no one was sure who had won. There was the long wait, the murmuring crowd, the timer blinking a new track record, and again, the soft whir of the finish photo slipping down to the stewards. The photo was murky, indistinct. The stewards made their ruling.

The winner was Stagehand.

Atop the grandstand, Marcela and Red huddled together and wept. The jockey pulled himself up and smiled. "He tried with every ounce, with every muscle in his body," he later said. "I am proud of my horse."

Howard and Smith sat cold and still in their box. By two noses in two runnings of the race he and his wife most wanted to win, Howard had lost $182,150, and Seabiscuit had been denied the title of history's greatest money winner. Howard pushed out a faint laugh. "Hell," he said. "We can't win all the time."

The press box wilted. Seabiscuit had delivered what many of them thought was the greatest performance in racing history, and had lost simply because of a fluke in the weight system, and a foul from another horse. "The best horse," wrote turf scribe Salvator, "was unjustly beaten."

Stagehand cantered back to the winner's circle. "That's the greatest racehorse in the world," Nick Wall would say of Seabiscuit. "He had enough trouble to stop a locomotive. . . . At equal weights, there's nothing that wears racing plates that's a mortal to beat him."

Seabiscuit returned to the grandstand, where Smith and the Howards awaited him. Woolf was rigid with rage. He slid down and dragged his kangaroo-leather saddle off of Seabiscuit, so angry over the foul from Count Atlas that he could barely speak. It was the first time in his ten-year career that he had been beaten in a photo finish of a stakes race.

Howard looked at Seabiscuit. The horse's head was high, and light played in his eyes. He didn't know he had lost. Howard felt confidence swell in himself once more.

"We'll try again," he said. "Next time we'll win it."

Seabiscuit, Tom Smith, and C. S. Howard
(© BETTMANN/CORBIS)

CHAPTER 13

Hardball

A few minutes after Seabiscuit lost, the Howards reeled out of Santa Anita, changed into formal attire, raised their chins once again, and walked into the Santa Anita Turf Club Ball, held in honor of Stagehand's victory. There was a buzz in the room. Hours before, beneath the swaying palms of Florida's Hialeah Park, War Admiral had logged his tenth consecutive victory, winning the Widener Handicap with ease. The Triple Crown winner had become so unruly that before many of his races, the battered assistant starters gave up on loading him into the gate and instead let him walk up to the break on the far outside of the gate while the other horses started from a standstill inside it. But once under way, he was better than ever. In the Widener, he had delivered a smashing performance, and everyone was comparing it to Seabiscuit's extraordinary run in the Santa Anita Handicap. The two horses were the talk of the ball and the nation. The next morning magazines and newspapers all over the country would be running side-by-side photographs of War Admiral's victory and Seabiscuit's defeat. Scores of sports columns in publications of every stripe focused on the merits of the two horses. The prospect of a meeting between the two was becoming an international obsession. All evening, reporters circled around Howard, asking if he'd be willing to match his horse against Riddle's colt. Howard, as always, said yes.

After the ball the operators of California's new Hollywood Park approached him with a formal match race proposal. Howard told them that if they could get Riddle on board, Seabiscuit was in. The officials agreed to consult Riddle at his home in Pennsylvania. Howard waited to see what would happen. Again, nothing did.

Howard's patience had run out. For a year he had practically pleaded for a match on any terms, but Riddle remained uninterested. Riddle did not believe that Seabiscuit was in War Admiral's league and may have felt that by agreeing to run against a western horse in a match race, he would be demeaning his colt. Even if he had held a higher opinion of Seabiscuit, he had nothing to gain from a match race. War Admiral had already won the Horse of the Year title without having to meet Seabiscuit. Because of the championship voters' pronounced bias toward eastern horses in general and War Admiral in particular, Seabiscuit almost certainly could not dethrone the Horse of the Year without beating him on the track. War Admiral was sucking up a fortune in purse money and barely needed to extend himself against the horses he did run against—in many of his races only two or three owners were willing to send their horses out to face him. Riddle had no reason to disrupt his colt's schedule to take on Seabiscuit and accept a risk, however small, that a fluke would cost his horse the championship. If Seabiscuit showed up for one of War Admiral's scheduled full-field races, that was fine, but Riddle could see no reason why he should agree to a match.

Howard was in the opposite position. Like Riddle, he understood that Seabiscuit had to conquer War Admiral on the track to be deemed his superior in the championship voting and in history. With so much riding on the meeting, he and Smith did not want their horse to meet War Admiral in a full-field race, in which he would run the risk of a third horse interfering with him, as Count Atlas had done in the hundred-grander. The risk of interference was not the same for each horse. War Admiral's early speed was so overpowering that he was nearly always able to blast out to a lone lead, on the rail and away from other horses, and the walk-up starts ensured that he broke by himself, unhindered by his opponents. In contrast, Seabiscuit broke with the rest of the field, and as a pace-stalker, he had to make his run from out of the crowded pack. Howard needed a match race, and he was ready to force the issue.

His target was a bespectacled former journalist named Herbert Bayard Swope, chairman of the New York Racing Commission, the governing body of War Admiral's home turf. If anyone could get the match arranged, Swope could. One afternoon in early March of 1938 Howard sat down with Swope and told him that he wanted Seabiscuit to meet War Admiral, and he wanted Swope to use his influence to arrange it. Swope suggested that he enter Seabiscuit in the Suburban Handicap at Belmont Park, in which War Admiral would meet a full field, and said he would try to get the purse raised from $20,000 to $50,000. It was not the scenario that Howard wanted, but he sensed it was not yet time to push the issue. He told Swope to work on it, and if things moved forward, they could talk again. Swope agreed.

In the aftermath of the Santa Anita Handicap, everyone at the track was buzzing about the foul Count Atlas had committed against Seabiscuit. Several reporters, remembering the foiled attempts to kidnap Woolf and tamper with Seabiscuit, speculated that the foul was the result of a race-fixing conspiracy. Santa Anita had made films of the race, but the stewards had not looked at them. A group of newspapermen petitioned the stewards to see the films. Expecting to see only Count Atlas fouling Seabiscuit, the newspapermen saw that and something more. They gave the films back with hearty encouragement that the stewards have a look. The stewards watched the race.

The film showed it clearly: Woolf had lifted his whip up and repeatedly cracked Johnny Adams on the flanks. Woolf was called on the carpet. When asked if he had hit Adams, he said sure he had, explaining that Adams had been laying his horse over on Seabiscuit. Woolf was suspended for the rest of the meet. Adams was not penalized.

Howard was furious. "If Woolf did not protect Seabiscuit," he seethed, "it was a cinch the stewards wouldn't. I notice that while Woolf has been set down, Adams still rides. Hence I think that it was up to Woolf to protect his own mount. It was unfortunate that he had to strike Adams, but there was no recourse. I don't blame Woolf for not standing idly by and allowing another rider to ruin his chances in a $100,000 race.

"Guess we'll have to teach the Biscuit to act up at the post—to kick and rear and plunge and otherwise misbehave himself," he said bitterly. "Then he'll be allowed to start outside the gate, where he can break free without risk of interference. That's War Admiral's act, and it seems to be an effective one. When they're out to get your horse you're a lot better off having him away from the crowd, I'm beginning to think."

His words fell upon deaf ears. Howard had to find a new jockey, and right away. He had accepted an invitation to run Seabiscuit in Tijuana during Woolf's suspension. In 1934, when Mexico banned gambling, the lively Tijuana that Woolf and Pollard had known faded. The recent relegalization of racing had done little to bring back the town's glory days. Agua Caliente Race Track, built for $3 million in 1929 but sold for just $140,000 in 1936, remained a shadow of its former self. Then Caliente official Gene Normile came up with the idea of renewing the track's namesake championship race and inviting Seabiscuit down for it. There was no surer sell in all of sports. Howard could hardly refuse. After the hundred-grander, Santa Anita's racing secretary had assigned Seabiscuit 135 pounds for the San Juan Capistrano, his next scheduled race. Howard never considered running his horse under such an impost, and Normile made the choice easier. Because Mexican racing officials were not bound by the mandate that every horse carry at least 100 pounds, they could give Seabiscuit 130 while assigning other horses fewer than 100 if they needed to. Howard accepted. Although still angry over Woolf's suspension, Howard didn't want to court more trouble with California racing officials by hiring Woolf for the Mexican race. California was still Seabiscuit's home base. With Smith's approval, Howard hired Spec Richardson to ride.

Normile had pulled off a coup in getting Seabiscuit to come down for the Agua Caliente Handicap, but now he faced another quandary. No one was willing to run against Howard's horse. Normile sweetened the pot for second through fifth places and offered extraordinary breaks in the weights, giving them between twenty-two and thirty-two fewer pounds than Seabiscuit. That did the trick: seven other horses were entered to try for second place.

Team Seabiscuit arrived in high style. Howard motored down in the first of eight Buick limousine coaches packed with thirty of his closest friends. Seabiscuit rolled in, the fans massing by the sides of his van like snowdrifts. The van door slid open, the horse appeared, the flashbulbs crackled, and the crowd pushed forward. Accompanied by two Pinkerton guards, Seabiscuit swept down the ramp and into the mob. He struck a handsome pose and held it. He had been posed so often that he seemed to know what was wanted of him when the press corps buzzed around, prompting the reporters to dub him "Movie Star." As always, he dutifully raised his head, pricked his ears, fanned his tail, and stood square when he saw the cameras raised. When he heard the shutters click, he relaxed. The track photographer asked for a profile shot, and Seabiscuit was turned for it. Each time the man prepared to snap the shot, the horse cocked his head and looked at the camera. The photographer tried hiding in the bushes while his assistant distracted the horse, but again Seabiscuit swung his head around to stare at him. After eight minutes, Smith pulled out a carrot and thrust it in the hand of the assistant. "Here," he said. "He loves these. Hold it just out of reach and let your man take the picture." It worked.

Pollard was finally well enough to travel and returned to the town in which he had once reigned supreme. He found it shriveled and spent. The great racetrack was now a hollow, rattling place. Most of the bars and shops that had sprung up around it had shuttered their doors. The pulsing avenues down which Woolf had steered his purring Studebakers and Cords were wind-whipped and quiet. Even the Molino Rojo girls were gone. The home of glorious smoke-blowing women had been born again, transformed into, of all things, a schoolhouse. It would later become a church. One of the few healthy businesses in town was the sad trade in divorces, handled quickly and easily in cold offices that had once been noisy saloons.

But for one afternoon in the spring of 1938, Seabiscuit resurrected the old Tijuana and Agua Caliente. Long before "Seabiscuit Day," the

Americans began arriving. Hotels filled up with Scabiscuit fans hailing from all over the United States. Officials, recognizing that they were playing host to the most adored visitor ever to cross city limits, rushed to prepare. The railroads scheduled special trains to carry the masses of humanity southward. Crews worked to widen all roads leading in from California. The track installed additional mutuel windows, constructed about a dozen bookmaking facilities in the infield, opened up all vacant areas of the clubhouse, and hired an army of extra personnel. Though the parking lot could hold fifteen thousand auto-mobiles, officials knew that that wouldn't be nearly enough. They began clearing out space for additional parking.

Their efforts didn't make much difference. Just after dawn on race day, March 27, the first headlights blinked over the border crossing. By noon, the Road to Hell was snarled with Seabiscuit fans. Border police were swamped, trying in vain to ease the gridlock by dividing traffic into four lanes. Within a few hours, cars had backed up from the track entrance all the way to the border. At the track, the additional parking was used up early in the day, and spectators began leav-ing their cars on the shoulders of the road and hiking in. When the shoulders filled up, they fanned out into the city golf club, then right onto residential lawns. Long before the first race, the track was filled well beyond capacity with the largest attendance in its history. The congregation at the paddock alone was greater than the track's total attendance the day before.

The mob devoured all the food in the clubhouse. They set an all-time wagering record and bet Seabiscuit down to the lowest odds ever seen at Caliente. The grandstand was soon so crammed that just before the race, masses of suffocating fans spilled over the fence and onto the racetrack. Unable to wedge them back into the grandstand, officials herded them into the infield. Police were stationed along the rails to prevent fans from seeping back onto the track in front of the horses. Photographers circled the course, their cameras ready.

The race was over the instant it began. Seabiscuit bounded out of the gate in front and galloped away from his competition. Bored, he began swinging his head around. According to Richardson, each time the horse passed a photographer, he would prick up his ears and hoist his tail until the rider reminded him of what he was there for. To enthusiastic applause, Seabiscuit cantered home. Richardson had a miserable time trying to pull him to a stop and turn him back toward the winner's circle, where Howard, Smith, and Bing Crosby awaited him. Someone swore that as Bing handed the gold trophy to Howard, Tom Smith smiled. It was only a rumor.

The crowds swarmed onto the roads once again, pausing to clean out Caesar's restaurant of every morsel of food well before the dinner hour. Cars were still stacked up at the border long into the night. It took two days for the town to clean up.

On March 29, 1938, two days after the Caliente triumph, the Sea-biscuit train drew into Tanforan. Several hundred fans were waiting. Howard traveled over to Bay Meadows. There he received a wire from Swope, who had a pleasant surprise. He had been true to his word. He had sold Belmont chief Joseph Widener on a full-field meeting between Seabiscuit and War Admiral in the Suburban Handicap on Memorial Day, May 30, with an augmented purse of $50,000. Now that the issue was in the works and Belmont was moving forward, Howard sensed that it was time to play hardball. He picked up the phone and called Swope.

After agitating for so long for the race, he said no to Swope's proposal. He made a string of demands. He wanted a one-on-one race. He wanted it run at Belmont, over a mile and a quarter, but not on Memorial Day, which would conflict with Seabiscuit's schedule. He suggested sometime between September 15 and October 1. He wanted the horses to carry equal weights, proposing 126 pounds but leaving himself open to any weight Riddle wanted, so long as both horses carried the same. And he wanted a much, much bigger purse. When Swope heard Howard's figure, he must have blanched.

One hundred thousand dollars.

Howard wasn't kidding. If Swope failed to get that much, Howard said, he could take Seabiscuit to a certain western track, which had already offered such a sum. Howard, who had long felt victimized by eastern disdain for western racing, now tried to exploit it. "Belmont Park, the country's leading racetrack," he said, "should be willing to at least meet that figure."

It was an audacious play. He was asking for a king's ransom, and he was bluffing. Hollywood Park had indeed mentioned $100,000, but Howard knew that Samuel Riddle would never take his horse west to race. He was counting on Swope's ignorance of that fact.

Howard knew he had to find a way to give Riddle a strong interest in running, so he had done his homework. He approached Riddle as he approached the marketplace, tailoring the proposal to the owner's desires. Horses have strong preferences for particular courses, and Belmont was War Admiral's home track, the site of his greatest performance. A mile and a quarter was War Admiral's optimal distance. Howard had learned that Riddle shared his ambition to break Sun Beau's all-time earnings record by season's end; the $100,000 purse would be highly appealing. And he knew that Riddle was deeply concerned about the weight his horse was asked to carry. Before the Widener Handicap, War Admiral had never carried more than 128 pounds. Riddle set a limit of 130, ranted at the Hialeah racing secretary when the horse received just that, then balked when another track's secretary assigned the horse 132 pounds for a later race. The weight issue was putting War Admiral's schedule in doubt, and Howard's offer to run under any weight provided an alternative. Riddle's image, never wonderful, also stood to benefit. With this proposal, he would be able to accept every one of Howard's conditions, casting himself as the good guy who was sportingly making concessions to his demanding opponent, even though it was he who was getting the bargain. Finally, Howard's proposal gave Riddle a built-in excuse. If War Admiral lost, Riddle could always say that Howard had dictated the terms of the race. It was an offer that was very hard to refuse.

It also must have been very hard to make. In his drive to bring Riddle to the table, Howard was gambling with his own horse's chances. Howard much preferred that the race be held in the West. If it were held at Belmont, Seabiscuit would have to endure a five-day,

3,200-mile train trip to get there. Belmont posed another problem. Seabiscuit had run there only once, under Fitzsimmons's care, and he had been humiliated. Smith warned Howard that Belmont's mile-and-a-half circumference was so large that the race would be run around just one turn, instead of the two turns necessary to complete a mile and one quarter at every other track in America. One of Seabiscuit's major weapons was his supremacy at running turns; racing around just one turn at Belmont would deprive him of one of his strengths. There was a strong possibility that if Howard secured the match race on these terms, his horse would be too compromised to win. It was a daring play, but Howard felt it was his only chance.

Swope must have swallowed hard. Howard had masterminded a situation that made refusal costly. Led to believe that Howard had very different conditions in mind, Swope had already sent Belmont officials scurrying to arrange a meeting between the two horses, and if the deal fell through now, his reputation within the organization might be tarnished. The reaction of the public was another problem. News of the race negotiations had broken the day before—Howard had undoubtedly leaked it to the press—and the response was nationwide jubilation. Telegrams applauding the proposal were flooding the Racing Commission offices. The papers were full of stories and cartoons about the prospect of the match. The phone in Swope's office never stopped ringing. Belmont was already talking with CBS Radio, which was offering to broadcast the race live worldwide, predicting that twenty million sets would be tuned to it. If the deal died now, there might be a public backlash against Belmont. Finally, Howard had raised the mortifying possibility that the most spectacular draws in racing would stage their epic meeting in the West, costing Belmont the opportunity to host what promised to be one of the greatest and most heavily attended sporting events ever held.

Swope was trapped. He returned with a complete proposal that met Howard's demands to the letter. He even agreed to the $100,000 purse, winner-take-all.

Swope rushed to complete the deal. He contacted Riddle, who did not immediately get back to him. With Belmont head Joseph Widener committed to the idea, the only remaining hurdle before the track could make an official offer was C. V. Whitney, a powerful member of the Westchester Racing Association's board of directors, the governing body for Belmont. The formal vote on the proposal would be made at the April 12 board meeting, but as the majority of voters could be expected to follow Whitney's lead, his opinion was everything. Swaying him was a tall order; a staunch opponent of match races and big purses, he was likely to come out against the plan. On April 6 Widener sent the proposal by wireless to Whitney, who was on his boat, fishing off the shores of Bermuda. Widener could not reach him.

The delay proved critical. All over the United States, track managers realized that Belmont had beaten them to the punch. They hustled to put together match proposals, and Howard and Riddle were suddenly bombarded with offers. On the same day that Widener was attempting to contact Whitney to finalize a race plan, Chicago's Arlington Park made a formal proposal to Howard and Riddle for a $100,000 match race in July, months before the Belmont race date. Howard, playing them against Belmont, said he was open to any proposals.

All eyes turned to Riddle. He was, at long last, willing to negotiate. On April 6 he shipped War Admiral to Belmont. The next day he wired Swope to tell him he was coming to town the following morning. But he, too, seemed to be toying with Belmont. To Swope's distress, Riddle sent a similar telegram to an Arlington official, who rushed to New York to meet with him the same day. Judging from his comments to his associates, his remarks about Chicago's infernal July weather, and his general aversion to racing in "the West," Riddle was almost certainly not considering the Arlington offer. But he was not above making Swope sweat it out. "Why not have two races, one at Arlington, the other at Belmont?" he said. "That should please everyone."

Swope was appalled. If both races were agreed upon, Belmont's race would be of far less interest, especially if the first event proved decisive. Complaining that "the Chicago people" were muscling in on his match race, Swope went into overdrive. He sent a flurry of wires to

Howard, extolling the superb racing strip, mild fall weather, and general beauty of New York. Howard telephoned him back, reminding him that it was $100,000 or nothing. Riddle sat down with Swope. As Howard had foreseen, he loved the conditions. His only suggestion was that the race be held sooner than September, as the form of either horse might tail off before then. Swope took his request under consideration. Riddle told the Arlington officials to hold their offer open.

The critical date, April 12, neared. Everyone waited for Whitney. En route from Bermuda, he was the focus of intense pressure. The press worked on him, talking of how much revenue New York would lose if Whitney turned it down, and inviting the fans, who at this point were in agonies of anticipation, to lay the blame squarely on his shoulders if the race fell through. On the morning before the meeting, Howard cranked up the pressure. "You can tell them Seabiscuit will meet War Admiral anywhere, weight for age, track fast, from a quarter mile to a couple of miles," he said. "I have been willing for a long time. Personally, I want to know which is the best horse. And there are a million racing patrons who would like to know the answer to the same question."

"When these two meet," he continued, "whether it be at Belmont Park, Bay Meadows, Tanforan or Pumpkin Corners, they can bet me until the bell rings."

While the world awaited Whitney, an event at Tanforan introduced a new wrinkle in the match plans. Only two months after being rescued as they lay side by side on the track at Santa Anita, Red Pollard and Fair Knightess emerged from the dim interiors of the Howard barn and made their first steps back out on the racetrack. The mare, brought back from temporary paralysis by Smith's exhaustive labors, moved stiffly and hesitantly through an easy canter. She was finally out of danger. Pollard, too, was tentative. Though he presented himself as fully healed, he was barely using his left arm and his ribs were still bound in tape. Smith let him make his own choices and slipped him up on Seabiscuit's back for a few light gallops. The jockey held up well. Howard contacted his personal physicians, who scheduled Pollard for X rays on April 13.

On April 12 Whitney finally materialized at the board meeting. Out in California, Howard waited for news. After a long interval, he was handed a telegram from Whitney. The board had voted unanimously in favor of the proposal. The race would be one-on-one, though not officially a match race; by antiquated racing rules, a match had to be a purseless race. There was one change: Complying with Riddle's wishes, they would schedule the race for Memorial Day, May 30, not September. Would Howard accept? Howard telephoned him back just as Riddle walked into Whitney's office. The three men settled in to an impromptu meeting. Howard agreed to the new date but inserted a new condition: Pollard must ride. If he was not able to, the race was off. They broke without final agreement.

Over the telephone late that night, Riddle and Swope talked it out. Riddle had a habit of raising his voice to a blasting volume when on the phone. He was booming so loudly that a man in the room with Swope said he would have had to leap out the window to avoid hearing every word. In the end Riddle barked his assent. "You know very well," he bellowed at Swope, "my horse will beat the stuffing out of him." After having demanded, and received, the concession that the race be held in the spring, Riddle grumbled that his horse would really do better against an older horse in the fall. Nevertheless, he said, he was willing to go ahead with a spring race.

The following day Pollard stripped for his X rays. Howard's physicians went over them. The fractures had healed. With a lot of conditioning, the jockey might be able to ride in May.

Howard picked up the telephone at his Burlingame home and gave Swope his acceptance. The Arlington officials bowed out gracefully. The news rippled over the world. The race, anticipated to be the greatest in the sport's history, was on.

Before the meeting, there was another race to be run. Bay Meadows had arranged to hold a charity day for crippled children on the April 16 date of its namesake handicap, and Howard couldn't say no. After Seabiscuit's extraordinarily easy win in Tijuana, the Bay Meadows racing secretary had proposed assigning him 136 pounds, but Howard had intercepted him and charmed 3 pounds off of his horse's impost. Still, 133 pounds was the highest weight any horse had ever lugged in modern California racing, and every other horse in the field would be carrying at least 20 fewer pounds. The only one who was happy about it was Woolf. Despondent over Seabiscuit's loss in the Santa Anita Handicap and seizing the opportunity to eat as his diabetes dictated while his suspension was in effect, he had gorged himself on steaks and ballooned up to 128 pounds. With tack, he only just made the weight.

The entire earth seemed to wedge itself into Bay Meadows to see Seabiscuit run. The track, flooded with by far the largest crowd ever to attend a horse race in San Francisco, was overwhelmed. Officials shunted thousands into the infield but still found the track so packed that people could barely move. The grandstand became an undulating, endless sea of earth-tone fedoras and ladies' spring hats. Fans lay on, stood over, and clung to every support structure, making the track appear as if it were constructed entirely of spectators.

They ran out of programs before the third race. The supply of hot dog buns, a key barometer of fan enthusiasm, was completely exhausted by early afternoon. Attendants served the dogs up on rye bread, and when that ran out, hungry fans had to hold their dogs in old newspapers and then discarded mutuel tickets. Though officials lengthened the time between races considerably, the wagering lines were so long that many bettors never caught a glimpse of a pari-mutuel window. "One unfortunate citizen," wrote a reporter, "got in line to buy a win ticket on Patty Cake in the sixth and was considerably bewildered to find himself coming out of the melee at the end of the seventh with a hot dog." The gridlock in the parking lot was so intractable that, even though the races ended at 6:30 P.M., it would be well into Sunday morning before everyone got out of the track.

It was all worth it. Seabiscuit buried the field, demolishing the track record by 1⅗ seconds. The fans went wild, taking up a raucous cheer: "Bring on War Admiral! Bring on War Admiral!"

For Woolf, the win was bittersweet. It was, he believed, the last time he would ever sit astride this little horse. He slid from the saddle, pulled the wreath of flowers from around Seabiscuit's neck, and wrapped it around his own shoulders. The Howards stood on each side of him, laughing with the crowd. Woolf didn't smile. He paused a moment, the camera flashes flickering off his cheeks. Pollard was looking down on him from the press box. Woolf consigned the horse back to him. He walked back to the jockeys' room, slipped out of the Howard silks, and hung them up.

A few days after the Bay Meadows Handicap, the *Overland Limited* clattered to a stop at the Tanforan siding for the long trek east. Team Seabiscuit was slated to stop off in Maryland to fulfill a promise to Alfred Vanderbilt to run in Pimlico's Dixie Handicap, then go on to meet War Admiral in New York. Grooms tramped on and off the train, loading a full car to the roof with rice-straw bedding, oats, and timothy hay. A multitude stood by to see Seabiscuit off. Howard pulled up in a long Buick packed with admirers. He stepped out with a big cake in hand and gave it to the grooms, who quickly devoured it, then said good-bye to his horse. He would follow him east later. Fans brought heaps of flowers, and a woman stepped forward and braided ribbons into Seabiscuit's mane while he posed for the inevitable photographers. The ceremony over, Seabiscuit clopped into his railcar, stacked chest-deep in straw. Pumpkin followed. Smith climbed in with them and set up his customary cot beside Seabiscuit. The train pushed off. A continent away, War Admiral stood in his stall at Belmont, waiting.

As the train lurched into motion, Seabiscuit was suddenly agitated. He began circling around and around the car in distress. Unable to stop him, Smith dug up a copy of *Captain Billy's Whiz Bang* magazine and began reading aloud. Seabiscuit listened. The circling stopped. As Smith read on, the horse sank down into the bedding and slept. Smith drew up a stool and sat by him.

The trainer had a dark feeling. Since the Bay Meadows Handicap he'd had a nagging sense that the horse was not quite right. Though Seabiscuit had won the race easily, running the final quarter in a blazing twenty-four seconds flat and obliterating the track record by 1⅖ seconds, he had dragged early in the race. Woolf had needed to hustle him to keep up with the front-runners. Howard had shrugged off the slow early fractions, attributing them to the difficulty of accelerating under 133 pounds, but Smith was uneasy. It wasn't just that the horse seemed a hair off form. The trainer was worried about match race strategy.

From his years holding Irwin's horses for relay races and matches, Smith knew something about one-on-one races: If one horse could steal a commanding early lead, he almost always won. Clearly, superior breaking speed in a match race was almost always a trump card. Against ordinary horses, Seabiscuit had enough early speed, but War Admiral was no ordinary horse. He was one of the fastest-breaking horses racing had ever seen. Conventional racing wisdom holds that a horse's natural running style cannot be altered. But to have any chance against War Admiral, Smith knew he was going to have to make the habitually pace-stalking Seabiscuit, who had to fight the inertia of a much blockier heavier body, into a rocket-fast breaker.

As the train snaked eastward, Smith abruptly made a change in plans. He didn't want Seabiscuit to run in the Dixie Handicap. He needed time to prepare for the race and feel out this sense of wrongness in the horse. Howard was reluctant to break his promise to Vanderbilt, but he was not about to overrule Smith when the trainer was so certain. The itinerary was changed. Seabiscuit was going straight to Belmont to prepare for War Admiral. They could make it up to Vanderbilt later.

Rocking on his stool as the train wound over the mountains, Smith began formulating a training plan. "We've got to tear off that guy's épaulets," he said aloud, "pull the ostrich feather out of his hat and break his sword in two early or we'll never even get close enough to the Admiral to give him the sailor's farewell."

Almost no one thought he could do it.

The prematch race photo session at Belmont Park,
May 4, 1938: War Admiral . . .
(© BETTMANN/CORBIS)

. . . and Seabiscuit
(© BETTMANN/CORBIS)

CHAPTER 14

The Wise We Boys

Seabiscuit slept for most of the trip to Belmont, rising only when reporters tramped aboard the train at the whistle-stops between San Francisco and New York. The newsmen had learned how to buy access to their source; several of them came on board laden with carrots, which Seabiscuit fished from their pockets. "Whenever food showed," Smith noted, "he was quick to get up." When the human buffet cleared out of the train, down Seabiscuit would go again.

On April 26, the horse completed his 24,265th mile of career rail travel. He was stretched out on his side in the straw when the *Overland Limited* drew up in New York. The big railcar door slid open and Seabiscuit got up, shook off the straw, and poked his head out. Two hundred people surged forward. Smith appeared and glared back at them from under the gray fedora. He led Seabiscuit down the ramp and stood for a moment, frowning as the horse blinked in the sun and yawned. Flashbulbs blinked and movie cameras whirred as Seabiscuit stood there, posing.

Several score of newsmen were scattered among the fans, eyeing the horse critically. Long before Seabiscuit arrived, the polls on the race had begun. Virtually every reporter and horseman in the East thought that War Admiral would prove to be Seabiscuit's master. The New York bookies were having a tough time trying to find anyone willing to put a few bucks on Seabiscuit; 95 percent of the wagers were on War Admiral. Down in Louisville to cover the Kentucky Derby, Oscar Otis found that he was about the only journalist who thought Seabiscuit could win. Other reporters thought he was addled. "There's going to be a pretty good horse race," wrote the *New York World Telegram*, "until Seabiscuit flattens out like a rug at the sixteenth pole." Seabiscuit, wrote another reporter, "was a hero in California and a pretty fair sort of horse in the midwest. In the east, however, he was just a 'bum.'"

Smith led Seabiscuit down the gangplank, past lines of trees heavy with spring foliage, around the walking ring, then toward the barns. A cluster of people trailed him. Seabiscuit, wired from the journey, was bucking and kicking out behind, so they kept their distance. On the backstretch the horse passed War Admiral's barn. On the wall near the Triple Crown winner's stall was a little shrine to Man o' War and Brushup, War Admiral's mother. Below photos of the two horses hung a sign: THEY GAVE US WAR ADMIRAL. War Admiral's trainer, George Conway, lingered by his horse's stall. He was a tall, cardiganed old man, formal and quiet. He hovered over the grooms while they curried his horse and prowled along behind when the horse went to the track. War Admiral stood quietly as Seabiscuit clopped past. The two horses didn't see each other. Seabiscuit moved on to Barn 43, to a freshly painted 168-square-foot stall with a cathedral ceiling. Howard had obtained special permission to knock down the wall between it and the next stall so that Pumpkin could take up his customary sidekick position.

On April 28 Pollard completed his long drive across the country. He went to the barns to see Seabiscuit, then hung up his tack. Woolf was there with him; Howard had insisted that Pollard ride in the match, but he was covering his bases. Woolf's presence was a constant reminder of Pollard's shaky position. He needed no reminding. The papers were full of questions about Pollard's ability and fitness. The newsmen gathered by the rails, watched Pollard ride, and commented on his obvious soreness. They began to wonder aloud what Howard was thinking. "It's probably a matter of sentiment with Owner Howard to put Pollard in the pilot-house, and it might turn out to be a good idea, despite," wrote reporter Jack James. "But right now it looks, from this distance, as just another 'worst of it' impost which our boy friend, the 'Biscuit, must carry to the post."

The moment Pollard arrived at the track, the hard training began. Because the starting gates of the day had no doors, the only breaking signal horses received was the ring of a bell. Smith wanted to sharpen Seabiscuit's response to it. He began by fashioning a homemade starting bell. He boosted Pollard onto Seabiscuit, picked up the starting bell and a buggy whip, and without a word of explanation, led them to the training track. Pollard must have expected that they would go to the gate, but Smith led them right past it. The jockey had learned enough to know that asking Smith what was going on would have been fruitless. He rode out to the track in silence, looking down at the contraption clutched in Smith's hand and wondering at the trainer's judgment. "I thought Tom," he remembered later, "had blown his topper."

Smith positioned Pollard and Seabiscuit on the track, then moved a few feet behind them. Pollard prepared himself for Smith's orders. Smith lifted the buggy whip and flicked it over Seabiscuit's flanks just as he hit the bell. The device raised a clanging racket, sounding, Pollard remembered later, "like all hell breaking loose." The jockey burst into frantic urging and Seabiscuit lunged forward, breaking into a dead run. Pollard galloped Seabiscuit out, brought him back, and he and Smith repeated the drill over and over. The lesson was perfectly conceived classical conditioning. Seabiscuit, like any prey animal, was hard-wired to bound forward at the whip's brush over his hindquarters, a simulation of a predator's grasp. By pairing the touch of the whip with the sound of the bell, Smith was teaching Seabiscuit to associate one with the other so that he would have the same reaction to the first as to the second: *run*. Seabiscuit proved to be a superb student. After a few tries, he was reacting so quickly that he was gone before Smith could wave the whip. The horse was alert, buoyant, animated, all of his faculties alive to his rider. Pollard could feel it under him: electricity pulsing up into his hands.

The jockey, too, needed a little conditioning. To prepare Pollard for a rocket start, Smith sent him out for races on every front-running sprinter in the Howard barn. Smith didn't care about the race results; all he wanted was swift starts and the fastest early fractions. The horses lost, but Pollard did as told, outbreaking the field in each race. His arm was loosening up every day, and for the first time since his fall with Fair Knightess, he began to look like the rider he had once been.

Seeing Pollard coming back into form, Smith changed training tactics. He took the rider and Seabiscuit out to the starting gate. Traditional gate schooling has always been a matter of standing still, teaching a horse to tolerate the huge, clattering metal contraption around him while he awaits the loading of other horses. But in the match race War Admiral would be his only competitor. Waiting would not be a problem. If Seabiscuit relaxed in the gate, War Admiral would leave him in his dust. The horse had to learn to be less patient, not more. Smith designed a new exercise. Sitting on Pumpkin by the gate, he ordered Pollard to rush Seabiscuit into the gate, pause for only an instant, then gallop out. Pollard did as told, and Seabiscuit bounded through. After a few repetitions Seabiscuit grew playful. He eagerly dove into the gate and streaked right through, then pivoted back for another run at it.

After a dozen or so starts, the horse was bouncing all over the track. It was time for a test. Starter George Cassidy stepped into the starter's box and Smith brought Seabiscuit up. This time Pollard halted him in the gate. For a moment Seabiscuit stood still, perched on his toes, hind legs braced, ready to roll. Cassidy rang the bell. Pollard threw the reins up on Seabiscuit's neck, and the two sprang out. Seabiscuit ran flat out for a sixteenth of a mile before Pollard pulled him up. Smith was satisfied that the horse understood the task before him. Seabiscuit skipped back to the barn, "obviously," said one railbird, "in a marvelous humor."

On May 11 Smith began the third phase of starting gate instruction. For horses, herd animals alert to clues of danger from each other, skittishness is contagious. War Admiral was a raging lion behind the gate, and Smith was concerned that Seabiscuit would take one look at his opponent's tantrum and throw one of his own. He needed to expose Seabiscuit to a similarly unruly gate horse and inure him to the sight of it. He already had just the right horse for the job. Months earlier, Howard had purchased a colt named Chanceview from Alfred Vanderbilt. The horse had proved fairly useful as a stakes horse, but he was an incorrigible rogue at the starting gate. Smith brought them out together, turned Seabiscuit toward Chanceview, and let him watch while the colt banged around like a rodeo bronc. Smith drilled them in the gate until he was satisfied that Seabiscuit had seen every trick War Admiral might pull.

The New York publicity machine heated up. On May 4 Seabiscuit and War Admiral were brought out on a grassy lawn before a pink flowering hedge to pose for an army of photographers. War Admiral emerged first. He was a splendid sight, his mane and tail braided in yellow ribbons, his coat glossy and his head high. He was in a mercurial Hastings temper, and a halter and chain looped over his bridle barely restrained him. As an attendant approached him with the saddle, he reared skyward, struck out with his forelegs, and began plunging around on the end of his lead. The saddle holder chased him around and around the enclosure. The man threw the saddle over the horse's back, and War Admiral flung it right off. They tossed it on him again, only to have it come sailing back in their faces. "Don't worry about that," said his nervous jockey, Charley Kurtsinger. "As soon as he starts running he's the easiest horse in the world to handle. All he wants is to get out in front and go."

Finally, they got the saddle on and the girth cinched. Kurtsinger, dapper in Riddle's legendary black and yellow silks, leapt onto his back, and again War Admiral flung himself around, bucking and thrashing and tearing divots out of the Belmont lawn. Kurtsinger gritted his teeth and hung on. The photographers began grumbling. "He's just a lively horse," trainer Conway said weakly as he was buffeted around.

A distant train whistle sounded. War Admiral spooked at it, jerking his head up. For one brief instant he stood still, ears pricked, head high, body stretched out in all its geometric magnificence. He was listening to the train. No one was foolish enough to try to pull off the ugly halter and nose chain to perfect the shot. The attendant on the end of the lead rope braced himself, Kurtsinger turned his head and grinned stiffly, and all the photographers snapped their shots.

Kurtsinger bailed out and War Admiral whirled off. Seabiscuit came out after him, sauntering in, wrote a reporter, "like he owned the place." Pollard strode out with him, buttoned into Howard's red and white silks.

The contrast between the two horses could not have been more glaring. Though a little lower at the withers and nearly half a foot shorter, nose to tail, Seabiscuit seemed a cumbersome giant in comparison. At 1,040 pounds, he outweighed War Admiral by 80 pounds, with six feet of girth and a markedly wider chest. But the big body was perched on legs a full two inches shorter. His neck was thick, his head heavy, his tail stubby, his boxing-glove knees crouched. Whitey had done his best to clean Seabiscuit up, braiding his mane, forelock, and tail, but the mane plaits didn't lay right and stuck out like quills. The horse stood straddle-legged, as if perpetually bracing himself against a strong wind.

But to the weary photographers, Seabiscuit was a relief. He stood perfectly still as he was being saddled, and Pollard hopped on his back. The photographers lifted their cameras, and Seabiscuit pricked his ears and struck his horizon-gazing pose. He held the position, without quivering a muscle, for nearly five minutes as the photographers scurried around him, cameras grinding, shooting him from every angle. They brought the noisy newsreels right up to his nose, but he never moved.

From the day of his arrival in New York, Smith was Smith; the New York press corps couldn't get a grunt out of him. "Tom Smith," wrote a reporter, "says almost nothing, constantly." The *New York Herald Tribune* found one reporter's valiant attempt to get more than a monosyllabic answer out of him so amusing that it published a transcript of the entire nonconversation. Smith was cooperative in only one respect. Probably at Howard's insistence, he let the press come into the barn to see the horse, albeit without narration from the trainer. This was a step better than George Conway. A similarly mute man described by one reporter as "lean, tall and indifferent," Conway wouldn't let photographers near the barn in the understandable fear that the jittery War Admiral would spook at the flashbulbs and whack his head. When Smith proved more welcoming, the reporters virtually moved into Barn 43, forcing the trainer to wade through them to get to his horse. When the horse left the barn, they tramped along en masse behind him, joining large throngs of spectators on the apron of the track. They hung around day and night, asking Smith if he *really* thought his horse could win.

By May 14, the honeymoon was over. "You won't be seeing this horse much anymore," Smith growled. He shooed the press out of the barn, slung a rope across the entrance, posted a guard, and retreated to his track cottage, sitting by an oil stove in a cramped room. Even Pollard, who had been jabbering gaily with reporters since his arrival, stopped talking. "Some suspect," wrote Jolly Roger, "that Tom may have removed his tongue." Team Seabiscuit effectively vanished. No one was allowed to see the horse. Pleas for information brought a vintage reply: "No."

The reporters assumed that Smith was just being curmudgeonly, but there was likely more to it than that. In a workout three days earlier, Seabiscuit had needed 1:48 to negotiate a mile. Though the track was somewhat soggy that day, Seabiscuit had been capable of ticking off miles in 1:36 throughout his career with Smith. It had been an unusually rainy spring in New York, and the track was difficult to handle even when dry. But the surface alone couldn't account for so sluggish a workout. The horse seemed off, yet Smith could find no problem. There was still plenty of time before the race, but the trainer was increasingly concerned. He knew that any sign that Seabiscuit was not himself would only make the press more intrusive. He parked himself in the cottage and kept his mouth shut. More than ever before, he sought to hide the horse's training, taking him out at 4:00 A.M. He got away with it until one morning when he was a little late leading the horse off the track. A group of clockers arriving for work at four-thirty saw Smith leading a winded Seabiscuit back to the barn. Smith moved the work times to 8:00 P.M. For the time being, no one caught him, but the press now knew he was fooling them.

The absence of news about the year's biggest story drove the reporters to distraction. At first they wrote whatever came to mind. One dreamed up an "interview" with Seabiscuit, in which the horse disowned his year-younger half-uncle, War Admiral. *Life* magazine ran a full-page photo layout of Seabiscuit's facial expressions. One bored clocker resorted to timing Smith as he walked down the track, catching him at a clip of thirty-five minutes for the half mile. Veteran turf writer John Lardner printed the information, "but this," he admitted, "had little or no bearing on the race."

The New York press corps went into a huddle. They dubbed their conflict with Smith "the Battle of Long Island." If Smith was going to be silent, so would they; they opted not to write another word about Seabiscuit. It was a bold move, but a bad one. An angry public outcry followed, and the plan was quickly scrapped. So they formed a conspiracy. They banded together to create the "Wise We Boys," a network of reporters and clockers operating in concert to catch Seabiscuit training. Someone followed Smith every hour of the day, and each reporter received assignments on where and when to be posted. Clockers were stationed at the track twenty-four hours a day, greeting one another with the phrase "What do you know?" Sentries were deployed in concentric circles around Barn 43, even, reportedly, perching in trees. Meetings were held to share information. It was, remembered one reporter, "an epic of espionage."

The Wise We Boys' most inspired decision was to send scouts to pick the brains of anyone who had witnessed Smith's secret training methods in the past. They pooled their findings and made a critical discovery. During his sojourn in the East in 1937, Smith had been caught working Seabiscuit at night four times. While this information wouldn't normally have been very useful, the reporters were able to pin down the exact times at which the workouts had been held. In every case, the horse had worked precisely at 8:00. Further investigation unearthed evidence that Smith had secretly worked Seabiscuit twice at Bay Meadows. Again, the time was 8:00 P.M. They had found Smith's witching hour.

A fearless clocker volunteered to verify the finding. On the night of May 17 he scaled the grandstand and slid out onto the roof. Shinnying out onto a perilous but hidden spot, he gripped the roof with one hand and his stopwatch with the other. He waited. The track was flooded in moonlight. He could see every pole along the course, glowing in lunar blue.

At exactly 8:00, Smith emerged. He walked the length of the grandstand, checking for spies. Seeing no one, he pointed his flashlight at the barns and flicked it on and off twice. Seabiscuit emerged under a rider and cantered up to the far turn. As he dropped into a run, the clocker punched his watch. Seabiscuit rolled around the track, then slowed to a walk and returned to the barn. The clocker stopped his watch and crawled back down.

The next morning, papers across the nation ran the workout time, which was slow, and attributed it to Seabiscuit. Not one paper mentioned the circumstances, reporting the work exactly as if the horse had gone out in the standard manner. Smith said nothing.

The following afternoon Smith emerged from the barn to swing Pollard up on a horse for a race. As he stood in the paddock, a reporter's voice sang out from the crowd.

"Is it true, Mr. Smith, you consider eight P.M. to be your lucky hour?"

"Tom answered," wrote a delighted Jolly Roger, "with a grunt of something akin to rage."

There was rejoicing among the Wise We Boys. "Score: Newsmen 1, Tom Smith 0," trumpeted Jolly Roger in the *San Francisco Chronicle*.

Smith executed a flanking maneuver. A few days later, reporters and clockers were startled to see him leading Seabiscuit out in broad daylight. He was heading toward the training track, which abutted the main track's clubhouse turn. Had Jean Harlow been dancing stark naked around the sixteenth pole, the press box could not have cleared out any faster. Thinking that Smith was surrendering and victory was at hand, the Wise We Boys grabbed their stopwatches and bolted from the booth, ran down through the bowels of the immense building and into the parking lot, piled into their cars, sped over to the training track, bailed out, and sprinted to the side of the course. There they sat, panting and congratulating one another, watching the gap in the track and waiting for Smith to lead Seabiscuit in and lay down his arms, like Lee at Appomattox.

Time passed. A breeze whistled over the empty track. Seabiscuit didn't come. The laughter gradually died out.

By the time the boys at the training track realized that they had been had, it was all over. Seeing that he had emptied out the clockers' stand and reporters' booths, Smith had simply turned Seabiscuit around and worked him over on the main track. He had fooled every single clocker and newsman on the grounds.

Knowing he wouldn't be able to pull that off twice, Smith tried his most ingenious move: hiding in plain sight. Since his pursuers were focused on discovering him working Seabiscuit late at night, before dawn, and on the training track, Smith scheduled a workout on the main track in the daytime, just after the last race. He knew that the clockers and reporters would never believe that he would do something so obvious, and would pay no attention to him.

Because Belmont rules stated that any workout in daylight after the last race had to be approved, Smith had to consult the stewards. He knew better than to walk over to the stewards' stand—a reporter stood by to tail him wherever he went—so he called the office instead.

When the phone rang, the stewards were tied up in meetings. By fantastic coincidence, a reporter named Eddie Farrell happened to have just taken a seat by the phone while he waited to speak with the stewards. Hearing the ringing, a steward yelled into the office, asking Farrell if he would pick up the phone. Farrell answered with a simple hello.

"This is trainer Tom Smith speaking," came the voice over the line. "I would like permission to work a horse after the last race."

Farrell couldn't believe his ears. He turned in his chair and called to the stewards. "Tom Smith would like permission to work a horse after the last race."

"Tell him all right," came the reply.

Farrell banged down the phone, dashed to the press box, rounded up the clockers, and delivered the news.

One half hour after the last race was run that evening, twenty-two giggling newsmen and clockers tiptoed to the top of the grandstand. They crammed into the press box and hid themselves, keeping the lights out and spying through peepholes. Grinning and giddy, they watched as Smith's charge worked over a mile and an eighth. The following morning the papers were full of stories on Seabiscuit's work-out, but again, the reporters made no mention of the circumstances. "Score, newsmen 2, Tom Smith 0," wrote Jolly Roger.

But there was something out of place about the incident. Some of the clockers, training their field glasses on Tom Smith's face as he led the horse back to the barn, noticed a glaring incongruity. Tom Smith looked *happy*.

"I'm wondering," Jolly Roger wrote later, "if that really was Sea-biscuit the boys were looking at." It occurred to him for the first time that Grog, who was supposed to be in California, hadn't made an appearance out there in a good long time.

The question was still eating at him later as he sat at his spy post outside Smith's cottage. Curious, he trained his field glasses on Smith through the cottage window. There sat the trainer, pushed up against the oil stove. Smith, Roger noted with despair, "had a slight, knowing smile."

Had Smith known he was speaking to a reporter when he called the stewards' office that afternoon? "I was just wondering which would be the winner in a contest such as this—an Indian fighter's intuition or that wily old boy, coincidence," Roger wrote later. "Personally, I'm coupling Seabiscuit and Intuition."

At the murky press of daybreak on May 20, Pollard took Seabiscuit to the track, jogged him around to warm up, then walked him to the training track and into the starting gate. It was immediately clear that Seabiscuit wasn't right. He started banging around the gate like Chanceview and refused to settle down. When the bell rang, he left it like a shot. Pollard flattened down for a hard mile workout. The first few furlongs went well, but gradually, Seabiscuit began to slow down. After a third quarter in 25⅗, Pollard reached back and delivered a crack with the whip. There was no response. The horse kept decelerating. After a final quarter in 27⅗, Pollard pulled him up.

The stopwatch told the tale. It had taken Seabiscuit 1:42 to negotiate eight furlongs on the training track, and that was under strong urging. Worst of all, it was by far the fastest mile the horse had worked since coming to Belmont. The reporters, for once, had caught the workout. "Somebody ought to tell him that he's going to fight War Admiral," one of them mused after watching Seabiscuit slog by. "If he goes into the ring that way against the Admiral, he'll be batted out in a helluva hurry."

The rumors that had been filtering down the backstretch, whispered in confidence between clockers and horsemen, suddenly became noisy public accusations: *Something is wrong with Seabiscuit.* The newsmen peppered the nation's papers with stories about the slow workouts. People were hollering suspicious questions at Smith everywhere he went. The atmosphere was growing hostile. Smith needed a little Howard image control, but he was on his own. The Howards were on a cruise around Bermuda. They had visited briefly in early May, just before embarking on the ship. Howard, chattering gaily about how he had been mobbed on the train by Seabiscuit fans who were coming to New York for the race, swung by the barn for a quick once-over of his horse.

"He never looked better," said Howard.

"Right," said Smith.

Then the Howards had sailed off. They had no idea that a problem had arisen since their departure or that Smith was in a terrible predicament. The reporters pestered the trainer over and over again: Is the horse okay? Seabiscuit, Smith said repeatedly, had "never been better."

One week before the match, Pollard rode out onto the Belmont course for his final test before the match race. He was aboard Fair Knightess, who was making her first start since she and Pollard went down in the San Carlos three months before. In this, the Handspring Handicap, she was a long shot; no one had thought that Smith could get her back into racing condition after her injuries. Firing her out of the gate, Pollard sent her up alongside the favorite, then drew off to a commanding lead on the backstretch. No one could catch them. Pollard and Fair Knightess, who might have died together on the track at Santa Anita, cantered home easy winners. Pollard was ready to go.

Seabiscuit was not. Smith was shaken. The horse's speed was gone, and Smith didn't know why. The issue was being treated as a scandal. The *New York Daily Mirror* was demanding that racing officials step in and investigate the horse's condition and either call off the race or assure the alarmed public that Seabiscuit was in good shape. Even Walter Winchell chimed in, questioning Seabiscuit's fitness. Smith's defenses were less and less convincing. Apparently in an effort to mollify the inflamed press, he let photographers back into the barn. If the horse was unsound, he said, he would never let him out of his stall to work out. The reporters wanted to see the horse in the daylight. Smith, his nerves at the breaking point, made an ominous statement implying that there would be no match race, then led the horse out.

Few seemed to have noticed what Smith had, which was that War Admiral looked even worse than Seabiscuit. On May 17, it had taken him a doddering 1:49 to negotiate a mile, a time even slower than Seabiscuit's. Four days later, it took him 2:08⅗, trotting horse time, to run the race distance of a mile and a quarter. On May 23 he had seemed so uncharacteristically narcotized in starting-gate drills that a bystander had remarked, "You'd swear he was a dull-witted lead pony instead of the high-strung animal he is." By many reports, Riddle and Conway were weighing whether or not to scratch their horse from the race, but they were waiting in hopes that Seabiscuit would be withdrawn first, saving them from being blamed for the massive disappointment. Smith was getting conflicting signals. Some people were telling him to stay in the race, that War Admiral was training so badly that Seabiscuit, bad form and all, could lick him. Others warned Smith that War Admiral's bad works may have been designed to fool Smith about the colt's condition. He didn't know what to do, and the reporters wouldn't stop pressuring him.

Was the horse lame?

"No."

Was he not in shape?

"If the horse is not in shape, I'll pull him out of there."

Was he sick?

"He galloped yesterday. Sick horses don't gallop. They act sick."

It was time to make a decision, but the Howards were hundreds of miles away. Smith patched through an emergency call to their cruise ship: Come to Belmont.

The Howards couldn't believe the state in which they found Belmont. Wild accusations were flying around, including one published charge that Smith was deliberately working the horse slowly in order to get long odds in the race. Everyone wanted to know if the horse would run. Howard was privately distressed but publicly reassuring and confident. To quiet the doubters, he gave his word that the public would be able to see Seabiscuit work a full ten furlongs—the race distance—at three-thirty on the afternoon of May 24.

On the morning of the appointed day, Smith took Seabiscuit to the track for a short morning gallop, in preparation for the afternoon's public workout. He studied his horse's action. His eyes fixed on the horse's knees.

There it was: a faint whisper of soreness. It was subtle, but it was there.

Howard had a terrible decision to make. Seabiscuit probably could run in the race. At best, he would probably lose. At worst, he could be injured. Howard's inclination was to scratch him, but the potential consequences were daunting.

Belmont officials, anticipating the largest crowd ever to attend a horse race in America, had worked themselves to exhaustion and spent $30,000 to publicize the race and prepare the track. In the Belmont grandstand, which, if stood on end, would nearly equal the height of the new Empire State Building, every seat was booked. Millions had been wagered. Silversmiths had already cast an elaborate trophy. Press coverage was at saturation levels. The buildup to the Memorial Day Indy 500, normally a huge sporting event, was all but squeezed out of the nation's press; in the *San Francisco Chronicle*, coverage of the auto ace was buried on page 24, alongside an interpretation of the tides. The horses were on the cover of *Newsweek* as well as the ubiquitous *Radio Guide*, which showed War Admiral galloping, Seabiscuit yawning. Billboards advertising the event rimmed every major road on Long Island. CBS Radio had taken out full-page ads to promote its international broadcast of the race. Several "Seabiscuit Limited" trains, packed to the doors, were already en route from the West Coast. Other chartered trains were coming from Kentucky, Chicago, Boston, and Philadelphia. Bing Crosby had booked a plane east with a huge party of his friends. Swope, Widener, and Whitney had gone out on a narrow limb to give Howard what he had demanded, putting up an enormous purse and postponing the Suburban Handicap, a fixture of the biggest racing day of the spring, to accommodate the race. There was even talk of shipping old Man o' War all the way from Kentucky to accompany his son and grandson to the post. The entire world awaited the race with rapt attention.

And should Howard decide to scratch the horse, he knew that it would only confirm the long-standing belief that his horse was a "cripple." "Now the one time out of so many times that the critics appear to be right," Howard said bitterly, "has to come just before a race like this."

Hours before Seabiscuit was to undertake his public workout, Howard and Smith retreated to the cottage by the barn. Nearby, the grooms stood with the horse they called "Old Pop," grim-faced, watching the door and saying nothing. Seabiscuit, oblivious, rooted around in his hay.

A passerby finally broke the silence.

"He *looks* all right."

"Yes, he looks all right," replied a groom.

"But he hasn't been working very well, has he?"

"No, he hasn't."

In midafternoon, the cottage door opened. Smith emerged, went to Seabiscuit's stall, and began preparing to send the horse out. Howard went to the stewards' stand, to which he called C. V. Whitney, Joseph Widener, and Herbert Bayard Swope. At the track, crowds began to gather to see the workout.

Smith led Seabiscuit toward the course. Howard disappeared into the administrative offices to explain the problem to Swope and Whitney and get their opinion. A few minutes later, he walked out. A crush of reporters pushed up to him. His voice wavered as he began to speak.

It was three-thirty. Back on the track, Smith boosted Pollard up on Seabiscuit, swung his leg over Pumpkin's back, and began moving down the course. The track announcer's voice cut over the grandstand.

The race was off.

The crowd sagged. Smith led Seabiscuit past the stunned fans and back into the barn.

At the stewards' office, Howard gave his profound apologies to everyone, then took Marcela back to their lodgings at the Garden City Hotel. She wanted to cry in private.

Howard was mortified over the disaster he had created. And he was worried about his horse. "I don't know if he'll ever come out of his soreness," he said. "We won't patch him up and send him out there to break his heart trying to win." The idea of retiring him and taking him home to Ridgewood began playing in his mind. Smith shook his head. The horse was not through yet. Smith could work through the lameness. Howard came to believe him. They began laying plans.

Howard was in a fix. His efforts to arrange a match at Belmont had not only fallen through, they had greatly diminished his chances of ever securing a meeting between the two horses. Riddle, who had never been more than lukewarm about it, could now say that he had tried to get the match race but that Howard had backed out. War Admiral could go into his scheduled retirement at season's end without anyone accusing him of dodging the best competition. Belmont officials were snakebit. Howard did his best to warm them to the idea of rescheduling the match, even setting aside his heretofore paramount goal of breaking Sun Beau's earnings mark. Forget the $100,000 purse, he said. Once Seabiscuit recovered, he would welcome a race at Belmont held merely on a sporting basis. Belmont officials grudgingly agreed to consider it, and there was talk of rescheduling the race for the fall meeting.

Riddle put an end to that. Belmont officials, trying to come up with some way to salvage the weekend, telephoned Riddle and offered War Admiral a berth in the Suburban Handicap, which had been moved to Saturday, May 28, to accommodate the match. Though War Admiral had been assigned 132 pounds, Riddle accepted. The day appeared to have been saved. Twenty-five thousand fans, many of whom had crossed the country expecting to see the race of the century, mobbed Belmont on race day. The papers were singing of Riddle's sportsmanship in starting War Admiral in the race. The crowd, which had greeted Howard's announcement with sympathy and understanding, was eager to see its consolation prize.

At the very last second, without any warning, Riddle and Conway refused to start War Admiral. They offered no explanation. Officials insisted that they give one, so they cited poor track condition. As the track was, by all accounts, perfect—the Suburban was run in record time—no one believed them.

War Admiral's scratch appeared on the jockey board in the infield. Most of the reporters, and much of the crowd, believed that Riddle had simply balked at the 132-pound impost and didn't care enough about the consequences of scratching to do the sportsmanlike thing. The crowd had run out of patience. A cacophony of boos and catcalls rolled down the grandstand for a full two minutes. Riddle, wrote one spectator, "was accused of everything under the sun save the shooting of Lincoln and the current recession."

C. V. Whitney listened to the din and was livid. Asked if he would agree to a War Admiral–Seabiscuit rescheduling, he snapped.

"Not if I could buy them for a dime a dozen. I'll never again consent to such a thing."

After seeing what Belmont had gone through, no other track managers were likely to agree to a race either. There was a rumor that Seabiscuit's lameness was a ruse designed to avoid a loss to War Admiral, and an awful lot of people believed it. Howard had, it seemed, only one chance left. If no one was willing to arrange a match, he was going to have to follow War Admiral to his next scheduled contest, to pit Seabiscuit against him in a full-field race.

The next suitable venue was the Massachusetts Handicap on June 29. War Admiral was slated to run in it, and though Suffolk Downs' officials made no effort to invite defending champion Seabiscuit, Howard had already entered him. Seabiscuit would have a full month to recover, ample time, said Smith, for him to work the soreness out of those knees.

Perhaps Riddle felt the sting of his public excoriation. On June 6, he ran his colt in Aqueduct's Queen's County Handicap despite a 132-pound impost. Many of the fans, eager to let Riddle know how they felt about the scratching of a week before, attempted to drown out any cheering with lusty howls. In spite of the mixed reception, War Admiral won. Then he loaded up and headed north to Suffolk Downs to prepare for the Massachusetts Handicap. On June 14, Smith and the Howards followed him. Pollard and his agent, Yummy, came with them. Woolf stayed behind. With Pollard in perfect condition, he thought they didn't need him.

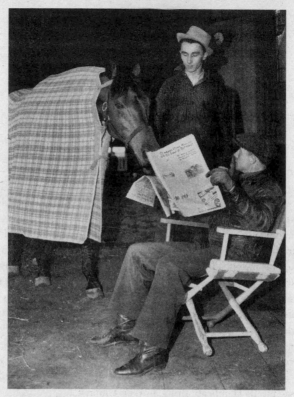

Seabiscuit and his walker visit with Pollard after a workout.
(© BETTMANN/CORBIS)

CHAPTER 15

Fortune's Fool

June 23, 1938, dawned golden and beautiful for Red Pollard. The great rolling wheel of his life had swung upward again, and he could not suppress his high spirits. He was riding in fine form, everything clicking, the broken bones mended, his timing right. Beneath him that morning was Seabiscuit, and Pollard could feel from the tension in the reins and the rhythm under him that Smith had worked his magic. The horse was, as they said, "sound as a Roosevelt dollar" and jumping out of his skin to run. He clicked past the track poles at a staccato pace. Pollard tipped back in the irons and Seabiscuit tugged on his hands, picking off six furlongs in 1:12⅕, marvelous time. The horse finished the mile sparkling and galloped out an eighth of a mile farther, still burning Pollard's arms in his eagerness to continue.

A smile shimmered over Smith's face. Six days to go until the Massachusetts Handicap. Bring on War Admiral.

Back at the barn, Pollard jumped off and handed the reins to a groom. He sat down in front of a shed row to rest and chat with friends. While sitting there, he caught sight of an old friend from his Tijuana days, owner Bert Blume, and the two began talking. Blume was in trouble. A rider had promised to gallop a green two-year-old named Modern Youth for him but hadn't shown up. There were no other riders available. The workout was critical; the colt was scheduled to race and needed a blowout. The race in question was a forgettable weekday event for a trifling purse, but Blume was strapped for money. Pollard, Blume remembered later, "had been broke often enough to know what it was like." And he had not forgotten a good turn Blume had done him back in his bush-league days.

"I'll work the bum," Pollard said. He hopped aboard the horse and trotted off. Had the rider given Blume a moment to consider the risk Pollard was taking in riding an immature colt just before a major race, Blume would not have let him go. But Pollard, as Blume noted, was impulsive with his generosity. He and Modern Youth were gone in an instant. All Blume could do was watch.

Flying past the three-eighths pole at breakneck speed, Modern Youth suddenly spooked, bolting to the right, and headed straight for the outer rail. Pollard couldn't stop him. The colt plunged through the rail, somehow got his hooves back under him again, and fled for the barns. Pollard clung to his back, unable to regain control. The horse was running in a blind terror, streaking down the shed rows. He was probably doing thirty or so when he tried to cut between two barns. He was moving too fast to make it. He skidded sideways and slammed into the corner of a barn, then fell in a heap.

A sickening noise ran down the long line of barns. It was Pollard. He was screaming.

His right leg was nearly sheared off below the knee.

All along the backstretch, men dropped what they were doing and ran toward the sound. They found Pollard lying on the ground, writhing spastically. The flesh of his leg had been ripped away, exposing the bone. Pollard's face was a rictus of agony, his lips peeled back over his teeth, and gusts of pain were rolling through his body and escaping through his mouth in deep guttural roars.

Someone ran for an ambulance, but the one that sat at the track during the day's races had not yet arrived. Someone else called Smith, who rang for an ambulance and then sped toward the barns. The stable hands, despairing of getting help to the track fast enough, fetched the only transportation on hand, a little runabout truck that the track starter used to motor around the course. The truck had no passenger seat, and the back was cluttered with gate equipment. So while Pollard lay on the ground, his cries distilling down to long strings of barked obscenities, the panicked stable hands heaved the gear out of the runabout. They sprinted down the shed rows, gathering pommel pads, horse blankets, and rub rags, and threw them on the truck bed to serve as a makeshift gurney mattress. They hoisted the screaming rider up from the foot of the barn wall and gently laid him on the horse paraphernalia. The starter jumped into the driver's seat while a host of stable hands climbed in around Pollard, who was swearing out every oath in his tremendous vocabulary. The little runabout chugged off onto the road.

Back at the barn, Blume was in tears. He sobbed uncontrollably for an hour and sank into a weeklong guilt-inspired bender. He never forgave himself.

Though Winthrop Hospital was only five minutes from the track, none of the stable hands knew where it was. The runabout driver steered the truck blindly through the streets, slowed by heavy traffic, trying to find someone to help Pollard. The jockey never stopped screaming. An excruciating forty-five minutes passed. Pollard was growing more and more frantic. Then, across lanes of traffic ahead, someone spotted a physician's bungalow. The runabout puttered toward it.

Just then an ambulance screamed up behind the starter's truck and pulled to a halt. Smith sprang out. After commandeering the ambulance at the track, he had been combing the streets for nearly an hour in search of the runabout. He found Pollard mad with pain, "hotter than a smoking .45," went one account, "and not holding back." They transferred their wailing patient into the ambulance. Smith climbed in beside him, and the driver hit the siren and slammed the pedal to the floor, darting in and out of lanes and swerving around cars. Along a road running perpendicular to a river, the traffic thickened, bogging the ambulance down. Pollard became wild, screeching and howling in the back.

"Tom!" he shouted. "Stop this wagon! I can't stand it any longer. Stop it, I tell you!" His voice was so loud that passersby across the river turned to see what the commotion was. Smith, shaken by Pollard's insistence, told the driver to stop.

Pollard sat up and began searching the lines of buildings. His eyes hit on one.

"STOP!" he bellowed. "That's the place." He pointed to a liquor store. "Tom, I tell you I cannot get to that hospital alive if you don't get on over there and buy me a bottle of beer."

Smith, a lifelong teetotaler who strongly disapproved of Pollard's drinking, probably waved off the jockey's plaintive wails for alcohol that morning. But his agent, Yummy, came through. Speeding to the hospital, he snuck a crock of bow-wow wine in to Pollard. He found the stricken rider distracting himself from his pain by firing off aphorisms from Ralph Waldo Emerson—"Old Waldo"—at the nurses.

Yummy saw Pollard's leg and was horrified. Both bones of his lower leg were splintered. Yummy knew what the injuries meant. He reeled over by the telephones and wept. He spent the morning calling Pollard's friends, crying into the phone as he broke the news. "The Cougar just got throwed off a horse he was working and busted his leg," he sobbed to David Alexander. Yummy stayed by Pollard all day, despondent, greeting the worried friends who came to see him. He would still be there long after nightfall.

Someone contacted San Francisco and told the Howards what had happened. Howard got on the telephone and pulled every string he had. Almost immediately he had a team of the nation's best orthopedic specialists on planes, flying in to Boston at his expense. They examined Pollard's leg. Somehow, they saved it from amputation, but it was a hollow victory.

Pollard, they announced, would probably never walk again. His career was declared over.

Smith wired the news to Woolf in New York, asking that he come up immediately. Woolf sped north.

Pollard stabilized. Woolf arrived to take his place on Seabiscuit. On the backstretch, there was only one reminder of the accident. At 6:00

one morning shortly after Pollard went down, a fully equipped ambulance rolled onto the racecourse, pulled over to the side, and parked. Suffolk Downs made sure that it would be there every morning from that day forward. No fallen rider, at least at Suffolk Downs, would have to go to the hospital in a starter's runabout again.

At the Howard barn, life had to go on. Smith prepared Kayak, the horse Lin Howard had bought in Argentina and sold to his father, for a purse race at Suffolk. As soon as the colt had disembarked in California, Smith had sent him to the Burlingame Polo Grounds near the Howards' house. He had put the best man he knew, his own son Jimmy, in charge of his breaking and early training. The son had clearly inherited his father's instincts. Returned to the elder Smith once he matured, Kayak showed promise. A very difficult horse upon his arrival, he was now as tame as a kitten. In his first start, at New York's Aqueduct Racecourse under Pollard on June 10, he had led into the stretch and lost narrowly, finishing second. Smith was starting to think that Kayak was going to be awfully good.

Seabiscuit took well to Woolf's guidance. His workouts for the Massachusetts Handicap were brilliant. All traces of knee soreness were gone, and his action was smoother than ever. Smith sent him out one morning for a three-furlong workout. He lined Seabiscuit up at the three-eighths pole, positioned a sprinting stablemate fifty yards ahead and set them off at the same time. Seabiscuit mowed his stablemate down with incredible speed, running the first eighth in 11 seconds, a quarter in 23, and three eighths in 36. "If that isn't running," Smith later said, "I don't know anything about horses."

War Admiral, meanwhile, was his usual combative self. Guarded by Spot, a surly Dalmatian who took hunks of flesh out of reporters who got too close, he stormed around the barn and fretted, pouted and balked in his workouts. At times he refused to run without a workmate. One day he backed himself up against a fence and froze there, Hard Tack–style, simply refusing to budge. His handlers scurried around, trying to coax him into moving. In the end the only way Conway was able to get him to move at all was to turn him the wrong way around the track.

On June 26 Smith was set to give Seabiscuit his last pre-race workout. Outside was a driving rain. Charles and Marcela were due in that afternoon, so Smith delayed the workout. The rain fell all day. At four-thirty the Howards arrived. The track was a quagmire. Howard and Smith stepped out into the muck and worried. In normal conditions, they wouldn't have worked the horse, but Seabiscuit couldn't afford to miss another workout before meeting War Admiral. Smith led the horse out. Seabiscuit flew through the slop to clock six furlongs in 1:12⅗, fast enough to win almost any sprint race in the country. Howard beamed.

On June 28, the day before the race, heavy rain was still raking the course. Entries were due by 10:30 A.M. At 9:30, War Admiral's entry was made. Conway was confident. "He can beat anything on four feet," he had told reporters upon arriving at Suffolk with the bucking, rearing War Admiral in hand, "and if anything beats him, we will know the miracle of the ages has happened." Seabiscuit, he said, was "just one more horse to beat."

Still Howard and Smith waited. The rain never let up. Smith went down to the track office with his entry but just stood there without entering the horse, watching the rain. Finally, just fourteen minutes before entries closed, he made the entry. The decision was not final; they could still scratch him at any point up to forty-five minutes before post time. "We're still on the fence," said Howard. If the track stayed loose and wet, the horse was in; if the rain stopped and the track turned into the kind of thick surface that would pull on Seabiscuit's legs, he was out. Smith went back to the barn and readied Kayak for his purse race. The horse was superb, skipping over the mud to win. His time was excellent.

That night David Alexander and a host of radio technicians arrived at Pollard's hospital room. NBC had asked Alexander to host a nationally aired, live interview with Woolf and Pollard, conducted from Pollard's hospital room. Woolf would be on a hookup from a Boston broadcasting studio. Alexander found Pollard lying prone with his leg up in traction, his misery greatly assuaged by a leggy private nurse named Agnes. The technicians set up a makeshift radio studio around his bed. Concerned that Pollard's famously mischievous ad-libs might get them kicked off the air, Alexander had come prepared. He presented Pollard with a complete script for the interview, leaving nothing to the jockey's rich imagination or questionable vocabulary. At the studio, Woolf was given the same script.

At first the interview went as planned. Woolf read his lines, and Pollard read his responses. When they reached the section devoted to race tactics, Woolf dutifully recited his line asking Pollard how he should ride the race. Just then, Pollard's script spilled to the floor. The pages fluttered everywhere. Alexander hurriedly tried to gather them up. He looked up, a mess of papers in hand, just as Pollard opened his mouth. In the jockey's eyes, Alexander saw "an evil gleam."

"Why, Georgie boy," said Pollard to the eager ears of the entire nation, "get on the horse—face to the front—put one leg on each side of him, get someone to lead you into the gate, and then *fuck it up like you usually do.*"

For a moment the only sound reaching the NBC radio audience was a brief *swish!* as the radio technicians lunged for their controls. Woolf collapsed into peals of laughter. Alexander forged on with the interview, but the discussion he had planned so carefully had broken down completely. Woolf couldn't stop laughing and was barely able to grunt out his responses.

NBC didn't think it was so funny. The quip was a national scandal. The network, horrified at Pollard, wrote up a sanitized transcript of the interview.

The harrows worked the track all night. Howard kept the reporters up late. He was careful not to raise expectations. "My horse is sharper than a fishwife's tongue, and I'm as anxious as the next man to see him race against War Admiral. But a 'holding track' definitely is against him, and if we have to miss Mr. Riddle's horse today, we'll catch up with him yet."

In the morning the rain stopped. Seabiscuit was taken to the track for a final blowout. He ran beautifully. Smith took him back to the stall, inspected his legs, found them clean and cool, and bound them up in bandages for the rest of the morning. As midday rolled past, seventy thousand fans spilled out of the hotels and special trains and poured into the track. It was the second-largest crowd ever to attend a horse race in North America. Among the fans was Samuel Riddle. It had taken a special effort to get him to the track that afternoon. He was in poor health and had to come with the assistance of his physician, who sat with him.

Howard and Smith went out to make their final decision. They walked down the track from the finish line to the far turn. Their feet sank to the ankles, but the mud was loose. They looked for the "cupping" that told of a sticky track, but they didn't find it. One hour before post time, fifteen minutes before the deadline for scratches, they decided to go. Seabiscuit's number blinked up on the board. The race was on. Smith had never been more confident in his horse. Not normally a betting man, he cleaned out his pockets and put it all on Seabiscuit's nose.

Forty minutes before post time, Smith walked into Seabiscuit's stall. The bandages were unraveled from the horse's legs. Smith slid his hands over the horse's joints and tendons, feeling for the uniform cool firmness of a healthy leg. Halfway down one foreleg, his fingers tracing the bones and soft tissues of the lower leg, Smith paused. Seabiscuit was flinching. Smith looked hard at the spot. There was no break in the skin, and the hair lay flat. He touched it again. He felt a slender vein of heat, running from the ankle to the knee. The leg was injured. Smith realized that the horse must have kicked himself while galloping that morning. Because the skin had not been nicked and the heat had been slow to settle in, Smith had missed it. He could not race this horse.

But the trainer was too late. The deadline for scratches had passed five minutes before. Already the other horses, War Admiral included, were trickling to the paddock. Smith would have to appeal to the stewards for special permission to withdraw his horse. Clutching a scratch form, he left Seabiscuit in his stall and ran for the stewards' stand.

He had to cut through the crowd to reach it, and the throng was packed in and tamped down. Minutes slipped by as Smith waded through the mass of spectators. Finally, he made it to the ladder that led to the stewards' stand, suspended from the grandstand roof. He cleared the ladder and burst into the room. Seabiscuit, he announced, was injured and could not run. The stewards stared at him, incredulous.

No one moved. Smith realized that they didn't believe him.

Smith's high jinks with the press and Seabiscuit's recent history of scratches had come back to haunt him. The stewards had probably heard rumors that Seabiscuit had not really been lame at Belmont, and they were determined not to be duped. Every one of them believed that Smith had simply decided to duck War Admiral and was using injury as an excuse.

Chief steward Tom Thorpe demanded that Smith run his horse. Smith refused. They traded charges and countercharges. A crowd of reporters gathered outside the room, looking in the windows. They could see Smith and the stewards making angry gestures at each other, but they couldn't make out the words. Finally, Smith walked around the room, holding the scratch form straight out in front of him, offering it to each steward in turn. Each one glared back at him and refused to take it. Furious, Smith shredded up the form and stormed out. No one, he snapped, was going to force him to race an injured horse.

The stewards sat there and mulled over what to do. Outside, the crowd sensed that something was up. Every horse but Seabiscuit was in the paddock. A few people began to boo.

Howard was brought in. The stewards wanted him to overrule his trainer. Howard knew that another scratching would bring down an avalanche of criticism, but he would not second-guess Smith. He proposed a compromise. Bring in the track veterinarians to decide. The stewards agreed. If two track vets could confirm that the horse was really injured, Smith could scratch him. Otherwise, the horse had to run. With that, everyone dashed off to find two veterinarians. Post time was now a few minutes away. After a frantic hunt, two veterinarians were finally located and taken to the stall. They went over the horse and delivered their verdict.

Smith was right. A tendon running up the back of Seabiscuit's left foreleg was strained. The horse, the veterinarians said, would probably never run again. The stewards backed down, but they were livid. In the jockeys' room, Woolf unbuttoned his silks and took them off.

Seabiscuit's number went dark on the tote board. The crowd began to boo. On national radio, commentators declared that Seabiscuit's career was over. At the track, the announcer's voice called out over the sea of heads, explaining Seabiscuit's condition. With his first few words, the boos grew in intensity. The crowd was determined to drown out the poor announcer, who became progressively more frustrated. By the end of his message he was screaming into the mike, concluding in an angry bellow, "*And this is positively the truth!*"

Howard listened to the hooting and was horrified. He rushed to the press box to administer some image control but met a hostile audience. Chief steward Thorpe came in at the same time, venting his rage. "No one coaxed Howard to put his horse in the race because we figured something like this would happen," he sniped. "I think it was poor sportsmanship."

The crowd was howling epithets, the stewards were infuriated, the reporters were unsympathetic. For once, no amount of Howard charm could help. He reeled back to his box and sat down to a chorus of catcalls. Gradually, the din died off. Howard was deeply embarrassed, but did not regret what he'd done. "If I had raced him that day," he remembered later, "I would have broken him down for good. I would have been a fool to do that, no matter what was said of me. The old boy had taken enough punishment in his lifetime without me piling any more on."

On the track, the race was about to go. War Admiral crashed through the gate several times before settling down to break with the field. His black and yellow silks bobbed along with the pack, then fell back. Somewhere in the race he stepped in a dip in the ground, nearly fell face-first to the track, and emerged with a cut hoof. He labored home far behind the winner, Menow, diving for a photo finish for third place. He returned bleeding, only to have the judges deem that he had lost the photo for third. It was the first time he had ever finished out of the money. Riddle stood up and left. Howard felt a pang of pity for him and his horse. "It seems things are all going wrong, what with Red in the hospital and the Biscuit hurt," he said. "But then, Sam Riddle probably feels worse than we do right now."

The crowd was sagging. The race caller, collecting himself and trying to salvage something out of the ruined afternoon, cheerily announced that the winning jockey, Nick Wall of Stagehand fame, was "an East Boston boy!" There was no response.

"If anyone proposes another match race between these two super horses," wrote a reporter after the race, "henceforth, he will be tried in the morning for treason, mutiny, mopery and *non compos mentis.*"

After the race, the New England Turf Writers Association held its annual dinner. Their evening program reflected the general view of the Seabiscuit crew. On the program cover was a handsome shot of War Admiral. Seabiscuit's photo was put on the back.

The next morning Smith packed Seabiscuit's leg in poultices, bundled him up with the rest of the Howard horses, and got the hell out of Boston.

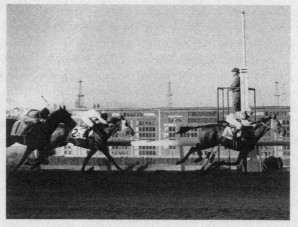

Hollywood Gold Cup, July 16, 1938
(© BETTMANN/CORBIS)

CHAPTER 16

I Know My Horse

Seabiscuit's train chattered west. They were bound for Arlington Park, just outside Chicago, in hopes that they would find some peace there. They didn't.

When the doors of the railcar swung open and Seabiscuit's head poked out, Smith was down on the platform waiting for him, standing in a sea of hostile reporters. Unraced for two and a half months, the horse was supercharged. He swung his head around edgily, his ears wagging from under his protective shipping helmet. Smith called out, "Hey there, boy, take it easy," and Seabiscuit caught sight of him, picking out his rigid form in the crush of men. He relaxed and walked down the gangplank with his usual ease.

Having heard the radio commentators state that Seabiscuit's injuries were career-ending—statements that no one in the Seabiscuit camp had uttered—and having heard persistent rumors that Smith had lied about the horse, the reporters were immediately suspicious when they saw Seabiscuit step out, walking soundly. They made no secret of their cynicism. "Does he really have a sore tendon?" asked one. "Why was he scratched from the Massachusetts?" yelled another.

"My," Smith replied, "but you must be having rainy weather around Chicago."

Someone suggested that Arlington Park officials would demand that Smith work Seabiscuit in their presence before his next scheduled race, the July 4 Stars and Stripes Handicap, to see that there was no "monkey business." Smith said that complying with such a demand was up to Howard. Then he swung up on Pumpkin, grasped Seabiscuit's halter, and led him, bucking and antsy, away from the reporters.

Seabiscuit had indeed been injured, but the veterinarians had been wrong. The injury was not as serious as they had feared. Under Smith's care, Seabiscuit's leg cooled and healed. He was soon dead sound.

The public pressure on the Howard barn was enormous. After seeing Seabiscuit walk from the train, a local reporter stated that the rumor that his injury had been faked had been "confirmed." Another called for the stewards to demand that Howard file a definitive guarantee that the horse would start. Arlington Park officials made a point of warning the public that if it rained, Seabiscuit probably would be scratched. But though the press and track officials were skeptical, the public was not. They bought up advance seats at an unprecedented pace, packed into special trains, and crammed into the track in record numbers to see the horse they called "the Great Traveler."

Right on cue, rain swamped Arlington on race day. Seabiscuit had been assigned 130 pounds, as much as 25 more than his rivals. He would be running on a course that clearly had no time to dry out. The only exercise Smith had time to give him was one slow gallop, followed by a brief half-mile sprint. The horse, idle since the Bay Meadows Handicap in mid-April, was as big as a house. He had no chance of winning the Stars and Stripes, and everyone in his camp knew it. But the pressure from the stewards and the press was too much to bear. Howard announced that as long as it wasn't raining at the time of the race, his horse would go.

The rain stopped, and the puddles on the track went still. Pumpkin, Howard, and Smith brought Seabiscuit to the paddock, and drew him up beside a swaying willow hedge. The crowds gathered ten deep for one hundred feet in each direction, a few spectators reaching through the slats of the fence to stroke Seabiscuit's chest as Smith cinched the girth on Woolf's kangaroo-leather saddle. Howard gave the nod and Woolf rode Seabiscuit out before a crowd of fifty thousand. Shuffled back to last in heavy traffic and carried hopelessly wide on the first turn,

Seabiscuit slipped through the mud, but still passed eight horses to finish second. The crowd was quiet. "The Seabiscuit myth," wrote a reporter, "is broken."

Smith loaded the horse back onto the train. Woolf and Howard climbed up with him. They were going back to California.

The destination was not Santa Anita, but the new Hollywood Park. The track was offering a $50,000 purse for the inaugural Hollywood Gold Cup, a ten-furlong race that promised to become one of the sport's premier events. The field was topped by a familiar face. Bing Crosby and Lin Howard's Ligaroti was finally coming into excellent form. On the day that Seabiscuit lost the Stars and Stripes, the "Argentine Jumping Bean" had broken the track record in the American Handicap. In the race he had defeated Whichcee, who had been universally regarded as California's second-best horse, behind Seabiscuit. Bing and Lin were overjoyed, and prepped him for the Hollywood Gold Cup. Lin was listed as the official trainer of the horse, but the actual conditioning had been done by Jimmy Smith, Tom's son. Track officials had been pleading with Howard to bring his horse to the race and make it a family affair, and though Seabiscuit had been assigned 133 pounds, between 13 and 28 pounds more than his competition, Howard accepted. Seabiscuit's stock was falling through the floor. No one in the Howard camp had any credibility left, and it was widely speculated that the horse's great days were behind him. Seabiscuit had to run in a big race, and he had to win it.

The race was scheduled for July 16, giving Smith only a week to prepare Seabiscuit after his arrival in California. The trainer did his best to keep him fit on the long journey west. Whenever the train pulled into a whistle-stop, he backed Pumpkin into a corner of the rail-car and trotted Seabiscuit around and around. Outside the train, admirers mobbed the platforms to watch him go. As the train pulled out, the fans cheered him on his way. With each stop, news that the horse was coming buzzed up the telegraph wires, and a new throng would gather farther along the route. In town after town, through

Kansas, New Mexico, and Arizona, the story was the same. At Albuquerque, even the reservation population turned out. As Smith walked the horse by, an ancient Indian leaned up and looked the horse over.

"Racehorse?" he said. Smith nodded.

"Looks like a cow pony to me."

Smith was pleased.

The rumors followed them west. The backstretch at Hollywood was thick with stories, chief among them that Seabiscuit was lame. The stewards listened and worried that they would be burned by Seabiscuit as Belmont and Suffolk Downs had been. They had some reason to be wary. Earlier in the meet, a much-anticipated meeting between Kentucky Derby winner Lawrin and Preakness winner Dauber had to be canceled at the last moment when Dauber suffered a minor injury. The event had been traumatic for the Hollywood Park officials and seemed to make them overly concerned about Smith.

On July 11, 1938, Smith walked Seabiscuit onto the track for his first workout at Hollywood. The trainer didn't like the looks of the track, which was so deep and crumbly that it was playing at least a second slower than usual. "It looked like they were trying to grow corn on the track," he said.

Before five hundred spectators, Seabiscuit breezed an easy mile under Woolf. He didn't show a trace of lameness, prompting Smith to announce that the horse was ready to run in the Gold Cup. But no one was ready to believe that things were as they appeared. The rumors about Seabiscuit's bad-leggedness continued to circulate, and the stewards' anxiety escalated. Two days later Smith stacked Seabiscuit with 133 pounds, including Woolf, and turned them loose for another workout. With Woolf pulling hard on the reins, Seabiscuit went smoothly and soundly, looking so fit that even the clockers were singing his praises.

The pair of workouts should have been enough to dispel the rumors. They weren't. As Smith led the horse back to the barn, someone gave him an incredible piece of news. The stewards had commissioned a veterinarian to go over to the Howard barn, pull Seabiscuit out, examine him, and determine whether or not Smith was lying about his horse's condition.

The action was unprecedented; no one had ever seen stewards treat a trainer with such blatant distrust. It was all the more extraordinary given the record of the trainer in question; aside from Fair Knightess, Tom Smith had reportedly never had a horse in his care suffer a serious injury. But Smith had played around with his pursuers for too long. Ever since Oscar Otis had discovered the trainer working Seabiscuit by moonlight in 1937, racing officials had been growing increasingly frustrated. It had finally boiled over.

Standing in the barn next to his perfectly sound horse, Smith was dumbfounded. "Nobody is going to inspect this horse if I know anything about it," he snapped. "He won't go postward if I don't think he's in good shape. We wouldn't have shipped Seabiscuit clear across the country if we didn't believe he was in good shape. And now that he's here, no clockers, newspapermen, or veterinarians are going to step in and tell me how to train my horse."

His words fell flat. The veterinarian arrived at the stall, ready to examine the horse whether or not Smith gave him permission. Smith blocked his way.

"Nobody is going to examine Seabiscuit but me," he snarled. He slammed the stall doors in the veterinarian's face. The vet gave up and left.

After trying and failing to reach Howard to get him to talk Smith into the exam, the stewards asked Smith to work the horse in their presence, and cleared a slot for him between the third and fourth races on the afternoon of July 14. An assembly of clockers lined up to see the work. They sat there and aged a little, seeing nothing but an empty track. Hollywood Park general manager Jack Mackenzie tried to make an end run around Smith, running up to Howard's box in hopes of winning his word that Seabiscuit was sound and would start. But Howard, like Smith and Seabiscuit, never showed up. Mackenzie camped out at the box all afternoon, then gave up and went to a telephone and tried to track Howard down. For once in his life, Howard was inaccessible.

That evening Smith finally emerged from the barn with Seabiscuit. Track representatives dropped in behind him, trailing him all over the track. After watching Seabiscuit work, they followed him around while he cooled out, searching for lameness that wasn't there.

The conflict turned bizarre on the day before the race. Smith sent his stable agent, Sonny Greenberg, to the racing secretary's office with an entry form. Mackenzie took one look at it and hit the roof. Smith had scrawled two words across it: "Doubtful starter."

Mackenzie booted Greenberg back out the door with a demand to see Smith in person. Greenberg ran back to Smith. The trainer scrawled another note and sent Greenberg back to the track offices. The stewards read his message: "I have a previous engagement."

That did it. Mackenzie was seething. Someone suggested that mercenaries be sent over to the Howard barn to forcibly haul Smith into the office. Setting that popular idea aside, the stewards fired the leg-weary Greenberg back to the barn again, bearing yet another message. "Seabiscuit will either be a positive starter tomorrow, or we will refuse his entry entirely."

A few minutes later, Greenberg dragged himself back to the offices with Smith's counterdemand: No one was to show up at his barn asking to examine the horse. The stewards complied, and Greenberg stumbled back to the Howard barn.

In late morning, the administrative office door swung open. The officials looked up, expecting to see Greenberg. It was Smith. The stewards sat blinking at him. "All right," Smith said. "Take the 'doubtful starter' off the blank. Seabiscuit will run all right."

Back at the barn, resting his sore legs, Greenberg saw Smith laughing. "The madder they got, the better he liked it," Greenberg remembered. "He just done that for bein' onery."

On July 16 a record sixty thousand people pressed into Hollywood Park to see Seabiscuit try for the Gold Cup, while millions more crowded around radio sets to hear NBC's national broadcast. The radio announcer spent fourteen of the fifteen minutes before the race talking about Seabiscuit. One question hummed through the crowd: Was Seabiscuit the same horse he was when he left California in April?

The fans cheered when Seabiscuit stepped out onto the track, then gave him two more ovations as he paraded to the post and loaded into the gate. Once in, Seabiscuit stood quietly. In stall number one, the quick-footed Specify began acting up, backing, ducking back and forth, and kicking at his handlers. He had been assigned just 109 pounds, and his jockey, Wayne Wright, had reduced himself half to death to make weight. Wright felt weak and woozy, and was having trouble holding the horse. A lot was riding on his being able to hold himself together: Specify's owner, Bert Baroni, was so confident that Seabiscuit was lame that he had placed a $5,000 wager on his horse.

Standing under his 133 pounds in the hot sun, Seabiscuit waited. After several minutes and the efforts of three assistant starters, Specify finally stood still. Starter Eddie Thomas reached for the bell. An instant before he rang it, Specify lunged forward. Wright couldn't hold him. Thomas hit the bell a millisecond later. Specify had lunged himself into a false start, but the race was on. Wright was under Baroni's orders to restrain the horse, but he simply couldn't. In a few strides, Specify was six lengths ahead of the field and running away with Wright.

Seabiscuit broke sluggishly and sank back through the field. Going into the first turn with only one horse behind him, Woolf asked Seabiscuit to move up. There was no response. From his post on the homestretch, Smith watched Seabiscuit's action and gritted his teeth. As he had foreseen, the track was crumbling like sand under the horse's hooves. In the saddle, Woolf could feel his mount fighting the surface. Seeing that he could not make up ground at this stage, the jockey changed his game plan, eased up, and settled in to wait. The fans grew concerned. Seabiscuit was dropping farther and farther out of the race. After half a mile, he was more than twelve lengths back and still sinking. Woolf was not moving at all, his chin in Seabiscuit's mane, his eyes on the horses ahead, his hands still. In the grandstand, the crowd pleaded for Woolf to do something.

The Iceman wasn't worried. "Let 'em run themselves out,"

someone heard him saying into Seabiscuit's ear. "It's a long way to go." Smith had given him orders to stay with Ligaroti, who was now galloping near him. Woolf knew that to put Seabiscuit into a drive to catch Specify would leave him vulnerable to a late rally by Ligaroti. He would not repeat the mistake he had made against Stagehand, moving too soon. He nudged his mount down onto the rail, where the going was smoother, and waited.

With eight horses ahead of him, Woolf couldn't see what was happening out front. Seabiscuit was built low to the ground, so Woolf's view was constantly obstructed by bigger horses. Somewhere in the backstretch, he lost sight of Ligaroti. He knew that there was a horse far out in front, but because the runner immediately ahead, Whichcee, was blocking his view, he couldn't tell if it was Specify or Ligaroti. It was critical to know. If it was Ligaroti, a horse with a sustained stretch drive, he would have to move now and hope Seabiscuit could hold his rally. If it was the shorter-winded Specify, whom he expected to collapse in the homestretch, he could afford to wait.

Late in the backstretch, Woolf shifted Seabiscuit to the outside and craned around Whichcee. He caught sight of the horse out in front, but he still didn't know who it was. He looked at the horse's jockey. He was leading with his left hand. Woolf knew that among the local riders, only Wayne Wright was left-handed. So it had to be Specify. He studied Wright's hands. He was holding the reins loosely, and they were flapping on Specify's neck. It was all Woolf needed to see. Specify was at the top of his speed, with nothing in reserve. Woolf was sure that he would soon burn out. He began to edge Seabiscuit closer but didn't ask him for his best, thinking that Ligaroti was tracking him. A tentative cheer rose out of the crowd. Seabiscuit was only making up ground in inches, and he was still at least eight lengths behind. Time was running out.

Leaning around the far turn, Woolf drew a bead on Specify again. Incredibly, the horse was still rolling. A pang of fear went through Woolf. Ligaroti was somewhere behind him; bumped and pinched hard on the backstretch, he had been knocked too far back, and would finish a fast-closing fourth. Woolf knew he could easily beat the others, but he was beginning to worry that he couldn't catch Specify. Dropping flat in the saddle, he gave his mount two taps with the whip and clucked in his ear. Up in the booth, caller Joe Hernandez saw him do it, and shouted into the microphone, "And here comes Seabiscuit!"

For a moment Seabiscuit faltered, the ground breaking up under his hooves. But all at once, his turn speed emerged. He bent his body to the arc of the rail and punched into the belly of the field. At the top of the stretch, he shot out of the front of the pack. Specify came into view, still leading by four lengths. Whichcee was on his outside. Woolf looked back for Ligaroti just as his mount caught sight of Specify. Seabiscuit's ears flipped back and flattened. Woolf didn't need to tell his horse what to do. Seabiscuit lunged forward, cutting inside of Whichcee and gunning for Specify.

Woolf felt like he was flying. He put his whip away. "There was nothing to do," he said later, "but give him his way." Specify's hindquarters neared, and Woolf pulled back a tick on his left rein to give Seabiscuit clear sailing. Seabiscuit swept up to Specify and finished him. He accelerated away and cruised under the wire all alone, breaking the track record.

As four pageboys struggled to haul the four-foot-high solid-gold trophy to Howard in the winner's circle, Woolf was wreathed in flowers. "I thought it would be easy," he said. "It was." Howard laughed and smiled and stroked Seabiscuit's nose. The awards presenter, the comely actress Anita Louise, handed Smith his trophy. The trainer's uncharacteristically bashful response became the subject of a banner headline: SILENT TOM SMILES!

Someone told Smith about Bert Baroni's $5,000 bet that the supposedly lame Seabiscuit would lose to Specify. Smith laughed so hard, said a witness, "I thought he'd bust."

Seabiscuit, sound, brilliantly fast, and impeccably prepared, had spoken on Smith's behalf. The reporters had been wrong, and they knew it. Up in the press box, they stayed late to bang out praises and apologies. Down on the track, the cheering went on and on.

*

After the last race of the day was run and the track had cleared, darkness gathered under the shed rows of the Hollywood backstretch. Virtually everyone was gone but Smith, standing alone with Seabiscuit.

"The clockers told me the horse wasn't right," a passerby heard the old trainer say, "and the handicappers said he wasn't in condition.

"But I know my horse."

*In one of the wildest and most controversial horse races ever run,
Seabiscuit (A) and Ligaroti barrel down the Del Mar
homestretch as Spec Richardson, on Ligaroti, repeatedly
fouls George Woolf, on Seabiscuit.*
(SAN DIEGO UNION)

CHAPTER 17

The Dingbustingest Contest You Ever Clapped an Eye On

L in Howard was in one of those moods during which crazy ideas
sound perfectly sensible. A bullish, handsome man with decisive eyebrows and more hair than he could find use for, Lin
had a great deal of money and a habit of having things go his way. So
many things in his life had gone his way that it no longer occurred to
him not to be in a festive mood, and he spent much of his time celebrating the general goodness of things and sitting with old friends
telling fat happy lies. But things had not gone Lin's way lately, and he
was not accustomed to the feeling.

Lin wanted in the worst way to whip his father at racing, to knock
his Seabiscuit down a peg or two, and he believed he had the horse to
do it in Ligaroti. He was sure enough about it to have made some
account-closing bets on the horse, at least one as a side wager with his
father, and he was a great deal poorer for it. The last race really ate at
him. Ligaroti had been at Seabiscuit's throat in the Hollywood Gold
Cup when another horse had bumped him right out of his game. He
had streaked down the stretch to finish fourth and had come back a
week later to score a smashing victory over Whichcee in a Hollywood
stakes race, firmly establishing himself as the second-best horse in the
West. Bing Crosby and Lin were certain that with a weight break and a
clean trip, Ligaroti had Seabiscuit's measure. Charles Howard didn't
see it that way. Since the race, he had been going around with pockets
full of clippings about Seabiscuit. Anytime anyone came near him, he
would wave the articles around and start gushing, like a new father.

The senior Howard probably didn't hold back when Lin was around. He was immensely proud of Lin's success with Ligaroti, but he enjoyed tweaking his son, and he was good at it. He had once given Lin a book for Christmas entitled *What You Know About Horses.* The pages were blank.

One night shortly after the Hollywood Gold Cup, Lin was sitting at a restaurant table across from his father and Bing Crosby. They were apparently talking about the Gold Cup, and Lin was sitting there looking at his father and doing a slow burn. Bing wasn't too happy either; his misadventures as a horse owner were becoming an embarrassment. An idea was kicking around in Lin's head, and it seemed as good a time as any to toss it out there. Why not have a match race between Seabiscuit and Ligaroti?

Charles snorted.

Crosby lit up. The year before, he had invested $600,000 in the building of a new track, Del Mar, a magnificent seaside racing palace near San Diego. Del Mar was a Bing paradise, featuring good racing by day and dinner, dancing, and crooning by night. But in its second year Del Mar needed a boost; daily attendance averaged just six thousand. A match race featuring Seabiscuit was just what the track needed. Crosby knew he could talk the board of directors into footing a big purse for the event. Crosby and Lin worked on Howard for the rest of the meal.

Howard began to see the merits of the race. For one, a sizable purse could get Seabiscuit that much closer to Sun Beau's money-winning mark; he was still $85,000 short. In addition, Smith might enjoy pitting his horse against one trained by his son, Jimmy, just as Howard would enjoy facing off against Lin. And Lin wouldn't let up on the needling. Howard gave in.

Lin wanted to make it interesting. He dared his father to make a side bet with him. Howard shook him off. He told him he couldn't bear to take any more money from his own son.

Crosby hustled off to make the arrangements. He returned with a fair deal. Del Mar would put up a winner-take-all purse of $25,000, 14 percent of the entire purse budget for the track's meeting. Seabiscuit would carry 130 pounds, Ligaroti 115. The race, slated for August 12, would be run over a mile and an eighth. Woolf would ride Seabiscuit, Spec Richardson would ride Ligaroti. Charles and Lin flipped a coin to determine post position. Charles won the toss and picked the rail.

At Del Mar the reporters followed Smith everywhere, but all they got out of him was a gusty *"Ugh!"* Unable to catch Seabiscuit working, the newsmen took a page from the Wise We Boys and staked out tactical positions around the track. Smith somehow evaded them. Someone wondered aloud if Seabiscuit was working "camouflaged as a diesel tractor." In the afternoon, racegoers streamed past Seabiscuit's stall. "It looked like a parade," Smith growled. When the races were on, Seabiscuit could see the fields go down the backstretch and would try to climb out of his stall to run with them. Smith had had enough and secreted the horse away to a new stall. The press couldn't find it.

In the week before the race, Howard took an unusual phone call. The caller was a track official, who told him that a New York bettor had sent $5,000 to wager on Ligaroti, challenging Howard to put up $15,000 against it. Howard was surely amazed at such a huge wager from a complete stranger, but he was not one to back down from a challenge. It took him a while to learn that he had been suckered. The mysterious "New York bettor" was in fact Lin, who had talked the track official into placing the call.

Meanwhile, Lin and Crosby were hard at work putting on a horse race Hollywood-style. Crosby arranged to have a large section of the clubhouse roped off and patrolled by guards, with admission restricted to Ligaroti rooters—the "I'm for Ligaroti" section. He went out on a promotional tour to gather a cast of thousands, contacting four hundred friends, mostly movie people, and talking them into coming to the track to cheer his horse on. He appointed Dave Butler, director of Shirley Temple films, head cheerleader, fitting him with a turtleneck emblazoned with the initials BL, for Binglin. He had four hundred Ligaroti pennants printed up in the horse's colors, cerise and white polka dots, and attached to canes for waving. Turf scribe

Jack McDonald surveyed the production and wondered if the net effect would be to inspire Ligaroti or scare him to death.

Crosby flooded the region with publicity. All over town, posters went up that read:

DEL MAR
AUGUST 12, 1938
SEABISCUIT VS. LIGAROTI

CHARLES HOWARD
VS. BING CROSBY
FATHER VS. SON
THE ICEMAN WOOLF
VS. SPEC RICHARDSON
AMERICA VS. ARGENTINA

ONE OF THE
GREATEST MATCH RACES
OF ALL TIME

From the race's conception, the press viewed it with skepticism. Sportswriters argued that the rich event was a farce arranged to pad Seabiscuit's bankroll. Del Mar, conscious of the potential conflict of interest for the Howards and Smiths, barred public wagering on the race. But the press's distrust and the absence of gambling did nothing to cool the enthusiasm of racing fans. On the sweltering race day, special trains and buses poured in from San Diego and Los Angeles, filling the track with well over twenty thousand people, many more than the track's official capacity. Lin plastered a twenty-foot LIGAROTI sign on the wall behind the "I'm for Ligaroti" section, and scores of Crosby's movie friends, including Clark Gable and Carole Lombard, Spencer Tracy and Ray Milland, took up their cerise and white pennants and filed in. "Is there anyone left in Hollywood?" wondered a spectator. Dave Butler led a chorus of Ligaroti cheers, and the crowd grew boisterous.

Crosby perched on the roof with Oscar Otis, who would call the race for a national radio broadcast. In the jockeys' room, Woolf suited up to man the helm on Seabiscuit while Richardson slipped on Ligaroti's polka dots. Just before the race, Woolf and Richardson made a deal. No matter who won, they would "save," or split, the purse between them.

It began as an exhilarating display of pure speed. To a gleeful shriek from the crowd, Seabiscuit and Ligaroti ripped out of the gate side by side. There was no clever strategy in either camp; each rider wanted the lead immediately. It was Seabiscuit who got it, tearing toward the first turn with his head in front. He couldn't shake Ligaroti off. They rounded the first turn and barreled into the backstretch locked together. Inch by inch, Ligaroti edged closer, then thrust his nose in front. A few strides later, Seabiscuit edged back to the lead again. After six furlongs, they were one fifth of a second faster than the track record. The mile marker clipped by, and the tote board flashed the fraction: 1:36⅕. The track record had been eclipsed by two seconds.

They couldn't, it seemed, keep up such a pace. With the crowd leaping and yelling, the two horses skimmed the far turn and straightened away for the run for the wire. Richardson was playing every card he had, hollering in Woolf's ear to try to distract him or provoke him into fouling himself out of the race.

With an eighth of a mile to go, Richardson felt Ligaroti beginning to weaken. The colt sagged inward, muscling his shoulder and hip into the smaller Seabiscuit. Hemmed in between Ligaroti and the rail, Seabiscuit had nowhere to go. He was driven to the left and for an awful moment nearly tumbled over the rail. He straightened himself out, grimly stood his ground, and held his head in front. Richardson kept right on yelling.

Seabiscuit had Ligaroti beaten. Richardson knew it. Desperate, the jockey resorted to an old bush-league tactic. Reaching across the gap between the two horses, he grabbed Seabiscuit's saddlecloth and pulled back hard. Woolf couldn't believe it. "What are you doing, Spec?" he shouted. Richardson didn't let go.

Seabiscuit was now towing Ligaroti down the homestretch. Woolf couldn't break him free. Anchored by Richardson's grasp, Ligaroti began to haul himself forward. The two horses drew together again, running stride for stride with Seabiscuit's head still in front. On their backs, Woolf and Richardson struggled. With seventy yards to go, Richardson abruptly released the saddlecloth and grabbed Woolf's whip hand. Woolf twisted around in the saddle, trying to snatch his wrist free. It was here, Richardson later said, that he locked his leg over Woolf's leg. If Seabiscuit moved up, Woolf would be scraped off his saddle and slammed into the track. The Howards' sporting gesture had disintegrated into a back-alley brawl.

With just a few yards to go, Woolf was frantic. Seabiscuit was fighting hard, but in Richardson's grasp, he could not break away. The wire was looming overhead, and Ligaroti was lunging for the lead. Races in that day were not yet filmed with head-on and side-shot patrol cameras to police for riding infractions, so there was a good chance that Ligaroti would not be disqualified if his nose hit the wire first. Woolf could not move Seabiscuit up. He had to move Ligaroti back.

With twenty yards to go, Woolf tore his hand free, threw out his right arm and grabbed Ligaroti's bridle, just above the bit. Just as the wire passed overhead, he pulled back, lifting the horse's head up and to the left as Seabiscuit's head bobbed forward. Seabiscuit flew under the wire first. Lugging 130 pounds, Ligaroti, and Richardson, Seabiscuit had run nine furlongs in 1:49. He had broken the track record by four seconds, the equivalent of some twenty-five lengths.

Up on the clubhouse, Oscar Otis looked quizzically at the finish line. He had seen Ligaroti's head jerk up oddly at the wire. A jubilant celebration was going on all around him; almost no one else had noticed anything amiss. The reporters were raving. One called it "the dingbustingest contest you ever clapped an eye on . . . a ripsnorting race." But the stewards, standing on an infield platform right above the finish line, had seen everything. The INQUIRY sign blipped up on the board.

Richardson galloped back first, jumped off the horse, bounded up the stairs three at a time, and muddied up the stewards' stand carpets. Shouting passionately and waving his arms as he spoke, Richardson charged that Woolf had fouled him. The stewards called Woolf in. With his usual frankness, the Iceman admitted everything he had done but explained why he had done it. The stewards sent the jockeys outside while they conferred. The crowd buzzed in confusion.

Woolf and Richardson waited side by side on the track, Woolf with his hands on his hips, Richardson with his arms folded on the rail. Each one peered angrily out of the corner of his eye at the other, and neither said a word. Woolf was sure that Richardson was about to smack him.

The ruling came down. The foul was not allowed, and the result was allowed to stand. The baffled reporters asked the stewards why they had held an inquiry at all, but the stewards refused to explain themselves. Clearly, something was up: Woolf and Richardson were told not to accept any more mounts pending a meeting by the stewards.

The riders stomped to the jockeys' room, snapping at each other. The newsmen, in agonies of curiosity, tailed them. They overheard Richardson accusing Woolf of grabbing his bridle, and Woolf retorting that Richardson had grabbed his whip. Woolf said if Richardson had just stopped shouting for one single instant to concentrate on riding, he might have gotten his horse's nose in front.

Down in the winner's circle, Crosby could smell disaster. Standing with Marcela, he waited, sober-faced and distracted, as his wife—universally known as "Mrs. Bing"—gamely presented the winner's trophy to Charles. Lin and his father, laughing, shook hands. With the ceremony over, Crosby rushed after Woolf and Richardson. He found them on the verge of blows in the jockeys' room, with all the reporters watching. Desperate to avoid bad publicity, Crosby stepped between them and told them to hold their tongues. Marcela, more excited than she had ever been over a race, downed several aspirin.

The next morning the stewards called Woolf and Richardson in and threw the book at them. Not only were both suspended for the rest of the meeting, but the officials recommended that the state racing board ban them from all California tracks until January 1, 1939. It was a punishment tough enough to demand explanation, but the stewards still refused to reveal what had happened. In their zeal to avoid resurrecting the sport's reputation for chicanery, they tried to bury the incident. Asked to release official photos, they declined. "I want the newspapers to forget this thing," said the presiding steward. "Consequently, I have no further information to give."

A more suggestive comment could hardly have been made. The press covering the race was already suspicious and scandal-hungry, and assumed that the stewards were hiding something shocking. Wild speculation was the order of the day. Someone was bound to make a public accusation of wrongdoing. Someone did.

It began four days after the race, with a *San Diego Sun* story trumpeted in an enormous front-page banner headline in two-inch-high letters: "INSIDE" ON BISCUIT RACE BARED. Anonymously written, the story charged that Woolf admitted he had been told not to win by too much, to "make it look close" and "make a race of it." Richardson, the story alleged, knew that Seabiscuit was being held back and tried to take advantage of it to steal the race so he could cash in on a $1,500 bet on Ligaroti. Woolf then had to resort to dirty riding to thwart Richardson. The article speculated that the stewards' "secret investigation" may have revealed "the identity of the race figure who gave Woolf his orders," but that the officials were not telling the public.

At first glance, it seems surprising that the story caused the stir it did. The uproar was not over the rough riding in the race—which was truly outrageous—but over a supposed shadowy conspiracy around it. Yet, however much the tone of the article suggested otherwise, even if true, the allegations were trivial. As long as Woolf intended to win, there would have been nothing wrong with minimizing his winning margin. At most, it would have created a more entertaining spectacle and saved Bing, Lin, and Jimmy Smith from the humiliation of seeing their horse routed. Likewise, there certainly was nothing wrong with Richardson trying to win the race. But the paper presented these allegations as scandalous bombshells, calling them "startling disclosures." In an era in which the sport's corrupt years were still a fresh memory, it was enough to set the ball rolling. The story was picked up by the wire services and distributed nationwide.

A massive controversy ensued. Richardson immediately denied placing any bet, and Woolf denied that he had ever made any such statement, or even spoken to any reporter. Though the allegations did not point to race-fixing, in the sensational atmosphere following the unexplained suspension of two jockeys, the race was now being referred to as a "frameup" and a "fix." Resting in the Del Mar Hotel, Howard saw the *Sun* story and exploded. He had long tolerated false allegations with tactful restraint, but he saw this as a strike against his honesty and an attempt to group him with the race-fixers from the sport's past. It brought him beyond rage.

Summoning a host of reporters to the hotel lobby, he lost his ever-genial composure for the first and only time in his public life. Barely able to contain his fury, he emphatically denied that he or Smith had given Woolf any such orders. He called the story "dirty and libelous." "The whole thing is not worthy of denial," he hissed, "excepting that it is so vicious that it cannot be overlooked." He said that he had told Woolf to gun to the lead and get far enough ahead of Ligaroti to move to the outside; letting Seabiscuit's rival assume the rail would prevent Ligaroti, who often drifted in, from bumping him. It was only because Ligaroti was so fast, Howard said, that Woolf was unable to execute the plan. Most compelling was his final point: Given that both his splits and final time for the race were record-shattering, the idea that Seabiscuit had been restrained was preposterous.

"Any fool writing racing ought to know that a race run in 1:49, with the first mile in 1:36⅗ and which was the time caught by numerous private clockers as well as the official track timer, couldn't be fixed in that manner," he said, glaring at the reporters. "I am deeply chagrined that any editor would accept a story without verification in which such obviously erroneous information is contained. . . . If the man who wrote that story had any sense, he would know you couldn't 'boat' a race run in that fast time."

Howard challenged the anonymous writer to produce proof of his charges and angrily defied anyone in the room to give him a plausible argument for how the allegations could have been possible. He concluded by addressing the implications that he was a race-fixer. "If Seabiscuit, or any other of my horses, can't win on their merits, I'd retire from racing today."

Howard followed up the press conference by publishing a signed statement that Woolf had not been told to check Seabiscuit. He wrote at least one prominent reporter personally, arguing that the race itself was testimony to the absurdity of the *Sun*'s charges and enclosing the finish photo of the race—the reporter had evidently questioned whether or not Seabiscuit had crossed the line first. In his letter, Howard pointed to what he thought was the motivation behind the attack on his integrity: the rivalry with War Admiral. "I realize," he wrote, "that there are a few people in the East who are becoming quite alarmed over the prospect of Seabiscuit ending up as the top winner of the American turf."

Back at Del Mar, officials supported Howard, stating that the accusations that Seabiscuit had been restrained, or that Howard or Smith had told Woolf to do so, were ludicrous. But they couldn't stop the flood of charges. A movement began to deny Howard the purse money or prevent it from being officially credited to Seabiscuit.

The California Turf Writers Association, recognizing that a lack of official information had created this absurd situation, demanded that the stewards clear things up. The morning after Howard's speech, the Del Mar officials finally issued a statement explaining in detail exactly what had transpired during the race: Richardson had grabbed Woolf's saddlecloth, then his whip, then Woolf had grabbed Ligaroti's bridle. They emphasized their agreement that without the fouling, Seabiscuit would have won anyway.

Though the accusations died off quickly after the stewards' statement, Howard was still in a jam. He was jockeyless. Unsure of what to do, he suspended all of Seabiscuit's engagements.

Lin inadvertently solved the problem for him. He firmly believed that Richardson had not fouled Woolf enough to merit banning him from the track for the rest of the year. He discovered that, evidently unbeknownst to anyone, someone had filmed the race. Lin bought the film and, before viewing it, asked the stewards and reporters to join him at a theater in Solana Beach to see it. Delighted at the chance to find out what really happened, a mob showed up. The lights dimmed and the film ran.

Lin turned crimson. The film showed Richardson committing every foul short of shooting Woolf off his horse. Woolf had clearly acted in self-defense. The press began to lobby to have the suspension overturned for Woolf. The state racing board, tired of the whole mess, realized that the race's nonbetting status gave them an out because the public had not been defrauded. They opted to lift the suspensions on both jockeys after the Del Mar meeting concluded.

The moment the result was handed down, Howard contacted Woolf. Pack up your things, he told him. We're going east to get War Admiral.

Smith led Seabiscuit along the road that wound up to the railroad siding. The train stood waiting, stocked for a long sojourn in the East. A flurry of Navy planes screamed overhead, low enough to part a man's hair. The horse didn't bat an eyelash. He tramped aboard the train and lay down. By the time Smith got settled in and the train whined into motion, Seabiscuit was fast asleep.

After drilling through walk-up starts with Smith's homemade
bell, Woolf and Seabiscuit streak over the Pimlico track
in a workout on October 26, 1938.
(MORGAN COLLECTION/ARCHIVE PHOTOS)

CHAPTER 18

Deal

The summer of 1938 gave way to fall. Through the window in his room at Boston's Winthrop Hospital, Red Pollard watched the sky darken. He was not getting better. Surgeons had operated repeatedly on his crushed leg, rebreaking it and resetting it, but it would not heal. Though nearly four months had passed since his injury, he could not stand. His powerful boxer's body had dwindled to a virtual skeleton. He weighed eighty-six pounds. His face had aged so dramatically that, on the twenty-ninth birthday he celebrated that November, he could easily have passed for fifty. He was so weak that basic tasks required tremendous effort. He kept a brave face before his friends, assuring them he would ride again, but they didn't believe it and neither did he.

The brisk New England October blew into Massachusetts. Pollard brooded. He pored over "Old Waldo" Emerson and ruminated on the philosopher's essay on "Compensation." He grasped for hope in Emerson's vision of natural polarities, in which all things are balanced by their opposites darkness by light, cold by heat, loss by gain. He thought about the career he had lost.

> *A makeweight flying to the void*
> *Supplemental asteroid*
> *Or compensatory spark*
> *Shoots across the neutral dark.*

He was falling in love with his private nurse. Regally lovely, Agnes Conlon caught the eye of every young man in the hospital. The child of a well-heeled, status-oriented Back Bay family of antique dealers, she was far out of the league of a jockey with a seventh-grade formal education and no fixed address. She was also spoken for, the steady girlfriend of a local physician. In disposition, she was Pollard's antithesis, governing her life with rigid reserve as he scattered his passions.

In their afternoons in the hospital, Pollard wooed her with quotes from Old Waldo while she tended to his leg. He apparently told her about his darkest secret, his blind eye. He trusted her completely.

Sometime that fall, Red proposed. Agnes's family was horrified. "It was as if you suddenly decided to marry someone from the circus," said his daughter, Norah Christianson. And Red was so emaciated and weak that Agnes was certain he was dying. But something about him was appealing. It would be said later by those who knew Agnes that Red was, for her, a liberation from herself. It seemed that there was a part of her that yearned to be as extravagant as he. Agnes did a crazy thing.

A letter from Red slid into the mailbox of the Pollard family home in Edmonton. Agnes had said yes. Old Waldo, Pollard told his friends, had been right after all.

A few hundred miles south of Winthrop Hospital, Alfred Vanderbilt was busy cultivating a passion of his own. Fresh from his honeymoon with Marcela's niece, the twenty-six-year-old operator of Baltimore's Pimlico Racecourse had never given up on the idea of staging a War Admiral– Seabiscuit match race. When the meetings at Belmont and Suffolk Downs had fallen through, Vanderbilt had begun contemplating the idea again. He had bided his time all summer, waiting for the horses to reach their peaks and the demand for the race to build again.

September of '38, the timing seemed right. While Seabiscuit had spent the summer pillaging the West, War Admiral had been plundering the East with four triumphs in succession. Then Riddle did something out of character. At a society dinner in mid-September, he announced that he would put up $25,000 as forfeit money for a race between his colt and Seabiscuit. Howard jumped at the offer. Knowing Riddle's fickleness, he opted not to call him directly to negotiate in private; with only the two of them talking, there would be few consequences to backing out. Instead, Howard cranked up the pressure by bringing in the press. He cracked open his address book and began calling reporters, asking them to announce that he'd gladly meet Riddle's sum, and War Admiral, anywhere and any time Riddle wanted. "We're ready," he said, "any time Samuel D. Riddle wants to send his horse against the Biscuit."

Vanderbilt decided that the time was ripe to get Pimlico involved. He was playing with a weak hand. Pimlico could offer only a tiny fraction of the $100,000 purse Belmont had put up. Riddle posed another problem. He was still angry over Pimlico starter Jim Milton's use of tongs on War Admiral the year before, and he was sticking to his vow never to run a horse at the track again.

Vanderbilt thought he could talk Riddle out of his boycott, but just as he was about to contact the owner, Riddle seemed to back out of his offer altogether. He announced that he would not allow any race to interfere with War Admiral's set schedule, which called for him to appear in Belmont's Jockey Club Gold Cup, then complete his season in two $7,500 races in New England. After that, the four-year-old horse would be retired.

Howard, who had already brought Seabiscuit to Belmont in hopes that a match could be arranged, was disconsolate. Neither he nor Smith wanted to run in the Jockey Club Gold Cup. They had never welcomed the idea of a full-field contest with War Admiral, and the October 1 race would interfere with a promise Howard had made to run Seabiscuit in the September 28 Havre de Grace Handicap in Maryland. Howard hoped to talk Belmont officials into another match, but they wanted no part of it. Any interest there might have been in a match declined further when Howard, knowing he could not scratch his horse at Belmont again, allowed him to run in the September 20 Manhattan Handicap under 128 pounds in the middle of a whirling rainstorm. Seabiscuit came home third, drenched to the bone, covered head to toe in mud, and miserable. Howard and Smith took Seabiscuit down to Maryland. Howard believed that his last chance for a match race had probably slipped away. Almost everyone agreed with him.

Except Vanderbilt. The young Marylander was an energetic diplomat and thought he could get a deal made. On September 28 Seabiscuit's stock rose after an overwhelming victory in the Havre de Grace Handicap. Taking advantage of this, Vanderbilt launched a vigorous one-man campaign to find an agreement between the Howard and Riddle camps. Desperate for the race and knowing that Riddle was in control, Howard was game to any of Vanderbilt's suggestions. So Vanderbilt began working on Riddle.

At first Vanderbilt had so much trouble just making contact with War Admiral's owner that he nearly gave up. When he did track him down, Riddle was cool. For a fortnight, Vanderbilt besieged him with wires, calls, and requests for private meetings. He used a good measure of flattery, assuring Riddle that War Admiral would of course beat the stuffing out of Seabiscuit. Vanderbilt gave him a reasonable starting proposal: He would make the Pimlico Special, the prestigious stakes race that War Admiral had won in 1937, into a two-horse event. He knew the Special's conditions would appeal to both owners, as both horses had won at Pimlico at the race's $1\frac{3}{16}$-mile distance. Knowing that the attendance for such an event would completely swamp his little track, which had seating for just sixteen thousand, Vanderbilt proposed a date of November 1, a Tuesday, hoping that work commitments would limit the crowd to a manageable level.

Then there was the painful subject of the purse. Vanderbilt knew that both men wanted $100,000. He tried to maneuver them out of it. "I told them," he remembered, "that this was just a little track and we couldn't put up a lot of money." He argued that running for a smaller purse was preferable, because fans would know the race was truly a matter of sport. "I told them," Vanderbilt continued, "'You're not running for the money, you're running in the most popular race you could have now.'" The argument appealed to Riddle and Howard, who probably expected Vanderbilt to offer something in the neighborhood of $75,000. They were in for a shock. The best Vanderbilt could do was $15,000. Vanderbilt was quick to point out to Riddle that $15,000 was exactly the sum of the two purses being offered in War Admiral's scheduled races in New England, at least one of which he'd have to miss to make the match. To reassure each man of his opponent's sincerity, Vanderbilt asked that each put up a forfeit fee of $5,000.

Riddle finally responded. "I'll race if they'll agree to my terms, but I don't think they will." Vanderbilt asked what those terms were. Riddle was willing to accept the purse, provided that each horse carry 120 pounds. He wanted starter Jim Milton booted out in favor of George Cassidy, the starter for War Admiral's home track, Belmont. Finally, fearing that War Admiral would exhaust or injure himself fighting a conventional starting gate, and wanting to take advantage of his horse's skill at breaking from a walk, Riddle insisted that the race be started from an antiquated, gateless walk-up.

The first demand was no problem. Howard would surely appreciate a relatively low and equal impost. The second was more difficult. Vanderbilt didn't want to be strong-armed into dismissing Milton, whom he and virtually all observers agreed had done nothing wrong in his effort to load War Admiral in the gate the year before. But Milton, upon learning of Riddle's wishes, solved the problem for him. He came to Vanderbilt and recused himself from the race. He knew that if War Admiral broke poorly, he would be accused of carrying out a grudge against Riddle. Vanderbilt accepted his decision, and Riddle got his wish.

The third demand seemed impossible to fulfill. Because horses who gain commanding early leads in match races generally win them, observers thought the bullet-breaking War Admiral held a considerable advantage over the historically slower-breaking Seabiscuit, even with a conventional start. With a walk-up, War Admiral would have the added edge of performing a start at which he was superb and experienced, while Seabiscuit would be trying it for the first time. There was almost universal agreement that if War Admiral broke from a walk-up, he would lead from wire to wire. But the issue was a deal breaker for Riddle. Vanderbilt had no choice but to put it before Howard and hope for the best.

In New York, where he had been lobbying Riddle in person, Vanderbilt had the proposal with Riddle's demands typed up as a formal contract and sent to Howard. Howard moaned about the walk-up. He called Smith, who mulled it over. The trainer told him to demand that the start be made with a bell, not simply the traditional walk-up flag, and without assistant starters. The jockeys, he said, would have to be able to handle their horses without aid. Howard passed this on to Vanderbilt, who agreed. The contract came back. Howard had signed it and enclosed his $5,000 forfeit fee.

With one man down and one to go, Vanderbilt went to seal the deal. He showed up at Riddle's New York hotel room, contract in hand. Riddle was gone. The owner had already departed for the train station, bound for Philadelphia. Vanderbilt jumped into a cab, sped across town, and dashed into Penn Station, where he caught up with Riddle just as he was about to board the train. Riddle was still wavering. Vanderbilt stood his ground and refused to let Riddle board the train until he had signed the paper. Riddle gave in, and Vanderbilt returned to Maryland to cheers from horsemen. The November 1 Pimlico Special, universally hailed as the race of the century, was on. Nothing, this time, was going to stop it from being run.

When news of the deal broke to an ecstatic public on October 5, horsemen were amazed that Howard had accepted the walk-up. One horseman, wrote *The New Yorker*'s Audax Minor, "wonders if Riddle forgot to ask for permission to bring his own judges, too." Yet during the negotiations, Vanderbilt had noticed something strange. Howard, who had been loudly and publicly lamenting Riddle's demand for the walk-up, seemed in private to be delighted. "Howard loved it," Vanderbilt remembered. "He loved it."

The reason was Tom Smith. Once again the old cowboy had something up his sleeve. All along, he had been secretly hoping that Riddle would demand the walk-up. By some accounts, he had actually instructed Howard to make a few protests before ultimately agreeing to it so that no one would suspect his game plan. The best anyone thought Smith could hope for was for Seabiscuit to somehow stay reasonably close to War Admiral in the early stages of the race. Smith was far more ambitious. Sitting on a tack trunk with his friend Bill Buck during the match negotiations, he made an amazing statement. "I'm going to give them birds the biggest surprise they ever had in their lives.

"I'm going to send Seabiscuit right out on the lead."

Pollard was lying on his hospital bed, chatting with David Alexander, when the phone rang. It was Woolf, and he wanted to get Pollard's opinion on the match. The Iceman, like virtually everyone else, disagreed with Smith. He thought War Admiral simply had more God-given speed than Seabiscuit, and that the Triple Crown winner would surely beat him off of the line. How, he asked Pollard, should he ride this race?

Pollard surprised him. If Woolf put the throttle to the floor right from the bell, he promised him, Seabiscuit would beat War Admiral to the first turn. He told Woolf to gun to the lead but to keep him in check on the backstretch. When jockey Kurtsinger launched War Admiral in his final drive for the wire, Pollard said, do something completely unexpected and probably unprecedented: Let him catch up.

It was a startling plan. "Maybe you would call it a kind of horse psychology," Pollard explained to Alexander. "Once a horse gives Seabiscuit the old look-in-the-eye, he begins to run to parts unknown. He might loaf sometimes when he's in front and thinks he's got a race in the bag. But he gets gamer and gamer the tougher it gets." Pollard was sure that if Woolf let War Admiral challenge him, Seabiscuit would run faster and try harder than if Woolf tried to hold the lead alone. "Seabiscuit is the gamer horse. I know that." From there on in, the instructions were simple. Once War Admiral hooked Seabiscuit, "race him into the ground."

Everything hinged on two assumptions to which virtually no one outside the Seabiscuit camp would have ever agreed: that Seabiscuit had the speed to beat War Admiral off the line, and that he had enough gameness to fight back and win when his jockey sacrificed his lead. On the first point, Woolf was quickly convinced. The second was more difficult. Pollard knew that what he was asking his friend to do went against every tenet of reinsmanship.

"Most jockeys would have thought me nuts," he told Alexander after hanging up. "When a horse drives on you at a time like that, it just seems logical to drive as hard as you can to stay in front. It's instinct. I tell you that what I told Woolf to do was tough to do." If Pollard was wrong about Seabiscuit, then his strategy would hand the victory to War Admiral. But Woolf recognized that his friend understood the horse better than he did. He came to view the race as Pollard did, as a test of toughness, and had never seen a horse as tenacious as Seabiscuit. "Seabiscuit's like a hunk of steel—solid. Strong," he once said. "Admiral has speed, good speed . . . speed when unopposed. But he's not game." Of Seabiscuit he said, "you could kill him before he'd quit."

Woolf agreed to do exactly what Pollard told him to do. He and Smith brought Seabiscuit to Pimlico and went to work.

On the day after the match race deal was finalized, Smith walked up the Pimlico track to the starter's stand. Climbing up to the bell, he rang it several times, studying the sound. It made a clang much like an alarm clock. He hopped down and went back to the barn, where he gathered up some redwood planks, a phone, and an alarm clock. Dismantling the clock and the phone, he rigged up a starting bell with the clock alarm and the telephone's five-inch batteries, then cut the redwood into a box to hold the works and wired a trigger button to the outside. When the box was complete, Smith tacked up Seabiscuit and Pumpkin, pushed Woolf up onto the former, swung himself onto the latter, and took them toward the track, carrying the box with him.

On most mornings, War Admiral preceded Seabiscuit onto the course. Invariably, hundreds of people fanned out around the track apron to watch the Triple Crown winner, who had come to Pimlico after crushing the field in the Jockey Club Gold Cup. Trainer Conway stood on the sideline and watched his horse from afar as he circled around the course, legging up for the stout mile-and-three-sixteenths distance of the match. War Admiral was, as always, fretting and fussing and glorious.

As War Admiral was led back to Man o' War's old barn, Conway stepped back to watch Smith and Pumpkin trotting onto the track alongside Seabiscuit and Woolf. Smith took the horses up to the race's starting point at the top of the homestretch. The crowd, which had been thinly dispersed around the track to see War Admiral's distance workouts, migrated up to the turn after Seabiscuit and stood in a thick mass by the rail.

Spectators murmured among themselves at Smith's homemade bell. They watched quizzically as Smith lined up his horse, stepped behind him, and hit the bell, sending Seabiscuit into a rocket start. Woolf hustled him deftly; having begun his career booting horses through walk-up match races in Indian country, he knew how to hit the gas on a horse. Most of the time, Woolf would only let the horse fly through a short sprint before pulling him up and circling back for another go. Day after day, Woolf and Smith repeated the drill, sometimes pairing him with Chanceview. The homemade bell worked perfectly, and the horse began blowing off the line with explosive power.

When the walk-ups were over, Smith would take the horse back to the barn. Just as always, in the afternoons most of the Eastern Seaboard streamed into the barn to stare at Seabiscuit. Smith didn't seem to mind. "Can't hurt a horse looking at him," he said. Smith probably did think you could hurt Seabiscuit by looking at him. Which is why he made sure that the horse they were all gawking at was Grog.

For the next month America hung in midair. The names War Admiral and Seabiscuit were on everyone's lips, stories on the horses were in every paper, and the inflamed division between the horses' supporters broadened and deepened into a fanatical contest of East versus West.

One reader became so furious when journalist Nelson Dunstan switched his allegiance from Seabiscuit to War Admiral that he threatened to attack him. "*Everybody*," Vanderbilt recalled, "cared about it." Even President Roosevelt was swept up in the fervor. A rumor that he was going to "denounce one of the horses" during a Fireside Chat made the rounds, but he kept his allegiances secret. "The whole country is divided into two camps," wrote Dave Boone in the *San Francisco Chronicle*. "People who never saw a horse race in their lives are taking sides. If the issue were deferred another week, there would be a civil war between the War Admiral Americans and the Seabiscuit Americans."

As October waned, the tension all over the backstretch heightened. Trainer Conway was a frayed wire, shouting at reporters to get the hell away from his horse. Vanderbilt, also wound up with stress, blew off steam in bruising morning football games with the exercise boys. Smith's perpetual frown deepened. He distracted himself by working hard with Kayak, and sent him out to win two more races. Charley Kurtsinger tried to soothe his wife, who was terrified for him. Charley had only recently gotten out of the hospital after crashing with a horse at Saratoga in August, and his wife was now so afraid for him that she couldn't bear to be at the track when he rode. The closest she could get to watching him was to sit in the track parking lot in their car. Charley promised her that if she came to the track to see him ride War Admiral, he'd win it for her.

Charles and Marcela Howard were similarly jittery. Marcela slept with prayer beads on her pillow every night and attended Mass every morning. She and Charles hovered by the barns, waiting. They were there one afternoon a few days before the race when a sharp rainstorm brushed over the racing oval. Charles and Marcela stood together, watching the lightning crackle over the Maryland countryside. The storm died out and dispersed, and sunlight broke over the track. Marcela found it comforting. She whispered a poem:

> *"The storm is past, no more repining*
> *Behold! the gentle sun is shining."*

"Yeah," muttered Charles, "but the track is still too heavy for Seabiscuit."

In the track offices, horsemen gathered for the post position draw. Both horses' handlers wanted the rail, which, if the horse could hold it, would ensure the shortest trip around the track. If Seabiscuit got the rail, the experts believed he might have a glimmer of a chance. If War Admiral got it, they believed the race would be over before it began.

War Admiral drew the rail.

For Pollard, the days were bittersweet. David Alexander spent time with him and found him in jovial spirits. He was in love, he was about to try to start walking again, and he had been told that by early November he could leave the hospital. His engagement had brought his optimism back, and he was sure he would be able to ride again. A glance at his emaciated body, jutting out at harsh angles from under the sheets, testified to the contrary. He was up to his old pranks, sending a group of frostbitten horsemen on a wild-goose chase all over Boston in search of nonexistent "bull's wool" socks. Alexander couldn't get him to be serious. "George," Pollard told him, "will probably mess everything up as usual and try to get beaten a nose, but even George isn't bad enough to beat Seabiscuit in this one."

But as he spoke, the pain of his situation pressed through to the surface. "Maybe I'm conceited and maybe I'm not, but there still isn't anybody that can ride him like I can ride him," he said. "I can't tell you why. I just know how and he wants to run for me. I know that the minute I throw a leg over him, morning or afternoon. It looked for a while like I'd come out of here with a set of crutches as permanent equipment. Even if I'd have to use crutches, I still could have ridden the Biscuit. Maybe I couldn't ride any other horse, but I could have ridden him as long as there was somebody to shove me in the saddle."

Before Alexander and Pollard parted, the redhead gave him a prediction. Seabiscuit, he said, was going to win by four.

*

The War Admiral camp remained supremely confident. Conway quietly built his colt's endurance. Every day, he lingered by the rails to watch Seabiscuit's peculiar regimens, following his movements without comment, then returned to War Admiral. Everyone in the Riddle barn knew Smith was trying to coax early speed from Seabiscuit, but the idea of a horse outbreaking War Admiral was unimaginable. "I don't think Seabiscuit will give him much trouble," jockey Kurtsinger said. "And I don't care if Woolf elects to try to make a race of it. The Admiral will lick him any part of it."

The Howard barn preferred that their opponents keep thinking that way. They remained cryptic about strategy. Smith did little more than make a few grunts about Seabiscuit having good speed. Asked if War Admiral would set the pace, Marcela was coy. "That depends on whether or not he can outrun Seabiscuit in the first furlongs," she said. "Maybe he can't." Pollard went right ahead and lied to reporters, telling them the barn strategy was to concede the lead to War Admiral and then try to run him down in the homestretch. After listening to Woolf and Pollard discussing strategy, David Alexander asked them if he could state in print that Seabiscuit would outgun War Admiral for the early lead. Both said yes, providing that Alexander didn't quote them directly. "Both fully realized," Alexander wrote later, "that War Admiral's connections would pay no attention at all to the pipe dream of a mere newspaper columnist." So Alexander published the prediction. All it did was inspire a hearty laugh in the press box.

The laughter burned Howard. On the day before the race, with all the training done, there seemed no harm in letting people know what he thought. Sitting in the Pimlico clubhouse surrounded by reporters, Howard made a flat statement.

"War Admiral won't outbreak Seabiscuit," he said tersely, "he won't outgame him, and he won't beat him."

An uncomfortable silence followed. Someone politely changed the subject.

Sometime later that day, Woolf received a telegram. It was from Pollard: THERE IS ONE SURE WAY OF WINNING WITH THE BISCUIT. YOU RIDE WAR ADMIRAL.

Across the country that day, the ballots for year-end honors in Thoroughbred racing began arriving in journalists' postboxes. The writers collected them, leaving the spaces for Horse of the Year blank. They would wait until Tuesday evening to fill them in.

That night, Baltimore glittered and rang with exuberant prerace parties, the next day's racegoers singing out "Maryland, My Maryland" as they passed outside the track. Inside the Pimlico gates, it was hushed. A lone figure walked out onto the Pimlico dirt, clutching a flashlight. It was Woolf. The rainwater had not fully drained from the track, and he was concerned that Seabiscuit might struggle over the dampness. "Biscuit likes to hear his feet rattle" was how he put it. Turning down the lane, the jockey weaved back and forth, sweeping his flashlight beam from side to side, hunting for the driest, hardest path.

At the top of the homestretch Woolf stopped, testing the footing. In the soil beneath his feet, he could feel a firmer strip, the print of a tractor wheel that had lately rolled over the surface. The path was obscured by harrow marks. Walking the full length of the track, Woolf found that it circled the entire oval, a few feet from the rail.

He knew what he would have to do when the bell rang the following afternoon. "I figured to myself," he said later, "'Woolf, get on that lane and follow it.'" In the darkness of the last night of October 1938, George Woolf walked the course until he had memorized the path of the tractor print. Then he quietly stepped off the track.

"I knew it," he said later, "like an airplane pilot knows a radio beam."

*Midway through what is still widely regarded as the greatest horse
race in history, Seabiscuit and War Admiral turn out
of the backstretch and drive for the wire, November 1, 1938.*
(© BETTMANN/CORBIS)

CHAPTER 19

The Second Civil War

Beneath a translucent scrim of clouds at eight o'clock in the morning on November 1, 1938, Maryland Racing Commission chairman Jervis Spencer stepped out onto the smoky brown oval of Pimlico. With his hands pushed into the pockets of a gray overcoat, Spencer circled the track on foot, moving by a palette of colorful barns and turning leaves. Horses galloped past him. Vanderbilt stood in the winner's circle, awaiting the completion of the circuit. The course was rimmed in faces, all eyes on Spencer. Riddle and Howard had agreed that the chairman would be the final judge of the condition of the track; only if it was dry and fast would the race go. The issue was somewhat in doubt. As Woolf had noted in the darkness the night before, the week's rains had soaked into the dirt. But several days of crisp fall air and heavy labor by Vanderbilt's men had dried the surface well.

At eight-thirty Spencer stopped outside the winner's circle, looked up at Vanderbilt, and nodded. He turned to a microphone, cleared his throat, and spoke.

"In my judgment, there is no question that the track will be fast for the race this afternoon. The race is on."

As if somehow linked to the emotions of all present, the sun spilled out, bathing the overcoated men in warm Maryland sunshine. The coats came off and every man headed his own way. Vanderbilt walked out onto the track with a bucket, burning off a little nervous energy by picking up loose pebbles and clumps of dirt. Marcela Howard went off to host a prerace luncheon. A friend presented her with an exuberant Dalmatian as a gift. They named him Match in honor of the occasion and sent him over to the barn to cavort with Pocatell and Seabiscuit's guard dog, Silver. Up in the track secretary's office, a telegram arrived for Howard: PLEASE BET $200 FOR ME. OUR HORSE WILL WIN BY 5—POLLARD. Howard placed the bet for him, tossing in $25,000 of his own money for good measure.

He went to the backstretch and strolled around with Woolf. Somewhere along the shed rows, they came across Sunny Jim Fitzsimmons and stopped to talk about the race. Fitzsimmons liked Pollard's strategy of pushing for the early lead, but like Smith, Woolf, and Pollard, he believed that the match was not going to be determined by speed. The deciding factor would be resolve. One of the horses was going to crack in the homestretch. The other would come home the undisputed champion of American racing.

Vanderbilt had hoped that scheduling his race for a Tuesday would keep attendance within Pimlico's sixteen-thousand-seat capacity. It didn't. By 10:00 A.M., six and a half hours before the race, a vast, agitated throng was already banging up against the fences. Vanderbilt swung the gates open and unleashed a human stampede. All morning long, automobiles and special trains disgorged thousands and thousands of passengers from every corner of the nation and the world; the assembly of foreign dignitaries alone equaled a normal day's attendance. By midday, the grandstand and clubhouse were glutted, so Vanderbilt redirected fans by the thousands into the infield. The crowds kept coming in.

At three-thirty the horses began the long walk down the center of the track to the saddling paddock. War Admiral appeared first, spinning around in a white blanket, yellow ribbons in his tail. Two minutes later Smith and Pumpkin appeared with Seabiscuit, who was covered to the ears in a red blanket emblazoned with a white *H*. Thirty thousand people watched the horses from the grandstand and clubhouse. Ten thousand more teemed in the infield, lining up behind a small retaining fence about ten feet inside the track rail. Dozens of fans bristled over the tops of the steeplechase fences, leaving them teetering under the weight. A thick line of police fanned out to hold the masses back. Outside the track, some ten thousand fans who couldn't get in gathered ten-deep around the track fence and stood upon every rooftop, fence, tree limb, and telephone pole as far as a mile from the start, hoping to catch a glimpse of the race.

When the horses arrived in the paddock, they were greeted by the nervous faces of their handlers. The Howards fretted; Riddle looked small and old; Kurtsinger had the inward-focused look of someone at prayer. The saddling began. As Smith cinched the girth of Woolf's kangaroo-leather saddle around Seabiscuit's belly, Marcela stepped forward, clutching a medal of Saint Christopher, patron saint of travelers. Lifting up the horse's saddlecloth, she pinned the medal to it.

"This will bring you luck," she whispered. It was All Saints' Day.

Into this edgy scene breezed George Woolf. In dazzling contrast to everyone else at Pimlico, the Iceman was utterly relaxed. A lump of chewing tobacco bulged in his cheek. He strode in, smacked Pumpkin on the rump, swung lightly aboard Seabiscuit, and spat in the air.

There was a nervous stir. The bell on the starter's stand wouldn't work. The only other official bell at the track was attached to the starting gate. With no other options, the officials asked if they could borrow Smith's homemade bell. Smith said yes, and someone fetched the odd redwood box for starter Cassidy, who carried it up to his place at the top of the homestretch. Years later, *Daily Racing Form* reporter Pete Pedersen noted that "Tom's eyes were sparkling mirrors" when he recalled this incident, making one wonder if the old cowboy had a hand in the bell's demise.

Then another snag. Two assistant starters, almost certainly called in by War Admiral's handlers, showed up to lead the horses to the walk-up. Their appearance was in direct violation of the agreement, and Smith spoke up. For once, he wanted War Admiral to be required to behave himself at the post. Smith traded testy words with the officials, and there was a long delay. "No assistants," Smith snapped, "or no race." The assistant starters backed off.

*

At four o'clock, the two horses parted a sea of humanity and stepped onto the track before a crowd, wrote Grantland Rice, "keyed to the highest tension I have ever seen in sport." "Maryland, My Maryland" wafted over a strangely quiet grandstand. The spectators, wrote Rice, were "too full of tension, the type of tension that locks the human throat."

War Admiral walked up the track first, twirling and bobbing. Blunt-bodied Seabiscuit plodded along behind, head down. He looked up once, scanned the crowd, then lowered his head again. One witness compared him to a milk-truck horse. Shirley Povich of *The Washington Post* thought he exhibited "complete, overwhelming and colossal indifference." The appearance was deceiving. Woolf could feel it. In post parades, he was accustomed to the smooth levelness of Seabiscuit's walk, the gentle gait of a horse that puts his hooves down carefully. But this day Woolf felt something new, a gathering beneath him, something springlike. The horse was coiling up.

As the horses strode up the track, NBC radioman Clem McCarthy grabbed his microphone and turned to run to his race-calling post atop the clubhouse. The crowd was so dense that he couldn't get through. He struggled in vain against a current of bodies, then gave up, exhausted. He did the best he could, climbing up on the track's outer rail by the wire and settling in to call the race from there. His voice crackled over the radio waves to forty million listeners, including President Roosevelt. Drawn up next to his White House radio, F.D.R. was so absorbed in the broadcast that he kept a roomful of advisors waiting. He would not emerge until the race was over.

The reporters massed by the railings in the press box. War Admiral was the toast of the newsmen; every single *Daily Racing Form* handicapper had picked him to win, as had some 95 percent of the other writers. Only a small and militant sect of California writers was siding with Seabiscuit. Down in the stands, the allegiances were more muddied. War Admiral was the heavy favorite in the betting, but reporters mingling in the crowd found that most racegoers were rooting for the underdog.

Up in her box, Gladys Phipps gazed down on Seabiscuit with

pride. Her hard-tested faith in nasty old Hard Tack had finally paid off. After Seabiscuit began winning with Smith, the renowned Claiborne Farm, which had once politely but firmly rejected Hard Tack, changed its mind. Phipps retrieved her stallion from under the mulberry trees at the little farm where she had left him and shipped him to Claiborne, where the managers boosted his stud fee from nothing to a respectable $250. When Seabiscuit took the East by storm, they doubled the fee. Now, as the Biscuit challenged War Admiral, Hard Tack's fee was $1,000.

Nearby, Fitzsimmons watched the horses. He held a win ticket. It was on Seabiscuit.

As the track was one mile around and the race a mile and three sixteenths, the starting point was at the top of the homestretch, with the horses set to circle the course roughly one and one quarter times. As War Admiral walked to the line alongside the flagman and starter Cassidy, Woolf worked to fray the Triple Crown winner's famously delicate nerves. He put Seabiscuit into a long, lazy warm-up, sailing past his skittering rival and galloping off the wrong way around the track. Cassidy ordered him to bring his horse up. "Mr. Cassidy," Woolf called back cheerily, "I have instructions to warm Seabiscuit up before the start." Cassidy barked that he had not been forewarned of this. Woolf shrugged and kept right on going. He and Seabiscuit swung around the far turn and into the backstretch.

At the five-eighths pole, Woolf stopped Seabiscuit and turned him toward the grandstand. For a long moment, man and horse stood out on the backstretch. It was quiet. The infield crowds massed up against the rail by the grandstand, leaving the backstretch oddly vacant; most everyone thought the only time the horses would run together would be in that first trip down the homestretch, before War Admiral's speed put Seabiscuit away. Seabiscuit gazed at the throng, stirring gently in the sunshine; Woolf studied War Admiral, watching him unravel at the starting line, whirling in circles.

After an agonizing interval, Woolf cantered Seabiscuit back to the top of the homestretch. He drew up alongside War Admiral. The flagman raised his arm, and Cassidy poised his finger over the button of

Smith's bell. Seabiscuit and War Admiral walked forward together, each rider watching Cassidy. The immense crowd drew its breath.

At the last moment, something felt wrong to Woolf. He jerked his right rein and pulled Seabiscuit out. Kurtsinger reined up War Admiral, who bounced up and down in frustration. They lined up again and stepped forward, but this time it was Kurtsinger who reined out. The two horses trotted back to the turn. As they aligned for a third try, Woolf called over to Kurtsinger.

"Charley, we'll never get a go like this. We can't watch the starter and our horses at the same time. Let's walk up there watching the horses, and when we get even, let's break away ourselves. Cassidy will see us in line and will have to bang the bell."

Kurtsinger nodded. The two walked up a third time, each jockey watching the nose of his rival's mount. Woolf tightened his left rein, cocking Seabiscuit's head toward War Admiral to let him focus on his opponent. The horses were perfectly even. Woolf knew that this was it. As they approached Cassidy, Woolf suddenly blurted out, "Charley, look out because the Biscuit kicks like hell and I don't want you or your horse to get hurt."

Kurtsinger stared at Woolf in befuddlement, then cleared his mind and trained his eyes back on Seabiscuit's nose. The flagman's hand hovered high in the air. Up in the Howard box, Marcela squeezed her eyes shut.

The two noses passed over the line together, the flag flashed down, and the hushed track clanged with the sound of Smith's bell. War Admiral and Seabiscuit burst off the line at precisely the same instant.

The gathering Woolf had felt in Seabiscuit vented itself in a massive downward push. Lines of muscle along the horse's back, flanks, and belly bulged with the effort, cutting sweeping stripes into his coat. His front end rose upward. Woolf threw himself forward as ballast, thrusting his feet straight back. Seabiscuit reached out and clawed at the ground in front of him, then pushed off again. Beside him, War Admiral scratched and tore at the track, hurling himself forward as hard as he could. Seabiscuit drove over the track, his forelegs pulling the homestretch under his body and flinging it back behind him. Woolf angled him inward, keeping him close to War Admiral, letting him look at his rival. For thirty yards, the two horses hurtled down the homestretch side by side, their cutting, irregular strides settling into long, open lunges, their speed building and building.

A pulse of astonishment swept over the crowd. War Admiral, straining with all he had, was losing ground. Seabiscuit's nose forged past, then his throat, then his neck. McCarthy's voice was suddenly shrill. "Seabiscuit is outrunning him!" War Admiral was kicking so hard that his hind legs were nearly thumping into his girth, but he couldn't keep up.

An incredible realization sank into Kurtsinger's mind: *Seabiscuit is faster.* Up in the press box, the California contingent roared.

After a sixteenth of a mile, Seabiscuit was half a length ahead and screaming along. He kept pouring it on, flicking his ears forward. The spectators were in a frenzy. As the horses were midway down the first pass through the homestretch, the crowd suddenly gushed over the infield retaining fence ten feet inside the track rail. Thousands of fans surged toward Woolf and Seabiscuit. Caught at the infield rail, they bent themselves over it, pounding and clapping and flailing their arms in Seabiscuit's path. Seabiscuit, his ears flat and eyes forward, didn't even seem to see them.

Neither did Woolf. He had his eyes on the tractor wheel imprint, but War Admiral was on it. Woolf had to get far enough in front to cross ahead of War Admiral and claim it. He let Seabiscuit roll. By the time he and his mount hit the finish line for the first time, they were two lengths in front. Woolf looked back left and right, cocked back his left rein, and slid Seabiscuit across War Admiral's path until he felt the firm ground of the tractor imprint under him. He flattened his back, dropped his chin into Seabiscuit's mane, and flew toward the turn.

Behind him, Kurtsinger was shell-shocked. His lips were pulled back and his teeth clenched. In a few seconds, Woolf and Seabiscuit had stolen the track from him, nullifying his post-position edge and his legendary early speed. Kurtsinger didn't panic. War Admiral, though

outfooted, was running well, and he had a Triple Crown winner's staying power. Seabiscuit was well within reach. Conway had spent weeks
training stamina into the horse, while Smith had not done much for
Seabiscuit's endurance. Seabiscuit was going much, much too fast for
so grueling a race. He couldn't possibly last. Kurtsinger made a new
game plan. He would let Seabiscuit exhaust himself on the lead, then
run him down. He eased War Admiral over until he was directly
behind him, dragging off him, his mount's nose cabooses Seabiscuit's
tail. He took hold of his horse and waited.

As the two horses banked into the first turn, Woolf remembered
Pollard's advice to reel Seabiscuit in. He eased back ever so slightly
on the reins and felt the horse's stride come up under him, shorten-
ing. His action was little more than a faint gesture, but it meant that
Kurtsinger had to either slow down or commit to the outside.
Kurtsinger chose the latter, nudging War Admiral out.

Seabiscuit cruised into the backstretch on a one-length lead, with
Woolf holding his chin down. War Admiral chased him, his nose
nodding up and down behind Seabiscuit's right hip. The blur of faces
along the rail thinned, then vanished altogether, and the din from
the crowd quieted to a distant rumble. War Admiral and Seabiscuit
were alone. With nothing but the long backstretch ahead of him,
Woolf carried out Pollard's instructions. Edging Seabiscuit a few
feet out from the rail, he tipped his head back and called back to
Kurtsinger: "Hey, get on up here with me! We're supposed to have a
horse race here! What are you doing lagging back there?"

Kurtsinger studied the ground ahead. Woolf was dangling the rail
slot in front of him, inviting him to take it. Kurtsinger measured the
gap between Seabiscuit and the rail and saw that War Admiral was
narrow enough to get through. But Kurtsinger knew the Iceman well.
He knew that the instant he drove his horse up to full speed and
pointed him to the hole, Woolf would drop in toward the rail and slam
the door on him, forcing him to change course and lose momentum.
Kurtsinger tugged his right rein and moved War Admiral outside.

In a storied career of twenty-three races, through the Triple Crown
and virtually every fabled race in the East, no one had ever seen all

War Admiral could give. Kurtsinger asked the colt for the full measure. With five furlongs to go, he reached back and cracked War Admiral once across the hip. War Admiral responded emphatically. Bounding forward in a gigantic rush, he slashed into Seabiscuit's lead. A shout rang out in the crowd, "Here he comes! Here he comes!" Woolf heard the wave of voices and knew what was happening. In a few strides, War Admiral swooped up alongside him, his head pressing Seabiscuit's shoulder. A few more, and he was even. Kurtsinger thought: *I'm going to win it.* The grandstand was shaking.

Woolf loosened his fingers and let an inch or two of the reins slide through. Seabiscuit snatched up the rein, lowered his head, and accelerated. Pollard's strategy, Woolf's cunning, and Smith's training had given Seabiscuit a chance in a race he otherwise could not have won. From here on in, it was up to the horse. He cocked an ear toward his rival, listening to him, watching him. He refused to let War Admiral pass. The battle was joined.

The horses stretched out over the track. Their strides, each twenty-one feet in length, fell in perfect synch. They rubbed shoulders and hips, heads snapping up and reaching out together, legs gathering up and unfolding in unison. The poles clipped by, blurring in the riders' peripheral vision. The speed was impossible; at the mile mark, a fifteen-year-old speed record fell under them, broken by nearly a full second. The track rail hummed up under them and unwound behind.

They ripped out of the backstretch and leaned together into the final turn, their strides still rising and falling together. The crowds by the rails thickened, their faces a pointillism of colors, the dappling sound of distinct voices now blending into a sustained shout. The horses strained onward. Kurtsinger began shouting at his horse, his voice whipped away behind him. He pushed on War Admiral's neck and drove with all his strength, sweeping over his mount's right side. War Admiral was slashing at the air, reaching deeper and deeper into himself. The stands were boiling over. A reporter, screaming and jumping, fell halfway out of the press box. His colleagues caught his shirttails and hauled him back in. Below, spectators were fainting by the dozens.

The horses strained onward, arcing around the far turn and rushing at the crowd. Woolf was still, his eyes trained on War Admiral's head. He could see that Seabiscuit was looking right at his opponent. War Admiral glared back at him, his eyes wide open. Woolf saw Seabiscuit's ears flatten to his head and knew that the moment Fitzsimmons had spoken of was near. One horse was going to crack.

As forty thousand voices shouted them on, War Admiral found something more. He thrust his head in front.

Woolf glanced at War Admiral's beautiful head, sweeping through the air like a sickle. He could see the depth of the colt's effort in his large amber eye, rimmed in crimson and white. "His eye was rolling in its socket as if the horse was in agony," Woolf later recalled.

An instant later, Woolf felt a subtle hesitation in his opponent, a wavering. He looked at War Admiral again. The colt's tongue shot out the side of his mouth. Seabiscuit had broken him.

Woolf dropped low over the saddle and called into Seabiscuit's ear, asking him for everything he had. Seabiscuit gave it to him. War Admiral tried to answer, clinging to Seabiscuit for a few strides, but it was no use. He slid from Seabiscuit's side as if gravity were pulling him backward. Seabiscuit's ears flipped up. Woolf made a small motion with his hand.

"So long, Charley." He had coined a phrase that jockeys would use for decades.

Galloping low with Woolf flat over his back, Seabiscuit flew into the lane, the clean peninsula of track narrowing ahead as the crowd pushed forward. A steeplechase fence in the infield had collapsed, and a line of men had crashed through the line of police and now stood upright on the inner rail near the wire, bending down toward Seabiscuit and rooting him on. Clem McCarthy's voice was breaking into his microphone. "*Seabiscuit by three! Seabiscuit by three!*" He had never heard such cheering. Arms waved and mouths gaped open in incredulity as Seabiscuit came on, his ears wagging. Thousands of hands reached out from the infield, stretching to brush his shoulders as he blew past.

When he could no longer hear War Admiral's hooves beating the track, Woolf looked back. He saw the black form some thirty-five feet behind, still struggling to catch him. He had been wrong about War

Admiral; he was game. Woolf felt a stab of empathy. "I saw something in the Admiral's eyes that was pitiful," he would say later. "He looked all broken up. I don't think he will be good for another race. Horses, mister, can have crushed hearts just like humans."

The Iceman straightened out and rode for the wire, his face down. Seabiscuit sailed into history four lengths in front, running easy.

Behind him, pandemonium ensued. Seabiscuit's wake seemed to create an irresistible vacuum, sucking the fans in behind him. Tens of thousands of men, women, and children vaulted over the rails, poured onto the track, and began running after him. Police dashed over the track, but the fans simply ran past them, leaping and clapping. Ahead of them all, Woolf stood like a titan in the irons. He cupped his hand around his mouth and shouted something back at Kurtsinger. His words were lost in the cheering.

Up in the Howard box, Marcela's eyes opened and filled with tears. Howard, completely overcome, stood up and whooped. They smiled and bowed as hundreds of voices called out to them.

In his box nearby, Samuel Riddle lowered his binoculars, turned to the Howards, and smiled weakly. His eyes were wide and shining with the shock of it. He hurried from his box. "It was a good race," he said. The crowd solemnly cleared a path for him. One or two people put a hand on his shoulder as he passed.

Marcela sank back down, disconcerted. Howard wanted to take her to the winner's circle, but she decided to stay where she was. Tears were streaming down her face. She sat, drying her eyes with a hand-kerchief and laughing at herself. Howard burst out of the box and sprinted downstairs as fast as he could go, babbling and shaking hands with everyone he saw. He dashed onto the track and immediately dis-appeared in the swirling masses of revelers. Smith and Vanderbilt joined him, and the three of them fought to stay on their feet as reporters and fans pushed and pulled on them. Howard, unable to control his jubilation, jumped up and down with the fans. Police ran every which way.

The final race time lit up the tote board. A second roar erupted from the crowd. Seabiscuit had run the mile and three sixteenths in 1:56⅗. No horse in Pimlico's fabled and lengthy history, through thousands of races dating back to just after the Civil War, had ever run the distance so fast.

Woolf turned Seabiscuit and cantered him back into the mob. He was wrung out, "all in for breath," said McCarthy, "and he's almost as white as the sleeves of his jacket." Woolf pulled Seabiscuit up to the grandstand, and the crowd enveloped them, shouting, "Georgie! Georgie!" McCarthy shoved his way up to the horse and propped a microphone on Seabiscuit's withers. Woolf bent to it.

"I wish my old pal Red had been on him instead of me," he said in his easy drawl. "See ya, Red."

Hundreds of hands touched Woolf's legs and stroked Seabiscuit's coat. The horse stood quietly in the center of the chaos, his tail in the air and his ribs heaving in and out as the waves of fans pushed up to his sides. Smith elbowed his way up, and someone asked him for a statement. "I said mine on the track," the trainer said. The police fought their way in to them, then formed a square and drove the crowd outward, leaving Smith standing beside his horse. Pumpkin bulled in with a stable hand on his back. The police opened a narrow avenue into the winner's circle. Smith grasped Seabiscuit's rein and led his grand little horse down the avenue of guards. Smith kept his eyes straight ahead, chin up, his face proud and sober. He led Seabiscuit to Howard, who patted the horse's nose and beamed.

In the winner's circle, the police cordon gave way and the reporters and fans pressed in again, wedging Seabiscuit and his handlers into the corner. Smith lifted a blanket of yellow chrysanthemums over the horse's neck. Unperturbed by the near riot around him, Seabiscuit began gently plucking flowers off the wreath and eating them. Howard tugged a single chrysanthemum from the blanket. The crowd begged for souvenir blossoms. Smith pulled a flower out for himself, and in a rare moment of exuberance, heaved the whole blanket into the crowd. A happy yell went up, and the flowers vanished.

Kurtsinger steered War Admiral around the celebration and pulled him up in front of the grandstand. Kurtsinger sagged in the saddle. War Admiral had run the greatest race of his life, running by far his fastest time for the distance, but he had not been good enough. Conway pushed his way through the fans and emerged in front of his colt. He examined his legs, found them sound and cool, then turned away. A reporter asked him for a statement.

"No! No!" he said. "Nothing to say." Dazed, he disappeared into the mob.

Kurtsinger smiled bravely and slid from the saddle. He uncinched it and pulled it from War Admiral's back, then stood and looked at his horse for a moment. He stepped forward and whispered something in the horse's ear, then walked away. A groom threw a black-and-yellow blanket over War Admiral's back. The police cleared a path for him, and War Admiral, his head low, was led back to the barn to the lonely clapping of a handful of fans.

Woolf slid to the ground and stood with one hand on his hip, smiling confidently, as Vanderbilt handed Howard the silver victory vase. Someone dragged Smith over to the mike, and he muttered something about credit being due to horse and rider. The final odds lit up the board, and Howard burst out laughing. The crowd applauded.

It took fifteen minutes to clear a path wide enough for Seabiscuit to get out of the winner's circle. As Howard whirled off with the reporters, Woolf and Smith picked their way back to the jockeys' room, trailed by well-wishers. They stopped in the doorway. Kurtsinger was already inside. "I hate to beat Kurtsinger," Woolf said, "the cleverest jockey I ever competed against." The reporters buzzed around him with questions about Seabiscuit. "He's the best horse in the world," he said. "He proved that today."

Smith allowed himself a small smile. Woolf turned to him. "If only Red could have seen Biscuit run today," he said.

"Yeah," said Smith, his smile fading. "But I kinda think the redhead was riding along with you, George."

Woolf went into the jockeys' room. Down the bench, Kurtsinger was pulling off his boots and quietly crying. Someone gently asked him what happened.

"What can I say? We just couldn't make it," he said. "The Admiral came to him and looked him in the eye, but that other horse refused to quit. We gave all we had. It just wasn't good enough."

Smith went back to the barn to see his horse. He spent a few quiet moments with him, his arm thrown over his neck, the horse's head by his chest. Woolf dressed and joined them. He stood by the stall door, watching Seabiscuit settle in. The horse felt good. He trotted around the stall, playing. Woolf thought he looked as if he hadn't run the race yet.

The Howards packed up carloads of reporters and brought them all to their hotel room. In exactly two months, Seabiscuit would turn six, relatively old for a racehorse and an age at which most stallions were already at stud. The newsmen wanted to know if Howard was ready to retire his horse. Howard shook his head. Beating War Admiral had always been a secondary ambition. Charles and Marcela's greatest wish was for Seabiscuit to win the Santa Anita Handicap. The horse would stay in training.

When Howard finally let them go, the reporters went home and filled out their ballots for championship honors. Seabiscuit was, at last, Horse of the Year.

Smith arrived at the barn at four the next morning. The reporters, drowsing in the barn aisles, jumped up when they saw him. For once in his life, Smith couldn't stop smiling. "That War Admiral is a better horse than I thought he was," he quipped as he walked into the shed row. "I had been sure we'd beat him by ten lengths, and it was only four. It's funny that nobody'd believe me when I said this horse could run."

As he approached Seabiscuit's stall, he fell silent, walking tiptoe. He gently opened the door and peered inside. Seabiscuit was a dark lump half buried in the straw, dead to the world. Smith stepped back and quietly closed the door.

"He's earned his rest, all right," he breathed.

*

Up in Massachusetts, Pollard greeted reporters with a rhyme:

> *"The weather was clear, the track fast*
> *War Admiral broke first and finished last."*

David Alexander came in with congratulations.

"Well, what did you think of it?" Alexander asked.

"He did just what I'd thought he'd do."

"What was that?"

"He made a Rear Admiral out of War Admiral."

An envelope from Woolf arrived. Inside was $1,500, half the jockey's purse.

PART III

Moments after injuring his left foreleg at Santa Anita, Seabiscuit is attended by Howard (far right) and his grooms, February 14, 1939.
(© BETTMANN/CORBIS)

CHAPTER 20

"All Four of His Legs Are Broken"

In mid-November, after five months in bed, Pollard emerged from Winthrop Hospital, stabbing at the ground with his crutches and swinging his legs along. He returned to the world a changed man. His body was still wasted. His face was withered and old. His career was dead. He was homeless. And because he had no insurance, he hadn't a cent left to his name.

The Howards asked him to come live with them at Ridgewood. Pollard accepted. His doctor drove him to the airport, and Agnes rode along with them. Pollard promised her that once he was established, he would send for her and they would marry. Agnes watched him bump up to the plane and wondered if he would live to see her again.

When Pollard arrived in California, he went to Tanforan to see the racetrackers again. His appearance stunned everyone. On the backstretch, his old contract trainer, Russ McGirr, saw the young man whom he had once purchased as a bug boy for a bridle, a saddle, and a few sacks of oats. McGirr burst into tears as they embraced.

Pollard settled in at Ridgewood. He was determined to heal and get back to riding, so he tossed away his crutches and tried to walk. It was a mistake. On one of the Ridgewood hills, he set his foot down wrong in a ditch hidden in the grass. The leg came down at an oblique angle and snapped.

The Howards rushed Pollard to the hospital Charles had built in memory of his lost son and called Doc Babcock, the same country physician who had tried in vain to save Frankie. In examining

Pollard's leg, Babcock discovered that the Massachusetts doctors hadn't managed the setting and rehabilitation of Pollard's leg properly. The leg would have to be rebroken, but this time, he felt, it would heal. Pollard knew what suffering lay in store for him but didn't hesitate. He underwent the procedure.

Soon afterward, Woolf drove from Maryland back to California, where he arrived at Tanforan to general applause. Someone told him that Pollard had again been hospitalized, and Woolf was crestfallen. He got back in his car and headed north to Willits, where he spent several days visiting with Pollard.

November rolled through Maryland, bringing with it sheets of ice. The track at Pimlico became a virtual skating rink, and Smith limited Seabiscuit's outings to walks around the shed rows. The ice didn't melt, and the horse began gaining weight.

On December 1 Smith walked out of the barn and stooped over the dirt racecourse. The track was glazed in ice. He stood there a while, quietly humming, "I Hear You Calling, Caroline." Behind him, Seabiscuit fidgeted in his stall, fat and impatient, having not felt a saddle on his back for ten days. It was time to go. Smith went back inside and consulted with Howard. The next night, the trainer loaded the entire Howard barn onto boxcars for a trip south, to Columbia, South Carolina. There they could train in warm weather and on safe tracks.

The choice of South Carolina was a strategic one. Seabiscuit was nominated for the Santa Anita Handicap, to be run in March, but Howard had also named him for the Widener Challenge Cup at Florida's Hialeah Race Track. The races were to be run on the same afternoon. It is highly unlikely that he was considering passing up the hundred-grander for the Widener, but he thought the pretense might help in the touchy matter of weights. Santa Anita, undoubtedly because of Seabiscuit, had eliminated the 130-pound weight maximum for the handicap. The weights would be announced that winter, and given the results of the match race, the track racing secretary would obviously be inclined to assign Seabiscuit the biggest impost of his career. So Howard parked his horses between the two tracks and began playing one against the other, hoping to pressure Santa Anita out of giving Seabiscuit an excessive impost. Whenever he could, he made good use of his omnipresent entourage of newsmen. Sitting within earshot of a group of reporters at the Giants–Green Bay football game at the Polo Grounds in New York, Howard wondered aloud which race he would choose.

Even in the bucolic surroundings of Columbia, Seabiscuit could not escape the carnival atmosphere. Though the horse was not going to race in the state, carloads of fanatically devoted admirers drove hundreds of miles and swamped the town just to see him gallop in his morning workouts. Each time he cantered around the little training track, a happy whoop went up from his rooting section. Cameramen from the Universal Newsreel Company were crawling all over the town, creating a short-subject film of the horse's life. People were flooding the track every time Seabiscuit showed his face.

Late in December, Seabiscuit overstepped in a workout and kicked himself in the left foreleg, dinging the suspensory ligament. His leg came up with a little swelling, so Smith backed off on the workouts. Again, Seabiscuit began gaining weight.

The reporters came and went. Seabiscuit, bandaged to the elbows, frisked them from over his stall door. Over and over again, Smith was asked why Seabiscuit was bandaged, and over and over again, he explained that the wraps were merely protective. Just before Christmas, the umpteenth local reporter from the umpteenth little paper eyed the bandages and asked Smith for the umpteenth time what they were for. Smith kept an absolutely straight face: "All four of his legs are broken."

The shocked reporter rushed to his editors and banged out a story breaking the news: Seabiscuit had fractured all four of his legs, and he would never run again. The ridiculous story might have lived out a brief life in Columbia had the paper not put it out on the national wire, thinking it was the scoop of the season. The next day papers across the nation were reporting the stunning course of events.

Up in Burlingame, California, Howard had just arrived from the East. Seabiscuit had elevated him to superstardom. He was mobbed everywhere he went. While he attended the races at Tanforan with Bing Crosby, the crooner found himself abandoned as fans and autograph-seekers smothered Howard. The owner settled back into town to await the hundred-grander impost announcement. He killed time by mailing blown-up match race photographs to reporters and taking out ads celebrating the win.

On the day Smith made his statement about Seabiscuit's legs, Howard read the story in his evening paper, shrugged it off, and went to bed. He was by now all too familiar with false reports and knew that had anything happened to Seabiscuit, Smith would have been on the phone to him in minutes. But Howard didn't sleep well. Reporters and distraught fans phoned his house all night long.

The next morning, when he emerged from the barn, Smith was enveloped by a herd of agitated newsmen. Smith denied again and again that the horse was lame. "Some dumb farmer of a reporter saw Seabiscuit with his usual after-exercise bandages on and drew the wrong conclusion," he said. It took two weeks for the corrected story to make the rounds.

Howard's squeeze play didn't work. The track secretary at Santa Anita loaded Seabiscuit with 134 pounds. Howard swallowed hard. On the day after Christmas, Smith and Howard talked over the phone. The trainer wanted to bring Seabiscuit home from South Carolina without waiting for the Hialeah weights to be announced. Though the injury to the rapped leg was not serious—the horse was not even lame—he had always worried about that left front suspensory ligament and wanted to be at his home base if trouble developed. They had surely never seriously considered going to Florida anyway. Smith made his case to Howard. Howard wired him back: COME ON.

Seabiscuit would go in the hundred-grander. "One hundred and thirty-four is a lot of weight," said Howard, "but Biscuit is a lot of horse."

The next night, the town of Columbia gathered in the darkness to see Seabiscuit off on what would be the final cross-country journey of a career that spanned 50,000 railroad miles. The whistle sounded, the fans shouted their good-byes, and the train ground forward. For five days it pressed westward, parting oceans of fans and newsmen at each stop.

Somewhere along the railways in the heart of the country, Seabiscuit slipped out of 1938. That year, no individual had known fame and popularity that was as intense and far reaching. A study of news outlets revealed that the little horse had drawn more newspaper coverage in 1938 than Roosevelt, who was second, Hitler (third), Mussolini (fourth), or any other newsmaker. His match with War Admiral was almost certainly the single biggest news story of the year and one of the biggest sports moments of the century. "The affection that this inarticulate brown horse had aroused," journalist Ed Sullivan would write, "was a most amazing thing."

Fans scurried all over the unloading platform as Seabiscuit arrived at Santa Anita. The train-car door slid open, and the dogs Match, Silver, and Pocatell bounced out, followed by Pumpkin and Seabiscuit. A host of newsreel and newspaper men pushed forward. A line of exercise boys and horsemen stood with them. Smith leaned out the door with the horse, eyeing the crowd with disdain.

"We're back for more," he said blandly.

Howard dashed forward. "Tom!" he practically shouted. "He looks grand. And happy new year!" He trotted up to greet the horse.

"Someone ought to put a shank on Charlie and cool him out," a trainer cracked. "He's more excited than the hoss."

Smith and Howard walked off together, radiating pride. Seabiscuit, feeling his oats, bucked a little.

They had reason to feel good. Seabiscuit was sound and happy. He had no trace of lameness, and his speed was honed. The only hitch was his weight. He'd been idle in his stall for much of the time since the match, and his weight had crept up. Smith stripped him of his blankets on the morning after his arrival and walked him to the scales. Seabiscuit had gained thirty pounds. So Smith buttoned him into a bright yellow sweating hood and took him to the track at Santa Anita. Since the War Admiral race was over and the weights for the Santa Anita Handicap had been announced, the trainer was no longer trying to hide his horse's workouts. Smith's protectiveness had given way to confident magnanimity. "No longer will there be any secrecy to Seabiscuit's moves," he said. "We figure he is the people's horse, and we propose to train him in the open." The people loved the idea. Every time the horse set foot on the course, someone would cry out, "Here comes the Biscuit!" and the track would come to a dead standstill. Each of his workouts was attended by ten thousand or more spectators.

They were treated to a show. Smith had never seen the horse so good. His workouts were the fastest of the meeting. He careened around the turns with such reckless speed that Smith began to fear that he would be unable to hold his arc and would tumble over sideways. He took the horse back to the barn and pulled off all of his shoes. While Howard gathered up the old shoes to have them cast into silver ashtrays to give to reporters, Smith got a farrier to design special new turn-gripping shoes. "He's been working so fast," said Smith, "we're afraid he'll run right out of his hide. Already he has to run a bit sideways to keep from flying right in the air."

While Seabiscuit steamrolled around the Santa Anita turns, buzzing the infield spectators and scaring the hell out of everyone, Kayak began to come into his own. Smith had known from the beginning that the big black Argentine colt was going to be a hundred-grander horse. As he had done with Seabiscuit in 1936, Smith entered the horse in the Handicap, but was careful not to show the racing secretary too much, running him just eight times, always in middling undercard races, six of which he won. Kayak improved rapidly. By the time they got to South Carolina, Kayak and Seabiscuit were waging bitter morning workout battles. Seabiscuit was always faster, but no horse, not even Fair Knightess, had proven so worthy a sparring partner.

Smith's plan to keep Kayak's speed a secret worked. The horse drew just 110 for the Handicap. With the weights out, Smith had no reason to hide him any longer. Kayak roared into Santa Anita with guns blazing, staging an overpowering performance to win a handicap prep race, just missing a track record, running with ears up, tail fanned out behind him. Coming into the 1939 Santa Anita Handicap, Tom Smith was armed to the teeth.

It was time to get Seabiscuit into a prep race, but something always intervened. He was scratched out of one race because the field was gigantic, and the post position hung him out so far that he was practically starting the race from the parking lot. He was scratched a second time when the rain turned the track slick. January became February. The handicap was in March, and time was running out.

Two weeks into February, they entered him in the one-mile Los Angeles Handicap. Their luck held: On race day, the sky came up sunny and the field small. Smith spent the day sitting under the slope of the shed row roof. He was accustomed to the giddy ripples of fear that attended race days, but today they had a darker feel. Waves of uneasiness washed over him. Perhaps, he thought, he was giving too much work to an aging animal. The idea tugged at his head all afternoon. By the time he heard the rhythmic, rising chant of Joe Hernandez's voice as he called the undercard races, Smith had begun contemplating scratching the horse once again.

Out on the track, the racing secretary was surveying the crowd and worrying. Twenty thousand fans milled around the grandstand, and every one of them was here to see Seabiscuit. Another scratch would be a disaster. Climbing up to the boxes, the secretary found Howard and told him that the horse's fans mustn't be disappointed for a third time. A few minutes later, Howard appeared at Barn 38. He and Smith talked about whether or not to run Seabiscuit, and Howard stressed that he didn't want to ruin another day for Santa Anita and the horse's fans. Smith could offer no concrete reason to scratch. He swallowed his trepidation and opted to run.

Smith led Seabiscuit to the track. Woolf met him in the paddock, and Smith gave him a leg up. The Iceman leaned down from the saddle and bent his head toward Howard. "We'll set up a track record for you today, Mr. Howard," he said.

Woolf broke Seabiscuit smartly, rushing to the lead. On his outside, Today, his old rival from 1938, hooked up with him. Down the backstretch the two horses flew, noses together. The duel stretched on: an eighth, a quarter, a half. The fractions clipped off. Woolf was going to be good to his word. The track record was coming down.

Countless times on that long Santa Anita backstretch Seabiscuit's legs reached out over the track, stretching to gather up the ground, pounding down into the dirt, then folding up under his belly. With every stride, some two thousand pounds of force came down on the bones and soft tissues of each foreleg. Today and Seabiscuit, still moving at record pace, leaned together into the far turn. Seabiscuit switched lead legs, so that his left foreleg was bearing the greatest weight. With each stride, he pivoted on the leg, holding the line of the turn at close to forty miles per hour. Woolf had no idea that beneath him, something was about to go wrong.

Halfway around the turn, Today began inching away. Seabiscuit was fighting hard but slipping back. Today pushed a full length in front, then shifted down to the rail. Woolf angled Seabiscuit out to go around Today and gave him a whack with his whip. Seabiscuit surged forward, coming down heavily onto his left foreleg.

Woolf heard a sharp *crack!*

Seabiscuit took an awkward, skipping step. His head pitched downward. Woolf threw his weight back, snatched up the reins, and held Seabiscuit's head up as the horse swung his legs forward and caught himself. The horse pulled himself together and resumed running. Woolf held still for several strides, feeling for lameness, but detected nothing. Perhaps, had Pollard been on him, he would have felt the slight catch in the rhythm, like a playing card against the spokes of a wheel. But Seabiscuit's stride was hard to read. Woolf felt nothing wrong. He thought Seabiscuit had simply stumbled over a rough part of the track.

Woolf backed off. He would catch Today in the stretch. He banked into the homestretch, swung out to go around Today, and made the biggest mistake of his career. He reached back and struck Seabiscuit across the hip with the whip.

Seabiscuit accelerated, and something gave under him. Woolf could feel it now, the jar in the stride: *pain*. He stood in the irons and began pulling the horse up. Seabiscuit crossed under the wire, finishing second by slightly more than two lengths. Today had set a record.

Seabiscuit reeled down the track. Woolf wanted to get his weight off of his mount's back, but he was going too fast. If he jumped off now, Seabiscuit, obedient to equine instinct to flee pain, would probably tear over the track, exacerbating his injury. Woolf had to control the horse's deceleration. He leaned against the reins. By the time he reached the turn, he had slowed the horse enough to bail out. Woolf kicked off his stirrups, leaned his weight on his hands, swung his right leg over Seabiscuit's rump, and pushed himself into the air. He hit the ground running and hauled the reins back, dragging the horse to a halt.

He looked down at the leg. There was no blood, and the limb appeared structurally normal. Woolf led Seabiscuit forward a few steps. The horse's head nodded, his left foreleg hovering in the air. An outrider, a mounted attendant assigned to catch loose horses and assist injured ones, galloped up and grabbed Seabiscuit's bridle. Slowly, gently, the outrider led Seabiscuit back toward the stands. Woolf walked back alone.

Up in the clubhouse, Smith and Howard were running. Smith was ahead, slamming into people and shoving them out of the way. Howard followed him. They crossed onto the track and sprinted toward Seabiscuit.

The outrider drew Seabiscuit up before Smith. Seabiscuit held the leg up. Smith bent over it. Woolf stood and stared at his mount. His lips were white. Howard rushed up, looked at Seabiscuit, and then wheeled on Woolf. He was near panic.

"Why did you do it?" he shouted. "George, *why did you do it?*"

Woolf said something about having believed that the horse had simply stumbled. He said he had had no idea that the horse was injured. He watched them tend to Seabiscuit, then walked back to the jockeys' room and sat down, heartsick. He called trainer Whitey Whitehill in, asked permission to be taken off his last mount.

A horse ambulance sped up. Smith straightened and waved it away. He needed to see Seabiscuit's gait. Howard held the reins while a groom threw a blanket over his back. They started walking the horse toward the barns. His head nodded with every step. Howard fell in beside him. Smith dropped far behind, frowning and dipping his head to study his horse's stride. He could see that it was the ankle that had gone wrong.

The grim procession filed past the grandstand. The shocked fans watched him go.

At the Howard barn, there was shouting and running. Grooms dashed everywhere, rushing for ice, Epsom salts, and liniment. Seabiscuit was led up and halted. A groom dipped bandages in ice water laced with Epsom salts and wound them around the left foreleg. The Howards stood and watched, their faces fallen. Behind them, horsemen gathered in silent attendance. A groom walked Seabiscuit around and around the barn. The horse had run a mile at nearly a world-record clip, and injured or not, he had to be cooled out. Seabiscuit's head continued to nod. Periodically, the groom stopped him and poured ice water inside his leg bandage while the horse slurped water from a bucket standing on a bench. Howard walked up and looked the leg over. "He never deserved such hard luck," he said.

Marcela stood nearby. "The Handicap doesn't matter," she said. "He's got to be all right."

"Remember," Smith told Howard, "he went lame at Belmont."

"Yes," Howard responded, "but I never saw him pull up that way. Never before."

Smith had no response. A mournful hush fell over the barn, broken only by the long, low moans of a saddle pony who missed his absent stable companion. All evening long, the deep, sad sound drifted out from the shed rows.

When Seabiscuit had cooled out, Smith went over the leg. There was no disturbed hair, no broken skin. They led him back into his stall. He had stopped limping. A veterinarian went in the stall with him, and a ring of stable hands watched from the door while he worked. The veterinarian examined the leg, then painted it in liniment, packed it in mud, and wrapped it loosely in fresh bandages soaked in ice water. He emerged to the forlorn collection of grooms but offered no verdict. He said the injury needed time to declare itself. It could be as bad as a broken bone or a blown suspensory ligament. Or it could be as minor as a kick bruise. Whatever it was, the vet thought Smith was wrong. It was in the knee, he said, not the ankle.

Howard and Smith spent the night on their knees in Seabiscuit's stall, taking turns pouring ice water onto the horse's leg. Sometime in the night Seabiscuit folded up and sank down beside them. He drifted off to sleep, his legs stretched straight out. They kept working while he slept.

When Seabiscuit's eyes opened in the morning, Howard and Smith were still there. The horse raised his head and rolled his weight onto his chest, preparing to stand. Howard and Smith held their breath. Seabiscuit pulled his haunches up under him, straightened his forelegs, and pushed. In a moment Seabiscuit was up. He stood normally on the bad leg and dove into his feed bucket. Then he lowered his head to snatch hay off the floor of his stall. It was his habit to lean onto his left leg when he did so, letting his right knee bend so he could get his mouth to the floor. They watched as he dropped his nose. His right knee bent, just as it always had, and he leaned to the left, onto the bad leg. Howard and Smith exhaled.

They led him out into the shed row and eased him into the walking ring. A crowd gathered to see him walk. Looping in big circles, the horse didn't take a lame step. Then Smith asked him to turn sharply left, a trick he had learned to test the suspensory ligaments. The horse bobbled. Smith was right: It was the ankle, not the knee. The veterinarian took radiographs, which would take a while to develop. All they could do now was wait. The Howards spent their time sorting through myriad sympathy notes from fans, some of whom enclosed bottles of remedies for the horse. The X rays came back. There was no fracture. The injury was in the suspensory ligament. Maybe it was ruptured; maybe it was only bruised. The veterinarian said that if it was ruptured, the horse's career was over. Time would tell.

Days passed, and Seabiscuit improved dramatically. Smith walked him every day and studied his gait. The horse had no trace of lameness at the walk, not even when Smith turned him sharply. After three days there was no sign that he had been hurt at all. A few days later Smith took him out for a long, slow, riderless trip around the track, leading him from Pumpkin's back. Several hundred spectators came to see it. Howard stood by the rail and watched through binoculars. Again, the horse seemed perfectly sound and cooled out well. Smith began inching him back into work, giving him easy gallops. It appeared that he had only stung the leg, not incurred a deeper injury. Seabiscuit, they declared, was going to make the hundred-grander.

Meanwhile, the stable got a little insurance. Kayak won the San Carlos Handicap, nailing Specify at the wire and breaking the track record. And a curious dispatch came in from the San Francisco World's Fair. Fair promoters wanted Seabiscuit to be an exhibit. They offered to build a special paddock and walking ring and give Howard a handsome cut of the 50-cent viewing fee they would charge spectators. Howard declined, citing a most unlikely reason: "We do not care to commercialize Seabiscuit."

On February 23 Smith took Seabiscuit back to the track to continue his preparation. The horse sped over the track, level and even. Then there was a bobble. The rider abruptly stood up and threw his weight against the reins. The head nodded again. Smith and Howard didn't need to say much to each other. They both knew.

Seabiscuit's suspensory ligament was ruptured. Howard, his shoulders sagging with disappointment, stood at the clubhouse rail and told reporters that they weren't going to make it.

Smith pulled himself together and went on. He moved the special safety door from Seabiscuit's stall to Kayak's. Howard brought a man to the barn to make plaster casts of Seabiscuit's hooves for the production of souvenir ashtrays. The horse stood there calmly for an hour and a half as the man fooled with his feet. Howard stood by and watched. Neither he nor Marcela could muster any enthusiasm for the hundred-grander.

A week later it was Kayak, not Seabiscuit, whom Smith escorted to the track for the Santa Anita Handicap. Reporters queried him on his chances without Seabiscuit. "Watch my smoke," he said. On the way out, he stopped briefly before Seabiscuit's stall. Outside, a grandstand swollen with spectators awaited him. Several million people were tuned in to the radio broadcast. Buenos Aires was at a standstill: Kayak was Argentine. In the midst of the crowd at Santa Anita sat Charles and Marcela Howard, forced smiles papered over their faces.

A few minutes later Kayak cannonballed down the homestretch to win the 1939 Santa Anita Handicap. Marcela and Charles broke into tears. Someone asked Charles for a comment. "Oh, gosh, it was grand—" he said, his voice catching in his throat. He turned his back and hid his face among his closest friends, who ringed around him. "Kayak II is a good horse," he whispered. "But gee, it wasn't Seabiscuit . . ."

After the ceremonies, the Howards hurried from the track. That night they attended the Turf Club Ball. As always, Howard tried to get Smith to come, but the trainer never showed up. Santa Anita officials presented Howard with the traditional golden winner's trophy, then gave him a cup commemorating Seabiscuit.

"I am extremely proud of the horse," Howard said of Kayak, "but I can't help saying I would have been happier had Seabiscuit been the winner."

The Howards returned home. Marcela felt hollow.

Marcela and Charles Howard visit Seabiscuit at Ridgewood.
(LT. COL. MICHAEL C. HOWARD)

CHAPTER 21

A Long, Hard Pull

Agnes Conlon joined Red Pollard's strange world on April 10, 1939. Back in Willits, Doc Babcock had finally set Pollard's leg properly, and it was beginning to heal. He limped out of the hospital in early spring. Babcock sent him out with a stern warning: His leg would not stand the rigors of riding. If he went back to racing, he could be crippled for the rest of his life. He must never mount a horse again. Pollard smiled. "Then I reckon I'll have to find somebody to boost me up," he said.

Pollard took up residence at Ridgewood and immediately called for Agnes to come marry him. With no money to spare, they planned for a quiet, private weekday wedding and a modest honeymoon, and then Pollard would begin his long journey back to the saddle. Red wanted to be sure that she got the wedding gift she wanted most—a diamond watch—so he mailed her what little money he had so she could pick it out herself. Instead of buying the watch, Agnes bought an extra ticket west so her mother could see her marry. She had wanted to wear her sister's elaborate wedding dress, but their pennilessness called for something less formal. She packed up a simple navy pinstripe suit, hat, and sandals and embarked on her journey to California.

She was in for a surprise. Pollard greeted her with a beautiful wedding, undoubtedly financed and planned by Marcela. The ranch was decorated for the occasion, and legions of Pollard's friends, including Yummy, Spec Richardson, Doc Babcock, and a host of hospital staffers, were in attendance. Pollard, still underweight, was bundled into a double-breasted black suit, the left pant leg slid over his cast. Agnes was stunned by the preparations and a little mortified that all she had brought was the navy suit.

Under the sunlight in Willits, Agnes and Red Pollard spent their first married moments standing together, hearing the good wishes of their friends. Agnes smiled demurely, pressing the tips of her fingers into Red's palm and averting her eyes from the Associated Press photographer who was covering the wedding. Red stood by her, his bad leg angled out.

It was a melancholy season at Ridgewood. Smith, preparing to take Kayak east, vanned Seabiscuit to Ridgewood, said his good-byes, and left him in Pollard's care. The horse was led into his new home, a handsome stall adjoining his own private paddock. He was not ready for retirement. He was bred to seven mares, including Fair Knightess, but it didn't do much for his mood. Restive, he stalked the fences on his lame leg. Howard's spirits mirrored those of his horse. In Seabiscuit's racetrack days, Howard had made a habit of coming to the track every morning. Now he stopped going altogether. He and Marcela spent much of their time at the stallion barn, petting Seabiscuit. At times Howard lingered there for several hours. The papers referred to Seabiscuit as "retired," but Howard wouldn't use that word. He was hanging on to the idea that somehow the horse might race again.

Red and Agnes returned from a honeymoon on Catalina Island, and the broken-legged jockey began the period of his life that he would call "a long, hard pull." Red would go up to the barn, hitch a lead rope onto Seabiscuit, and head off into the meadows, swinging painfully along on his crutches while Seabiscuit limped beside him. "We were a couple of old cripples together," Red said, "all washed up. But somehow we both had a pretty good idea that we'd be back." Howard's friends stood on the hills and watched them go, shaking their heads at the sad sight of two athletes whose bodies had failed them. Sonny Greenberg came out to look the horse's leg over.

There is no way, he thought, that they'll get this one back on the track.

At first Pollard was too weak to go far, but he gradually built up his endurance. Hour after hour, day after day, Pollard and Pops walked together. When Pollard tired, he would lead Seabiscuit back and leave him off in the hands of his new groom, Harry Bradshaw. Bradshaw was a backstretch legend, a man with such magical skills at tending lameness that once, when a man was negotiating to buy an elite horse in Bradshaw's care, he refused to take the horse unless Bradshaw was part of the bargain. Smith had made a special effort to get him out to the farm and had given him detailed instructions on how to care for the horse. Bradshaw took his job seriously, staying at the barn day and night to nurse Seabiscuit's ankle.

Agnes and Red began their marriage. Red taught her to drive a car along the roads lined with redwoods. He took her out to the barns, helped her up on the backs of the horses, and watched her ride. For Agnes, every moment was stolen time. Red was so frail that she feared his life was still in danger. She discovered that he was already deep into alcoholism. And she learned how he tortured his body to make weight. Horse racing had made him a cripple and an addict. And now he was going back to it.

Slowly, painfully, horse and rider healed. Pollard was soon off his crutches and took to leaning on a cane. He wore weighted shoes to strengthen his wasted leg muscles. The bones of his leg were so weak that he needed to wear a fur-lined metal brace to prevent them from buckling, but they held up. Seabiscuit's lameness at the walk disappeared. Howard began slipping out to the barn in the morning with Pollard, and one day when the urge was too strong they got out a stock saddle and cinched it on Seabiscuit. Howard gently lifted Pollard into the saddle. The redhead was far too weak to hold the horse, so Howard swung aboard a pinto horse named Tick Tock, took Seabiscuit's lead rope, and led the two around the meadows, gradually increasing the length and speed of each outing. Soon, Howard had a little track of three eighths of a mile cut out of the flat valley land. He began leading Seabiscuit and Red onto it for long, slow walks.

Seabiscuit was starting to feel fine. Within hours of his birth, he had known how to run, and speed had been the measure of his life ever since. He knew what the track was for, and it wasn't walking. He was frantic to run. His whole body gathered up behind the bit, and he skittered around like a downed electrical wire, begging Pollard to turn him loose. Howard had left a bushy gully in the center of his makeshift track, and one morning the sight of the horses and men spooked the deer hiding out inside. They bolted for the hills, streaking past Seabiscuit. "Good Lord!" Howard remembered later. "The first time he spotted one he thought the race was on!" Seabiscuit yanked the reins loose and bounded off after the deer, imitating the animals' pogo-stick strides. Pollard somehow hung on, Howard kept his grip on the lead rope, and they pulled Seabiscuit to a halt.

A few hundred miles south, Tom Smith sat in the sun by the barns at Hollywood Park. His eyes were trained on Kayak, who hung his head out of his half door, surveying the backstretch.

Smith was in the midst of a trying season. First Seabiscuit was injured. Then Kayak was hurt in a freak accident when something blew across the track and caused him to bolt. He came down wrong, gashed himself badly, and wound up out of training. After a period of convalescence, the horse returned to racing, only to be injured again. All Smith had to cling to was a wild thought that Seabiscuit might someday return.

Smith's eyes played over Kayak. A reporter walked up.

"Wouldn't it be great," the newsman said, "if the Biscuit could stage a comeback?"

Smith slid up in his chair.

"I suppose," he said, an edge to his voice, "you think he won't come back?"

The reporter, flustered, stammered out something about the rarity of successful comebacks.

Smith stood up. "The Biscuit will come back," he said in a voice more emotional than he meant it to be. "He'll come back and fool the whole turf world."

Smith seemed uncomfortable. He drew himself together and smiled at the reporter.

Kayak continued to gaze out the door.

Pollard had learned a thing or two about training from Smith, and he managed Seabiscuit's rehabilitation carefully. By early summer, walking turned to a gentle canter, first a mile, then two, then three. Seabiscuit kept pulling, but Pollard never gave in; the turns on the little track were too tight, the leg too delicate. Howard walked out to the barn every morning with a quiver in his gut, afraid that they might make a mistake and reinjure Seabiscuit. But the horse kept getting stronger and sounder. An idea was working around in the heads of everyone at Ridgewood. Howard and Smith might be right. Seabiscuit might make it back to the races. Outside the ranch, it was considered an absurd idea. Inside, it seemed somehow possible.

Everyone went to work. Bradshaw began strapping Seabiscuit into a fur-lined muzzle to get the extra pounds off him, and they weighed the horse every week. When a groom was caught sneaking carrots to Seabiscuit, Pollard ran him off with a pitchfork and the groom was summarily fired. Seabiscuit took to stomping and bellowing for food day and night. His moans rang off the barn walls and worked on everyone's nerves, but no one gave in. "The whole ranch became centered on the job," Howard said. "Even the pigs quit grunting at him and the chickens kept out of his way."

By summer's end, Seabiscuit had made surprising progress. He was now soundly negotiating five miles a day. Beneath Pollard, there was something different. Seabiscuit was developing a new stride. No longer did he stab out with a foreleg as he ran, producing the curiously choppy duck-waddle gait that so many observers had mistaken for lameness. He now folded his legs up neatly under him when airborne, directing all of his motion forward and back, not side to side. It was a beautiful, smooth gait, and probably a sounder one. Seabiscuit was in fighting trim and hard as rock, and Pollard, though still a wreck, was at least strong enough to handle him.

"Our wheels went wrong together, but we were good for each other," he said. "Out there among the hooting owls, we both got sound again."

On her trips to the barn, Marcela also noticed something new. Seabiscuit was pacing around his stall, as he had done in his days with Fitzsimmons. When he paused, he directed his gaze at the horizon, distracted. Howard saw that look and knew what it meant. "You knew he wanted to race again," he said, "more than anything else in the world."

In the fall Howard called Smith in. The trainer motored up to the ranch and silently watched as Seabiscuit, looking blocky in his winter coat, was galloped in front of him. Smith scrutinized the horse from head to toe. He was deeply impressed with the work Pollard had done with him.

They were all thinking the same thing. Seabiscuit was ready to take another run at the Santa Anita Handicap.

The idea was outlandish. The comeback, if successful, would be unprecedented. No elite horse had ever returned to top form after such a serious injury and lengthy layoff. Few great horses have competed beyond age five or through more than forty races; in a couple of months Seabiscuit would be a bewhiskered seven years old, more than twice the age of many of the horses he would be facing, and he had already raced eighty-five times. When word got out, the Howard team would be widely ridiculed. But Smith, Howard, and Pollard believed he could do it.

Pollard wanted to go with him. He had never lost his belief that he could ride in races again, though no one who looked at him as he leaned on his cane, his leg grotesquely thin and discolored, his body weak and emaciated, would have agreed with him.

His desire became urgency. Agnes began experiencing unusual symptoms and paid a visit to her doctor. He told her that she was pregnant. She thought he had to be wrong. She was certain that Red was too weak to be capable of fathering a child. But the doctor's verdict was unequivocal: Agnes was going to have a baby.

For Pollard, the news was at once wonderful and terrifying. He was still living on the Howards' good graces. He had no money, no home, no career. He had only Seabiscuit. He told Howard he wanted to go back to the track with the horse. Howard was frightened for him. Doc Babcock had said that Pollard was never to go near a horse again. One bump, one twist, and he could lose his ability to walk forever. All Howard would agree to was to let him come along. On a cool day in the late fall of 1939, Pollard and Seabiscuit set out for Santa Anita to chase the one dream that had eluded them.

At Seabiscuit's stall, Pollard awaits
Howard's decision, December 1939.
(*LOS ANGELES EXAMINER*)

CHAPTER 22

Four Good Legs
Between Us

C harles Howard knew something about making an entrance. In the predawn hours of one December morning in 1939 the Seabiscuit crew came whooping and hollering into Santa Anita in a manner only a man as spectacular as Howard could have pulled off. Their vehicle was a streamlined "palace" horse van painted in Howard crimson and white and featuring two musical horns, eight headlights, fourteen cigar lighters, and a luxurious stall with kapok-stuffed walls. The back doors dropped open, and Smith and Seabiscuit emerged. Smith took the horse straight down the shed rows, pulled him up at the Kaiser Suite, and evicted Kayak. "Have to give the better horse preference," he grunted. The first fans arrived at daybreak. All morning long, hundreds of them streamed into Barn 38 to greet the old warrior. Among them was Woolf. Seabiscuit came to the door and rubbed his face against the jockey's fedora.

Smith, knowing that returning the horse to racing was controversial, took the offensive with the press. With a host of newsmen congregated outside, he led Seabiscuit out and stood him in an open space between the barns. He announced that anyone who was suspicious of the horse's soundness could step right up and have a look. He asked the photographers to take close-up shots of the horse's left ankle. "If anybody thinks I am training a cripple," he said, "I want these pictures definitely to prove otherwise."

The 1940 hundred-grander was on March 2, giving Smith about three months to prepare the horse. He got to work. He had Seabiscuit's heavy winter coat clipped off and took him to the scales. The horse weighed in at 1,070, twenty pounds too much. Smith was worried that the load would strain the leg, so he pulled out the yellow sweating hood and gave the horse slow gallops. In the barn they strapped the horse into a muzzle each evening to stop him from eating his bedding. Seabiscuit put up a fight, but the groom managed to get it on without losing any fingers. Gradually, the weight vanished from the horse's ribs.

On December 19 Smith felt the horse was ready to be tested. He tacked him up and took him out for his first fast workout since the injury. As the grooms watched and fretted, Smith waved the exercise rider on. Venting months of frustration, Seabiscuit burned rubber off the line and sped past the grandstand. He came back perfectly sound. The grooms sagged with relief.

The mood didn't last long. Late that afternoon Smith went into the track secretary's office to see the weight postings for the Santa Anita Handicap. He couldn't believe his eyes: Though he had been idle for a year, Seabiscuit had been assigned 130 pounds; Kayak, 129. As he ran his eyes down the list, the highest number Smith saw for any other horse was 114.

Smith lit up like a firecracker. He stormed around the office and shouted about the irresponsibility of the handicapper. A gathering of horsemen gaped at him. Silent Tom's tirade lasted a full five minutes. After giving vent to his anger, he pulled himself together and stalked off.

"So what?" he grumbled. "We'll run one-two anyway."

The year 1940 rolled in with heavy black clouds. Snow brushed over the tips of every peak up in the San Gabriels, but down on the track there was only rain and slippery mud. Smith tucked Seabiscuit away in the barn and waited for a break in the weather. It didn't come. Day after day, the rains kept falling. Over and over again, Smith postponed Seabiscuit's workouts. He spent every minute with the horse, sleeping in the barn, watching him eat, personally wrapping his legs in stall bandages, but he wouldn't let him out to work. Pressure began to build. Seabiscuit was entered in several races, and each time he had to be scratched. The crowds booed and the press picked at Smith and Howard. "If Seabiscuit is scratched again," wrote a reporter, "he will be an etching." The whole barn was in a funk. Kayak was trounced in his first race of 1940. Not a single Howard runner won.

Seabiscuit may have been trapped in the barn, but his idleness didn't hurt his celebrity. He was the hottest name in the nation. Fans thronged into the Uptown Theater in Pasadena to see *The Life of Seabiscuit*, a compilation of the horse's newsreel footage. The film relegated a much anticipated Jimmy Stewart movie to second billing. The stylish "Seabiscuit" ladies' hat, with a fishnet veil, was all the rage in department stores on Manhattan's Fifth Avenue. The hat was the first of myriad lines of signature products: toys, commemorative wastebaskets, two varieties of oranges. All kinds of businesses from hotels to laundries to humor magazines were using the horse's likeness in their ads. The horse even had his own parlor game, the first of at least nine.

When Pollard hung up his tack in the Santa Anita jockeys' room, he found the riding colony in an uproar. Just before the track's season had begun in December, Pollard's old colleague Tommy Luther had sat down for coffee in the Santa Anita golf club with a handful of other riders. They began chatting about the alarming number of jockeys who had been wiped out by injuries, including Pollard. Luther had never gotten over the death of poor little Sandy Graham, thrown from a horse Luther was to have ridden. He had an idea: Why not ask each rider to contribute 10 cents for every ride, plus $20 a year, to a community fund that could help injured riders? The five riders liked the idea and agreed to have a second meeting at the golf club, each man bringing two riders with him.

The next morning, when Luther arrived to pick up his jockey's license for the track's winter meet, he was called before old Pink Whiskers, steward Christopher Fitzgerald, who asked about the meetings. Luther explained his fund idea. Pink Whiskers accused him of starting a union. Luther denied it. Pink Whiskers promptly banned him from riding for a full year for his "defiant and threatening attitude." The ban was upheld everywhere in the country.

Luther refused to back down. He rallied the jockeys around him, and each week the riders streamed across the street to the golf club. Woolf was there, as were Spec Richardson and Harry Richards. But Pollard refused to go. No man in the riding colony needed a community fund more. He had twice narrowly escaped dying in riding accidents that had landed him in the hospital for months on end, wiped him out financially, and caused near crippling injury. Now he was forcing himself back into the saddle at the risk of his leg because he hadn't a cent to his name to support a coming baby. Red Pollard should have been the community fund's poster boy.

But all he could think of was Charles and Marcela Howard. With the jockeys' efforts widely perceived as the formation of a union against stewards, owners, and trainers, Pollard feared that he might offend the Howards by crossing the street and walking into the golf club. To the exasperation of his fellow riders, Pollard stayed away.

For Pollard, it was a season of incredible strain and humiliation. Before arriving at Santa Anita, he had tried to resume his career at Tanforan. At first he found a few trainers who wanted to help him get back on his feet. The result was nearly catastrophic. He had come away hopping from two horses, in obvious pain. He had looked very weak, and everyone, including the newsmen, had noticed. And he hadn't won a race.

He came down to Santa Anita resolving to do better. Yummy, still as fiercely loyal as he had been back in their Thistle Down days, joined up with him again and promised to get him mounts. Red and Agnes settled into a little rental house near the track. Pollard built his strength, hit the sack early, and rose well before dawn to head back to the track. But his declarations of readiness were received with awkward silence. Everyone knew what had happened at Tanforan. Yummy scoured the backstretch for trainers willing to put the Cougar on their horses. He didn't find one. Every trainer on the grounds believed Pollard was finished, and no one wanted to be responsible for crippling him.

The biggest disappointment was Howard. Even when he had been at the top of his game with Seabiscuit, Pollard had never established himself with any other major stable, so Howard was his only real hope. Smith wanted Pollard on the horse for the hundred-grander. Howard wanted to grant the redhead his wish, but both he and Marcela were tormented by the thought of what it would cost him. He let Pollard ride Seabiscuit in slow gallops but kept him off the horse's back for most of his fast workouts. At first, Howard would not allow Pollard to ride in races on any of his horses. Then, one afternoon in late January, he finally relented and assigned the jockey the race mount on a filly. But when the track came up muddy, Howard abruptly snatched Pollard off the horse and put someone else in his place, fearing that the filly might slip and jar the jockey's leg. From then on, when jockeys' names were posted for Howard's horses, Pollard was never among them. In a sport in which men are measured by their toughness, he must have felt humiliated.

Pollard was left with nothing to do. His anguish deepened. He sat in Pops's stall, thinking about Agnes's pregnancy and wondering how he would find the money to support the baby. He told Howard again and again that he was fit to ride in the hundred-grander, but got nowhere.

The truth was that Pollard couldn't even convince himself. The leg didn't feel right in his boot. The bones felt like matchsticks. He was sure that it wouldn't take more than a light bump to shatter them. A secret terror began to rack his mind: What if Howard let him ride and his leg snapped in midrace?

And then there was Woolf. Seeing that Howard might bar Pollard from riding, Smith had started letting Woolf gallop Seabiscuit. There was widespread speculation that either Woolf or Buddy Haas, Kayak's jockey, would be signed on to ride Seabiscuit in the big race. Almost everyone at Santa Anita thought that anyone but Pollard should ride. Pollard called his naysayers "my left-handed rooting section."

Pollard watched Woolf canter off on Pops. Despair rushed up under him like a riptide. "And none so poor," he muttered to a reporter, echoing *Julius Caesar*, "to do me reverence."

Pollard began to crumble under the pressure. He had become a binge drinker. He made a point of temperance during working hours—

"Never let it be said," he once told his friend Bill Buck, "that Pollard was drinking when he was riding"—but during off-hours he sometimes drank heavily. "Tonight's the night," he once shouted as he ran into Buck's apartment near the end of a race season, "the Cougar howls!" When he drank, he endured monstrous hangovers and appeared to suffer from delirium tremens. "I got to wear glued shoes when I'm hung," he said, "because I shake the nails out of the other kind."

Yummy was frightened for him. If Pollard began drinking too heavily, he would lose any chance he had to ride Seabiscuit. Yummy did everything he could to keep the jockey from going on benders. He asked Pollard to come stay with him at the Turkish baths. Pollard refused. So Yummy shadowed him everywhere. He made a point of knowing exactly where his client was twenty-four hours a day. He asked David Alexander to stay around Pollard as much as possible to keep him from overimbibing. In an apparent bargain to keep him dry until the race, Yummy made a deal with the rider. If Pollard won the hundred-grander, Yummy promised to sneak him a swig of bow-wow wine in the winner's circle.

Pollard wasn't the only one feeling the strain. Smith was racked with anxiety. "His whole life," recalled Sonny Greenberg, "was gathered around Seabiscuit." Howard, too, was at the breaking point. Over a five-year partnership, these two radically different men with often conflicting priorities had forged a surprisingly harmonious relationship, but decisions about Seabiscuit's racing and training schedule had repeatedly caused tension between them. When under pressure, each man had a tendency to become more controlling, and never was the pressure higher than in the winter of 1940.

One morning at Santa Anita, Howard pushed Smith hard to take a course with Seabiscuit that Smith was not prepared to take, apparently to rush his very conservative training regimen. In front of a barnful of horsemen, Smith laid down the law. Let me train my horse as I see fit, he snapped, or find a new trainer. Everyone within earshot froze, listening for Howard's response.

Howard said nothing and walked away.

*

January waned, and still Seabiscuit had not raced. Whichcee, Heelfly, all his rivals were preparing well. The rains didn't relent. Smith couldn't wait any longer. He took Seabiscuit and Kayak out for a hard work on the training track. For once, Pollard was allowed to ride Seabiscuit for speed. In a driving rainstorm that sent everyone running, Seabiscuit and Kayak blistered six furlongs in 1:13 with Pollard leaning all the way back against the reins, his feet "on the dashboard." Horse and jockey returned intact. A few days later Smith sent Seabiscuit back out again, and again his time was superb, 1:12⅖ for six furlongs. Pollard said the horse had never been sounder.

After the workout, Smith entered Seabiscuit in the San Felipe Handicap, scheduled for January 30. Pollard awaited a decision on whether or not he would be in the irons. Smith announced that Pollard would ride. But Howard added an escape clause: Pollard would ride only if he was fit to do so. If he wasn't, Howard said, Woolf had the mount. He said nothing about the hundred-grander, now just a month away.

Woolf and Pollard fell into the first crisis of their friendship. To Pollard, the mount on Seabiscuit could not have been more important. The horse meant financial rescue, the ability to meet his responsibilities as father and husband, professional redemption, and the end of a long, public humiliation. But Woolf must have burned with the frustration of the nose loss in 1938, and the guilt for having possibly exacerbated the horse's injury in 1939. In announcing publicly that it was Woolf or Pollard, Howard had inadvertently set the two against each other.

Somewhere along the backstretch, Woolf and Pollard had a bitter argument over Seabiscuit, nearly coming to blows. When they walked away, their friendship was broken.

January 29 dawned sunny and clear. Howard started the long walk to the track offices to enter his horse in the next day's San Felipe. As he ambled around the course, the barometer in the track secretary's office leaned toward rain. He entered the horse. Seeing that Seabiscuit was in, NBC Radio began setting up at Santa Anita to broadcast the race nationally. The barometer continued to sink. Overhead, the clouds furrowed. The next morning, just as Seabiscuit stepped on the track for his final blowout, it began to rain. Then it cleared again, and Howard went to the track and crossed his fingers.

After the third race, David Alexander interrupted Howard in the Turf Club.

"It's raining, Charley."

"No!" Howard shouted, a little too loud. "Three times in a row! This just can't happen."

He stared out at the rain. "It might stop," he said weakly.

It rained harder and harder. A half hour before the race, Howard and Smith got into a station wagon and toured the track. The rain pinged off the roof. The horse needed the work badly, but the track was just too muddy to risk it. When the scratch appeared on the board, the crowd booed. The sun promptly came back out.

The scratchings were becoming a joke. "For hire: One Rain-Maker Racehorse," wrote David Alexander. "Answers to the name of Sea-biscuit. Guaranteed to cause rainstorms wherever he goes. Capable of solving all irrigation problems of dust bowl farmers. Can vastly simplify Federal reclamation projects in all drought areas. All busi-nesses now operating under Federal Bankruptcy Law 7-B can become liquid at once by employing services of this miraculous animal. . . . Clockers have given up timing Seabiscuit with a stopwatch. They're using a barometer instead."

The rain kept falling. A week later Seabiscuit had to be scratched again.

Howard was driven to distraction and needed something to keep himself busy. Overhearing a valet lamenting the lack of funds to create an all-jockey baseball team, he jumped in.

"Let me take care of it," he said. "What will it cost?" The valets came up with an estimate of $23.80 per jockey.

"Go to it," said Howard. "Go first-class."

Arriving to watch them play, Howard was delighted to see that the jockeys had memorialized his generosity by ordering their uniforms in

Howard red and white, with the Howard signature triangle on them. Instead of their own names, the jockeys had stenciled the names of Howard's horses on the back. Howard attended every game, playfully rooting for the opposition.

Days slipped by. The Santa Anita Handicap was just weeks away. Seabiscuit had not raced once. His fans were so eager to see him that as many as forty thousand showed up just to watch him canter around the track in his workouts. The exercise was not doing the trick. "He's gaining weight," moaned Smith, "and we aren't feeding him enough to satisfy a full-grown canary bird." Seabiscuit was far behind in his preparation. The chances of his making the hundred-grander were dimming every day. Woolf couldn't wait any longer. Pressured by trainers who wanted his services in the race, he gave up and signed on to ride Heelfly.

The sky finally cleared for Seabiscuit on February 9, and Smith sent him out for his first race, the La Jolla Handicap. Pollard begged Howard for the mount, and the owner relented. It was Pollard and Seabiscuit's first race together since 1937. It was not a happy reunion. Seabiscuit broke in a tangle. Pollard tried to rush him into contention, only to be pocketed in. As Pollard waited for a gap to run through, a horse blew past. It was Heelfly, with Woolf in the stirrups. Pollard swung Seabiscuit out of the pack and asked him to chase Heelfly. There was no response. Seabiscuit finished third. Up in the press box, a *San Francisco News* reporter typed out the story. "We are afraid that on Handicap Day they'll be passing the 'Biscuit, pappy, passing the 'Biscuit by."

Pollard slid slowly to the ground in front of the grandstand. He was crying.

Smith came out to meet him. He looked over Seabiscuit's legs. The horse was perfectly sound. Smith wasn't worried about the loss. "I'm satisfied. He was a short horse," he said, using the horseman's term for an animal who is not fully fit. "He ran like one."

Pollard pulled himself together. Over the weekend, Yummy took him down to his old haunt, Caliente. The visit gave the rider confidence. "Can we do it? I say we can," he told Alexander. "It's me and the Biscuit, for the big money." Pollard handed Yummy a stack of dollars and sent him to a future book operator to place a bet on the Santa Anita Handicap. "Seabiscuit," he told him. "To win."

A week later, Kayak and Seabiscuit paraded out for the San Carlos Handicap, the same race in which Pollard and Fair Knightess had fallen two years before. The 1940 running turned out better, but not by much. Given clear sailing, neither horse could even get into contention. At the half-mile pole, Seabiscuit abruptly propped. Pollard managed to hang on, but when he asked him to run, again the horse didn't respond. Pollard crouched over his neck, urging him on and getting nothing, watching helplessly as horses flew past. A heartbreaking thought crossed his mind: *He has nothing left.* The horse had never felt this way under him. As his old rival Specify flew to the victory, Seabiscuit labored in sixth, Kayak eighth. The crowd booed. "Seabiscuit seems definitely through as a top fighter," wrote Jack McDonald. "Seabiscuit [is] apparently washed up."

This time, Smith was rattled. He couldn't understand what had happened. He wondered if his talents had failed him, if he had, in trying to compensate for months of undertraining, thrown too much work at his horse at once. He had two weeks to fix the problem and he wasn't sure if he could.

Pollard left the track in despair. Around Santa Anita, people were blaming him for Seabiscuit's losses, and he must have heard them. But as the days passed, something about the race kept pulling at him. At the half-mile pole, Seabiscuit had propped. He hadn't done that since back in 1936, in the first race against Myrtlewood in Detroit. The horse hadn't seemed tired before he did it, so it was strange that he tired abruptly afterward. Pollard began to wonder if the Biscuit had just been fooling around. Perhaps, he thought, he'd done it because he was feeling good and a little mischievous. Howard and the stable hands clung to the propping incident as a good omen. It was all they had.

Smith was adamant that Pollard was the man for the job. Howard couldn't commit to it. Shortly before Seabiscuit's final prep race, the San Antonio, Pollard learned that Howard had sent a $500 retainer check to jockey Buddy Haas, asking him to come west. Howard then made Seabiscuit's entry for the Santa Anita Handicap.

He left the jockey space blank.

Later that week there was a rap at the door of David Alexander's rental house in the Hollywood hills. It was Pollard. Alexander had never seen him in such a state. He was falling apart. He was, Alexander wrote, "nervous and worried and distraught."

Alexander ushered Pollard into his den. He tried to make small talk, telling the jockey that Bing Crosby's hit "Pennies from Heaven" was written in that den by earlier tenants.

"That's what I need," Pollard muttered. "Pennies from heaven. And I've got just one more ride to get 'em."

"How's Pops?" Alexander asked.

"Pops's leg is no worse than usual, but how's the Cougar?" Pollard replied. Alexander watched as Pollard pulled his trouser leg up. The jockey's leg was purple. A broad welt ran the entire length of it. It looked, Alexander wrote, "like a charred, knobby broomstick."

"One little tap," Pollard said. "Just one. But it's got to last for one more ride."

He shrugged. "Old Pops and I have got four good legs between us," he said. "Maybe that's enough."

They talked about Pollard's fears. The leg was only part of it. Buddy Haas's impending arrival had him overwrought.

"I've got to ride that horse." Pollard's voice had a deadly urgency to it.

Alexander promised Pollard that he would talk to Howard. The following day he tracked the owner down and asked him point-blank if he was going to take the mount away from Pollard.

"What would you and the other newspaper boys do if I rode Haas?" Howard asked.

Alexander said he couldn't speak for the whole press corps, but "I said I would crucify him and use a whole keg full of nails for the job."

"If Red breaks that leg again," Howard said soberly, "it will cripple him for life."

Alexander told him that maybe it was better to break a man's leg than his heart.

February 23 was the day before the San Antonio. Howard was pacing around Santa Anita, a rabbit's foot working overtime in his pocket. With only a week remaining before the Santa Anita Handicap, Seabiscuit had to run well or his attempted comeback would have to be deemed a failure. Kayak, too, had his reputation on the line. The whole barn was failing. Howard had never doubted his chances so much, and Smith had said nothing that reassured him.

A clerk met Howard on the bridge between the grandstand and clubhouse.

"Do you happen to have a rabbit's foot, Mr. Howard?"

Howard said yes and pulled it out of his pocket.

"Give me that damn thing," said the clerk. "It's the unluckiest thing you can have on a racetrack."

Howard handed it to him, and the clerk threw it away.

Beneath a hazy winter sky the following afternoon, Smith pushed Pollard up on Seabiscuit for the San Antonio, then went up to Howard's box and sat down. Seabiscuit and Kayak walked out to the post. Smith said nothing, watching the horses. Howard worried. For what was surely the first time, he had not placed bets on his own horses. Marcela was so worried about jinxing the horses that she hadn't come to the track.

Seabiscuit approached the starting gate. Smith studied his motion. He saw something there he hadn't seen in a year. He leaned toward Howard and said five words: "It's Seabiscuit, wire to wire."

Howard wheeled on Smith in amazement. He jumped up, ran to the betting booth, and emptied his pockets into the clerk's hands.

The crowd of thirty-five thousand hushed, and the bell rang. Seabiscuit broke alertly and bounded up with the early leaders. The field flew off into the backstretch. In his box, Howard was in agonies. The crowd murmured and waited.

A minute later the field bent around the far turn and rushed at the grandstand. There was one horse in front and pouring it on. His silks were red. It was Seabiscuit. The crowd roared. Pollard and Seabiscuit glided down the lane all by themselves, reaching the wire in track-record-equaling time. Kayak was right behind him. It was Pollard's first win since 1938. Howard swept down the steps to shake his hand.

As Pollard and his horse moved past the grandstand, hundreds of men spontaneously rose together and doffed their hats to him, their eyes shining. The cheering rolled over the track for more than fifteen minutes.

A few minutes later, Pollard sauntered out of the jocks' room, smiling. "If the track is fast like it was today for next Saturday's big race, we'll win as far as a country boy can throw an apple," he said. "We made our comeback together. I guess me and the Biscuit both needed those first two races, but we are ready to meet all comers now." He went to the barn to check on Seabiscuit. Smith was there, marveling at the horse. He was sounder than he had been in two years.

Howard had seen enough. Buddy Haas would ride Kayak. Pollard had won the mount on Seabiscuit. "Just give us a fast track," Pollard said. "That's all we want."

Howard went home to celebrate. It began to rain.

*Trapped behind a wall of horses on the final turn of the 1940 Santa
Anita Handicap, Pollard and Seabiscuit make a desperate attempt
to run between Whichcee (rail) and Wedding Call.*
(© BETTMANN/CORBIS)

CHAPTER 23

One Hundred Grand

Every night Smith drifted off to the sound of raindrops ringing off the barn roof. Every morning he woke to the same sound. The National Weather Service switchboard took more phone calls in that week than ever in its history, with nearly every caller asking if the skies would clear for Seabiscuit's run at the Handicap that Saturday. The rain didn't relent and Smith had no choice but to work the horse in the mud.

Early in the week, Smith brought Seabiscuit and Kayak out together. Howard stood by the barns and blinked at the clouds, a sarcastic smile on his face. He watched as the horses slogged through the mud, Seabiscuit dogging and taunting until Kayak pinned his ears and abruptly quit. They took the two horses back to the barn and cooled them out together. Kayak, clearly frustrated, took a lunge at Seabiscuit, dragging a groom with him. Smith was pleased. Seabiscuit was his old nasty self. Got to stop working these two together.

The rain kept falling. Smith kept working the horses. Kayak handled the mud well; Seabiscuit didn't. "You know," said Howard, "I wish one thing. It's that Kayak's four mud-running legs might be attached to Seabiscuit's racing heart. Then I'd have something." The tapping of rain carried his words away.

Two days before the race, the heavens finally relented. The drying irons rolled out. Fifty track workers slogged over the course, sponging the mud out of the puddles. Slowly, the track dried.

Early on the morning of March 2, race day, groom Harry Bradshaw came down the shed row, poured a helping of oats into Seabiscuit's bucket, then stepped out from under the shed row roof. At last the sun was breaking through. Bradshaw turned his face toward it. "Be with him today," he said.

Smith came up, working a strip of buckskin in his fingers.

"He's right as rain, Mr. Smith," said Bradshaw.

"Wrong word, Harry."

The trainer stood back to let the horse eat. Seabiscuit heard his voice and nosed over his half door. Smith lay the flat of his hand on him.

"Today's the day," he said.

At eight o'clock Howard's stable agent stepped into the track secretary's office, scrawled the name Seabiscuit onto an entry slip, and dropped it into the entry box. He was the first horse entered. Then the agent dropped Kayak's name in. Rain or shine, both horses would run.

The sun was still straining to clear the east end of the grandstand when the Howards pulled up to the barn. Pollard was already there. Howard looked anxiously at the jockey's leg, the brace swelling the boot, and put his hand over Pollard's shoulder. Pollard assured him that he'd be okay. Smith swung Pollard up on Seabiscuit to stretch his legs. Howard got up on his saddle horse, Chulo, Smith got on Pumpkin, and the sextet trotted out to the course for a prerace blowout. Marcela walked with them to the track apron and watched them go, her hands tight on the rail. The track was dry and fast. Smith signaled to Pollard, and Seabiscuit broke off and kicked over the track. Pollard talked in Seabiscuit's ear as they whirled through a quarter mile in a scorching twenty-two seconds. Seabiscuit was ready to go. Pollard dismounted and went home to spend a few hours with Agnes.

People had begun gathering by the track gates just after dawn. By nine-thirty, the parking lot was already swollen with cars. Many people had driven across the nation to see the race; virtually every state in the union was represented by a license plate. They threw the gates open at ten. Five thousand fans gushed into the grandstand and clubhouse, staking out their territory with blankets and spring jackets. "It looked," wrote *Thoroughbred Record* correspondent Barry Whitehead, "like the Oklahoma landrush." The fans found Santa Anita decked out in all its splendor. In the clubhouse and turf club, arches of acacias, columns of jonquils, and giant gardenias with fifteen hundred blossoms stretched overhead, while peat beds of irises, white primroses, peach blossoms, and tulips lined the entire interior.

By ten-thirty, the grandstand was filled to capacity. By noon the parking lot couldn't fit another car, and the overflow spilled out onto the track's decorative lawns. A horse-loving priest from the church across the street opened his yard to let fans park there for free. Still the cars kept coming, snarling every local road for the entire day. Trains chugged up all afternoon; one of them, from San Francisco, had all seventeen cars filled to bursting with Seabiscuit fans. Up in the press box, reporters from all over the world arrived. Over the next few hours they would churn out half a million words on the Morse wires, Teletypes, and typewriters. The clubhouse roof and the top of the tote board were lined with newsreel cameras. In the luxury boxes, celebrities filed in: Clark Gable and Carole Lombard, Jack Benny, Sonja Henie, James Stewart, and Mervyn LeRoy. Bing Crosby had stayed up all night recording at Universal so he could have the day off, and came with Mrs. Bing, rooting for yet another hopeless long shot from their barn, Don Mike.

By midafternoon, seventy-eight thousand people had crammed into the track, more than ten thousand in the infield alone. It was officially the second-largest crowd ever to attend a horse race in America, but because the record tally, at the Kentucky Derby, was famously exaggerated, the attendance at this hundred-grander was undoubtedly the largest. Radios all over the world were tuned to the broadcast from Santa Anita. The town of Willits was at a standstill. Up in Flint, Michigan, Howard had arranged to have the loudspeakers in the Buick salesroom rigged to broadcast the race.

The afternoon ticked on. The race approached.

At home, Pollard made his final preparations. Agnes strung a Saint Christopher medal onto a necklace and gave it to him. He slipped it on under his shirt. Before he left, he promised Agnes that he'd bring her flowers from the winner's wreath.

The first big gust from the crowd came as Seabiscuit was led from the barn to the paddock. Marcela, who had stood with him in the barn, stayed behind. "I'd seen Johnny's leg," she said. "I just couldn't watch it."

When Pollard walked into the paddock, he was greeted by Doc Babcock, who had flown down from Willits. The doctor carefully unrolled Pollard's leg bandages.

Yummy, who was there at the start, was there for the end. David Alexander was with him. Yummy, Alexander remembered, "sidled up to me like some character out of a spy novel."

"I've got it," Yummy whispered.

When Alexander asked what he had, Yummy flashed a little bottle of bow-wow wine, secreted away in his coat pocket. He told Alexander about his promise to Pollard: If he won, Yummy would sneak it to him.

Pollard strode over to his mount. Smith pulled the saddle over Seabiscuit's withers and tightened the girth. Marcela's Saint Christopher medal shone against the saddlecloth. Howard was beside himself with anxiety. When he was nervous he was talkative, and he had spent the afternoon calling Marcela at the barn over and over again and chattering at her. Now he prattled on at Pollard, giving him every needless detail of how to ride the race. Pollard humored him, then turned to Smith. The old cowpuncher lifted Pollard onto Seabiscuit's back.

"You know the horse, and the horse knows you," said Smith, winking. "Bring him home."

Howard tapped out a cigarette and tried to light it. His hands were trembling so much that his match went out. He lit a second match, then a third, and they too sputtered out. Alexander wished him luck.

"You're shaking like a leaf," he said, watching Howard work on the fourth match.

"I guess I'm a little nervous," Howard replied, smiling.

Seabiscuit and Pollard stepped down the long lane toward the track. Howard was whispering, "I hope he can. I hope he can. I hope he can." His jaw quivered.

As Seabiscuit stepped onto the track, swinging his head left, then right, the fans erupted in a massive ovation, drowning out the bugler playing "Boots and Saddles." There was no question about the crowd's allegiance. In the paddock the horsemen, virtually to a man, were hoping that if they didn't get it, the old Biscuit would. "I'd like to see Seabiscuit win," said a rival owner, "even though I'm running against him." Up in the press box, Jolly Roger and all the other Wise We Boys had dropped their objectivity. Even Oscar Otis was up there, cheering Pollard on.

Alexander looked up at Pollard as he passed. The Cougar, Alexander later wrote, had "the old impish go-to-hell grin" on his face. Alexander thought of Huck Finn.

Seabiscuit walked to the gate, the applause building and building. In the hush of the barn, Marcela suddenly changed her mind. She ran down the shed row, cut out into the daylight, and rushed toward the track. She knew she couldn't get to the grandstand in time. She spotted a water wagon parked ahead, track workers perched up on top of it, and ran toward it. Her dress whipped in the wind.

The bell rang in Pollard's ears, and he felt Seabiscuit drop and push beneath him, hammering the track and powering forward. There was the rushing sound of seventy-five thousand voices and the tumbling motion of horses and the flight of wind and dirt and the airy unreal feeling of mass and gravity slipping away.

They rolled down the homestretch for the first time, and Pollard felt the rightness of Seabiscuit's stride, the smooth strumming under him. Whichcee had the lead. Pollard let Seabiscuit hunt him. They bent through the first turn, Pollard holding his mount one path out from the rail, an open lane ahead. A splendid spot.

Pollard could sense the pace as they straightened down the

backstretch: blistering fast. But he knew Whichcee had stamina, and he couldn't let him steal away. He had to drive Whichcee hard to break him. He held Seabiscuit a half length behind him, keeping just far enough out from the rail to give himself clear running room. Whichcee strained to stay ahead. The two horses blazed down the backstretch together, cutting six furlongs in 1:11⅗; though they were set to run a grueling mile and a quarter, the fastest sprinters on earth would have been drained to the bottom to beat such a time. Whichcee screamed along the rail, stretching out over the backstretch, trying to hold his head in front. Seabiscuit stalked him with predatory lunges. Wedding Call tracked them, just behind and outside of Seabiscuit as they pushed for the far turn. They clipped through a mile in 1:36, nearly a second faster than Seabiscuit and War Admiral's record-shattering split in their 1938 match race. Seabiscuit still pushed at Whichcee. Pollard, up in the saddle, was a lion poised for the kill.

They leaned around the final turn, and Seabiscuit pulled at Pollard's hands, telling him he was ready. The rail spun away to the left, and Whichcee's hindquarters rose and fell beside them. Wedding Call made his move, throwing his shadow over them from the right. Pollard stayed where he was, holding his lane one path out from the rail, leaving himself room to move around Whichcee when the time came.

The field was gathering, and the space around them compressed. Horses were all around, their bodies elongated in total effort. Then, in an instant, they came inward with the synchronicity of a flurry of birds pivoting in the air. Wedding Call clattered up against Seabiscuit, bumping him toward the rail behind Whichcee. The path ahead closed.

Seabiscuit felt the urgency and tugged at the reins. Pollard had nowhere to send him. He rose halfway up in the saddle, holding Seabiscuit back, his leg straining under his weight. Whichcee and Wedding Call formed a wall in front of him. A terrible thought came to Pollard: *There is no way out.*

A jockey in the pack heard a deep, plaintive sound rise up over the shouts from the crowd. It was Pollard, crying out a prayer. A moment later, Whichcee wavered and sagged a few inches to his left just as Wedding Call's momentum carried him slightly to the right. A slender hole opened before Seabiscuit. Pollard measured it in his mind. Maybe it was wide enough; maybe it was not. If Pollard tried to take it, it was highly likely that he would clip his right leg on Wedding Call. He knew what that would mean. He needed an explosion from Seabiscuit, every amp of his old speed and more. He leaned forward in the saddle and shouted, "*Now*, Pop!"

Carrying 130 pounds, 22 more than Wedding Call and 16 more than Whichcee, Seabiscuit delivered a tremendous surge. He slashed into the hole, disappeared between his two larger opponents, then burst into the lead. Pollard's leg cleared Whichcee by no more than an inch. Whichcee tried to go with Seabiscuit. Pollard let his mount dog him, mocking him, and Whichcee broke. Seabiscuit shook free and hurtled into the homestretch alone as the field fell away behind him. Pollard dropped his head and rode for all he was worth. Joe Hernandez's voice cut over the crowd, calling out Seabiscuit's name, and was instantly swallowed in the uproar from the grandstand. One of the stable hands yelled to Marcela that Seabiscuit had the lead. She shrieked.

In the midst of all the whirling noise of that supreme moment, Pollard felt peaceful. Seabiscuit reached and pushed and Pollard folded and unfolded over his shoulders and they breathed together. A thought pressed into Pollard's mind: *We are alone.*

Twelve straining Thoroughbreds; Howard and Smith in the grandstand; Agnes in the surging crowd; Woolf behind Pollard, on Heelfly; Marcela up on the water wagon with her eyes squeezed shut; the leaping, shouting reporters in the press box; Pollard's family crowded around the radio in a neighbor's house in Edmonton; tens of thousands of roaring spectators and millions of radio listeners painting this race in their imaginations: All this fell away. The world narrowed to a man and his horse, running.

In the center of the track, a closer broke from the pack and rolled into Seabiscuit's lead, a ghost from his past. It was Kayak, charging at him with a fury. Pollard never looked back. He knew who it was.

Pollard felt a pause. For the last time in his life, Seabiscuit eased up to tease an opponent. Kayak came to him and drew even. Up on Kayak, Buddy Haas had never heard such thunder as was pouring from the grandstand and infield. He drilled everything he had at Seabiscuit. Kayak's black nose nodded into the lead.

Pollard let Seabiscuit savor this last rival, then asked him again. He felt the sweet press of sudden acceleration. A moment later, Pollard and Seabiscuit were alone again, burning over the track, Kayak spinning off behind, the wire crossing overhead.

The world broke over Santa Anita. Howard ran from his box with his fist in the air. Smith went with him. Yummy banged around the winner's circle, jumping up and down. Agnes stood in the throng, sobbing. All around them, men and women hurled their hats in the air, poured onto the track, drummed on the rails, and slapped one another on the back. Hundreds of spectators were weeping with joy. "Listen to this crowd roar!" shouted Hernandez. "Seventy-eight thousand fans going absolutely crazy, including this announcer!" The sound was ear-splitting; virtually every journalist reported that he had never heard shouting so loud and sustained.

Sun Beau's money-winning record had finally fallen. Seabiscuit had clocked a new track record that would stand untouched for a decade: a mile and a quarter in 2:01⅕. It was the second-fastest ten furlongs ever run in American racing history.

Galloping out in the backstretch, Pollard lingered over his last few moments of solitude with Seabiscuit. Then he turned him and quietly cantered him back. He rode back into the world sitting tall and regal in the saddle, his back straight, his head up, his face gravely dignified. Tears were cutting down his face and streaming to his chin. He looked, someone said, like "a man who temporarily had visited Olympus and still was no longer for this world."

He walked Seabiscuit through the masses of shouting fans to the winner's circle. The horse was strutting like a prizefighter. "Don't think," Pollard said later, "he didn't know he was the hero." Howard rushed up to him, slapping his horse and shouting to Pollard. They led Kayak into the winner's circle with Seabiscuit, the camera flashes playing off of them like lightning. The winner's blanket of roses fell over Pollard's lap. Beneath it, he felt Yummy's hand in his, slipping the flask of bow-wow wine into his hand. Pollard dropped his head as if to smell the roses. "Best-smelling drink I ever tasted," he would later say. The horse stood calmly, serenely, plucking the roses off the blanket as souvenir hunters yanked hairs from his tail.

Pollard, his hair running with sweat, pulled the blanket over his shoulders and slid down from Seabiscuit's back. Yummy, still pouncing up and down, jumped onto him. The blanket was torn from Pollard's back, dragged away, and shredded by eager hands before he could pull out Agnes's promised blooms. Howard never even saw it. Pollard uncinched his saddle and walked up the track to a chorus of wild cheering, tears still flowing over his cheeks. Fans were fighting to get close to him, to shake his hand. He slipped into the jockeys' room and pulled off his silks. Agnes's Saint Christopher medal glinted against his chest.

Woolf stood across the room. Whatever had separated him from Pollard had vanished. Both knew it. The redhead was whisked off to the press room. He bummed cigarettes off of the reporters as he praised Smith and Bradshaw and old Doc Babcock, then took a few shots at Woolf again, as he always used to.

There was no trace of bitterness in Woolf's voice when he spoke of the race. He didn't mind losing. "There was just too much Seabiscuit," he said. "Just the greatest horse I ever saw."

Long after the horses and their handlers had left the track, the din died away and the crowds trickled out. Workmen crisscrossed the grounds. A lone fan still stood at the east end of the grandstand. As the sun dropped in the winter sky, the man called out to the empty track.

"Ha-ray for Seabiscuit! Hoo-ray for Seabiscuit!"

His voice carried up to the press box, where the reporters were banging out their stories. The room was still ringing with the sensation of what had happened.

"Oh," wrote Jolly Roger, "that I lived to see this day."

*

Back at the barn, the Howards gathered to watch the horses cool out. Howard was wheeling all over the grounds, singing out, "What a race! What a horse! It was perfect!"

Smith barely looked up from Seabiscuit.

As dusk fell, Pollard walked up. Smith put his hand out to him.

"Red, you put up a great ride today."

"I got a great ride," Pollard said. "The greatest ride I ever got from the greatest horse that ever lived."

"Little horse, what next?" a newspaper would read the next morning. In six years, Seabiscuit had won thirty-three races and set thirteen track records at eight tracks over six distances. He had smashed a world record in the shortest of sprints, one half mile, yet had the stamina to run in track record time at one and five-eighths miles. Many of history's greatest horses had faltered under 128 pounds or more; Seabiscuit had set two track records under 133 pounds and four more under 130 while conceding massive amounts of weight to his opponents. He was literally worth his weight in gold, having earned a world record $437,730, nearly sixty times his price.

Howard wavered on whether or not to race him again. Pollard urged retirement. When asked about it, Smith said, "Seabiscuit is Mr. Howard's horse. I will abide by whatever decision Mr. Howard makes."

Later, someone heard him whisper under his breath, "I hope he doesn't race anymore."

Howard heeded his trainer's wishes. The partnership was over.

Charles and Marcela whirled off to the Turf Club Ball at the Ambassador Hotel Fiesta Room, where they laughed and celebrated and slurped champagne from a gigantic golden loving cup. Howard's eyes scanned the faces of the revelers, searching for Smith. He was hoping that this one time the trainer would show up. He had a 1940 Buick estate wagon that he wanted to give him. But Smith never came. Sometime in the evening, Howard snuck away to a telephone.

The phone rang in Smith's room. Howard's voice bubbled over the line, begging him to join the festivities. Smith declined; he was already in bed. Howard accepted it. He wished the trainer good night, put down the telephone, and returned to his element.

Red, Agnes, David Alexander, and Yummy spent the evening in The Derby, a tavern Woolf had bought in preparation for his retirement. The place was vintage Woolf, decorated floor to ceiling in flamboyant cowboy memorabilia.

They gathered around a table and talked. Outside, the Depression was playing itself out, and with it would go the world that had been shaped by it. War was coming, and America was turning its long-averted face upward. It would soon be dawn.

Red Pollard sipped his scotch and reminisced about Seabiscuit and quietly slipped out of history. The smoke from his cigarette curled up from his fingers and slowly faded away.

Smith slept briefly, then woke. Before the sun fingered over the tips of the San Gabriels, his stiff, gray form passed down the shed row at Barn 38. The air carried the hushed sound of stirring straw, and the horses shook the sleep from their bodies. In the darkness, they didn't see Smith coming, but they knew he was there.

Charles Howard and Seabiscuit
(LT. COL. MICHAEL C. HOWARD)

Epilogue

On a soft April day in 1940, Smith led Seabiscuit out of the Kaiser Suite for the last time. There had been countless requests for appearances—the promoters of the Golden State International Exhibition, having secured the attendance of F.D.R., wanted to host "that other great American, Seabiscuit"—but Howard declined them all. It was time to let the horse rest. Howard had preceded Seabiscuit up to Ridgewood and had coaxed every reporter, newsreel man, admirer, and friend in his address book into driving up to attend the horse's homecoming. He proudly introduced everyone to Seabiscuit's first foal, still wobbling on new legs. The owner passed out cigars and showed off the sacks of fan mail addressed to "Daddy Seabiscuit" and "Pappa Seabiscuit." The foal delighted Pollard in particular; he was a redhead. Howard named him First Biscuit.

Smith wasn't going to join the celebration. He preferred to say his good-byes at the track. He slipped his fingers into Seabiscuit's halter and led him down the shed row. A somber group of newsmen, spectators, and horsemen quietly parted to let them pass. Seabiscuit paused and looked toward the track, and Smith's eyes clouded over. He led his horse up the ramp and disappeared into the darkness. A moment later, he emerged alone.

The men who handled Seabiscuit quietly scattered. Woolf continued his dizzying ascent, becoming the leading rider in America. On the day in 1942 when he rode Triple Crown winner Whirlaway to break Seabiscuit's earnings record, Pollard was up in the stands cheering him on with his usual lack of restraint, bouncing around the box, rooting himself hoarse, and drawing the stares of everyone nearby. Dismounting, Woolf was swamped by reporters asking him to confirm that "Whirly" was the best horse he had ever ridden. Woolf was as impolitic as ever. "Seabiscuit," he said, "is the greatest horse I ever rode."

On a January day in 1946, Woolf rode into the Santa Anita starting gate for a weekday race. At thirty-five, he was preparing to end one of history's greatest athletic careers. He was struggling with his diabetes, and friends had noticed that he was unusually thin that winter. That afternoon, Woolf wasn't feeling well enough to ride, but a friend needed a jockey for a horse named Please Me. Woolf didn't need to think about it. "There was one thing special you can say about George," Smith would say of him. "He remembered the little fellows who were his friends when he needed them. He never forgot about his friends. Say that about George." Please Me was an ordinary horse in an ordinary race, so Woolf used weekday tack. When he walked out to the paddock, he left his lucky kangaroo-leather saddle in his trunk.

For George Woolf, the last sensations of life were the sight of Santa Anita's russet soil and the curve of Please Me's neck, the coarse feel of mane in his hands, the smell of the horse's skin, the deep roll of his breathing. As Woolf and his mount passed the grandstand and banked into the first turn, some witnesses thought they saw Please Me stumble. But most saw Woolf sink from the saddle, unconscious, his dieting and diabetes finally taking their toll. He slid into the air. There was the awful dissonance of a lone horse galloping riderless. There was terrible speed and terrible, sudden stillness.

The sound of the Iceman's head striking the track carried over the crowd. Woolf's friends turned away.

Fifteen hundred people came to say good-bye to Woolf. Genevieve, widowed at thirty-two, sat in a front pew. Gene Autry sang "Empty Saddles in the Old Corral," his voice wafting out over rows and rows of faces, spilling back to the church's opened doors, down the steps, and filling the street. Pollard was among them, sobbing for his best friend. "I wonder who has Woolf's book?" he said later. "Saint Peter, or some other bird?"

Three years later a wistful bugle cry carried over the empty track at Santa Anita, and sixteen thousand people gathered by the paddock to witness the unveiling of the George Woolf memorial statue. Much of the price had been footed by Please Me's owner, Tiny Naylor, who sold a horse at auction and donated the proceeds to the statue fund. The rest had come from the California Turf Writers Committee and countless contributions from trackers and fans the world over. Genevieve joined Charles Howard in the center of the paddock to hear a eulogy delivered by Joe Hernandez, the man who first called Woolf "Iceman." The jockeys lined up in silent attention before Woolf's veiled likeness, their hats over their hearts.

The cloth was slid from the statue.

Woolf's handsome face looked out across Santa Anita once again. He stood just as he always had in life, hand on hip, chin up, radiating insouciance, the kangaroo-leather saddle over his arm. His gaze fell to the east end of the paddock and rested on the life-sized bronze image of Seabiscuit that Howard had placed there.

"George Woolf is at Santa Anita, there near the paddock, facing [sculptor Tex] Wheeler's magnificent figure of Seabiscuit," wrote the *Thoroughbred Times*'s Jack Shettlesworth. "He'll be there as long as Santa Anita stands. Santa Anita will be there as long as people feel anything about anything in racing."

Howard lobbied to get Smith named champion trainer of 1940, but Smith would never have the respect he deserved. Owner and trainer continued to work together until the spring of 1943, when Smith underwent back surgery and wound up in a yearlong convalescence that forced Howard to replace him. They parted amicably, and Smith went, of all places, to the East, signing on as trainer for cosmetic queen Elizabeth Arden Graham.

Graham was a woman of famously dubious sense, and working for her was a tall order. She demanded that her trainers apply her beauty products to her horses. Prone to premonitions, she once dreamt that her filly had climbed a tree and called her trainer in the middle of the night to see if the dream had come true. "I climbed all the way up in that tree," replied the much abused trainer, "and if [the filly] was up there, she got back in that stall all right." She was also famous for firing workers for absurd reasons; she once dismissed an exercise boy because his hair was "remarkably bushy and profuse." She went through trainers like chewing gum. But once she found Smith, she was sold. She loved the way he nurtured her horses. "There's something about Tom Smith," she said, "that gives you confidence." He humored her insistence that stalls be perfumed and horses be slathered in cold creams, trained just as he wanted, and won everything in sight. "I try not to hurt her feelings," he once said, "and yet do it my way." He soon became the leading trainer in America.

Smith was sitting in Graham's box one afternoon when an ancient man hobbled up to him. It was Samuel Riddle, easing down in his last years of life. For years, Riddle had burned with resentment over War Admiral's loss to Seabiscuit, turning his head away when he saw Smith, never speaking a word. But this day Riddle halted in front of Smith and directed his first words to him since the race. "Tom," he said, "you and that George Woolf are the only ones who ever outdid me."

On November 1, 1945, one of Smith's horses, a claimer named Magnific Duel, was being prepared for a New York race when a Jockey Club official saw a groom spraying something up the horse's nostril. The atomizer he took from the stall contained 2.6 percent ephedrine, a decongestant. Smith was in deep trouble. New York did not allow any medications in racing horses. Though Smith was not present when the incident occurred and there was no evidence that he knew what his groom was doing, by racing law he was responsible for anything his employee did. The Jockey Club suspended him immediately, pending a hearing. Smith was aghast. "I am absolutely innocent," he said.

At the hearing, pharmacologists testified that the dosage in the atomizer was far too low to have any effect on the horse's performance. The horse had tested negative for any trace of the drug. In a quarter century of training, Smith hadn't received a single black mark on his record. It made no sense that, while training the leading barn in America, winner of half a million dollars in purses in 1945, he would have had any interest in tampering with a $1,900 claimer. From a betting standpoint, he had even less to gain; the horse was a heavy favorite, and would have paid only a few cents on the dollar. His defense convinced nearly everyone in racing and the public that he was not deserving of punishment, but it was not enough for the Racing Commission. In an extremely controversial decision, Smith was banned from racing for one year.

In his seventy years, Smith had never known a life apart from horses. He had nowhere to go. He came to Santa Anita, but officials wouldn't let him in. He spent his days sitting alone out on Baldwin Avenue, just outside the track fence, watching his sport go on without him. Graham may have been the strangest of eccentrics, but she was loyal. She paid for a prominent lawyer for Smith, hired his son Jimmy to train in his place, and gave him back his job the minute he was reinstated in 1947. He repaid her by promptly winning the Kentucky Derby with her horse Jet Pilot.

But the damage had been done. Unquestionably one of the greatest trainers who ever lived, Smith was excluded from racing's Hall of Fame for more than forty years after his death. His reputation was ruined; racing officials tailed him around after his reinstatement, trying to catch him in some nefarious act. Smith was bitter for the rest of his life. He toyed with the officials, pretending to hide things in the hay and sending his pursuers on wild-goose chases, hoping to be accused again so he could be exonerated and make fools of the officials. When *Time* asked him to speak about the Racing Commission, Smith was typically pithy. "Those bastards."

He descended into obscurity just as he had risen from it. He eventually parted with Graham and wound up training a single horse at Santa Anita. When he was seventy-eight, a stroke stilled him. He was sent to live his last days in the antiseptic confinement of a sanatorium. At

Forest Lawn in Glendale, California, on a cold day in 1957, they buried the man the Indians called the Lone Plainsman. Almost no one came.

Pollard had exhausted every physical and emotional reserve to get himself back to the Santa Anita Handicap, and he emerged near collapse. Agnes was afraid for him. They finally had some money, so the two left town immediately for a long vacation. There Pollard coped with what he called his "nervous reaction" to the strain, and the two of them discussed their future. When Pollard came back, he had an announcement to make. "My pal's quit racing," he said. "I'm not getting any younger, and I've had more than my share of serious accidents. Maybe I won't be lucky in escaping with nothing worse than broken bones next time."

"I'll never throw a leg over another horse," he said, "unless it's for a canter in the park."

Howard offered him a job as his stable agent. Impressed with the work Pollard had done to get Seabiscuit back to the track, Howard hoped to have the redhead succeed Smith when the old trainer finally took down his shingle. Pollard took the job.

One day in early May 1940, Pollard limped down the shed rows at Santa Anita in his best impersonation of a run. Agnes was in labor, and he was desperate to find someone with a car. He found a teenaged kid who could drive, dragged him out to his car and pressed him into service. Pollard reached the hospital a few minutes later and promptly fainted from the excitement. He was hospitalized alongside his wife, who delivered a little girl that Pollard named after his sister Norah. Pollard would have known her anywhere; her voice, even as a baby, was a deep baritone like his. In a few years, a son, John, would follow.

Eventually Pollard took out a trainer's license and tried to do for a barnful of horses what he had done for Seabiscuit in 1939. It didn't work out. Describing himself as "a barnacle on the wheels of progress," he quit. With nothing better to do, he took out a jockey's license, strapped his fur-lined leg brace back on, and returned to riding. This time he had a safety net. Evidently with Howard's blessing, he had joined the newly established Jockeys' Guild, the final realization of Tommy Luther's community-fund insurance idea. He was voted onto its first board of directors. They were too late for one rider, John Giangaspro, who was killed in a race two hours after Lloyds of London agreed to insure the riders. Giangaspro had not yet had the chance to join, but the other jockeys stood by him, ensuring that his family received the $5,000 death benefit.

The war came down on Santa Anita a few months later. The horses were shipped out and men and women and children were shipped in, Japanese-Americans interned in stalls meant for animals. The Kaiser Suite became home to an entire family, the Satos. When the Satos and their unfortunate brethren were moved out in 1943, the track became Camp Santa Anita, a massive ordnance storage site and open-air Army barracks for thousands of soldiers.

Seized by patriotic fervor, Pollard galloped off to join the military. Due to his innumerable injuries, he was deemed such a spectacularly unfit soldiering prospect that all three services rejected him. He went back, once again, to race riding.

Agnes had had enough of lugging her babies through hotels and rental places. They journeyed east and bought a little house in Pawtucket, Rhode Island. He rode with less and less success, winding up back in the bush leagues. He spent part of each year on the road, traveling alone from motel to motel, and the rest booting horses around Rhode Island's declining Narragansett Park, soon to meet the bulldozer, where he and Pops once raced.

He continued to endure horrific injuries, falling so often that he quipped about having a "semiannual comeback." He never received anything but the worst care. He went down one day at Narragansett and was taken to the hospital, but no one ever came to look him over, so he just got up and went home. It wasn't until much later that he learned that he had walked out on a broken hip. After breaking his back in a spill in Maryland in 1942, he was carried to a hospital in a laundry basket. The injury knocked him out of the sport for a year and left him with one leg shorter than the other. A 1945 head injury incurred in a Florida race cost him a handful of teeth and nearly his life. "When I woke up, the parish priest leaned over me and whispered, 'The Devil has no stall for you,' so here I am," he told reporters after awakening. "And I guess I'll be here forever, me and Methuselah."

He nearly was. His brilliant red hair slowly went gray, his blind eye paled, his battered body aged, and still he rode racehorses. He rode alongside kids who hadn't even been born when he first offered a sugar cube to Seabiscuit, but he never let the latest teenaged hotshot get the best of him. Shouting, "No room at the bar!" he would cut off the rail route and make some poor kid go around the long way.

He came home at night and Agnes tended to him. So many phone calls told her of terrible crashes that she came to fear the phone's ring. On some mornings the back door banged open to reveal a host of muddy racetrackers, carrying a bloodied Red in from another fall. She prayed for his safety every day, but never complained to him. She understood, as would her children, that her husband would have suffocated in any other life. He was in constant and serious pain, but didn't speak of it. He still carried a rosary and little volumes of poetry in his pocket, and still gave away most of the money he earned. His children grew up knowing to be careful around their father's game leg, which never fattened up to anything much thicker than a broomstick. Pollard wove his books into his children's lives but did not try to teach them about horses. He never once brought them to the track to see him ride and didn't tell the stories of his youth. The closest his daughter, Norah, ever came to the races was to comply with his request to paint a cougar on his helmet.

By 1955, when he was forty-six, he couldn't make it any longer. "Maybe I should have heeded the rumble of that distant drum when I was riding high," he once said. "But I never did. Trouble is, you never hear it if you are a racetracker. Horses make too damned much noise." He called David Alexander from across the country to tell him the news. "I'm hanging up my blouse for good," he said. "I wanted you to be the first to know. You can't first-past Father Time."

"It's about time," said Alexander. When the writer paid tribute to him in a lengthy article in *Time*, Pollard called him up and sang every verse of "You Made Me What I Am Today, and I Hope You're Satisfied," then hung up.

Pollard wound up sorting mail in a track post office, then working as a valet, cleaning the boots of other riders. His racetrack injuries worsened as he aged, and he slowly became a prisoner in his own body. He struggled as hard as he could against his alcoholism but never beat it.

One day in the waning years of his life, Red Pollard stopped talking. Perhaps it was a physical problem. Perhaps the old raconteur just didn't want to speak anymore. When on rare occasions a reporter turned up to ask about Seabiscuit, Agnes answered the questions while Red sat by, mute.

In 1980 Agnes was hospitalized with cancer. Though only seventy, Pollard was suffering from so many physical problems that he could no longer get along without her. His children had no choice but to place him in a nursing home. He knew this ground. The home had been built over the ruins of Narragansett Park.

The Cougar slipped away one day in 1981, uttering not a word in parting. Agnes was with him when he stopped breathing. His heart kept beating for several minutes, then went still. No cause of death was ever found. It was as if, Norah remembers, "he had just worn out his body." Agnes died two weeks later.

Seabiscuit and Howard grew old together in the slow rhythms of Ridgewood. Howard's hair thinned; Seabiscuit's muddy bay coat darkened. Howard kept the horse with Kayak in a handsome red barn and installed a walking ring that led right up to the door of Howard's house. He hung a sign on the pillared gates to the ranch, out on the Redwood Highway, that read: RIDGEWOOD, HOME OF SEABISCUIT. VISITORS WELCOME.

The visitors came, fifty thousand over the years, as many as fifteen hundred at a time. Howard erected a little grandstand by his horse's paddock and ushered the spectators in to watch him. Kayak thrilled the crowds by galloping around his adjacent paddock in all his black splendor. Most of the time, all Seabiscuit did was stretch out on his side, drowsing in the shade of his paddock oak tree. Occasionally, he would raise his head and look the spectators over, then drop off to sleep again. Once in a while he'd get up and amble over to his admirers, licking their cameras and sticking his tongue out to be scratched.

With each spring the foals came. Howard doted on them as if they were his own children. "They are the finest foals I have ever seen," he said when the first crop came, "and I am not prejudiced when I say this." They all had their father's amiable personality, and most of them had his homely little body too. Nearly all were homebreds, the products of Howard's moderately bred mares; the ranch was more than six hundred miles from the nearest major breeding farm, and few breeders wanted to subject their mares to such a long haul. So Howard used his own mares, pampered and overfed their babies, and sent them into training fat and happy.

When the "Little Biscuits" reached racing age and went south to the tracks, the public flocked in to see them. Thousands of admirers came out to watch their workouts, and on race days full houses packed in to cheer for them and for proud old Howard. The owner issued Christmas card photos of Seabiscuit standing with his foals. The cards became hot items across the nation. One racetrack, Chicago's Arlington Park, re-created one in a giant mural.

A few of the Seabiscuits could run. Sea Sovereign and Sea Swallow became stakes winners, as did a chip off the old block, a grandson named Sea Orbit, who ran sixty-seven times, winning twenty-two, including a long list of elite stakes races in California. One of Fair Knightess's foals, Phantom Sea, became stakes-placed. But most of the Seabiscuits were poor racehorses, and because Howard refused to let them suffer the indignity of running at their ability level, in claiming races, few of them won anything on the track. Howard didn't seem to notice. After an advisor talked him into selling an especially slow one, Howard quietly bought him back. "You don't understand," he explained. "This one used to eat sugar cubes out of my hand."

Hollywood took the tale of Seabiscuit's life, deleted everything interesting, and made an inexcusably bad movie, *The Story of*

Seabiscuit, starring Shirley Temple. They cast one of Seabiscuit's sons in the title role. When they set up to film the War Admiral match race, they deliberately chose a woefully sluggish horse to play War Admiral. Unfortunately, the Seabiscuit son was even slower. Every time they tried to shoot the race, the colt playing War Admiral beat the colt playing Seabiscuit, no matter how hard the jockeys tried to prevent it. Eventually, they gave up and substituted film of the actual race.

Seabiscuit settled well into his retirement. Knowing he needed activity, Howard taught him how to herd cattle. The horse loved it, nipping at the animals' rumps and torturing them as he had once tortured War Admiral and Kayak. Every day the ranch hands rode him out with Pumpkin on a five-mile jaunt, trotting up and down the California hills, cantering alongside the lake, pausing to graze on the mountain grass. He became very fat—1,250 pounds—and blissfully happy. Every fall he would pose for family portraits, sometimes with Marcela aboard, and Howard would have the photos printed in huge numbers and mailed to everyone he knew.

When the war came, Howard looked into building a bomb shelter for the horse but eventually gave up the idea. He worked to help the war effort, donating an ambulance to the British Red Cross, which named it *Seabiscuit*. Howard printed patriotic messages on all the Seabiscuit Christmas cards and mailed Seabiscuit's shoes off to bomber pilots as good-luck charms. One bomber, which survived 694 missions over Japan, was named for the horse and painted with his smoke-breathing likeness.

As Seabiscuit aged, Howard faded. His heart began to fail him, and his life slowly contracted. Marcela, who adored him to the last, nursed him through his final years. He showered her in flowers and little love notes, written in a wavering hand. He found one last success on the track, this time with the great Noor, winner of the Santa Anita Handicap and conqueror of Triple Crown winner Citation. "Guess you've got another Seabiscuit on your hands," said a reporter after Noor's greatest win. Howard, thin and unsteady, straightened up and raised his chin. "Sir," he said, "there will never be another Seabiscuit."

When his heart became too frail for him to endure the thrill of seeing his horses run, Howard came to the track anyway, sitting in the parking lot and listening to race calls on the radio in his Buick. In what is believed to be the last photograph ever taken of him, he was at the racetrack, standing in the winner's circle. After leaving the track, he would go back to Ridgewood to be near the horses. On beautiful days, he would throw a saddle over Seabiscuit, and together they would walk into the hills to lose themselves in the redwoods.

On the morning of May 17, 1947, Marcela met her husband at breakfast and told him his rough little horse was gone, dead of an apparent heart attack at the relatively youthful age of fourteen. The onetime bicycle repairman, whose own heart would fail him just three years later, was beside himself with grief. "I never dreamed," he said, "the old boy would go so quickly." Someone broke the news to Pollard, who was plugging away on claimers at Suffolk Downs. His mind rolled back over all those years. "It seems only yesterday," he said.

Howard had the body carried to a secret site on the ranch. After Seabiscuit was buried, the old owner planted an oak sapling over him. Howard, a vigorously public man, made his last gesture to his horse a private one. He told only his sons the location of the grave and let the oak stand as the only marker. Somewhere in the high country that once was Ridgewood, the tree lives on, watching over the bones of Howard's beloved Seabiscuit.

Acknowledgments

If you found yourself in a red-light district in the spring of 1951 and you had a spare quarter, you could purchase *SIR! A Magazine for Males* and read the story behind this cover headline. The magazine was the strangest of hybrids, a girlie gazette straining to pass itself off as a scientific journal. As pornography, it was a crashing failure. The featured model in an article on "Latin Quarter Lovelies" is shown hopping around in nothing but four one-quart-capacity Egyptian fezes—only one of which is on her head—with pasties stuck to the bottoms. The cover story asserts that corpulent people tend to be jolly and helpfully offers shots of nude models as proof. In another piece, "PURE SCIENCE UNCOVERS ANCIENT VICE," the life's labors of a University of Chicago classics professor are distilled into a discussion of how "The Antics of the Ancient Greeks Would Make Modern Playboys Drool with Envy." Somehow the magazine endured, thanks to advertising from "rupture control" companies and a pharmaceutical outlet that sold thirty days' worth of "genuine Male Sex Hormones" in a plain brown wrapper for $5.

 SIR! came to grace my bookshelf after I typed the name George Woolf into an Internet auction search engine and turned up the magazine as a match. I didn't have much hope for it, but the mystery of how an unpornographic, unscientific jockey landed in a pseudo-scientific porn magazine got the best of me. I shelled out $2.50 and gave *SIR!* a home. When it arrived, I flipped through and discovered, sandwiched between the trusses and jolly jiggling women, a wealth of tales of the Iceman's exploits: setting his tack on fire, sleeping on the jocks' room roof, riding pantless down a homestretch before a grandstand full of fans. I called Woolf's old friends and asked them about the stories. They verified all of them and even provided details the magazine had missed. *SIR!* had merit after all.

Writing this book has been a four-year lesson in how history hides in curious places. I obtained the narrative's basic framework from the usual suspects—newspapers in the Library of Congress and other archives, official track chart books, racing histories, magazines. But the narrative they offered, though intriguing, was incomplete. The textures of my subjects' personalities, their complex relationships, motives, fears, thoughts, and secrets, all remained elusive, as did the small but telling details that give historic figures immediacy and resonance in the imagination. My subjects had long since died, but I was convinced that they must have left behind some detritus. I began prowling Internet search engines, memorabilia auctions, and obscure bookstores, writing letters and placing "information wanted" ads, and making hundreds of calls to strangers in hopes that someone or something could illuminate what seemed to be a lost past.

The story wasn't lost. It was scattered all over North America, tucked in back pockets and bottom drawers. A remarkable quantity of information came from an odd assortment of memorabilia, most purchased, some borrowed from a proselytizing sect of collectors. A few items were bad investments—a disco tribute to Seabiscuit springs to mind—but most yielded something of value, sometimes a note that gave an added dimension to a man, sometimes a forgotten anecdote or a critical explanation. In faded magazines and moldy newspapers I discovered rare photos, long interviews with my subjects, conversations between them, and exhilarating eyewitness accounts of events in their lives. My subjects' private lives and the world they inhabited unfolded in the pages of almost a dozen forgotten autobiographies of horsemen stretching back to 1913 Kentucky Derby-winning rider Roscoe Goose. On a crackling audiotape I heard George call out to Red from the back of Seabiscuit, standing in the midst of a roaring throng. A 1945 Jockeys' Guild yearbook found in a Virginia bookshop yielded details on Frenchy Hawley and the stomach-turning mechanics of reducing. I unearthed Seabiscuit's signature board games, pinball machine, wastebasket, postcards, and "endorsement" ads for two beer brands, two lines of Seabiscuit oranges, whiskey, a hotel, a humor magazine, a dry-cleaning service, and ladies' hats. I was the only bidder in an auction for what turned out to be a rare film of the Seabiscuit–War Admiral match race, one of a half-dozen race films and newsreels I was able to obtain.

My greatest source was living memory. An ad placed in the *Daily Racing Form* on Breeders' Cup day yielded a stack of letters. At least ten were written on the backs and in the margins of tip sheets and racing programs. One was composed in crayon on a slip of paper torn into a rough hexagon. Nearly all were penned in the sweeping Victorian script of a lost age. I picked up the phone and started calling these people and the hundred or so potential sources I found through racing contacts. Once or twice, my call wasn't well received. "How old do you think I am?" snapped an angry octogenarian when asked if he had known any of the Seabiscuit crew (he died of old age a few months later). Some were a little too eager to talk. "You sound like a young girl!" a gravelly ninety-something man thundered into the phone. "I *like* young girls!" Some told me more than I ever imagined, like the aged horseman who described his bodice-ripping romps with the Molino Rojo girls, then asked me not to print his name "'cause my ex-wives might not like it." Most of the time, my interviewees welcomed me into what one source called "those dear, dead days" and allowed me to linger as long as I wished.

The luxury of researching those who achieve the extraordinary is that their lives play out before many observers. I spoke with people who saw Red Pollard hitch his toboggan to his pony, tumble down under Fair Knightess, spout Shakespeare and throw fists in the jock's room, draw his last breaths in a nursing home built on the ruins of a track on which he once rode. I followed Woolf through the memories of friends, from a grade school classmate to a man who saw him die and sat vigil over his body on the day of his funeral. I found a groom who handled Seabiscuit for Fitzsimmons, the boys who galloped him for Smith, and several dozen witnesses to his races. I was even contacted by a nearly hundred-year-old former groom living in a telephone-less trailer in the desert, who is evidently the last person on earth who recalls the Lone Plainsman telling of his youth on the mustang ranges. The Detroit cemetery worker; the wife speaking for a husband muted by a stroke; the ancient trainer living through his last summer tethered to an oxygen tank; the clerk at a mail-order seafood company; the operator of the Seabiscuit liquor store in Hercules, California: each had something to contribute. Again and again, when I was able to check their testimony against records kept at the time, the accuracy of their statements was verified: the color of War Admiral's blanket, the precise time of Seabiscuit's half-mile split, a quip Red made seventy years ago. Ultimately, I gathered an almost uninterrupted memory record of the story I wished to tell from those who recall the sound, the smell, the feel of it, and who divulged secrets, such as Red's blind eye, that finally solved mysteries more than half a century old.

*

The completion of this book is tinged with sadness, as several of those who helped create it didn't live to see it in print. Among them was Sonny Greenberg. A bug boy with Red Pollard and George Woolf, Sonny was, he cheerfully admitted, a pathologically bad jockey, once steering a horse around a turn with such ineptitude that he "lost more ground than when the Indians sold Manhattan for a string of beads and a bottle of whiskey." Sonny may not have had Woolf's skill, but he was an astute observer of life in the Howard barn and racing in its golden era. Putting up with at least seven hours of my questions, Sonny animated life in Seabiscuit's time—the purr of Woolf's blue Cord roadster, the torment of reducing and the taste of jalap, the wicked, misunderstood humor of Tom Smith. Sonny, who in racetrack lingo told me that his advanced age left him "on the 'also eligible' list—I could draw in at any time," drew in on May 6, 2000. It was Derby day.

On two of the most fascinating days of my career, Alfred Gwynne Vanderbilt, Jr., told me in candid detail how he masterminded one of the most spellbinding sporting events in American history, the meeting between Seabiscuit and War Admiral. Vanderbilt went on to own a magnificent gray horse named Native Dancer, who lost only one race, the Kentucky Derby, by less than a foot. Vanderbilt stayed in racing for two thirds of a century, even after macular degeneration left him unable to see his beloved runners. In November 1999, he spent the last hours of his life at the track, handing out cookies at Belmont Park. I will never forget his eloquence, his wit, and his magnanimity.

Other generous contributors who passed away before the completion of this book include the brilliant trainer Woody Stephens, who spent a couple of long afternoons telling me about his youth as a jockey; his equally accomplished archrival and friend Charlie Whittingham; Lucien Laurin, trainer of Secretariat; former jockey Sam Renick; former *Turf and Sport Digest* editor Raleigh Burroughs ("Honey," he told me a few months before his death, "there is nobody else who is older than I am; I've got patina all over me"); and trainer Henry Clark.

The list of others whose stories fill this book is lengthy. I long ago ran out of words of gratitude for Lieutenant Colonel Michael C. Howard, United States Marine Corps. The great-grandson of Charles Howard and the grandson of Lin Howard, he trusted me with the treasures of his family— scrapbooks, photographs, cards, personal notes, clippings—and gave me immeasurable assistance and encouragement in reconstructing this story. From the beginning of this project to the end, Lieutenant Colonel Howard went to enormous effort to furnish me with the information that has given this story color and depth. His kindness and generosity will always be an inspiration to me.

I contacted Helen Luther and her husband, Tommy, one of the finest jockeys of his era and the true father of the Jockeys' Guild, in hopes of finding a little information on Red Pollard; I emerged with a lifetime of stories and a set of surrogate grandparents. Abundant thanks also go to Pollard's daughter, writer Norah Pollard Christianson, and his sister, Edie Pollard Wilde, who entrusted me with intimate and sometimes painful details of the life of the Cougar. Wad Studley, who can talk horse with the best of them, taught me about the wilder side of Tijuana and the stranger nicknames of the racing oval. Bill Buck, who grew up with Red and George, was my greatest source on their bug boy days. Noble Threewit, without whom Tom Smith and Charles Howard would never have met, told me about rooming in a stall with Smith in Tijuana; Noble's wife, Beryl, shared her recollections of George. The gifted horsemen Keith Stucki and Farrell "Wild Horse" Jones thrilled me with tales of what it was like to skim over the track aboard Seabiscuit and offered an inside view of the Howard barn. Bill Nichols re-created Ridgewood, where he worked as a ranch hand. Jane Babcock Akins, daughter of Doc Babcock, told me of the day Frankie Howard died. Johnny Longden took me back to George's school days.

I am also grateful to trainer Jimmy Jones, who survived the rampage of Tijuana's manure mountain and the leviathan that was Ten Ton Irwin. Harold Washburn told me about Smith's homemade bell, the match with War Admiral, and the legend of the Iceman. Joe "Mossy" Mosbacher taught me about life on the road for bug boys. Leonard Dorfman put me in the grandstand as Seabiscuit accelerated alongside Stagehand in the 1938 hundred-grander, a performance so extraordinary and heartbreaking that it brought him to tears. Ralph Theroux, Sr., gave me a glimpse of the Seabiscuit–War Admiral match race from the infield, at least the part he saw before the steeplechase fence he was standing on collapsed. Jack Shettlesworth told me what Red *really* said to George in their notorious 1938 NBC radio interview. Mike Griffin, disabled in a 1930s racing spill, taught me about the perils of a jockey's life. Eddie McMullen spoke of Pollard as an older rider. George Mohr and Larry Soroka took me inside the Fitzsimmons barn. Thomas Bell, Jr., reminisced about Tom Smith and his father's life on the racing circuit.

Gerard Oberle described the day Seabiscuit was to meet War Admiral at Suffolk Downs.

Kathy Gold, RN, of the Diabetes Wellness and Research Foundation, explained diabetes treatment in the 1930s. George Pratt, Ph.D., of the Massachusetts Institute of Technology, instructed me on the physics of the racehorse. Matthew Mackay-Smith, DVM, medical editor of *EQUUS,* treated me to his boundless wisdom on equine veterinary medicine. Marvin Bensman, Ph.D., University of Memphis (www.people.memphis.edu/~mbensman/ welcome.html), answered my questions on the history of radio.

Thanks also to Frank Whiteley, Joe Perrato, Howard "Gelo" Hall, Betty Raines, Bill Boland, Hugh Morgan, Barbara Howard, Michelle and Charles Howard III, Warren Stute, Bart Baker, John Wilke, John Nerud, Rex Henshaw, DVM, Mike Salamy, Daniel Guiney, Bob Nanni, Richard Holland, Bobby DeStasio, Joe Dattilo, Ken Hart, J. R. Buck Perry, Jr., Buddy Abadie, Elmer L. Taylor, Achilles Zephirius Achilles ("Ace"), Dale Duspiva, Fred Dayton, Don Mankiewicz, and Art Bardine.

Many people assisted me in tracking down facts and sources. The freakishly efficient Tina Hines provided indispensable help as a research assistant, digging up documents at the Keeneland Library; Keeneland's Cathy Schenck and Phyllis Rogers pored over their archives in search of books and photos. Chick Lang, who knows where all the bodies are buried, scoured the industry to locate interviewees. Jane Goldstein and Stuart Zanville at Santa Anita found sources and photos. Debie Ginsburg, Karen Bowman, Joanne Tober, and Jessica Appleby at the *Thoroughbred of California* and the Burke Memorial Library mailed reams of information. Patricia Ranft at the *Blood-Horse* made up an infinitely useful index. Tom Gilcoin and Dick Hamilton at the National Museum of Racing answered racing history questions. Kip Hannon sent terrific archive video of Seabiscuit's races. Dorothy Ours, who knows the lives of Man o' War and Samuel Riddle better than anyone on earth, answered a long string of questions.

Jenifer Van Deinse, Bob Curran, Eric Wing, Joan Lawrence, Howard Bass, and Tom Merritt of Thoroughbred Racing Communications and/or its successor, National Thoroughbred Racing Association Communications, answered questions, located sources, and helped check facts. Lynn Kennelly at the Willits, California, Chamber of Commerce raided her local library archives and emerged with priceless information. Vicki Vinson sent me memorabilia and wrote a marvelous article on this book. Jan Romanowski helped me discover information I'd missed and tracked down one of my most important sources when all my efforts failed. Jane Colihan at *American Heritage* advised me on obtaining photos. Susan Kennedy picked through Bay Meadows's records in search of one elusive photo.

Suzan Stephenson at the Bowie, Maryland, Public Library's Selima Room, a treasure trove of racing literature, helped me unearth volumes of information; Dian Hain told me of the Selima Room's existence. John Ball and John Giovanni of the Jockeys' Guild helped me gather facts on the lives of jockeys of the 1930s. Paula Welch, formerly Special Projects Editor of the *Daily Racing Form*, found articles and helped in the photo hunt. Victoria Keith, founder/editor of *Thoroughbred Champions* (www.Thoroughbred Champions.com), and researcher/co-editor Kathleen Jones, served as valuable sources of facts and encouragement and sent Triple Crown-themed flowers. Dace Taube at the University of Southern California Library worked late to sift through photos. Joe Hirsch and Jay Hovdey of the *Daily Racing Form*, Tommy Trotter and Julie Hazelwood of Vessel Stallion Farm, Joseph Martin and Rick Snider of the *Washington Times* pointed me to excellent sources. Jim Maloney sent clippings. Richard Needles sent his fine artwork of Seabiscuit. Richard Brunner sent racing records.

Thanks also to Billy Turner, trainer of Seattle Slew; Kit Collins; Diane Brunn at the University of Kentucky Agricultural Library; Arlene Mott at Interlibrary Loan in Rockville, Maryland; Martha Canterini at the historical racing site *Second Running* (www.secondrunning.com); Steven Crist, Irwin Cohen, and Logan Bailey of the *Daily Racing Form*; Mark Shrager; Dale Austin; Ronnie Nichols; Leon Rasmussen; Andrew Beyer of *The Washington Post*; Tracy Negrin; Sean Lahman; John Thorn; Bob Kaplan; Steve Murtaugh; Cricket Goodall; Debbie McCain; Becky Shields; Dave Hicks of NYRA; Gary McMillen; James Lehr; Warren Bare; Gary Madieros; and the National Agricultural Library.

My special thanks go to Richard F. Snow, editor of *American Heritage*, for helping me get this project off the ground. In the fall of 1996, Richard saw the potential of this story in my query letter and gave me the honor of contributing to his splendid magazine, which has been my addiction for as long as I can remember.

Perhaps the greatest privilege I have enjoyed in producing this book has

ACKNOWLEDGEMENTS

been the opportunity to work with my agent, the exceptionally skilled, kind, invincible Tina Bennett. A woman with the perfect solution to any dilemma, Tina helped me transform an article into a book proposal, then into a manuscript, assisting me in shaping my thoughts, offering valuable criticism, and making my dream of telling this story to the world a reality. My eternal gratitude goes to Isaac Barchas for introducing me to Tina. Thanks also go to Tina's assistant, Svetlana Katz.

Susan Avallon read at least ten drafts of one section of this book, but never complained, and her criticisms improved the work enormously. My *EQUUS* editors, Emily Kilby and Laurie Prinz, pored over my rough draft and gave me the benefit of the expertise that has made their magazine a paragon of excellence. Professor Megan Macomber, who has been gently guiding my work since my freshman year at Kenyon in 1985, once again treated me to her marvelous instinct for words. Journalist Susie Hiss Thomas did a careful reading of the first stabs at this story and offered her wisdom. Thanks also to my mother, Elizabeth Hillenbrand, who helped in innumerable ways to get me through this long and sometimes difficult process.

I am deeply indebted to my editor at Random House, Jonathan Karp, who saw the promise in this story and gave me the best possible forum in which to tell it. Jon was always enthusiastic, made house calls when I could not come to him, and studied the manuscript with a sharp eye. My work is vastly better for his keen judgment. I also send thanks to Jon's assistant, Janelle Duryea.

Since the day in 1996 when it first occurred to me that a book should be written about these men, Borden Flanagan has given his unwavering support, infinite patience, and tireless assistance. He has set aside much of his own life to pore over each of my drafts, offer insights, and smooth my prose. My manuscript has benefited immeasurably from his command of language and ideas. Without him, this story would have remained untold. He has my most profound gratitude.

My final thanks go to Tom Smith, Charles and Marcela Howard, Red Pollard, and George Woolf for living lives of singular vigor and grace, and for giving us the incomparable, unforgettable Seabiscuit.

Laura Hillenbrand
September 2000

Notes

A note on sources: As I researched my subjects for this book, Lieutenant Colonel Michael C. Howard, great-grandson of Charles and Marcela Howard, generously gave me access to the private scrapbooks of Charles and Marcela Howard. These books included a wealth of newspaper and magazine clippings, photographs, telegrams, and letters, some of which do not include complete publishing information. In the following section, I indicate these incompletely annotated sources with the abbreviation *SB*. In a few cases, it is unclear whether the dates on these materials indicate the dates on which the articles were filed by their authors, or the dates on which they appeared in print. In instances in which the date specified is a filing date, I have used the abbreviation *FD*. In most cases, articles appear in print on the day after they are filed.

PREFACE

xi   the year's number-one newsmaker: "Looking 'Em Over," *San Francisco News*, *SB*, January 1939; B. K. Beckwith, *Seabiscuit: The Saga of a Great Champion* (Willfred Crowell, 1940), p. 33.

xi   forty million listeners: "Seabiscuit Stands Out," *The Pay Off*, November 1938.

xi   population was less than half its current size: Irvine, E. Eastman, ed., *World Almanac 1938* (New York: New York World-Telegram, 1938), p. 241; Robert Famighetti, ed., *The World Almanac and Book of Facts 1997* (New Jersey: K-III Reference Corp., 1996), p. 377.

xi   seventy-eight thousand people witnessed his last race: *There They Go:*

Racing Calls by Joe Hernandez, album released by Los Angeles Turf Club, n.d.

xi attendance comparable to Super Bowl: Jorgen Lyxell, "Super Bowl" online article (San Francisco: Jorgen Lyxell; accessed September 13, 2000); www.acc.umu.se/~lyxell/superbowl/.

xi forty thousand fans see workouts: "40,000 See Howard's Champion," *The Baltimore Sun*, November 2, 1938.

xii fifty thousand exhausting railroad miles: M. A. Stoneridge, *Great Horses of Our Time* (New York: Doubleday, 1972), p. 34.

CHAPTER 1

3 21 cents: "Charles S. Howard," *San Francisco Chronicle*, June 7, 1950, p. 1.

4 cavalry: Michael C. Howard, telephone interview, January 18, 1997.

4 racing bicycles: Terry Dunham, "The Howard Automobile Company," manuscript from the papers of Marcela Howard, July 1975.

4 "devilish contraptions": "My Thirty Years in the Press Box," *San Francisco Chronicle*, February 6, 1937.

4 anti-automobile laws: Floyd Clymer, *Those Wonderful Old Automobiles* (New York: McGraw-Hill, 1953), p. 30.

5 automobile ban at Stanford: "Charles S. Howard," *San Francisco Chronicle*, June 7, 1950, p. 2.

5 "Accessories": "My Thirty Years in the Press Box," *San Francisco Chronicle*, February 6, 1937; Clymer, *Those Wonderful Old Automobiles*, p. 67.

5 refueling at pharmacies: William M. Klinger, "Pioneering Automobile Insurance" online article (San Francisco: Museum of the City of San Francisco, accessed February 24, 1998); www.sfmuseum.org.

5 "windshield hats": Clymer, *Those Wonderful Old Automobiles*, p. 22.

5 road signs ... erected ... by insurance underwriter: Klinger, "Pioneering Automobile Insurance."

5 "picnic parties": Ibid.

6 Automobile-repair shops: Ibid.; Michael C. Howard, telephone interview, January 18, 1997.

6 first American race: Clymer, *Those Wonderful Old Automobiles*, p. 57.

6 The European race . . . halted due to "too many fatalities": Ibid., p. 26.

6 Howard gains Buick franchise: Dunham, "The Howard Automobile Company."

6 three Buicks: "Automotive Highlights," *Los Angeles Times*, March 24, 1940, p. 3.

7 housed automobiles in parlor of bicycle-repair shop: Tom Moriarty, "California Sportsman," *Rob Wagner's Script*, March 18, 1938, p. 8.

7 four city blocks per hour: Louise Herrick Wall, "Heroic San Francisco" online article (San Francisco: Museum of the City of San Francisco; accessed February 24, 1998); www.sfmuseum.org/1906/06.html.

7 "We suddenly appreciated . . .": Emma Burke, untitled article, *Outlook*, June 1906.

7 cars used as ambulances: Michael C. Howard, telephone interview, January 18, 1997; Dunham, "The Howard Automobile Company."

7 Van Ness as firebreak: Wall, "Heroic San Francisco."

8 blew up shop: Moriarty, "California Sportsman," p. 8.

8 day's rental of a horse and buggy: Wall, "Heroic San Francisco."

8 Robert Stewart: Michael C. Howard, telephone interview, January 18, 1997.

8 auto racing in 1906 San Francisco: Klinger, "Pioneering Automobile Insurance."

9 Howard racing cars: "Charles S. Howard," *San Francisco Chronicle*, June 7, 1950, p. 2; Dunham, "The Howard Automobile Company."

10 Howard advertises wins: Dunham, "The Howard Automobile Company."

10 "horse is past . . .": Ralph Moody, *Come On Seabiscuit* (Boston: Houghton Mifflin, 1963), p. 22.

10 sold eighty-five White Streaks: "Charles S. Howard," *San Francisco Chronicle*, June 7, 1950, p. 2.

10 Durant gave Howard sole distributorship: Dunham, "The Howard Automobile Company."

11 GM bailout: "Charles S. Howard," *San Francisco Chronicle*, June 7, 1950, p. 2; "Yea, Verily," *SB*, fall 1937.

11 Charles S. Howard Foundation: "Howard, Charles Stewart," *National Cyclopedia of American Biography*, p. 27.

11 expedition to Galápagos: Dunham, "The Howard Automobile Company."

12 Frank's accident and aftermath: "Frank Howard Killed," *The Willits*

News, May 14, 1926, p. 1; Jane Babcock Akins, telephone interview, November 12, 1999.

13 Howard cries over painting: Bill Nichols, telephone interview, January 14, 1998.

13 Tijuana: T. D. Proffitt, III, *Tijuana: The History of a Mexican Metropolis* (San Diego: San Diego University Press, 1994), pp. 190–98; Wad Studley, telephone interview, February 6, 1999.

14 target practice: Wad Studley, telephone interview, March 2, 1999.

14 Three hundred tracks had been operating: Tom Biracree and Wendy Insinger, *The Complete Book of Thoroughbred Horse Racing* (Garden City, N.Y.: Doubleday & Company, 1982), p. 143.

15 departing Hollywood film crew: Sonny Greenberg, telephone interview, December 24, 1999.

15 Howard to Tijuana: Carter Swart, "The Howards of San Francisco," *Northern California Thoroughbred*, fall 1981, p. 111.

15 Howard loses interest in automobiles: Tom Moriarty, "California Sportsman," *Rob Wagner's Script*, March 18, 1938.

15 Meeting Marcela: Swart, "The Howards of San Francisco," p. 111.

16 Blooey: "A Blue Monkey Visits New York," *New York American*, SB, 1935.

17 Giannini: Joe Estes, "Thoroughbred Farms in California," *Blood-Horse*, SB, n.d., p. 676.

17 "Doc" Strub: David Alexander, *A Sound of Horses* (New York: Bobbs-Merrill Company, 1966), pp. 51–70; Mary Fleming, *A History of the Thoroughbred in California* (Arcadia, Calif.: California Thoroughbred Breeders Association, 1983), pp. 95–97.

18 1935 average income: Eastman, *Almanac 1938*, p. 288.

18 "hunnert-grander": "Seabiscuit's Past," *Los Angeles Times*, SB, winter 1938.

18 America's most heavily attended sport: Tom Gilcoin, telephone interview, February 28, 1997.

CHAPTER 2

21 A journalist who had watched Smith: "Like Mike and Ike," *San Francisco Chronicle*, SB, n.d.

21 chop off his own toe: Alexander, *A Sound of Horses*, p. 185.

22 "Lone Plainsman": "Like Mike and Ike," *San Francisco Chronicle*, *SB*, n.d.

22 Smith's history: Obituary, *Blood-Horse*, January 19, 1957, p. 338; "Alarm Clock for Training," *San Francisco Chronicle*, *SB*, 1936; "Seabiscuit Makes Debut," *Los Angeles Times*, December 28, 1936; "They Do Come Back," *San Francisco Chronicle*, *SB*, fall 1939; Moody, *Come On Seabiscuit*, pp. 23–29; "Seabiscuit Trainer History," *Morning Telegraph*, *SB*, fall 1937.

24 "Cowboy Charlie": Willard Porter, "Big Charlie Irwin," *True West*, September 1987, pp. 38–43; "Riddle Walked In," *SB*, fall 1938; "Old West Cowboy Dies," *The New York Times*, March 24, 1934, p. 1; "450 Pound Horseman," uncredited clipping, n.d.; Bill Buck, telephone interview, January 28, 1998; Wad Studley, telephone interview, February 6, 1999; Tommy Bell, telephone interview, June 22, 1999; Keith Stucki, telephone interview, March 25, 1998; Noble Threewit, telephone interview, January 17, 1998; Jimmy Jones, telephone interview, February 3, 1999; "Seabiscuit's Trainer Pupil of Famous Cowboy Irwin," *SB*, 1937.

25 Work under Irwin: "Tom Smith Sets Sights," *San Francisco News*, March 27, 1939; Keith Stucki, telephone interview, March 25, 1998.

26 Indian reservations: "Riddle Walked In," *SB*, fall 1938.

28 Knighthood: "They Do Come Back," *San Francisco Chronicle*, *SB*, fall 1939.

30 squatting down on floor: "Alarm Clock for Training," *San Francisco Chronicle*, *SB*, 1936.

30 watching a horse . . . for hours: "Kayak II and the 'Biscuit'; A Namesake Turns Out Well," *Blood-Horse*, February 24, 1951, p. 432.

30 "I'd rather depend on my eye . . .": Ibid.

30 "It's easy to talk to a horse . . .": Theodus Carroll, *Firsts Under the Wire: The World's Fastest Horses* (New York: Contemporary Perspectives, 1978), p. 29.

31 "Learn your horse . . .": "Seabiscuit Makes Debut," *Los Angeles Times*, December 28, 1936.

31 Oriley: Bill Buck, telephone interview, January 28, 1998; "History of Silent Tom Smith," *Morning Telegraph/Daily Racing Form*, *SB*, March 1939; "Silent Tom Smith," *SB*, March 16, 1940.

31 living out of a horse stall: Noble Threewit, telephone interview, January 17, 1998.

32 "the best trainer . . .": Joe Estes, "Thoroughbred Farms in California," *Blood-Horse*, *SB*, n.d., p. 676.

CHAPTER 3

35 Smith's clothes: "Best San Francisco Horse," *San Francisco Chronicle*, *SB*, late 1936.

35 hat story: "Silent Tom Smith," *SB*, March 16, 1940.

35 alarm clock: "Alarm Clock for Training," *San Francisco Chronicle*, *SB*, 1936.

37 Smith discovers Seabiscuit: Beckwith, *Seabiscuit*, p. 25; "Hey for Seabiscuit," *San Francisco Chronicle*, May 14, 1938.

38 duck waddle: Stoneridge, *Great Horses of Our Time*, p. 35.

38 "mostly in his heart . . .": Ibid.

38 "I'll see you again": Beckwith, *Seabiscuit*, p. 25.

38 Fitzsimmons: Jimmy Breslin, *Sunny Jim: The Life of America's Most Beloved Horseman* (Garden City, N.Y.: Doubleday & Company, 1962).

38 track built around house: Breslin, *Sunny Jim*, pp. 78–79.

39 Hastings/Man o' War: Peter Chew, "The Mostest Hoss," *American Heritage*, April 1971, pp. 24–29, 90–95.

40 War Relic: Tommy Luther, telephone interview, February 2, 1998.

41 Hard Tack: Joe Hernandez, "The Horse of Iron," *Turf and Sport Digest*, November 1938, p. 26.

41 foreleg jabbed out: "Seabiscuit, the All-American Winner," *San Francisco Chronicle*, *SB*, spring 1938.

42 "Runty little thing": Moody, *Come On Seabiscuit*, p. 3.

42 "so small . . . you might mistake . . .": "A Testament," *SB*, November 1938.

42 equine sleeping habits: Dale Leatherman, "While You Were Sleeping," *EQUUS*, April 1996, pp. 36–38; Bobbie Lieberman, "Your Horse's Biological Clocks," *EQUUS*, February 1984, pp. 40–45.

43 had to wake horse up in morning: Charles Hatton, "This Is a Horse," *Turf and Sport Digest*, January 1939, pp. 16–32.

43 left him in a van: "Seabiscuit's a Dempsey Sort," *San Francisco Chronicle*, *SB*, n.d.

43 Seabiscuit's behavior: Ibid., pp. 16–32; "Sports," *Newsweek*, *SB*, March 1940.

43 "I thought he simply couldn't run": "Seabiscuit's Story," *San Francisco News*, March 6, 1940.

43 "He struck me . . . as a bird . . .": Hatton, "This Is a Horse," pp. 16–32.

44 Use of whip: "Seabiscuit's Story," *San Francisco News*, March 6, 1940; "Seabiscuit's Final Test Today," *New York Sun*, May 24, 1938; Hatton, "This Is a Horse," pp. 16–32; "The Judge's Stand," *Morning Telegraph/Daily Racing Form*, *SB*, n.d.; "Sports," *Newsweek*, *SB*, March 1940.

46 "mean, restive, and ragged": Beckwith, *Seabiscuit*, p. 21.

47 "He had something when he wanted . . .": B. K. Beckwith, *Step and Go Together* (South Brunswick and New York: A. S. Barnes and Company, 1967), p. 113.

48 "pretty nice hoss . . .": "In the Paddock," *SB*, February 1939.

48 pawning off horse as polo pony: "Things and People," *Blood-Horse*, February 18, 1950, p. 400.

49 Howards find Seabiscuit/lemonade wager: Beckwith, *Seabiscuit*, pp. 25–26; Michael C. Howard, telephone interview, January 18, 1997.

50 "Better come and see . . .": Beckwith, *Step and Go Together*, p. 113.

50 "Get me that horse . . .": "Turf King," *San Francisco Chronicle*, *SB*, n.d.

50 "I fell in love with him . . .": Beckwith, *Step and Go Together*, p. 114.

50 trial race: "Smith Recalls Stipulation That Could've Stopped Seabiscuit Sale," *Daily Racing Form*, February 13, 1953; "Biscuit's Best Race Recalled," *SB*, November 3, 1938; "The Judge's Stand," *Morning Telegraph/Daily Racing Form*, March 7, 1940.

51 "I can't describe the feeling . . .": Beckwith, *Seabiscuit*, p. 27.

51 Seabiscuit might . . . win another purse: "Turf King," *San Francisco Chronicle*, *SB*, n.d.

51 "Deal or no deal?": Beckwith, *Seabiscuit*, p. 27.

52 "Looks like they got a new saddle horse . . .": Farrell Jones, telephone interview, November 4, 1998.

CHAPTER 4

56 Red Pollard's history: Edith Wilde, telephone interview, February 2, 1998; Bill Buck, telephone interview, January 28, 1998; "Pollard's Bricks Helped Build City," *Strathcona Plaindealer*, Summer 1983, p. 1; "Jockey Pollard Recovering," *Morning Telegraph/Daily Racing Form*, *SB*, July 1938; David Alexander, "Four Good Legs Between Them," *Blood-Horse*, December 24, 1955, pp. 1558–63.

57 bartering gasoline for groceries: Edith Wilde, telephone interview, February 2, 1998.

57 hitching the horse to his toboggan: Ibid.

57 "the body of a dancer . . .": Norah Christianson, telephone interview, January 26, 1998.

58 ovals cut through hayfields: Keith Stucki, telephone interview, March 25, 1998.

58 quarter horse can sprint at some fifty-five miles per hour: George Pratt, e-mail interview, April 10, 1998.

59 abandoned at track: Edith Wilde, telephone interview, February 2, 1998.

59 dirty tactics: Bill Buck, telephone interview, January 28, 1998; Keith Stucki, telephone interview, March 25, 1998.

60 "I was trying to kill that Cuban . . .": "Eddie Arcaro, 'The Master,' Is Dead at 81," *Los Angeles Times*, November 15, 1997, p. C11.

60 "To succeed in those days . . .": Eddie Arcaro, *I Ride to Win!* (New York: Greenberg, 1951), p. 45.

60 boxing: Alexander, "Four Good Legs," pp. 1558–63; Alexander, *A Sound of Horses*, p. 182.

60 nicknames: Wad Studley, telephone interview, February 6, 1999.

61 bug boys: Tommy Luther, telephone interview, February 2, 1998; Bill Buck, telephone interview, January 28, 1998; B. K. Beckwith, *The Longden Legend* (New Jersey: A. S. Barnes and Co., 1973), p. 33.

61 imposts and lengths: Biracree and Insinger, *The Complete Book of Thoroughbred Horse Racing*, p. 210.

62 "I was hungry . . .": "Long Ride Over for Jockey Neves," *Los Angeles Times*, July 8, 1995, p. C1; "Neves, Howard Rider," *SB*, n.d.

62 "Father" Bill Daly: Alexander, *A Sound of Horses*, pp. 170–72.

63 "Who hit you in the butt . . .": Bill Buck, telephone interview, January 27, 1998.

64 Preservator: "There They Go!," *Daily Racing Tab*, *SB*, fall 1939.

64 two saddles, a handful of bridles, and two sacks of oats: "There They Go," *Daily Racing Tab*, *SB*, fall 1937.

65 riding with somewhat longer stirrups: Eddie McMullen, telephone interview, February 5, 1999.

65 Woolf's clothing: David Alexander, "New England Racing," *Blood-Horse*, August 1, 1942, p. 160.

66 "fightin' bulldog": Alan Goodrich, "All-Time Greatest Jockey," *SIR!*, March 1951, p. 22.

66 Woolf's history: Bill Buck, telephone interview, January 28, 1998; "Seabiscuit Cinch," *San Francisco Examiner*, October 27, 1938; "Georgie Woolf," *SB*, n.d.; "The Sun," *Baltimore Sun*, October 30, 1938, p. 1; "Georgie Woolf Tops Jockeys," *San Francisco Examiner*, April 16, 1938, p. 22.

66 "Must have been born on one": Carey Alexander, "Woolf Is Top Money Rider in America," *Cheers*, March 1941, p. 6.

66 "as natural as walking . . .": "By Bud Spencer," *Los Angeles Times*, November 4, 1944.

66 "I'll be with them until I die": "The Iceman Dies," *Blood-Horse*, February 23, 1946, p. 86.

66 Pickpocket: Bill Buck, telephone interview, January 28, 1998.

67 "hold an elephant . . .": "Great Stakes Reinsman Honored Today," George Woolf Memorial pamphlet, February 10, 1949, p. 1.

67 skill: Goodrich, "All-Time Greatest Jockey," p. 66; Joseph Mosbacher, telephone interview, November 19, 1998.

67 visualize race: Bill Buck, telephone interview, January 28, 1998.

67 George sets tack on fire: Goodrich, "All-Time Greatest Jockey," p. 66.

68 "He was a better rider . . .": Joseph Mosbacher, telephone interview, November 19, 1998.

68 "saying . . . the wrong thing at the wrong time": Alexander, "New England Racing," p. 160.

69 "We got a party of our own": Bill Buck, telephone interview, January 28, 1998.

69 rodeo story: Harold Washburn, telephone interview, November 9, 1998; "Match Race," *SB*.

69 teasing Whitey: "Great Stakes Reinsman Honored Today," p. 4.

69 beaten in a photo finish: "Woolf Blames Bumping," *SB*, March 5, 1938.

70 "Big head, little ass . . .": Bill Buck, telephone interview, January 28, 1998.

70 "icemen and traveling salesmen . . .": Alexander, "New England Racing," p. 160.

70 "the strength to blow out a candle": Ibid., p. 159.

CHAPTER 5

73 Thomas Dowell: "Death of Jockey Dowell," *Thoroughbred Record*, July 1938.

74 "will all but saw their legs off . . .": Arcaro, *I Ride to Win!*, p. 49.

75 eating dehydrated lettuce: Ibid.

75 sight of water agonizing: Breslin, *Sunny Jim*, p. 128.

75 "road work": Chick Lang, telephone interview, January 23, 1998; Woody Stephens, telephone interview, January 13, 1998.

75 DeLara: Joe H. Palmer, *This Was Racing* (New York: A. S. Barnes and Company, 1953), p. 22.

76 virtuosos of defecation: Helen Luther, telephone interview, March 6, 1998.

76 "Frenchy" Hawley: *Jockeys' Guild Year Book, 1945* (New York: Jockeys' Guild, 1945), pp. 47–49; Tommy Luther, telephone interview, February 2, 1998; Helen Luther, telephone interview, March 6, 1998.

77 Greenberg's reducing: Sonny Greenberg, telephone interview, December 24, 1999.

78 lost *thirteen* pounds: Breslin, *Sunny Jim*, pp. 130–32.

78 "biggest disappointment of my life": Woody Stephens, with James Brough, *Guess I'm Lucky* (New York: Doubleday & Company, 1985), p. 39.

79 athleticism study: *Jockey* (video), Tel-Air Productions, 1980.

79 "a situation of dynamic imbalance . . .": A. E. Waller, et al., "Jockey Injuries in the United States," *Journal of the American Medical Association*, 2000; vol. 283, no. 10.

80 "the ultimate impossibility . . .": Beckwith, *The Longden Legend*, p. 33.

80 lengths lost on turns: Eric Wing, National Thoroughbred Racing Association e-mail interview, May 2000.

81 two hundred or more falls: *Jockey* (video), Tel-Air Productions, 1980.

82 three thousand pounds of force: George Pratt, e-mail interview, February 13, 1998.

82 current jockey injury rates: John Giovanni, telephone interview, January 23, 1998.

82 Rehabilitation Institute of Chicago: *The Jockey News*, June/July 1999, p. 58.

82 one in every five injuries is to head or neck: Waller, et al., "Jockey Injuries in the United States."

82 13 percent of jockeys suffered concussions: J. M. Press, P. D. Davis, S. L. Wiesner, et al., "The National Jockey Injury Study: An Analysis of Injuries to Professional Horse-Racing Jockeys," *Clinical Journal of Sports Medicine*, 1993; 5:236–40.

82 nineteen jockeys killed between 1935 and 1939: Ron Farra, *Jockeying for a Change* (Saratoga Springs, N.Y.: Saratoga Mountain Press, 1998), p. 69.

82 jockey headgear: Mike Griffin, telephone interview, January 23, 1998; Johnny Longden, telephone interview, January 13, 1998; Woody Stephens, telephone interview, January 13, 1998.

83 "Sandy" Graham: Tommy Luther, telephone interview, February 2, 1998.

84 Donoghue: Steve Donoghue, *Donoghue Up!* (New York: Charles Scribner's Sons, 1938), pp. 234–42, 126–30.

84 Ralph Neves: "Long Ride Over for Jockey Neves," *Los Angeles Times*, July 8, 1995, p. C1; "Resurrected," *San Francisco Chronicle*, May 9, 1936, p. A1; Barbara Mikkelson, "Jockey Shorted," online article (Urban Legends Reference Pages; accessed September 14, 2000); www.snopes.com/spoons/noose/neves.htm.

87 "it could get awfully rough out there": Arcaro, *I Ride to Win!*, p. 45.

87 "You didn't talk about it . . .": Farrell Jones, telephone interview, November 4, 1998.

87 "cannot be blotted out": Arcaro, *I Ride to Win!*, p. 42.

88 Empire City: Tommy Luther, telephone interview, February 2, 1998.

90 "The horse . . . he *takes* you . . .": Steve Murtaugh, telephone interview, May 2000.

90 living "all the way up": Ernest Hemingway, *The Sun Also Rises* (New York: Charles Scribner's Sons, 1926), p. 10.

CHAPTER 6

93 Molino Rojo: Sonny Greenberg, telephone interview, December 24, 1999; Joseph Mosbacher, telephone interview, November 19, 1998; Farrell Jones, telephone interview, November 4, 1998.

93 "the house of the wilted pigeons": Wad Studley, telephone interview, March 2, 1999.

95 Quoting Shakespeare in the jocks' room: Farrell Jones, telephone interview, November 4, 1998.

95 Bear story, twitch story: "The Post Parade," *Morning Telegraph/Daily Racing Form*, September 2, 1937, *FD*; Horace Wade, "Tales of the Turf," *Turf and Sport Digest*, October 1958, p. 16.

96 fight . . . over checkers match: Farrell Jones, telephone interview, November 4, 1998.

96 "Ride 'em, cowboy!": Carey Alexander, "Woolf Is Top Money Rider," *Cheers*, March 1941, p. 6.

96 Phar Lap's kangaroo saddle: Alan Goodrich, "All-Time Greatest Jockey," *Sir!*, March 1951, p. 67.

97 black market in his shoes: Joseph Mosbacher, telephone interview, November 19, 1998.

97 "I am going to be a jockey!": Harold Washburn, telephone interview, November 9, 1998.

97 rides half naked: Bill Buck, telephone interview, January 28, 1998; Goodrich, "All-Time Greatest Jockey," p. 66.

98 Woolf and Genevieve: Sonny Greenberg, telephone interview, December 24, 1999.

98 "How can I keep away?": "Me and the Biscuit," *San Francisco Chronicle*, February 15, 1940, p. 4H.

98 manure sitting/flood: Jimmy Jones, telephone interview, February 3, Wad Studley, telephone interview, March 2, 1999; Tommy Luther, telephone interview, February 2, 1998; Bill Buck, telephone interview, January 28, 1998; Chick Lang, telephone interview, January 23, 1998.

99 Woolf and Gallant Sir: Noble Threewit, telephone interview, January 17, 1998.

100 George sleeping: Goodrich, "All-Time Greatest Jockey," pp. 65–66; Bill Buck, telephone interview, January 28, 1998.

100 diabetes: "Turf in Review," *Daily Racing Form*, January 8, 1949;

Jockeys' Guild Year Book, pp. 40–41; Bill Buck, telephone interview, January 28, 1998; Kathy Gold, RN, telephone interview, Diabetes Research and Wellness Foundation, 1999; Sonny Greenberg, telephone interview, December 24, 1999.

102 *three times* as many horses: "By Bud Spencer," *Los Angeles Times*, November 4, 1944.

102 "the Desperate Dude": Goodrich, "All-Time Greatest Jockey," p. 65.

102 reinforced saddle: "Turf in Review," *Morning Telegraph/Daily Racing Form*, January 8, 1949.

102 Red blinded: Edith Wilde, telephone interview, February 2, 1998; Norah Christianson, telephone interview, January 26, 1998.

103 "only word he knows is yes": "Sports," *New York Journal American*, *SB*, fall 1938.

103 Mexico banned gambling: "Biscuit Given Big Edge," *SB*, March 26, 1938, *FD*.

104 Yummy: David Alexander, "Four Good Legs Between Them," *Blood-Horse*, December 24, 1955, pp. 1558–63; Alexander, *A Sound of Horses*, pp. 184–85, 187; Harold Washburn, telephone interview, November 9, 1998; Keith Stucki, telephone interview, February 11, 1999; Sonny Greenberg, telephone interview, December 24, 1999.

104 car wreck: "King of Horses," *Morning Telegraph/Daily Racing Form*, March 17, 1940.

105 27 cents: Alexander, *A Sound of Horses*, pp. 184–85.

105 Pollard meets Seabiscuit: "King of Horses," *Morning Telegraph/Daily Racing Form*, March 17, 1940; Moody, *Come On Seabiscuit*, pp. 35–37.

CHAPTER 7

109 so thin that hips could have made a passable hat rack: "Both Barrels," *San Francisco Call-Bulletin*, March 2, 1940, *FD*.

109 Seabiscuit's condition and behavior, Smith's treatment: Keith Stucki, telephone interview, March 25, 1998; Beckwith, *Seabiscuit*, p. 30; "Seabiscuit Makes Debut," *Los Angeles Times*, December 28, 1936; "Seabiscuit Was Bad Boy," *SB*; "Seabiscuit Trainer Says He's Another Discovery," *San Francisco Chronicle*, February 13, 1937; "Seabiscuit Crossed Up Clockers," *Los Angeles Times*, March 1, 1937; "Seabiscuit Was a Stall Walker," *SB*, fall 1937.

109 wooden-legged racetrack cat: Palmer, *This Was Racing*, p. 226.

110 goat: "Seabiscuit Was Bad Boy," *SB*; Beckwith, *Seabiscuit*, p. 36.

110 JoJo, Pocatell: Joe Hernandez, "Horse of Iron," *Turf and Sport Digest*, November 1938, p. 66; Beckwith, *Seabiscuit*, p. 40.

111 feed: "Hey for Seabiscuit," *San Francisco Chronicle*, May 14, 1938; Moody, *Come On Seabiscuit*, p. 89; "Both Barrels," *San Francisco Call-Bulletin*, March 5, 1940.

111 *Let him go*: "Seabiscuit Makes Debut," *Los Angeles Times*, December 28, 1936.

112 allowing horse to do as he pleased: "Hugh Bradley Says," *New York Post*, *SB*, May 1938.

113 "Why rate him?": "To the Point," *San Francisco Examiner*, March 3, 1940, section 2, p. 2.

113 swerving around dogs: "Seabiscuit Crossed Up Clockers," *Los Angeles Times*, March 1, 1937.

113 adjust the horse's speed with steering: Keith Stucki, telephone interview, March 25, 1998.

114 gate training: Beckwith, *Seabiscuit*, p. 34.

114 "You got to go . . . slowly . . .": Ibid.

115 Horse's affection for Pollard, Smith: Charles Hatton, "This Is a Horse," *Turf and Sport Digest*, pp. 16–32; "Hugh Bradley Says," *New York Post*, *SB*, May 1938; "Hey for Seabiscuit," *San Francisco Chronicle*, May 14, 1938.

115 "the best horseman . . .": Keith Stucki, telephone interview, March 25, 1998.

116 Race against Myrtlewood: Hatton, "This Is a Horse," pp. 16–32; "Biscuit Trainer Hails," *San Francisco Examiner*, March 12, 1940.

116 "that horse can win the Santa Anita!": "The Sun," *The Baltimore Sun*, October 30, 1938, p. 1; "Difference of Opinion," *San Francisco Chronicle*, February 21, 1940, *FD*.

118 "more natural inclination to run . . .": "Seabiscuit Trainer Says He's Another Discovery," *San Francisco Chronicle*, February 13, 1937.

118 "as gentlemanly a horse . . .": "Smith Recalls Stipulation That Could've Stopped Seabiscuit Sale," *Daily Racing Form*, February 13, 1953.

119 "You don't have to tell good horses . . .": Alan Goodrich, "All-Time Greatest Jockey," *Sir!*, March 1951, p. 66.

119 Exhibit workout: "Like Mike and Ike," *San Francisco Chronicle*, *SB*, winter 1936–37.

120 Sabueso: "Ligaroti Is Best Pampas Horse," *San Francisco Chronicle*, SB, fall 1937.

120 "Did you ever see two stallions fight?": Beckwith, *Seabiscuit*, p. 43.

121 "Let's head for California . . .": Ibid., p. 33.

121 Seabiscuit and trains: Ibid., p. 30.

122 "hang on to your hats": Ibid., p. 33.

CHAPTER 8

126 put on two hundred pounds: "Seabiscuit's Odds Cut," *San Francisco Chronicle*, February 11, 1937, *FD*.

126 *He's burning the top right off the racetrack:* Beckwith, *Seabiscuit*, p. 34; "Best San Francisco Horse Is Seabiscuit," *San Francisco Chronicle*, SB, late 1936.

127 world record workout: "War Admiral Race Causes Comment," *San Francisco Examiner*, SB.

127 Smith scared by Seabiscuit's speed: Beckwith, *Seabiscuit*, p. 34.

128 stable hands were shocked: "Seabiscuit Looms as Favorite," *SB*, December 1936.

129 Pollard brags about having time to shop during race: "May Import Foe from South," *SB*, n.d.

130 Seabiscuit "overrated": "Keep an Eye on Collier Candidate," *Pasadena Star-News*, December 25, 1936; "Mutuel Bells," *Glendale News-Press*, December 24, 1936; "Seabiscuit Fails to Warrant Position," *Los Angeles Times*, December 17, 1936.

130 rash: "Seabiscuit Gains in Skin Trouble," *Glendale News-Press*, January 22, 1937; Moody, *Come On Seabiscuit*, pp. 65–66; Farrell Jones, telephone interview, January 28, 1998.

130 "Don't tell me about bad breaks . . .": Ibid.

130 Ollie overfeeding: "Seabiscuit Crossed Up Clockers," *Los Angeles Times*, March 1, 1937.

132 Smith knew he had the best horse in America: "Seabiscuit's Trainer Says He's Another Discovery," *San Francisco Chronicle*, February 13, 1937.

133 "If Seabiscuit loses . . .": "Sports," *New York Journal American*, August 7, 1937.

133 Howard betting: "Seabiscuit Threat to Sun Beau's Record," *Los Angeles Evening Herald and Express*, August 9, 1937.

134 running of '37 hundred-grander: "The Inside Track," *Los Angeles Herald and Express*, March 1, 1937; "Too Close for Comfort," *Los Angeles Times*, February 28, 1937.

136 wire . . . close enough to touch: "Too Close for Comfort," *Los Angeles Times*, February 28, 1937.

136 "Faster, baby, faster . . .": Ibid.

137 Howard's premature celebration: "Sports," *New York Journal American*, August 7, 1937, *FD*.

137 "Fortune . . . kissed the wrong horse . . .": "There They Go," *Daily Racing Tab*, *SB*, summer 1937.

137 Red and Harry talk: "The Inside Track," *Los Angeles Herald and Express*, March 1, 1937; "Too Close for Comfort," *Los Angeles Times*, February 28, 1937.

139 Neither he nor Smith blamed him: "Seabiscuit Totes 120," *Los Angeles Times*, March 4, 1937; "The Inside Track," *Los Angeles Evening Herald and Express*, August 11, 1937.

CHAPTER 9

141 85 million people a week: William Manchester, *The Glory and the Dream: A Narrative History of America 1932–1972* (New York: Bantam Books, 1973), p. 120.

142 Radio history: Dr. Marvin R. Bensman, "Broadcasting History" online article (Memphis: Department of Communications, University of Memphis; accessed September 18, 2000); www.people.memphis.edu/~mbensman/homes30.dat.

142 Rural Electrification Administration, begun in 1936: "Rural Electrification Administration" online article (Kansas: Kansas Electric Cooperatives, Inc.; accessed September 18, 2000); www.kec.org.

143 Golden Rod beer: "Yea, Verily," *SB*, fall 1937.

144 Smith taciturn: Sonny Greenberg, telephone interview, December 24, 1999.

144 "He's a horse": Alexander, *A Sound of Horses*, p. 185.

144 "long distance conversationalist . . .": "Seabiscuit Scores Hollow Triumph," *San Francisco News*, *SB*, n.d.

144 sneak the horse out: "California Has New Turf Sensation in Seabiscuit," *SB*; Keith Stucki, telephone interview, March 25, 1998.

144 "Damned if I know": "Smithiana," *Thoroughbred Record*, February 23, 1957.

145 set out Seabiscuit's bridle: Moody, *Come On Seabiscuit*, p. 163.

145 electrified a park bench: Bill Buck, telephone interview, January 28, 1998.

145 "Turf writers and clockers swear . . .": "Silent Tom Smith," *SB*, March 16, 1940.

145 "Runs, though": Alexander, *A Sound of Horses*, p. 185.

146 "Seabiscuit and Greta Garbo . . .": "Seabiscuit Turns in Sizzling Work," *San Francisco Chronicle*, April 6, 1937, *FD*.

146 Howard goes to press box before races: "Seabiscuit Nips Track Record," *The Boston Globe*, August 8, 1937, p. 24.

146 Howard tells reporters of itineraries: "Seabiscuit Rides Home," *San Francisco Chronicle*, November 18, 1937.

147 Howard sends silver shoes to reporters: "Sports Mirror," *SB*, December 1937; "Hit or Miss," *Los Angeles Examiner*, February 15, 1938.

147 Howard's champagne: "Cap's Good Loser," *SB*, March 4, 1937, *FD*.

148 "He'll probably win . . .": Alexander, *A Sound of Horses*, p. 178.

148 Oscar Otis's excoriation of Pollard: "Jockey Richards Gives Rosemont Great Ride," *Los Angeles Times*, February 28, 1937.

148 "Pollard deserves at least half the credit . . .": "Seabiscuit Totes 120," *Los Angeles Times*, March 4, 1937.

149 San Juan Capistrano: "Boots and Saddles," *Santa Monica Outlook*, March 3, 1937, *FD*; "Hit or Miss," *SB*, March 1937.

151 Grog: "Like Mike and Ike," *San Francisco Chronicle*, *SB*, n.d.; Bill Buck, telephone interview, January 28, 1998; Wad Studley, telephone interview, February 6, 1999; Keith Stucki, telephone interview, March 25, 1998.

152 reporter sneaks to track cook's house: "Turf King," *San Francisco Chronicle*, *SB*, n.d.

152 "bring the old Biscuit out": Bill Buck, telephone interview, January 28, 1998.

152 artist painting Grog: Keith Stucki, telephone interview, March 25, 1998.

152 Stucki and Whitey fool horseman: Keith Stucki, telephone interview, March 25, 1998.

152 Seabiscuit was insured for $100,000: "Santa Anita Horses Worth Millions," *SB*, October 1937.

153 Bay Meadows Handicap, "Who finished second . . .": "Grand Manitou Runs Second," *San Francisco Examiner*, April 17, 1937, *FD*.

153 Smith wants to hide horse from eastern handicappers: "Seabiscuit Must Carry Weight," *San Francisco Examiner*, May 19, 1937, p. 27.

154 Pollard collapses: "Biscuit Iron Horse," *Los Angeles Evening Herald and Express*, May 1937.

154 Pollard hits Otis: Farrell Jones, telephone interview, November 4, 1998.

CHAPTER 10

158 "One end bites . . .": Dorothy Ours, e-mail interview, September 14, 2000; John Clark, *Trader Clark: Six Decades of Racing Lore* (Lexington: Thoroughbred Publications, Inc., 1991).

158 War Admiral compared to sire: "Admiral Likely Wilson Choice," *SB*, n.d.

160 Stucki rides past Fitzsimmons barn: Keith Stucki, telephone interview, February 11, 1999.

161 "A single steed . . .": "Turf King," *San Francisco Chronicle*, *SB*, n.d.

161 "Hail the conquerin' hero . . .": "Seabiscuit Wins Massachusetts Handicap," *Boston Herald*, August 8, 1937, p. 24.

162 "Let's have some applause . . .": "The Post Parade," *Morning Telegraph/Daily Racing Form*, September 2, 1937, *FD*.

162 *Los Angeles Daily News* poll: "Biscuit Leads by a Nose," *Los Angeles Daily News*, August 27, 1937.

162 Bing's telegram: Bing Crosby, telegram to Charles Howard, August 7, 1937.

164 Seabiscuit in mud: "The Inside Track," *Los Angeles Evening Herald and Express*, *SB*, n.d; "The Post Parade," *Morning Telegraph/Daily Racing Form*, October 11, 1938; "Seabiscuit," *San Francisco Chronicle*, July 19, 1938, p. 1H; Beckwith, *Seabiscuit*, p. 41.

165 "Bring on your War Admiral!": "The Judge's Stand," *Morning Telegraph/Daily Racing Form*, October 16, 1937, *FD*.

166 asked about training: "Smith Training System," *San Francisco Chronicle*, *SB*, November 1937.

166 Fitzsimmons asks to hold Seabiscuit: Ibid.; "Seabiscuit," *San Francisco Chronicle*, July 19, 1938, p. 1H.

167 Howard mocked for being afraid of War Admiral: "Belmont Board of Directors Meet Today," *San Francisco Call-Bulletin*, *SB*, April 1938.

167 Vanderbilt: David Schmitz, "A Presence Well Known" online article (Lexington: *Blood-Horse*; accessed November 13, 1999); www.blood-horse.com/features/vanderbilt1115.html.

168 "I believe Seabiscuit can beat War Admiral . . .": "Turf in Review," *Morning Telegraph/Daily Racing Form*, November 3, 1937, *FD*.

168 tongs: "The Judge's Stand," *Morning Telegraph/Daily Racing Form*, *SB*, n.d.

169 *He is befuddled:* "War Admiral Race Causes Comment," *San Francisco Examiner*, *SB*, n.d.

169 "Seabiscuit . . . will lick him sure . . .": "Seabiscuit Will Beat War Admiral," *San Francisco Call- Bulletin*, November 23, 1937.

169 Crusader incident: "Milton Asks New Starter," *SB*, October 6, 1938.

169 Howard kept his horses in town: "Seabiscuit to Stay . . .": *Baltimore Evening Sun*, November 3, 1937.

170 awaiting War Admiral: "Seabiscuit to Stay," *Baltimore Evening Sun*, November 3, 1937.

170 telephones Otis: "Seabiscuit Rides Home," *San Francisco Chronicle*, November 18, 1937.

171 homecoming: "Royal Welcome for Seabiscuit," *San Francisco Chronicle*, *SB*, November 1937; "Seabiscuit Set to Race," *Oakland Tribune*, November 22, 1937; "Home Town Fans Greet Seabiscuit," *San Francisco Chronicle*, November 22, 1937, p. 6H; "Even Europe Knows," *San Francisco Chronicle*, November 22, 1937.

CHAPTER 11

173 Exhibit: "Seabiscuit Voted Standout Horse," *San Francisco Examiner*, December 10, 1937; "Seabiscuit's Jockey Gets Suspension," *San Francisco Chronicle*, *SB*, December 1937; "Looking 'Em Over," *San Francisco News*, *SB*, December 1937; "Owner Refuses Entry," *Los Angeles Examiner*, December 22, 1937, *FD*.

175 Horse of the Year: "Seabiscuit Voted Standout Horse," *San Francisco Examiner*, December 10, 1937.

176 fog workout: "Clockers See Seabiscuit in New Workout," *SB*, n.d.

176 Monday workout: "Howard Horse Has Three Quarter Run in 1:12," *Los Angeles Examiner*, February 1, 1938.

177 dipping Seabiscuit's hoof in ink: "Can Seabiscuit Cop?" *San Francisco Call-Bulletin*, 22, 1937.

177 minimum imposts in California: "Seabiscuit Weight Still in Question," *San Francisco Chronicle*, SB, late March 1938.

178 lameness rumors: "Seabiscuit Sound?" *San Francisco Examiner*, SB, February 1938.

178 newsmen got down on their hands and knees: "Seabiscuit Works Out," SB, fall 1937.

178 " 'mystery' of Seabiscuit . . .": "The Post Parade," *Morning Telegraph/Daily Racing Form*, February 10, 1938.

179 "Doggone those clockers . . .": "Smith Feuds with Clockers," *Los Angeles Times*, February 2, 1938.

179 HOWARD HORSE PULLED UP "GROGGY . . .": "Howard Horse Pulled Up Groggy After Work," *Los Angeles Evening Herald and Express*, January 31, 1938, FD.

180 "Sponging": "Betting Coup," *Los Angeles Examiner*, February 1, 1938; "Horse Is Well Guarded," *Morning Telegraph/Daily Racing Form*, February 2, 1938.

180 Howard acts as decoy: "Seabiscuit Works Out," *San Francisco Chronicle*, February 12, 1938.

181 Fair Knightess fall: "Santa Anita Jockey Hurt," *San Francisco Chronicle*, February 20, 1938, p. 3H; "Before and After," SB, n.d.; "Harry Richards Expected," SB, mid-February 1938; "Pollard Will Be Idle," SB, mid-February 1938; Moody, *Come On Seabiscuit*, p. 109.

182 hind end was paralyzed: "Harry Richards Expected," SB, mid-February 1938.

183 Pollard asks Howard to hire Woolf: "Owner Refuses Entry," *Los Angeles Examiner*, December 22, 1937, FD.

183 "Seabiscuit will run . . .": "Howard Hunts New Jockey," *San Francisco Examiner*, February 21, 1938, p. 16.

184 "as good as hands can make him . . .": "Seabiscuit's Sizzling Work," *Morning Telegraph/Daily Racing Form*, February 21, 1938, FD.

185 Pollard meets with Workman: "Hit or Miss," *Los Angeles Examiner*, March 4, 1938; "Biscuit Trainer Raps Jockey," *San Francisco Examiner*, March 1, 1938.

185 San Antonio: "Workman Told to Hit Horse Twice," SB, n.d;

"Seabiscuit Beaten by a Neck," *San Francisco Chronicle*, February 26, 1938, *FD*.

185 Pollard listens to San Antonio: "Pollard Defends Workman," *Los Angeles Evening Herald and Express*, February 28, 1938, p. A12.

186 Smith watches San Antonio: "Biscuit Trainer Raps Jockey," *San Francisco Examiner*, March 1, 1938.

188 "All I want is a jockey who will obey . . .": "Biscuit Trainer Raps Jockey," *San Francisco Examiner*, March 1, 1938.

189 Woolf offered $1,000 to get out of contract: "There They Go," *SB*, 1937.

189 Woolf meets with Howard, Smith: "Ice Man Jockey," *San Francisco Examiner*, March 1, 1938, *FD*.

189 he'd split the riding fee: "Woolf Offers to Split," *SB*, March 1938; "Small Field . . .," *Los Angeles Examiner*, March 3, 1938.

CHAPTER 12

191 barn security: "Stagehand Winner," *San Francisco Chronicle*, March 6, 1938; "Owner Debunks Yarn on Seabiscuit Sponging," *SB*, February 2, 1938.

192 plot to kidnap Woolf: "Stagehand Winner," *San Francisco Chronicle*, March 6, 1938.

193 trainer . . . had to send . . . to Miami to get . . . Wall: "Seabiscuit Was Best Horse in Handicap," *SB*, n.d.

193 Red bows: "Jockey Pollard Recovering," *Morning Telegraph/Daily Racing Form*, *SB*, July 1938.

193 Marcela in press box, Bing: "Wonder Horse Nibbles," *SB*, February 11, 1938; "Sports," *New York Journal American*, May 1938.

194 bet between Howards: "As Bill Leiser Sees It," *San Francisco Chronicle*, March 5, 1938, *FD*.

194 Stagehand and Sceneshifter's caps: "Turf in Review," *Morning Telegraph/Daily Racing Form*, January 8, 1949; "Bill Henry Says," *Los Angeles Times*, *SB*, March 1938.

194 All I need is luck: Salvator, "Marginalia," *Thoroughbred Record*, *SB*, March 1938, p. 203.

196 McCarthy's call of race: Salvator, "Marginalia," *Thoroughbred Record*, *SB*, March 1938, p. 203.

196 half-mile world record broken: Beckwith, *Seabiscuit*, p. 44.

197 George realizes error: "Turf in Review," *Morning Telegraph/Daily Racing Form*, January 8, 1949.

197 "We've got the race!": "Bill Henry Says," *Los Angeles Times*, SB, March 1938.

197 *I am going to gallop by him . . .*: "Sports," *New York Journal American*, April 26, 1938.

198 Pollard and Marcela watch race: "Pollard Praises Stagehand," *Los Angeles Examiner*, March 6, 1938, p. 7; "The Post Parade," *Morning Telegraph/Daily Racing Form*, March 7, 1938; untitled, *San Francisco Examiner*, SB, March 1938; "Bill Henry Says," *Los Angeles Times*, SB, March 1938.

198 Pollard thought it was over: "Hugh Bradley Says," *New York Post*, SB, May 1938.

198 spectators would remember race for as long as they lived: Leonard Dorfman, telephone interview, November 12, 1999.

198 clapped a hand over Marcela's mouth: untitled, *San Francisco Examiner*, SB, March 1938.

199 "the greatest racehorse in the world . . .": "Sports," *New York Journal American*, April 26, 1938.

199 "We'll try again . . .": Beckwith, *Seabiscuit*, p. 44.

CHAPTER 13

201 Howard asked about match: "Sports," *New York Journal American*, SB, May 1938.

203 newsmen petition to see films: "Biscuit Jockey Blamed," SB, March 10, 1938.

203 Howard protests suspension: "Seabiscuit Withdrawn," *Los Angeles Times*, March 11, 1938; "Hit or Miss," *Los Angeles Examiner*, March 11, 1938.

205 Seabiscuit poses: "Hit or Miss," *Los Angeles Examiner*, March 31, 1938; "Sports Mirror," *San Francisco Chronicle*, February 12, 1938, p. 12; Charles Hatton, "This Is a Horse," *Turf and Sport Digest*, January 1939, pp. 16–32; "Hit or Miss," *Los Angeles Examiner*, March 31, 1938; "Sports Mirror," *San Francisco Chronicle*, February 12, 1943, p. 2H.

205 Agua Caliente: Jerry Brucker, "Seabiscuit's Overlooked Chapter," *Thoroughbreds of California*, September 1986, pp. 18–27; "Lure of

Handicap Day," *Morning Telegraph/Daily Racing Form*, March 25, 1938; "Seabiscuit Top Heavy Race Favorite," *Los Angeles Times*, March 26, 1938; "Crowd Sets New Mark," *Los Angeles Examiner*, March 28, 1938; "20,000 Watch Seabiscuit," *San Diego Union*, March 28, 1938; "The Inside Track," *Los Angeles Evening Herald and Express*, March 28, 1938, p. A11; "Seabiscuit Goes North," *Los Angeles Times*, March 28, 1938, *FD*; "Yea, Verily," *SB*, n.d.

207 Match negotiations: "War Admiral and Seabiscuit Match for $100,000 Proposed," *Daily Racing Tab*, *SB*, April 1938; "War Admiral, Seabiscuit Duel Arranged," *Baltimore Sun*, April 13, 1938; "Biscuit vs. War Admiral?" *San Francisco Chronicle*, *SB*, April 1938; "Three Big Offers," *San Francisco Chronicle*, *SB*, n.d.; "Coast Seeks," *San Francisco Examiner*, April 6, 1938; "Biscuit Runs in Bay Meadows Handicap," *Los Angeles Examiner*, April 14, 1938, *FD*; Marvin Drager, *The Most Glorious Crown* (New York: Charles Scribner's Sons, 1975), pp. 61–75.

209 Two turn concern: "Pimlico Next on List," *San Francisco Chronicle*, *SB*, April 1938.

211 "Seabiscuit will meet War Admiral anywhere . . .": "Board of Directors Meet Today on War Admiral–Seabiscuit Match Race," *San Francisco Call-Bulletin*, *SB*, April 1938.

212 "beat the stuffing . . .": "Sports," *New York Journal American*, April 26, 1938.

213 highest weight in California: "Biscuit First, Then Rest," *San Francisco Call-Bulletin*, April 16, 1938.

214 Pollard in press box: "Record Crowd Sees Seabiscuit," *San Francisco Examiner*, *SB*, April 1938.

214 Seabiscuit leaves: "Seabiscuit Shoves Off," *San Francisco Chronicle*, *SB*, April 1938.

214 *Captain Billie's Whiz Bang* magazine: "Biscuit Plays Duck," *SB*, n.d.

215 "We've got to tear off that guy's epaulets . . .": Ibid.

CHAPTER 14

217 slept for most of the trip: "Biscuit Good Sleeper," *San Francisco Examiner*, *SB*, May 1938.

217 24,265th mile of career rail travel: "Seabiscuit's Travels," *SB*, May 1, 1938.

217 95 percent of the wagers were on War Admiral: "Little Money Wagered on Seabiscuit," *San Francisco Chronicle*, May 7, 1938, *FD*.

218 tears down wall between stalls: "Biscuit Will Duck Pimlico," *San Francisco Chronicle*, *SB*, n.d.

219 gate training: "Off Fast!," *San Francisco Chronicle*, *SB*, May 1938; "Biscuit Goes to School," *San Francisco Chronicle*, May 11, 1938, *FD*.

219 "Tom . . . had blown his topper . . .": "Seabiscuit Gets Recognition at Last," *San Francisco Examiner*, February 2, 1944.

224 Wise We Boys: "Silent Tom Smith," *SB*, March 16, 1940; "Silent Tom Can't Keep a Secret," *San Francisco Chronicle*, May 21, 1938; "Howard Crosses Up Clockers," *Los Angeles Evening Herald and Express*, May 17, 1938; "Biscuit Bows Out," *SB*; "Bill Leiser," *San Francisco Chronicle*, May 22, 1938, p. 3H; "Seabiscuit Tom," *San Francisco Chronicle*, May 21, 1938, p. 1H; "Biscuit Bows Out," *San Francisco Chronicle*, May 24, 1938, *FD*.

228 "He never looked better . . .": "Howard Visits New York," *SB*, n.d.

229 paper wants racing board to step in: "State Racing Board Inquiry Is Suggested," *Daily Mirror*, May 23, 1938, *FD*.

229 War Admiral's bad training: "Howard Tells of Seabiscuit Program," *Los Angeles Evening Herald and Examiner*, June 16, 1938; "Biscuit's Knee Good," *San Francisco Call-Bulletin*, June 16, 1938, *FD*.

231 "Now the one time out of so many . . .": "$100,000 Match Race Called Off," *New York Journal American*, May 25, 1938.

232 scratch decision: "Down in Front," *New York Herald Tribune*, May 26, 1938; "Biscuit Admiral . . .," *SB*, May 1938; "$100,000 Match Race Called Off," *New York Journal American*, May 25, 1938.

232 "I don't know if he'll ever come out . . .": "On the Line," *Daily Mirror*, June 8, 1938.

233 Howard willing to race for no purse: "$100,000 Match Race Called Off," *New York Journal American*, May 25, 1938.

233 War Admiral scratched: "By Joe Williams," *New York World-Telegram*, May 31, 1938; "The Great Race," *Newsweek*, June 6, 1938.

234 "I'll never again consent to such a thing": Drager, *Most Glorious Crown*, p. 75.

234 spectators boo War Admiral: "On the Line," *Daily Mirror*, June 8, 1938.

CHAPTER 15

238 Pollard's accident: "Howard's Ace Loses Regular Jockey," *Providence Journal*, June 24, 1938; "There They Go," *Daily Racing Tab*, July 16, 1938; "King of Horses," *Morning Telegraph/Daily Racing Form*, March 17, 1940; Alexander, *A Sound of Horses*, pp. 181–82; Edith Wilde, telephone interview, February 2, 1998.

240 Howard flies in orthopedists: Edith Wilde, telephone interview, February 2, 1998.

241 "If that isn't running . . .": "War Admiral's Trainer Balks," *SB*, n.d.

241 War Admiral . . . balked in workout: "War Minstrel Proves He Will Be 'Cap Contender," *Boston Evening Transcript*, June 22, 1938.

242 "the miracle of the ages . . .": "In Best Condition of Career," *Boston Evening American*, June 15, 1938.

242 "We're still on the fence . . .": "War Admiral Runs at Suffolk," *The New York Times*, June 29, 1938.

242 NBC radio interview: Alexander, *A Sound of Horses*, pp. 180–81; David Alexander, "Four Good Legs Between Them," *Blood-Horse*, December 24, 1955, pp. 1558–63; Jack Shettlesworth, telephone interview, March 1998.

243 "My horse is sharper than a fishwife's . . .": "Sports," *New York Journal American*, June 29, 1938.

244 second-largest crowd ever to attend: "War Admiral 'Just Another Horse,'" *Wilmington Journal*, June 30, 1938.

244 Massachusetts scratch: "Setting the Pace," *New York Sun*, June 30, 1938; "New England Weathers 1938," *Morning Telegraph/Daily Racing Form*, *SB*, n.d.; untitled article, *SB*, June 1938; "Seabiscuit's Racing Career at End?" *SB*, June 1938, "The Race Track," *New Yorker*, June 9, 1938.

247 "It seems things are all going wrong . . .": "Menow Wins $50,000 Race," *Boston Herald*, June 30, 1938.

CHAPTER 16

252 "Looks like a cow pony . . .": Beckwith, *Step and Go Together*, p. 117.

252 condition of track: "War Admiral Next," *SB*, July 17, 1938.

252 "It looked like they were trying to grow corn . . .": "Stewards Issue Ultimatum," *SB*, July 15, 1938.

252 Stewards vs. Smith: "Seabiscuit Is Impressive," *Los Angeles Evening Herald and Express*, July 13, 1938; "Seabiscuit's Trainer Bans," *Los Angeles Times*, July 14, 1938; "The Morning After," *Daily News*, *SB*, July 15, 1938; "Stewards Issue Ultimatum," *SB*, July 15, 1938; "Seabiscuit in Late Breeze," *Los Angeles Examiner*, July 15, 1938.

253 Smith . . . never had a horse in his care: "Starting Gate for Match Never Built," *San Francisco Chronicle*, *SB*, May 1938.

254 Greenberg runs between barn and office: Sonny Greenberg, telephone interview, December 24, 1999; "Seabiscuit Runs at Hollywood," *Los Angeles Times*, *SB*, mid-July 1938; "Seabiscuit to Run," *Los Angeles Evening Herald and Express*, July 15, 1938; "Stewards Issue Ultimatum," *SB*, July 15, 1938.

255 Wayne Wright reducing: Leonard Dorfman, telephone interview, November 12, 1999.

255 "Let 'em run themselves out . . .": "Woolf Gives All Credit," *SB*, July 1938; "The Inside Track," *Los Angeles Evening Herald and Express*, July 1938; "Praise Woolf for Ride," *Los Angeles Evening Herald and Express*, July 19, 1938, p. A12.

257 "SILENT TOM SMILES!": "Seabiscuit Wins Race," *San Francisco Examiner*, July 17, 1938.

258 "I know my horse": "Seabiscuit Heads for Chicago," *Evening News*, July 18, 1938, p. 15.

CHAPTER 17

261 Lin–Charles rivalry: Noble Threewit, telephone interview, January 17, 1998.

262 Bing invested $600,000: Giles E. Wright, "30 Years of Surf and Turf," *Blood-Horse*, July 23, 1966, p. 1921.

262 side bet: Michael C. Howard, telephone interview, January 18, 1997.

263 "*Ugh!*": "It's Biscuit to Win," *San Diego Sun*, August 11, 1938, p. 15.

263 "camouflaged as a diesel . . .": Ibid.

263 Bing outfits track: "Rumors of Howard, Son Rift," *San Francisco Call-Bulletin*, August 12, 1938.

264 scare him to death: Ibid.

266 "What are you doing, Spec?": "Biscuit Race Riders Get Works," *San Francisco Chronicle*, August 13, 1938, *FD*.

266 fouling: "At Last!," *Los Angeles Examiner*, August 17, 1938, *FD*.

266 "the dingbustingest contest . . .": "Pilots of Biscuit and Ligaroti Set Down for Rest of Meeting," *Morning Telegraph/Daily Racing Form*, August 14, 1938, p. 1.

267 Woolf scolds Richardson on yelling during race: "Great Stakes Reinsman Honored Today," George Woolf Memorial Pamphlet, February 10, 1949, p. 4.

267 newsmen hear Woolf and Richardson arguing: "Stewards Rule Woolf, Richardson off Del Mar," *San Francisco Call-Bulletin*, August 13, 1938, *FD*.

267 Marcela . . . downed several aspirin: untitled article, *SB*, n.d.

268 "I want the newspapers to forget . . .": "Riding Orders Poppycock," *San Francisco Call-Bulletin*, August 17, 1938, *FD*.

268 public accusation of wrongdoing: "Inside on Biscuit Race Bared," *San Diego Sun*, August 16, 1938.

268 "make it look close . . .": "Hit or Miss," *Los Angeles Examiner*, *SB*, August 1938.

269 race was now being referred to as a "frameup" and a "fix": "Riding Orders Poppycock," *San Francisco Call-Bulletin*, August 17, 1938, *FD*; "Seabiscuit-Ligaroti Fixed Race," *Los Angeles Times*, August 16, 1938, *FD*; "Seabiscuit's Owner Denies Frameup!," *San Francisco Chronicle*, August 16, 1938, *FD*.

269 Howard's reaction: "Biscuit Owner Fights New Charges," *Los Angeles Examiner*, August 16, 1938, *FD*; "What Nots," *SB*, n.d.; "Seabiscuit-Ligaroti Fixed Race," *Los Angeles Times*, August 16, 1938, *FD*.

270 "there are a few people in the East . . .": "Sports," *New York Journal American*, *SB*, August 1938.

271 viewing of film: "Just a Case of Jockeying," *Los Angeles Times*, August 12, 1938, section III, p. 3; "Del Mar Cleans Up," *SB*, September 8, 1938.

271 Navy planes: Beckwith, *Seabiscuit*, p. 30; Beckwith, *Step and Go Together*, p. 118.

CHAPTER 18

273 leg broken and reset twice: Alexander, *A Sound of Horses*, p. 185.

273 Eighty-six pounds: "Sports," *New York Journal American*, *SB*, n.d.

273 Pollard's reading: David Alexander, "Four Good Legs Between Them," *Blood-Horse*, December 24, 1955, p. 1553.

273 "*compensatory spark* . . .": Carl Bode, ed., *The Portable Emerson* (New York: Viking, 1984), p. 165.

274 Red woos Agnes: Norah Christianson, telephone interview, January 26, 1998.

274 Agnes was certain he was dying: Ibid.

274 letter from Red: Edith Wilde, telephone interview, February 2, 1998.

274 Old Waldo . . . had been right after all: Alexander, *A Sound of Horses*, p. 187.

275 Match negotiations: Alfred Gwynne Vanderbilt, Jr., telephone interview, January 29, 1997; "By Joe Williams," *SB*, n.d.; Drager, *Most Glorious Crown*, pp. 61–75.

277 Milton recuses himself: "Milton Asks New Starter," *SB*, October 6, 1938.

278 secret desire for walk-up: Alfred Gwynne Vanderbilt, Jr., telephone interview, January 29, 1997; "Thrilling Seabiscuit Story," *San Francisco Examiner*, *SB*, November 1938; Tommy Bell, telephone interview, June 22, 1999.

279 "I'm going to give them birds the biggest surprise . . .": Bill Buck, telephone interview, January 28, 1998.

279 Pollard and Woolf strategize: "The Post Parade," *Morning Telegraph/Daily Racing Form*, November 3, 1938.

280 "Seabiscuit's like a hunk of steel . . .": "Starting Gate for Match Never Built," *San Francisco Chronicle*, *SB*, May 1938.

280 "you could kill him before he'd quit": Alan Goodrich, "All-Time Greatest Jockey," *Sir!*, March 1951, p. 66.

280 Smith and homemade bell: "Smith Recalls Stipulation That Could've Stopped Seabiscuit Sale," *Daily Racing Form*, February 13, 1953; "Tom Smith Reminisces About Woolf, 'Biscuit," *Daily Racing Form*, February 1953; Bill Buck, telephone interview, January 28, 1998.

281 Grog in Seabiscuit's stall: "Smithiana," *Thoroughbred Record*, February 23, 1957.

282 "a civil war between the War Admiral Americans and the Seabiscuit Americans . . .": "No Matter Who Wins," *San Francisco Chronicle*, November 1, 1938, p. 1H.

282 Kurtsinger's wife: "Seabiscuit Shows Speed in Workout," *SB*, October 27, 1938.

282 "*The storm is past* . . .": "Passing By," *SB*, November 1938.

283 "bull's wool" socks: Edith Wilde, telephone interview, February 2, 1998.

283 "even George isn't bad enough . . .": "The Post Parade," *Morning Telegraph*, October 11, 1938.

283 "I still could have ridden the Biscuit . . .": Ibid.

283 Seabiscuit . . . to win by four: "The Post Parade," *Morning Telegraph/ Daily Racing Form*, November 3, 1938.

284 Howard barn on strategy: "The Post Parade," *Morning Telegraph/ Daily Racing Form*, October 30, 1938; "Blue Bloods of the Turf," *Baltimore Evening Sun*, October 28, 1938, p. 30; Alexander, *A Sound of Horses*, p. 180.

284 "War Admiral won't outbreak . . .": Jimmy Loftus, "Talk o' the Turf," *Turf and Sport Digest*, December 1938, p. 32.

284 THERE IS ONE SURE WAY . . .: "Obituary: Red Pollard," *Blood-Horse*, March 21, 1981, pp. 1771–72.

285 Woolf and tractor path: "Now It Can Be Told," *Blood-Horse*, April 5, 1941, p. 59.

CHAPTER 19

287 Spencer inspects track: "40,000 See Howard's Champion," *The Baltimore Sun*, November 2, 1938.

288 OUR HORSE WILL WIN BY 5 . . .: "Sports," *New York Journal American*, *SB*, n.d.

288 $25,000 of his own money: "This Way," *Washington Times*, November 2, 1938, p. 19.

288 Fitzsimmons's prediction: "Seabiscuit's Victory Over War Admiral," *New York Press*, *SB*, November 1938.

288 fans outside track: "Biscuit Wins by Four," *New York Daily News*, November 2, 1938, p. 62.

288 paddock scene: "Roamer's Ramblings," *Thoroughbred Record*, November 5, 1938, p. 305.

289 Staint Christopher medal: Jimmy Loftus, "Talk o' the Turf," *Turf and Sport Digest*, December 1938, p. 32; "Cohn-ing Tower," *SB*, November 1938.

289 Bell on stand broken: "Tom Smith Reminisces About Woolf, 'Biscuit," *Daily Racing Form*, February 1953.

289 "No assistants . . . or no race": Ibid.

290 "keyed to the highest tension . . .": Grantland Rice, "Seabiscuit vs. War Admiral," *The Fireside Book of Horse Racing*, ed. David Woods (New York: Simon and Schuster, 1963), p. 243.

290 forty million listeners: "Seabiscuit Stands Out," *The Pay Off*, *SB*, November 1938.

290 Roosevelt listens to race: Stoneridge, *Great Horses of Our Time*, p. 27.

290 War Admiral favored in press box: "Woolf Shares Purse," *San Francisco Chronicle*, *SB*, November 1938.

291 prerace: "Thrilling Seabiscuit Story," *San Francisco Examiner*, *SB*, November 1938.

291 George canters Seabiscuit to backstretch: Ibid.

292 "we'll never get a go . . .": Loftus, "Talk o' the Turf."

292 "kicks like hell . . .": "Thrilling Seabiscuit Story," *San Francisco Examiner*, *SB*, November 1938.

294 "get on up here with me!": Harold Washburn, telephone interview, November 9, 1998.

294 War Admiral never extended: "Seabiscuit Shows Speed in Workout," *SB*, October 27, 1938.

295 writer falling from press box: Jack Mahon, "The Day the Biscuit Beat the Admiral," *Turf and Sport Digest*, February 1974.

295 fans fainting: Ibid.

296 "His eye was rolling . . .": Loftus, "Talk o' the Turf," p. 33.

296 tongue shot out the side of his mouth: "Thrilling Seabiscuit Story," *San Francisco Examiner*, *SB*, November 1938.

296 "So long, Charley": Harold Washburn, telephone interview, November 9, 1998.

296 steeplechase fence collapsed: Ralph Theroux, telephone interview, February 1, 1999.

297 "He looked all broken up . . .": "Winner Pays $6," *San Francisco Chronicle*, November 2, 1938, *FD*; "Biscuit Choice," *SB*, n.d.

297 George yells back at Kurtsinger: *1938 Pimlico Special*, downloaded

video (New York: ABC Sports, May 14, 1996; accessed March 26, 1997); America Online, ABC Sports racing page.

297 fans vault rail: *1938 Pimlico Special*, video; America Online, ABC Sports racing page; "Seabiscuit Defeats Admiral," *Daily Mirror*, November 2, 1938, p. 34.

297 Riddle's reaction: "In the Paddock," *SB*, November 1938; "Wife of Biscuit's Owner in Tears," *SB*, November 1938.

298 "old pal Red...": Audiotape, "Clem McCarthy's Call of the Seabiscuit–War Admiral Match Race."

298 paddock scene: "40,000 Watch Seabiscuit Defeat War Admiral," *The New York Times*, November 1, 1938; "Seabiscuit Beats War Admiral," *SB*, n.d.

298 "I said mine on the track": Ibid.

299 Kurtsinger whispers in War Admiral's ear: "Rodger H. Pippen," *SB*, n.d.

299 "If only Red . . .": "Rider's Views," *SB*, November 1938.

299 Woolf, Kurtsinger postrace quotes: "He's the Best Horse," *San Francisco Examiner*, November 2, 1938; "Rival Jockey Lauds Biscuit," *SB*, November 2, 1938.

300 morning after: "War Admiral's Trainer Balks," *SB*, November 1938.

301 Pollard after race: "The Post Parade," *Morning Telegraph/Daily Racing Form*, November 3, 1938; "He's the Best Horse," *San Francisco Examiner*, November 2, 1938; "Rider's Views," *SB*, November 1938.

301 $1,500: "Woolf Shares Purse," *San Francisco Chronicle*, *SB*, November 1938.

CHAPTER 20

305 Red rebreaks leg; George visits: "There They Go," *SB*, December 1938.

305 Babcock fixes leg: Edith Wilde, telephone interview, February 2, 1998; "Howard May Retire Seabiscuit," *Los Angeles Evening Herald and Examiner*, March 4, 1940, p. A16.

306 ice in Maryland: "Biscuit, Work Balked by Weather, to Quit Pimlico," *Baltimore Evening Sun*, December 1, 1938.

307 crowds form in Columbia: "Seabiscuit Will Race at Santa Anita," *SB*, n.d.

307 "All four of his legs are broken": "Seabiscuit Here in Fine Condition," *Los Angeles Evening Herald and Express*, January 2, 1939, p. A10.

308 "dumb farmer of a reporter . . .": "Smith Denies Biscuit Not in Good Shape," *SB*, December 25, 1938.

308 "One hundred thirty-four is a lot of weight . . .": "Seabiscuit Will Race at Santa Anita," *SB*, n.d.

309 horse had drawn more newspaper coverage: "Looking 'Em Over," *San Francisco News*, January 1939.

309 "The affection that this inarticulate brown horse had aroused . . .": "Hollywood," *SB*, March 3, 1940.

309 arrival at Santa Anita: "Seabiscuit, Sound and Eager, at Santa Anita," *SB*, January 2, 1939.

310 "No longer will there be any secrecy . . .": "Seabiscuit's People's Horse, Says Boss," *Los Angeles Evening Herald and Express*, *SB*, January 1939.

310 "Here comes the Biscuit!: "Rival Trainers, Owners," *San Francisco Examiner*, *SB*, early 1939.

310 new turn-gripping shoes: "Seabiscuit Gets Special Type Shoe," *Los Angeles Evening Herald and Express*, January 24, 1939, p. A12.

310 hiding Kayak: "Argentine Takes Worst," *Los Angeles Examiner*, March 5, 1939; "Kayak Trainer Given Credit," *Los Angeles Examiner*, March 3, 1939; Salvator, "Horse of the Month," *Horse and Horseman*, April 1939, p. 22.

311 Smith worries over starting Seabiscuit: "Seabiscuit out of Cap," *SB*, February 16, 1939.

312 two thousand pounds of force: George Pratt, e-mail interview, February 13, 1998.

312 Seabiscuit's injury: "Champ Goes Lame," *Los Angeles Examiner*, February 15, 1939; "Fear Seabiscuit's Career at End," *Los Angeles Evening Herald and Express*, February 15, 1939, p. B7; "X Ray Leg," *SB*, February 1939; "Howard Star Pops Knee at Santa Anita," *SB*, February 14, 1939; "Seabiscuit's Condition Better," *SB*, February 1939; "Seabiscuit Still a Puzzle," *SB*, February 1939.

312 Woolf heard a sharp *crack!*: Moody, *Come On Seabiscuit*, p. 151.

313 "Why did you do it?": "Seabiscuit Still a Puzzle," *SB*, February 1939.

314 Postinjury scene at Howard barn: "Fear Seabiscuit's Career at End," *Los Angeles Evening Herald and Express*, February 15, 1939, p. B7; "Leg Injury," *Los Angeles Evening Herald and Express*, February 15, 1939, p. B7; "Track Observers Predict," *Pasadena Star News*,

February 15, 1939, p. 16; "Howard Star Pops Knee at Santa Anita," *SB*, February 14, 1939; "Seabiscuit's Fate Still in Doubt," *San Francisco Examiner*, February 15, 1939, *FD*; "Seabiscuit Still a Puzzle," *SB*, February 1939; "Seabiscuit Scratched," *SB*, February 1939; "Seabiscuit out of Cap," *SB*, February 1939.

316 ruptured suspensory: "Seabiscuit to Stud," *Blood-Horse*, March 18, 1939, p. 456.

317 Buenos Aires was at a standstill: "Kayak to Pass," *SB*, March 6, 1939.

317 Howard reaction to '39 hundred-grander win: "There They Go," *SB*, March 1939.

317 Marcela felt hollow: Moody, *Come On Seabiscuit*, p. 153.

CHAPTER 21

319 "Then I reckon I'll have to . . .": Moody, *Come On Seabiscuit*, p. 153.

320 Howard stops going to track: "Biscuit May Come Back," *Los Angeles Times*, *SB*, summer 1939.

320 "a long, hard pull": "Howard May Retire Seabiscuit," *Los Angeles Evening Herald and Examiner*, March 4, 1940, p. A16.

320 "We were a couple of old cripples . . .": Beckwith, *Step and Go Together*, p. 120.

321 horse and rider healed: Beckwith, *Seabiscuit*, p. 58.

322 chasing deer: Ibid.

322 "The Biscuit will come back . . .": "Biscuit Secret Kept by Smith," *San Francisco Examiner*, February 26, 1940, *FD*.

323 "The whole ranch became centered on the job . . .": Beckwith, *Step and Go Together*, p. 121.

323 new stride: "Champ Ready," *SB*, n.d.

324 "Our wheels went wrong together . . .": "Obituary: Red Pollard," *Blood-Horse*, March 21, 1981, p. 1773.

324 "You knew he wanted to race again . . .": Beckwith, *Step and Go Together*, p. 121.

324 No elite horse had ever returned to top form: John Hervey, *American Race Horses 1940* (New York: Sagamore, 1941), pp. 200–201.

324 Agnes sure Red can't father child: Norah Christianson, telephone interview, January 26, 1998.

CHAPTER 22

327 "I am training a cripple . . .": "Big Three of Racing on List for Handicap," *SB*, December 6, 1939, p. 23.

328 "We'll run one-two anyway . . .": "Smithiana," *Thoroughbred Record*, February 23, 1957.

329 Tommy Luther banned for "defiant and threatening attitude": Farra, *Jockeying*, p. 63; Tommy Luther, telephone interview, February 2, 1998; John Giovanni, telephone interview, January 23, 1998.

330 Pollard won't join jockey meetings: Tommy Luther, telephone interview, February 2, 1998.

330 Yummy fighting: "The Post Parade," *Morning Telegraph/Daily Racing Form*, March 8, 1940.

331 Howard takes Pollard off filly: "The Post Parade," *Morning Telegraph/Daily Racing Form*, February 3, 1940.

331 Pollard's secret terror: Alexander, *A Sound of Horses*, p. 186.

331 Pollard criticized: Barry Whitehead, "Seabiscuit's Santa Anita Handicap," *Thoroughbred Record*, March 9, 1940, p. 195.

331 "my left-handed rooting section . . .": "The Post Parade," *Morning Telegraph/Daily Racing Form*, February 27, 1940.

331 "And none so poor . . .": untitled, *Morning Telegraph*, *SB*, winter 1940.

331 Pollard's drinking: Bill Buck, telephone interview, January 28, 1998; Alexander, *A Sound of Horses*, p. 187.

332 "I got to wear glued shoes . . .": Ibid.

332 Yummy worried about drinking: Ibid.

332 Smith and Howard argue: Sonny Greenberg, telephone interview, December 24, 1999; "Both Barrels," *San Francisco Call-Bulletin*, March 4, 1940, *FD*.

333 Woolf and Pollard argue: Farrell Jones, telephone interview, February 25, 1999.

334 "It's raining, Charley": "The Post Parade," *Morning Telegraph/Daily Racing Form*, February 1, 1940.

334 "For hire . . .": Ibid.

334 all-jockey baseball team: "Seabiscuit May Soon Be Shortstop," *San Francisco Chronicle*, *SB*, n.d.

335 "passing the 'Biscuit by . . .": "Seabiscuit Is Still Big Question Mark," *San Francisco News*, February 20, 1940.

335 Red weeps on track: "Seabiscuit Runs Third," *San Francisco Chronicle*, February 10, 1940, p. 4H.

335 Red and Yummy to Caliente: "Me and the Biscuit," *San Francisco Chronicle*, February 15, 1940, p. 4H.

336 Seabiscuit props: "Difference of Opinion," *San Francisco Chronicle*, February 21, 1940, *FD*.

336 *He has nothing left:* "Hundred Grand," *San Francisco Chronicle*, February 18, 1940, p. 2H.

336 propping as omen: "Difference of Opinion," *San Francisco Chronicle*, February 21, 1940, *FD*.

337 Howard sends retainer to Haas: "Seabiscuit Charges to Victory," *San Francisco Chronicle*, February 25, 1940, "Great Ride to Victory," *SB*, February 25, 1940.

337 Pollard visits Alexander: Alexander, *A Sound of Horses*, pp. 186–87.

338 rabbit's foot: "Racing Pays If You're Lucky," *San Francisco Chronicle*, winter 1940.

338 "It's Seabiscuit, wire to wire": "A Cinch," *SB*, February 25, 1940.

339 men doff hats to horse: "The Post Parade," *Morning Telgraph/Daily Racing Form*, March 2, 1940.

339 "as a country boy can throw an apple . . .": "The Biscuit—As Far as You Can Throw an Apple," *San Francisco Chronicle*, February 25, 1940; "Great Ride to Victory," *SB*, February 25, 1940.

339 sounder than he had been in two years: "A Cinch," *SB*, February 25, 1940.

339 "Just give us a fast track . . .": "Pollard Confident," *SB*, n.d.

CHAPTER 23

341 weather bureau calls: "Hollywood," *SB*, March 3, 1940.

341 "Kayak's four mud-running legs . . .": "Rain Renews Seabiscuit's Anita Jinx," *San Francisco Call-Bulletin*, February 29, 1940, p. 21.

341 morning of race: Beckwith, *Seabiscuit*, pp. 10–13.

341 "Be with him . . .": Beckwith, *Step and Go Together*, pp. 108–109.

342 prerace blowout: "Turnstiles Clicking," *SB*, early March 1940; Beckwith, *Seabiscuit*, pp. 10–13.

342 scene at Santa Anita: Barry Whitehead, "Seabiscuit's Santa Anita Handicap," *Thoroughbred Record*, March 9, 1940, p. 195.

343   half a million words: "Turnstiles Clicking," *SB*, early March 1940.

343   history's largest crowd: "Seabiscuit Great in Victory," *Los Angeles Examiner*, *SB*, March 1940.

343   Saint Christopher medal: "Kayak Could Have Won," *San Francisco Examiner*, March 3, 1940.

344   "I'd seen Johnny's leg . . .": Alexander, *A Sound of Horses*, p. 188.

344   "sidled up to me . . .": Ibid., pp. 187–88.

344   "You know the horse . . .": "The Biscuit Is Too Tough!," *San Francisco Examiner*, March 5, 1940.

344   Howard at the paddock: "The Post Parade," *Morning Telegraph/Daily Racing Form*, March 5, 1940; Alexander, *A Sound of Horses*, p. 188.

345   Alexander thought of Huck Finn: Ibid.

345   Marcela runs toward wagon: Beckwith, *Seabiscuit*, p. 61.

346   sprinters hard-pressed to equal time: *American Racing Manual 1938* (New York: Regal Press, 1938), pp. 196–360 (top sprint race times).

346   crying out a prayer: "I Just Sat and Watched," *San Francisco Chronicle*, March 3, 1940, p. 3H.

347   "*Now*, Pop!": "Sports," *New York Journal American*, *SB*, n.d.

347   Hernandez's voice cut over the crowd: *There They Go: Racing Calls by Joe Hernandez*, album released by Los Angeles Turf Club, n.d.

347   *We are alone:* "I Just Sat and Watched," *San Francisco Chronicle*, March 3, 1940, p. 3H.

347   Marcela up on the water wagon: "The Post Parade," *Morning Telegraph/Daily Racing Form*, March 5, 1940.

347   leaping, shouting reporters: "As Bill Leiser Sees It," *San Francisco Chronicle*, *SB*, March 1940.

348   Haas had never heard such thunder: "Haas Impressed," *SB*, March 1940.

348   crowd reaction: Whitehead, "Seabiscuit's Santa Anita Handicap," p. 195; "So Seabiscuit Took the Hundred Thousand," *San Francisco Chronicle*, March 2, 1940, p. 3H; "Chalk Brigade Reaps Harvest," *San Francisco Chronicle*, March 3, 1940; "Hollywood," *SB*, March 3, 1940.

348   Haas says he could not have beaten Seabiscuit: "Howard May Retire Seabiscuit," *Los Angeles Evening Herald and Examiner*, March 4, 1940, p. A16.

348   "Listen to this crowd roar!": *There They Go: Racing Calls by Joe Hernandez*.

348   "like a man who temporarily had visited Olympus . . .": "Sun Beau's Mark," *SB*, early March 1940.

349 "Best-smelling drink I ever tasted": Alexander, *A Sound of Horses*, p. 189.

349 Red takes shots at George: "To the Point," *San Francisco Examiner*, March 3, 1940, section 2, p. 2.

349 "Ha-ray for Seabiscuit!": "Extra Cheer for Biscuit," *SB*, early March 1940.

349 "Oh . . . that I lived to see this day": "Can Challedon or Kayak Whip Him?" *San Francisco Chronicle*, March 3, 1940, *FD*.

350 "you put up a great ride . . .": "Seabiscuit Gets Recognition at Last," *San Francisco Examiner*, February 2, 1944.

350 "Little horse, what next?": Stoneridge, *Great Horses of Our Time*, p. 34.

350 worth his weight in gold: "Seabiscuit First Worth Weight in Gold," *SB*, March 1940.

350 "Seabiscuit is Mr. Howard's horse . . .": "Biscuit Trainer Hails," *San Francisco Examiner*, March 12, 1940.

350 Howard calls Smith: "Silent Tom Smith," *SB*, March 16, 1940.

351 gathering at The Derby: Alexander, *A Sound of Horses*, pp. 189–90.

EPILOGUE

353 Seabiscuit leaves Santa Anita: "Turf Champion Leaves," *SB*, April 11, 1940.

354 "Seabiscuit . . . is the greatest horse . . .": David Alexander, "New England Racing," *Blood-Horse*, August 1, 1942, p. 159.

354 George sick, thin: "Turf in Review," *Morning Telegraph/Daily Racing Form*, January 8, 1949.

354 "There was one thing special you can say about George . . .": "Tom Smith Reminisces About Woolf, 'Biscuit," *Daily Racing Form*, February 1953.

354 left lucky kangaroo-leather saddle in trunk: Jenifer Van Deinse, e-mail interview, March 27, 2000.

354 Woolf's fall: "The Iceman Dies in California," *Blood-Horse*, February 23, 1946, p. 86; Bill Buck, telephone interview, January 28, 1998; Sonny Greenberg, telephone interview, December 24, 1999; Wad Studley, telephone interview, February 6, 1999.

354 friends heard Woolf's head hit track: Wad Studley, telephone interview, February 6, 1999.

354 Woolf's friends turned away: Ibid.

354 George's funeral: Bill Buck, telephone interview, January 28, 1998; "Turfdom Pays Final Tribute to Woolf," *Los Angeles Times*, January 8, 1946; Mike Griffin, telephone interview, January 23, 1998.

355 "who has Woolf's book?": "A Report on Pollard," *Blood-Horse*, March 9, 1946, p. 669.

355 "George Woolf is at Santa Anita . . .": Jack Shettlesworth, "Woolf Statue Unveiled," *Thoroughbred Record*, February 19, 1949.

355 Elizabeth Arden Graham: Bolus, *Remembering the Derby* (Gretna, La.: Pelican Publishing Company, 1994), pp. 179–96; "Ladies' Day in Louisville," *Time*, May 6, 1946, pp. 57–63.

356 Riddle speaks to Smith: "Tom Smith Reminisces About Woolf, 'Biscuit," *Daily Racing Form*, February 1953.

356 Smith accused of drugging horse: "Tom Smith and His Atomizer," *Blood-Horse*, November 17, 1945, pp. 1007–1009; "Tom Smith Ruling Stands," *Blood-Horse*, February 23, 1946, pp. 521–28.

357 Smith not deserving of punishment: "Ladies' Day in Louisville," p. 63.

357 Graham hires attorney, Jimmy Smith: Bolus, *Remembering the Derby*, p. 188.

357 "Those bastards": Ibid.

357 training a single horse: Leonard Dorfman, interview, November 12, 1999.

358 Almost no one comes to Smith's funeral: Tommy Bell, telephone interview, June 22, 1999.

358 "I'll never throw a leg over another horse . . .": David Alexander, "Four Good Legs Between Them," *Blood-Horse*, December 24, 1955, p. 1558.

358 "a barnacle on the wheels of progress": "Barnacle Red," *Blood-Horse*, February 2, 1957, p. 301.

359 Giangaspro's death: Sam Renick, telephone interview, December 5, 1997.

359 Satos in the Kaiser Suite: "New Guests in Seabiscuit's Stable," *SB*, n.d.

359 Pollard tries to enlist: Alexander, *A Sound of Horses*, p. 184.

359 taken to hospital in laundry basket: Edith Wilde, telephone interview, February 2, 1998.

360 "me and Methuselah": "Obituary: Red Pollard," *Blood-Horse*, March 21, 1981, p. 1773.

360 "Maybe I should have heeded . . .": Alexander, *A Sound of Horses*, p. 183.

360 "I'm hanging up my blouse for good . . .": Alexander, "Four Good Legs," p. 1558.

361 "You Made Me What I Am . . .": Alexander, *A Sound of Horses*, p. 178.

361 Pollard's post-riding jobs: Ibid., p. 168.

361 never beats alcoholism: Norah Christianson, telephone interview, January 26, 1998.

361 Red sat by, mute: Ibid.

361 hospital built atop Narragansett: Ibid.

361 No cause of death was ever found: Ibid.

361 "he had just worn out . . .": Ibid.

361 Howard hangs sign on Redwood Highway: "Both Barrels," *SB*, n.d.

361 Fifty thousand visitors: Jack McDonald, "Seabiscuit," *Spur*, August 1983, p. 33.

361 Fifteen hundred at a time: "Both Barrels," *SB*, n.d.

362 Seabiscuit's life at Ridgewood: Ibid.

362 Seabiscuit sleeps under tree: Bill Nichols, telephone interview, January 14, 1998.

363 herding cattle: Jane Goldstein, "Seabiscuit Cover-Up," *Blood-Horse*, March 13, 1978, p. 1244.

363 bomb shelter: "Seabiscuit Gets Own Bomb Shelter!," *SB*, December 25, 1941.

363 ambulance: "Howards Give U.S. Ambulance," *San Francisco Examiner*, *SB*, October 16, year unknown.

363 gives Seabiscuit shoes to pilots: "Seabiscuit Shoe Races Across German Skies," *SB*, n.d.

363 bomber: "Seabiscuit Bomber," *SB*, n.d.; "Navy Bomber Crew Back," *SB*, n.d.

363 "there will never be another Seabiscuit": Jack McDonald, "Seabiscuit," *Spur*, August 1983, p. 33.

364 listened from car: Jack Shettlesworth, "The Melancholy Knell," *Thoroughbred Record*, June 11, 1950, p. 24.

364 Howard rides Seabiscuit: Bill Nichols, telephone interview, January 14, 1998.

364 Marcela met her husband at breakfast: Carter Swart, "The Howards of San Francisco," *Northern California Thoroughbred*, fall 1981, p. 111.

364 "I never dreamed . . .": McDonald, "Seabiscuit," p. 33.

364 let the oak stand as the only marker: Michael C. Howard, telephone interview, January 18, 1997.

Index

Andy Dougan

Dynamo

Defending the Honour of Kiev

In 1942 in German-occupied Ukraine a football match took place between the Luftwaffe and a team from a local bakery, largely comprised of members of the sparkling pre-war Dynamo Kiev team. The match became an allegory of resistance; its consequences were brutal. In this moving tribute to the heroism of the Ukrainian footballers, Andy Dougan has uncovered the truth behind a legendary encounter, restoring to the centre of World War Two a moment of extraordinary poignancy and complex bravery.

'We are reminded once again of football's power to galvanise nations, express political will, and carry any amount of symbolic baggage . . . *Dynamo* is written from the heart.'   *Sunday Times*

'Just as you think you've read every good book about the war another one is published . . . Excellent.'

Philip Kerr, *Sunday Times*

'You don't have to have an interest in football to read Andy Dougan through the night.'   *Spectator*

James S. Hirsch

Hurricane

The Life of Rubin Carter, Fighter

'A great story. What can be seem on the outside is marvellous, but it is only a hint of the magnificence within.'   Denzel Washington

'A biblical tale of persecution, punishment and redemption.'
New York Times

'I was unjustly accused of killing three complete strangers. For what? Nobody could tell me. But I was black and the victims were white, and the police were white, and the lawyers were white, and the jury was white. So you tell me ... Everything that happened to me was deliberate. I was sent to prison to be destroyed, and not because of any murders. Only my innocence kept me going. That was the strongest thing I had.'   Rubin Carter

Rubin Carter was more than a boxer, a man who once knocked out a horse with a right cross. A former juvenile criminal in between a spell as a US paratrooper, he ran guns for Steve Biko in South Africa, and was a passionate advocate of black power in the 1960s. He was also a victim of one of America's most celebrated legal battles and drew support from, among others, Bob Dylan and Muhammad Ali. His is a fighter's story of jailhouse and heroic endurance.

'Engrossing'   *The Times*

'A great story like this is drenched in the shame of those who made such a travesty possible.'   *Irish Independent*

David Francis

Agapanthus Tango

'David Francis's first novel takes Midwest American boiled-down prose to the Australian outback, in a story of love stunted in a sunburned country.'   *Times Literary Supplement*

At twelve years old, Day sees his mother's body dumped from a wheelbarrow into the scorched earth of New South Wales. Stunned and in fear of his father, Day leaves the family farm, transforms himself into an expert groom and escapes Australia with a racehorse called Unusual. In the alien landscape of Maryland, his undiminished, painful love for his mother is challenged by the arrival of Callie, whose heart is set on becoming the world's first female jockey. As Day's passion for Callie takes hold, he is forced to confront his past – and to accept that the only way forward is to go back.

'Coolly poetic . . . Francis manages to hold the reader's attention with striking, descriptive prose and an unexpected final twist.'
                                                                 Guardian

'Francis is a vivid and original writer capable of prose to cut your throat.'   *Time Out*

'Blunt, poetic, almost Faulknerian in places.'   *Big Issue*

All Fourth Estate books are available from your local bookshop.

For a monthly update on Fourth Estate's latest releases, with interviews, extracts, competitions and special offers visit
www.4thestate.com

Or visit
www.4thestate.com/readingroom
for the very latest reading guides on our bestselling authors, including Michael Chabon, Annie Proulx, Lorna Sage, Carol Shields.

London and *New York*